THERE GOES THE NEIGHBORHOOD

DAVID R. REYNOLDS

THERE GOES THE NEIGHBORHOOD

RURAL SCHOOL CONSOLIDATION

AT THE GRASS ROOTS IN EARLY

TWENTIETH-CENTURY IOWA

University of Iowa Press   Iowa City

University of Iowa Press, Iowa City 52242

Copyright © 1999 by the University of Iowa Press

www.uiowapress.org

Printed in the United States of America

Printed on acid-free paper

Library of Congress Cataloging-in-Publication Data

Reynolds, David R.

There goes the neighborhood: rural school consolidation at the grass roots in early twentieth-century Iowa / by David R. Reynolds.

p.   cm.

Includes bibliographical references (p.   ) and index.

ISBN 978-1-58729-497-6 (pbk)

ISBN 978-1-58729-307-8 (ebk)

1. Schools—Centralization—Iowa—History—20th century.

2. Rural schools—Iowa—History—20th century.   I. Title.

LB2861.R49   1999

379.1'535-dc21   99-29743

FOR DEIRDRE

CONTENTS

PREFACE AND ACKNOWLEDGMENTS

According to popular accounts, the American public school system is in crisis. Schools fail to involve parents effectively in the education of their children. Schools fail to impart the job skills necessary to restore U.S. competitiveness in the global economy. And schools would fail to meet national standards of student achievement—*if* agreement on these standards could be reached. The focus of most of these criticisms is on performance. Although local control of education appears to remain a core American value, criticism of the public schools seldom entails analysis of schools as local democratic institutions and as important sources of community and individual identity. Indeed, when debates over American public education have touched upon issues of democracy and community at all, they have been preoccupied with identifying the appropriate articulation between various publics and professional educators in determining educational policy—or more colloquially, "Who should control what?" Such has not always been the case.

Alexis de Tocqueville, certainly one of the earliest critical observers of American democracy, pointed to the high level of centralization of social power in a single government and complete lack of administrative centralization in the United States in the early 1830s. He defined *centralization of government* as the concentration of authority to enact general laws common to all parts of the nation under a single directing power, and *administrative centralization* as the concentration of authority over matters of special concern to only certain localities or parts of the nation in that directing power.[1] Tocqueville also stressed that while individualism had been important in the founding of the Republic, he feared that it could become its undoing unless effective local political institutions (he used the term "provincial" instead of "local") could be maintained and strengthened. Without effective local institutions to ensure *administrative decentralization*, he feared that democracy could evolve into a form of soft fascism.[2] His solution was to merge state and civil society by linking individuals to a larger political and moral community by way of family, friends, local communities, religion, and other forms of political association.[3] For Tocqueville, local community and democracy were mutually, and necessarily, dependent upon one another. Community without democracy was fascism; democracy without community was unbridled greed and anarchy.

The founders also understood the importance of community and democracy in the tensions between the individual, civil society, and the state in the American system. In Thomas Jefferson's view, a predominantly agrarian society of small property owners with families working their own land would ensure individual liberty, check the rise of social inequality, foster local cooperation, and limit the encroachment of the state into the private realm. Private life and public life would be inseparable—a system not dissimilar from that described by Tocqueville. However, "Jefferson's friend and constitutional antagonist, James Madison, looked out on the same political landscape and came to very different conclusions about what must be done to guarantee the survival of the body politic."[4] He too saw the rise of inequality but, unlike Jefferson, saw it as a permanent feature of an essentially competitive human nature about which little could or should be done except to protect individuals from one another by preventing any one group from dominating the others. As a means of achieving this, Madison was much less sanguine about the prospects of democratic rule; instead he saw such protection being provided only by a strong central government. Alexander Hamilton's views paralleled those of Madison, but were more utilitarian and corporatist. In his view, people would be happy only when their economic interests were maximized, but they could not do this by themselves; a strong probusiness government was necessary. The implication was "that prosperity would solve the problem of liberty."[5] This was precisely what Tocqueville feared. Prosperity would allow "each citizen to isolate himself from the mass of his fellows and withdraw into the circle of family and friends," leaving the central government as the only apparent power capable of protecting them from anarchy.[6] The price paid would be the severing of ties between the public and the private and the failure of the democratic experiment. Lost also would be the promise of democracy—the willingness of a society to consider alternative political and economic systems.

Lawrence Goodwyn has argued that in this broader sense democracy died in America with the failure of the Populist revolt in 1896 when McKinley defeated Bryan in the presidential election.[7] Eighteen ninety-six was also the year when the reform of rural education was placed on the national political agenda of education leaders for the first time. Was the timing of these events purely coincidental? An underlying theme emerging from this inquiry into rural school consolidation is that they were not. After the depression of the 1890s, efforts to expand modern systems of public schooling into the countryside led to the use of the public school as an agent for transforming the nature of rural people and rural places in ways that reformers hoped would avoid or mitigate the class conflict then engulfing American cities. Although certainly not politicized that way at the time, rural school reform became a substitute for a more radical democratic transformation of the U.S. political economy. This substitution was aided not only by the defeat of populism but by the birth of American Progressivism and the rising influence of the professional or expert in the social division of labor in American society.

During the Progressive Era the relations between the individual, civil society, and the state defining what kind of democracy and what kinds of communities were to characterize American society were transformed. The reform of public education was a central feature in that transformation. Decision making regarding public education in both urban and rural areas became less subject to the vicissitudes of local communities, more bureaucratic, and more centralized administratively, but not without encountering widespread resistance in many localities. Resistance to rural educational reform was particularly virulent in the rural neighborhoods of the Midwest. Resistance was both place- and class-based and proceeded in the only way it could in the American system of democracy—in a highly decentralized, localized manner. In most instances, elites did not recognize rural resistance to school reform as deriving from farm people's concerns that the implementation of the principal policy prescription of reformers—rural school consolidation—would undermine the existing social relations, and the longer-run sustainability, of family farming itself. Instead, rural resistance was perceived to be based on irremediable ignorance or reactionary perniciousness to be ignored, if possible, and marginalized, if not. In the chapters below, an attempt is made to show how a richer and indeed more accurate interpretation of the struggle over rural education in the Midwest can be gained by situating that struggle within the complex interplay between the geography of class and place formation, regional class structure, and individual agency. While the narrative appears to give voice to midwestern farm people almost a century too late, it is a voice that still resonates in a way that can and should inform current debates over the future of American public education.

The University of Iowa supplied the support necessary for funding the research and writing involved in this project. The Graduate College provided me with graduate assistants to help with the archival work, and University House (now Obermann Center for Advanced Studies) provided a stimulating and supportive environment during the semester-long research assignment in which the project began to take shape. Many colleagues have contributed insights and criticisms, particularly in reacting to early drafts of papers from which this book would eventually be distilled. Emery Castle, Mickey Lauria, Dick Peet, Jennifer Reynolds, Abdi Samatar, Sonya Salamon, and Richard Walker are especially deserving of thanks; their critical comments and encouragement were invaluable. My best critic, most enthusiastic supporter, able editorial assistant, and trusty sidekick in logging countless hours searching through the correspondence of the Department of Public Instruction, in the Archives of the State Historical Society of Iowa in Des Moines, was Deirdre McGuinne.

Thanks go to Toby Moore. He was the only one, other than Deirdre, to wade through the woefully long first draft of the manuscript. I acknowledge also my graduate research assistants, Fran Ufkes-Daniels, Chris Merrett, Cecil Seethal, Jen Miau Lin, Bilal Ahmad, Pratyusha Basu, and Jim Wilson, who spent countless hours searching through the Iowa newspaper archives and other relevant sources at the State Historical Society of Iowa in Iowa City. I am also grateful to the University Press of Kansas for allowing me to draw liberally upon a paper of mine that first appeared as "Rural Education: Decentering the Consolidation Debate," in *The Changing American Countryside: Rural People and Places* (1996), edited by Emery Castle. That paper appears in a much revised form as the epilogue to the present work.

Finally, to my informants in Delaware County I extend my heartfelt thanks. They generously and graciously gave of their time as I strove to confirm and piece together their oral histories of the events surrounding rural school consolidation in their respective neighborhoods more than three-quarters of a century ago. Without their assistance, my reconstruction of the early rural school consolidations in Delaware County and Buck Creek could not have been attempted, much less completed. I am more grateful than I can say.

I

THEORETICAL AND

HISTORICAL CONTEXTS

A spatial structure of production is not a distribution of jobs but a geography of social relations. Thinking in terms of relations starts from the interdependence of phenomena and thus of the spaces they construct: this applies to jobs within a division of labour and to regions within an economy. What is at issue is the spatial form of certain aspects of social power.
— Doreen Massey, Spatial Division of Labor

I

INTRODUCTION: PLACING RURAL EDUCATIONAL REFORM

The so-called Progressive Era (ca. 1895–1925) is a period of critical importance for those seeking to understand the emergence of new forms of social and economic regulation in the United States. It was a period of rapid change. The cultural and ideological forces of Modernism increasingly took hold of the American psyche. The federal and state governments began to assume their modern bureaucratic forms. A professional middle class rose to fill new positions of authority in both the state and civil society and transformed the structure of power in American society. The introduction and widespread acceptance of new transportation and communication technologies changed the social meanings and valuations of space and time irreversibly, while space-time itself became more compressed as revolutions in the control and use of time annihilated geographical space. Leading these cultural, political, and material transformations was a new set of elites — the Progressives — who evinced great optimism that the powers of the state under their leadership could harness the productive capacity of capitalism to ensure the material progress of all classes. Perhaps no terms better capture the economic and political ideology of the Progressive Era than "progress" and "consolidation." [1] Material progress was the desired end; institutional and organizational consolidation was the means to that end.

In the Midwest, the more visible expressions of space-time compression and social transformation were rapid industrialization, urbanization, and rural out-migration. While some of the social relations of production characterizing midwestern agriculture in this period still involved spatial and temporal rhythms quite different from those prevalent in cities and towns, efficiency experts urged that attempts be made to synchronize them wherever and whenever possible. Though far less visible in the landscape, the social impacts of this process were as significant in the countryside as they were in the city. Rural free delivery (RFD), improved roads, the automobile, the increased circulation of newspapers and magazines, and the telephone all helped to reduce social isolation in rural areas. For the first time, many farm families clearly recognized how different their lifestyles were from those of the cities. If they subscribed to urban, middle-class values, rural life seemed antiquated, aberrant, parochial, and passé. Although many newspapers and magazines of the time rang with declarations of the virtues and moral superiority of farm life, increasingly experience seemed to contradict them. For growing numbers of rural people, the city and city jobs were more alluring than the rural neighborhood and farm chores. As rural-to-urban migration continued and urban values penetrated rural areas more deeply, bonds of reciprocity between farm people gradually gave way to the more fully commodified social relations of the market.

The Country Life movement was arguably the Progressive Era's most important rural reform movement. Its leaders sought to identify and implement an alternative future for rural people, especially for farm families. They believed that through appropriate spatial and economic planning and public investment, a new form of rural community combining the advantages of both city and country could be created. Previous research on the Country Life movement has emphasized the intellectual roots of the movement, the social backgrounds of its principal architects and operatives, and its ideological staying power, particularly among the new urban middle class in America. It has, however, failed to illuminate the central role that one particular reform, the consolidation of rural schools, played in engineering the desired transformation of rural life, especially in the Midwest. Indeed, in the Midwest, efforts to consolidate rural school districts became one of the most significant social movements of the Progressive Era. Initially, however, there were two sets of reformers, each advocating rural school consolidation but for different reasons. Leaders in the new field of educational administration saw school consolidation as a possible means of improving the quality of educational opportunities available to children in rural areas. Those in the Country Life movement came to champion rural school consolidation as a sociospatial means of engineering new forms of rural community. By about 1910, these two groups of reformers had combined their considerable rhetorical and political skills and formed a relatively cohesive social movement. For a time, they succeeded in creating a powerful discourse in support of rural school consolidation — one in which consolidation appeared to be *the* solution to a host of country life problems.

Whereas the common school movement had its origins in New England, the rural school consolidation movement was decidedly a midwestern phenomenon. Reformers took the first steps to implement rural school consolidation through legislative action in the Midwest. They succeeded in mobilizing a modicum of support for the idea at the grass roots, but it was also here where opposition ran deep and where the movement incurred its most serious defeats.[2] This book focuses on two questions. How did rural school consolidation become the principal policy prescription for the reform of rural life in the Midwest? Why did its supposed beneficiaries oppose it so vociferously? The objective is to take seriously and illustrate concretely the often-quoted aphorism usually attributed to Marx, "Men and women create history but not in circumstances of their own choosing." Rather than treating resistance to rural school consolidation as a reactionary aberration deriving from an irremediable and necessarily anachronistic localism, a richer and indeed more accurate interpretation is gained by considering it the result of the complex interplay between class and place formation, regional class structure, and individual agency.

An Overview of Central Arguments

Leaders of educational reform in the Midwest attempted to build educational systems that would assist in restructuring social relations in the countryside in ways more consistent with the needs of the larger, more clearly urban capitalist society rapidly gaining momentum in the region. They believed that success in this endeavor required greater control of rural education by educational professionals. They had little confidence in any system in which the locus of control and supervision over public schooling remained in the hands of farmers and their families. Educational reforms, however, had to wend their way through state legislatures dominated by rural economic interests, if not by farmers themselves. The particular reforms implemented in the various states were the result of struggles encountered and compromises made along the way in specific localities and in the states' larger political arenas. The reforms did, however, share two common elements. First, reform efforts focused almost exclusively on remediating the supposed ills of the rural schools, ignoring education in the cities and larger towns almost entirely. Second, reformers invariably selected rural school consolidation as the necessary first step in any program of reform.

Reformers failed to recognize the limitations of "annihilating space with time" through rural school consolidation. Instead, they persisted in their efforts to restructure spatial conceptions of rural community in ways that would make more revenue available for the provision of an expanded, more standardized, more modern public school curriculum. They maintained that increased spending on the existing rural schools was a waste of resources, and that only by investing additional revenue in newly created consolidated districts would the educational opportunities of farm children be equal to those available to children in the cities and towns.

Reformers argued that the one-room country schools had too few pupils to be divided into meaningful grades and administered efficiently. On this score they were undoubtedly right. The country schools may have been cheap, but they certainly were not efficient by any of the contemporary definitions of that term. The graded elementary school that had come to dominate the school systems in the cities, however, was only one model of efficiency. Another was available in the progressive educational ideas and practice of John Dewey and his coworkers at the University of Chicago. Ironically, Dewey's model was based on the practical modes of learning that had characterized rural education historically. While this might have found support among farm families for this reason, it found little support among educational administrators because it would also have required significant changes in the way in which urban schools operated.[3] Educational administrators argued that, compared with country schools, city schools were already managed efficiently. Rather than make city schools more like country schools, what was needed was to make rural schools more like urban schools. The reformers' apparent rejection of the "progressive" model in favor of the "factory" or "industrial" model was controversial and helped ensure that their proposals encountered significant opposition among farm people throughout the Midwest.

Rural school consolidation was resisted vigorously throughout the region and resisted successfully in a number of places. Nevertheless, we know little about why resistance occurred where it did or why it took the particular forms it did. Although writing about resistance to school reform in American cities in the nineteenth century, Michael Katz could just as well have been referring to rural resistance to reforms in rural education in the twentieth century when he wrote: "Insofar as most of the resistance came from inarticulate people, it is the hardest and most maddening aspect of nineteenth century educational history to document."[4] This has not prevented contemporary educational historians from trying to characterize this resistance using principally documentation left behind by the supporters of reform. Most of the alternative interpretations offered cleave into two polar extremes. One interprets resistance to the school reform as the expression of a fundamental allegiance to local autonomy and Jeffersonian democracy and the other interprets it as the expression of a deeply engrained, regionally specific, anti-intellectualism evincing profoundly antidemocratic tendencies.[5] More recently, educational historian Paul Theobald provides a third alternative. His work draws on contemporary scholarship in rural history focusing on the high levels of mobility and population turnover among the settlers and the problems yeoman freeholders had in placing their offspring on the land. He hypothesizes that the "majority of settlers in the Midwest in the nineteenth century were kept landless and on the move by a landed minority" who used the rural independent school districts they controlled as "instruments of exclusion."[6]

All three of these interpretations of rural resistance to common schools and later to rural school consolidation are in one way or another seriously flawed. By ignoring the regional structure of class power and by failing to inquire very deeply into the relationships between rural neighborhoods, rural schools, and rural culture, each undercontextualizes resistance. The interpretation offered in the present study was not arrived at a priori. The project began as an attempt to provide support for the revisionist view that resistance to school consolidation was an expression of the desire for local autonomy. It was not long, however, before this approach had to be abandoned as oversimplified and as begging more questions than it answered. While the abortive Populist revolt of the 1890s surely led to a critical reappraisal of the limits of bourgeois democracy among some farmers, it simply was not tenable that family farmers as a whole opposed rural school consolidation out of some local democratic impulse or simply because they distrusted the concentration of state power. The view that they sought to preserve core rural values was an attractive alternative, but this too required more specificity and appropriate contextualization. The existing literature provided few clues. What set of values were farmers fighting for or against? Why? This book seeks to provide answers to these questions.

Farmers, Place, Class Analysis, and Resistance to School Reform

While contemporary social history has emphasized the historical specificity of social relations, it has generally failed to acknowledge a similar specificity geographically — in terms of regions and localities, or more generically in terms of places.[7] This neglect has resulted in confusion over such key concepts as class, community, place, and region. In an attempt to overcome this deficiency as well as to avoid some of the major pitfalls of extending neo-Marxist class analysis to midwestern agriculture, this study interprets rural school consolidation as a place-based class movement.[8] Objectively, class is determined by the intergroup social relations characterizing the creation and disposition of surplus value in a mode of production. Groups of people occupying the same structural position in the mode of production constitute a class. While mode of production is an abstraction, it is a concrete one deriving from observable social relationships in actual, historically specific social formations. Hence, it is possible to speak of *capital* and *labor* in the *capitalist mode of production* characterizing the *social formations* of the industrial societies of Europe and North America in the late twentieth century. It is also possible to characterize a social formation as consisting of dominant and subordinate modes of production. For example, in the United States' social formation, the capitalist mode of production has been dominant for at least a century, but it continues to exhibit regional vestiges of petty commodity production as a subordinate mode. For a class to be mobilized into a movement (somewhere), its members must identify a set of class interests around which class consciousness can develop and establish an organizational infrastructure to further these interests. A class movement necessarily entails struggle for power among classes over the conditions leading to the creation of surplus value and to its distribution. That struggle has a geography as well as a history. A class movement is also "one in which the participants are involved in a struggle over the very definition of their political, economic and ideological interests."[9]

A place-based class movement is one in which class consciousness and a sense of place (and community) are inextricably entwined and mutually reinforcing. Not only do struggles occur in particular places, but the nature of these places as social and territorial entities significantly mediates whatever class consciousness exists among people in a locality. Struggle also implies resistance and a minimum of two sets of participants; hence any historical analysis of a class movement must concern itself with both the proponents and opponents of a social movement. Students of social reform movements dealing with education, even those employing class perspectives, have tended to focus on either the reformers or on the opponents of reform rather than directing attention to both. This is a serious deficiency in the literature. While it is also possible for class consciousness to significantly mediate a collective sense of place, class consciousness must form in the *first place*. Any historical class consciousness necessarily has some form of regional or place identity embedded within it. Social historians and social scientists, while recognizing the spatial and territorial boundedness of social and economic life, have tended to use the term "community consciousness" instead of "regional identity" or "place identity." Typically, "community" denotes one of two quite different phenomena: a territorially circumscribed set of social relations giving form and substance to the everyday lives of people, or any cultural basis for association other than economic class.

Place-based class movements fundamentally involve relationships of power rooted in concerns over the material reproduction of everyday life in particular localities and necessarily involve economic dimensions; but they must entail other cultural dimensions as well. But what of class and class consciousness? In what sense does their place-based nature have affect and not simply register an existential claim? One approach is to adopt E. P. Thompson's view that classes are emergent and not just reflections of the dominant power relations in a mode of production. In his view, a class is a group of people who have developed "a *disposition to behave* as a class, to define themselves in their consciousness in relation to other groups of people in class ways." Class is emergent in the sense that this disposition derives from sharing "the same categories of interests, social experiences, traditions, and value-systems."[10] Thompson's view of class is implicitly place-based in that it recognizes that such sharing requires forms of communication that historically could occur only in territorially circumscribed communities of various spatial extents. This perspective is satisfactory as far as it goes, but it does not go far enough. While recognizing that class is a process, it provides few clues as to how shared cultural experiences in a place are converted into a disposition of groups within it to behave as a class. In a way it links two forms of structural analysis — the cultural with the economic — and does so dynamically, but it still emphasizes structure over agency.

What is needed is a means of mediating individual and local communitarian actions with the collective pursuit of class interests. While formal organizations like political parties, cooperatives, unions, churches, and the local governmental organizations are primary vehicles in accomplishing this, the organizational capacity of a group is affected by its internal divisions and the objective class structure of the place (region or locality) in which it resides — a place's *local class structure*. At any given moment, the class structure of a place is made up of diverse economic locations or positions. Some people are members of a profession, some are skilled production workers, others are managers or executives, or, in the case in question, they may be traditional family farmers, "progressive" farmers, merchants, or workers. Each of these groups possesses a differing structural position within a place and/or a system of places characterized by territorially specific cultures, and these positions are intimately related to the group's organizational capacities for mobilizing as a class. For instance, miners have traditionally had high levels of interaction with one another both in the pits and in their typically small, single-industry communities and have usually seen themselves as occupying a distinct position in their localities and society. On the other hand, family farmers' interactions with one another historically were confined more to the social relations of neighborhood reproduction rather than those of production on the farm and were structured along gender lines. The differences between the class positions of farmers and merchants, facilitated by the spatial separation between city/town and countryside, however, were typically transparent to farmer and merchant alike. The result was that farmers tended to have a well-developed consciousness of their position in the regional economy, although they seldom described it specifically in class terms. The place-building and neighborhood-maintenance activities of farm family members, especially those of women, were the key cultural means by which farmers could on occasion operate as a "class for itself," albeit primarily locally. Farm men's relative lack of interaction and cooperation with one another in their daily chores and their relative spatial isolation at regional and national scales severely restricted their structural capacity to act in unison as a class in the realm of production.

The structural capacity of family farmers as a class was also affected by the extent to which those places in which their daily lives unfolded were divided by religion and ethnicity. While local and regional cultures affect structural capacity, they can be expected to produce quite different effects from place to place. The class capacity of any group is also affected by the state of class struggle in the larger society. A group that defines its class interests only in terms of members of a local community remains a place-based class organization. Place-based class organizations cannot amalgamate into a class in a broader societal sense without first articulating a cultural agenda that cuts across and transcends the potential parochialism of locality, region, or even nation. Unless challenged by subordinate classes, structurally favored classes can organize at whatever territorial scale necessary for them to retain or enhance their power. Subordinate classes have little choice but to begin their struggles as place-based class movements; the difficulty is in transcending their geographical confines.

In the analysis of the rural school consolidation movement in the Midwest that follows, the hypothesis that traditional family farmers viewed themselves as constituting a subordinate class is evaluated. Did family farmers' opposition to rural school consolidation stem to some significant extent from their desire to preserve themselves and their neighborhoods as places amidst the whirlwind of social and economic change characterizing the period? If so, was this a rational class response or simply another example of a complex class struggle becoming so hopelessly divided by place and region as to disintegrate into a reactionary politics? At the turn of the century, did family farming and the neighborhood-based social relations upon which it was dependent still offer a viable alternative vision of what rural life in America could be like?

Throughout most of the post–Civil War period, farmers had argued unsuccessfully for justice and a fair rate of return for the products they produced. As commodity chains from farm to final consumer became attenuated and production monopolized, family farmers were increasingly viewed by elites as marginalized holdovers from an earlier, competitive phase of capitalism in which most production was petty commodity production. The global depression of the 1890s dealt a severe blow to the archetypal system of petty capitalism or simple commodity production. Theretofore, production had been dependent on family labor expended on small farms nested within a neighborhood-based structure of social relations in which reciprocity and mutual aid were central features. By the time the depression finally ended in 1896, many midwestern farmers had given up and joined the urban middle class or the urban proletariat, contributing in many areas to actual population decreases in the countryside that threatened to undermine rural community life still further for those who remained.[11]

As the new century ushered in a period of rising prosperity for farmers in the Midwest, those farmers remaining on the land increasingly divided themselves into distinct subclasses. Subclass differentiation cleaved along such dimensions as the amount of land held and/or worked by family members, the acceptance of the legitimacy of capitalist social relations of production, and dependence on traditional patterns of community. Could these subclasses coexist amicably in the same places, or was one destined to become hegemonic both economically and ideologically? While farmers themselves appeared to persist in their belief that coexistence was both possible and desirable, most reformers did not and few identified with the farmer and his conceptions of class and community. Ideologically the reformers were closer to being Hamiltonians than Jeffersonians.[12]

As a system of simple commodity production, family farming was remarkably functional within the larger system of agrarian capitalism of which it was a part and in the creation and reproduction of a distinctive regional class structure in the Midwest. In an important sense, family farming helped underwrite the costs of rapid industrialization in the country from about 1870 onward. Family farming was not only a means of ensuring the provision of cheap food for the reproduction of the working class in the burgeoning cities, it was also effective in supplying the cities with a relatively steady stream of new workers. The farm needed the labor power of children, but rural localities were increasingly unable to absorb all of them when they reached adulthood. Once all the farmland in a locality was alienated and worked by families, one or two children in a family were all that were necessary to ensure the reproduction of the farm unit and the rural neighborhood; any additional children were "surplus." A few found jobs in the artisanal production that remained in the countryside, and some secured positions as service workers in nearby towns; but most had little choice but to seek working-class jobs in the larger towns and cities.

The rural school was an important institution in determining whether farm children became farmers themselves, engaged in some other form of rural-based petty proprietorship, joined one of the professions, or entered some fragment of the working class. The boy who didn't "take to schoolin'" was typically encouraged to carry on in farming or to head for the city to begin earning a living when he reached adulthood or was no longer needed on the farm. Boys who did "take to schoolin'" were encouraged to enter one of the traditional professions — the ministry (priesthood), medicine, and the law. Girls were encouraged to enter teaching or one of the growing number of service occupations available in the larger towns and cities. As localities in the Midwest began to manifest more "settled" demographic characteristics beginning about 1895, fewer "surplus" children were produced. The reduction in family sizes, however, was not sufficient to permit all, or even most, farm children to take up family farming in or near their home localities.[13]

The call for equality in opportunity in the education provided in the rural and urban schools, increasingly voiced by educational reformers from the late 1890s onward, was a powerful call and one echoed by many farmers.

Perhaps only through greater public investment in education could farm children destined for the cities arrive there with the educational qualifications necessary for them to escape working-class status and enter adult society as potential members of the bourgeoisie. If rural neighborhoods could voluntarily consolidate without necessarily undermining class identities, perhaps the structural capacity of family farmers could be enhanced in situ. If not, family farmers confronted a profound paradox. For those clinging to agrarian values rooted in place, school consolidation could be seen as one more means of ensuring the demise of the small family farm and the rural neighborhood altogether and the further peripheralization of family farmers in the regional class structure. To those more worried about the positions of their children in that structure, the consolidated school seemed to offer the promise of better educational opportunities and class mobility.

Family farmers seldom occupied positions of leadership in education above the rural district or school-township level. Consequently, despite their numbers they lacked the organizational infrastructure to help shape educational policy. Their place-based, territorial power, however, tended to be a negative blocking power — a power that stimulated resistance and slowed the centralization of authority over education in the hands of middle-class professionals, but militated against their success in organizing as a *class for itself*. Institutionally and organizationally, it was difficult for family farmers to establish a class consciousness outside the local context. When they did, it tended to lack congruence with the objective agrarian class structure of the region. As will be made clear in succeeding chapters, midwestern family farmers were unable to transcend locality and develop educational reforms different from those offered by middle-class reformers and supported by the increasing numbers of "progressive" farmers who embraced middle-class status and the fuller commodification of land, labor, and social life. Was this primarily the artifact of the parochialism of family farmers, or did it derive more from the structure of class power in the region and nation? Could family farmers have organized as a *class for itself* in this context? Were their struggles against school consolidation simply indicative of a retrograde yearning for place-based communities, with little or no potential for charting an alternative conception of rural progress? These are among the several questions addressed in the succeeding chapters. In confronting questions of educational provision today, we need, perhaps more than ever before, to understand not only how to structure alternative agendas democratically but how to make those agendas a reality. Perhaps we can learn from past failures.

Context of the Study: Iowa during the Progressive Era

The analysis of rural school consolidation offered here focuses on the early twentieth century and concentrates largely on a single state — Iowa. Nonetheless, it attempts to situate the struggles involved in that movement in their appropriate political, economic, and cultural contexts. The relevant geographical scales of these contexts range from the global and national to the state and to the locality. The choice of Iowa derives in part from the fact that the author has lived and studied there for more than a quarter century. It also derives from the belief that, in a cultural and ideological sense, Iowa is the most midwestern of midwestern states. Since the 1880s, more of Iowa has been under the family farmer's plow than any other state in the union. If ever there was a place for family farmers to exercise political and cultural power, it was Iowa.

At the turn of the century, Iowa had a dual system of public schooling that approximately matched the supposed dual urban-rural nature of its social relations. The school districts of the larger towns and cities possessed graded elementary schools and up-to-date, four-year high schools, while rural school districts and small towns continued to cling to their traditional common schools. Leading educators were well aware of these urban-rural differences in public schooling, as indeed they had been influential in creating them. Nonetheless, they saw in them inequalities, which advances in pedagogy, technology, and the material well-being of farmers made unnecessary. A few reformers attempted to revitalize the country school and country life by experimenting with better ways of linking instruction to the everyday lives of students and their families. More, however, sought to equalize the educational opportunities of children in the cities, towns, and rural areas of the state by deploying principles of scientific management, by utilizing improvements in transportation, and by tapping the enhanced wealth of rural communities. The solution they hit upon — the consolidation of the rural school districts — was analogous to the consolidation of the meatpacking industry that had been so crucial in the restructuring of midwestern agriculture in the last third of the nineteenth century. As in the meatpacking industry, equality of opportunity was to be achieved through oligopolistic practices, including but not limited to managing the supply and demand of education. Many farm people, however, were quite uncertain that they wanted equal opportunities for their children, if achieving them resulted in the even more rapid destruction of those aspects of rural life and culture they most cherished.

In 1913, Iowa had almost 14,000 country school districts and subdistricts, most with their own locally controlled, one-room schools. Beginning in that year and continuing for almost a decade, Iowa became the center of national, even international, attention as the newly established Department of Public Instruction and the state's leaders in education conducted the nation's first fully coordinated campaign to consolidate its rural school districts and subdistricts. Iowa was the first state in the nation to mount such a campaign and the only one to achieve a modicum of success along these lines before the Great Depression of the 1930s. For this brief period, as delegation after delegation of educational dignitaries from other states and nations visited its consolidated schools to observe the new "farmers' schools" and how to implement them, Iowa was very much in the educational spotlight. Ironically, the consolidated school did not represent an educational innovation per se when the campaign began. Although clothed in the rhetoric of farmers' schools by proponents, the "new" consolidated school entailed a rather straightforward extension of urban school systems to rural areas — the bringing of the city to the country. Consolidated schools would look like urban schools, would be administered like urban schools, and would employ the uniform, age-based pedagogy of urban schools. The principal difference between urban schools and consolidated schools was that the latter would be located either in "rural-minded" urban places or in the countryside. When the statewide campaign to consolidate the rural schools began in 1913, the Iowa State Teachers College trained teachers for the graded elementary and high schools. It had no program for training teachers or supervisors either for the traditional one-room schools or for the new consolidated schools that were to replace them.

At the turn of the century, Iowa farmers, like those elsewhere in the Midwest, found the rhetoric if not the practice of educational equality attractive. Most wanted their children to have educational opportunities comparable to but different from those available to town children. They expected that only some of their children would benefit from and/or want to attend high school. In this regard, the parents of farm children were not unlike working-class parents in the burgeoning cities. "Like parents everywhere, farmers of the Midwest generally had high aspirations for their children. They did not necessarily want them to be farmers. Rather they wished their children to be whatever they wished to be, to rise to whatever station in life their talents might take them." [14] They wanted high schools to be available for their children but they did not expect all of their children would or should attend them. They also worried about the increased costs of providing public high schools for farm children. Most farmers were unwilling to incur large increases in taxation to pay for the additional education that would benefit only a minority of farm children. If a farm child's aptitude and interests seemed to destine him or her for work in the city, farmers preferred to send that son or daughter to a really good high school — one located in one of the larger towns or cities in the area where the child might board with a friend or relative. If a son took an interest in farming, then a good common school education available in the country school, combined with the practical experience gained on the family farm, hard work, and attentiveness to innovations described in the farm journals, was considered all that was necessary for success in farming. Farm families generally did expect that at least one of their children would continue in farming on the "home place" and encouraged their other children to remain nearby. Farm households unable or unwilling to employ hired men also worried about how they would succeed economically with the loss of the child's labor power.

While the image of the "little red (or white) schoolhouse" is now one of nostalgia — an idealized abstraction of a bygone age — such was not the case at the turn of the century. The country school was then an institution directly controlled by the residents of small rural neighborhoods and the site at which 65 percent of Iowa's schoolchildren received their public schooling. It was, however, an institution under attack. The purpose of this book is to document the nature of that attack and the cultural and economic circumstances that spawned it, to analyze the political struggles it engendered, and to interpret them within the context of the political economy and geography of the period. How and why did farmers resist rural school consolidation? What were the intended and unintended impacts of rural school consolidation on local social relations? What were the lasting institutional effects? What is their relevance today?

Gabe said, think of the wildlife of an area as a rural community of people. Within its borders people are born, live, and die without getting very far from their birthplace. It is a complex place. The young and the old, the smart and the dumb, the gossips, the silent ones, the workers, the loafers, and the alarmists. All different and yet all have one thing in common, they know what goes on in their area.

— G. Nunnery, The Old Pro Turkey Hunter

2

FAMILY, NEIGHBORHOOD, CHURCH, AND SCHOOL

Until recently most historians and geographers have failed to probe very deeply into the nature of the social relations, rural institutions, and culture that characterized midwestern family farming throughout most of its history. One well-respected historian has even suggested that a distinctly rural culture failed to develop in the United States and that the American system of family farming was bereft of any authentic conception of community.[1] Recent scholarship calls these contentions into question and has presented substantial evidence that they are seriously flawed, if not false. This suggests that earlier scholars found no distinctive rural culture and an absence of community in rural areas either because they did not look for them or because they looked for them in the wrong places. Before the emergence of the new rural history in the late 1970s, most rural historians were geographical determinists. Clinging to European conceptions, they found no equivalent of a rural peasantry and mistakenly looked for community in towns and villages rather than in the countryside. Community as gemeinschaft was assumed to require regular, face-to-face interaction in tight-knit, family-based communities. They presumed that this in turn required a village-centered pattern of rural settlement; not dispersed farmsteads in the open country. Institutions like churches and schools also required village locations to be viable, according to this perspective on community.

The consensus of historians is that, in the United States as a whole, locality-based, communitarian social relationships were increasingly eclipsed by new forms of community from about 1870 onward. Growth in the scope and complexity of local life coupled with important losses in local autonomy encouraged people to restructure their conceptions of community. Increasingly, they identified with only selected aspects of their localities and only fragments of the larger society rather than with the totality of places in which their daily lives unfolded. Instead of breaking down or otherwise being destroyed, community took on a radically new form and quite varied meanings. No longer could community easily be equated with a social and territorial whole consisting of particular places linked through intensive spatial interaction. "The foundations of an older localized way of life were being eroded by new attitudes toward centralized authority and by innovations in transportation, communications, and organizational structure." [2] "Work, once securely planted in the context of family and locality, became separated from its traditional social context. Whereas work, family, and town once supplied mutually reinforcing personal orientations, they became crosscutting sources of identity in the bifurcated society that emerged in the late nineteenth century." People became involved in "different kinds of social relationships and held different statuses depending upon whether they were acting out a role as a member of a family, as political men and women, as followers of religious persuasions, or as participants in the economy." These changes did not occur uniformly in space or time and arrived later and proceeded more slowly in the rural Midwest, South, and Great Plains than elsewhere in the United States. While these roles had once been mutually reinforcing, creating territorialized sets of overlapping social relations easily recognizable as place-based communities, after 1870 they became more differentiated and even contradictory. "In time, each [role] developed its own autonomous conceptual framework within which social actions were framed. . . . Even in small towns, life became segmented, with major divisions following fault lines introduced by the intrusion of translocal institutions and role identities." [3]

As people in the towns and cities forged new social relationships and new forms of community at the turn of the century, older forms of community persisted in the rural areas even though the new social and economic realities were slowly undermining them as well. This resulted in sharpened cultural and class distinctions between farm people and townspeople — between traditional conceptions of community and more modern ones. In the countryside, exigencies stemming from the continued availability of relatively cheap land, a scarcity of labor, and the American practice of dispersed rural settlement conspired to make the family the preeminent social, economic, and educational institution of rural society. [4] Success or failure in any of these three senses was a family success or a family failure. Most rural historians have emphasized that these conditions also helped foster rural individualism and familial self-reliance as well as the relative isolation of farm families from the rest of society. Some have also maintained that the relative isolation of the rural family helped produced an intensely local orientation of politics in rural areas.[5]

Family, Neighborhood, and Class

Recent scholarship suggests that while emphasis on the family is appropriate, that on individualism is overdrawn, even misguided, and that on isolation is misspecified. It now appears that forms of community based on the rural neighborhood continued to persist in the Midwest because the family farming practiced there required them for its survival.[6] Economically, family farming relied upon the labor of family members and neighbors. Although farm families produced commodities for the market, they also needed to produce "goods that could be used directly on the farm or by the family or could be exchanged" in local nonmarket transactions. Otherwise, they could not meet their consumption needs and those of their neighbors.[7] The local social relationships of what W. J. Cash called a "kindly neighborhood communism persisted well into the twentieth century."[8] These relationships persisted because they were compatible with commercial farming and provided farm families with the vital safety net they needed to survive during hard times.

> American farmers lived within a dynamically growing capitalist world economy that encompassed the entire North American rim. Nearly all of them participated more or less regularly in commodity markets, to procure money to pay taxes and buy imported manufactured goods. Nonetheless, a system of noncommercial exchange developed in most rural communities based on male householder reciprocity . . . and . . . upon exchanges between women . . . rather than competitively set market prices. This system was imbued with great cultural significance by farm families, for it sustained their independence, their ability to live "competently" without being forced into abject financial dependence on creditors.[9]

Family labor power alone was seldom sufficient to meet the heavy labor needs of the farm at critical times in the cropping and livestock rearing cycles and during family emergencies or natural disasters. The uncompensated labor inputs from neighbors were not only necessary for the survival of the family farm, they were what made the midwestern system of family farming as productive as it was.[10] While "profits from cash markets were unpredictable because prices and weather" were "beyond the control of farm people; profits of production for home use and neighborhood exchange were more stable and helped assure survival."[11] Without the interest, the advice, and actual work rendered by family members and neighbors, family farming could not succeed. The help provided by neighbors was especially significant in times when the prices received for farm products were low.

Even though commodities produced on the family farm were bought and sold in the larger society, midwestern family farmers resisted easy categorization either as capitalist entrepreneurs or as members of the working class. Most preferred instead to view themselves as a "class apart." Family farmers did not fit very comfortably into the Marxist category of petty commodity producer either. Objectively, however, family farmers certainly seemed to fit that category. The contributions of individual farms and rural neighborhoods to the total agricultural production of the country were certainly small and family farmers remained among the fiercest defenders of private property. Nevertheless, the communal nature of neighborhood labor and its role in production was too important for the term petty commodity producer to be fully apt. Farmers were not ignorant or otherwise degraded peasants. Indeed, many surely viewed themselves as possessive individualists, and some even came to view themselves as a special class of businessmen. Nevertheless, the social relationships that sustained their production for the market gave meaning to the daily lives of their families and their neighborhoods.[12]

Money was typically in short supply in rural neighborhoods, even in the best of times. That which was available was needed to pay taxes and mortgages, and to buy machinery, hardware, and livestock. Uncompensated work exchanges within the neighborhood allowed families to minimize their expenditures on hired workers. Even when more money was available to more farm families during the first two decades of the twentieth century, farmers typically were loath to hire the labor services of other adult neighbors. They preferred instead to engage in informal nonmarket "exchanges" — exchanges set by local custom rather than through barter.[13]

"Breaking the sod, even with a moldboard plow, was a slow process. Barns, sheds, fences, and houses had to be built. Construction went on continuously for years, in addition to the ongoing work of raising crops and tending livestock. Within a family, children, older people, and women were all recruited to the workforce along with the working-aged men."[14]

At harvest time, the time for butchering, and "the laying in of firewood," family labor alone was insufficient. It was at times such as these that the neighborhood-based system of "changing" work was so important. Whereas capitalist farmers had to pay their workers in cash, this was not necessary in the "neighborhood system of family farming" characteristic of the Midwest.[15] Only a relatively small part of the payment family farm workers received was in cash. The major share came as in-kind transfers usually extended over long periods of time — even generations. Reciprocity was the expected form of exchange between neighbors. Reciprocity entailed obligation, not debt.

The relationship between geographical isolation and patterns of cultural maintenance and the intergenerational transfer of values has also been opened for reinterpretation in the new rural social history. Rather than foster individualism, as Turner argued, the relative isolation of farm families from markets forced a reliance on the extended lineal family and the neighborhood.[16] In many midwestern localities, immigrants from Germany constituted the largest single ethnic group engaged in family farming. Here the reliance on the extended lineal family and rural neighborhood was a basic goal of the system of family farming they had brought with them from Europe. In German neighborhoods, land was a "sacred trust maintained by achieving continuity of family land ownership and an agrarian way of life in a particular ethnic community." Land was sacred in the sense that a family's identity became bound up with the land it owned and worked, and the land in turn protected the family by providing it with security.[17]

Recent work also suggests that the family farm characterizing settled rural areas was not as isolated socially as had been assumed by earlier writers. Instead, the family farm was embedded in a dense web of community ties that connected farms and families in rural neighborhoods and integrated them into larger regional class structures. In short, whereas neighborhoods could be quite isolated from one another socially, family-farm households typically were not. For most rural communities, the "potentially disrupting forces from the larger society were mitigated to a large degree" not by their isolation from that society but "by the stability and constancy of family and social ties and the localism that continued to dominate the world view of settled rural inhabitants." Family farmers "were at once tied to larger national markets and also entwined in a face-to-face local life."[18] Farm people in the Midwest understood their lives in terms of these social relationships and structures, created as they were by social interaction and by the natural processes and labor processes that dominated their lives. Whether this produced a peculiarly myopic, local orientation to political activity is open to question. The clash between gemeinschaft and gesellschaft, so evident in urban and industrial contexts in the late nineteenth and early twentieth century, was far less evident in the lives of midwestern farm families. Indeed, the persistence of rural neighborhoods tended to structure social interaction such that the clash was quite place specific. It was more obvious in the dealings farm people had "in town" but often largely absent from the social and economic relationships they had with one another.

Midwestern family farms produced in excess of what was needed to reproduce and sustain family and neighborhood life and did so intentionally. Indeed, most were and always had been small commercial enterprises producing cash crops for regional, national, and world markets; but they were also significantly noncommercial, communal enterprises producing goods and services needed in rural neighborhoods. Both as commercial enterprises and as local institutions of cultural reproduction, farm families participated in the larger society's functions, crises, and history. Immigrants moved into rural neighborhoods while emigrants — typically young adults who either could not or preferred not to take up farming in or near the home neighborhood — fanned out from them. Farm families developed a distinct, yet subordinate class position in an overall system of agricultural production.

The overall system of agricultural production was capitalist, but relatively few family farmers in the early twentieth-century Midwest thought of themselves as capitalist businessmen. Few, if any, were averse to earning profits, for profits were necessary if the family was to remain in farming. The goal of family farming, however, was not capital accumulation for accumulation's sake, but only to improve the land and acquire what additional land was needed to maintain the family in farming intergenerationally. Family farming insulated farm families from the direct impacts of the changes in social relations linked to the emergence of wage labor and the factory system in the cities. Nonetheless, farm families were acutely aware of these changes. They realized that farm youths furnished much of the labor power needed in the burgeoning cities of the region. Even though the social relations of family farm production and reproduction were preindustrial, they were flexible enough to permit farm people to adapt to the exigencies of the early twentieth century.[19] The result was that social relations characterizing family farming changed more slowly than they did in the cities and larger towns. Farm people resisted changes that were patently destructive of those aspects of rural culture and social life they most valued.[20] The technical organization of production, however, was remarkably dynamic and very much up-to-date. Indeed, faced with a critical shortage of labor, family farmers showed little hesitancy in adopting mechanical innovations to lessen family labor inputs and enhance productivity. Objectively, the American system of family farm production had become fully integrated into the capitalist world economy by the 1890s.[21] Nevertheless, subjectively and socioculturally, family farmers remained members of preindustrial microsocieties struggling to adapt to the larger, more clearly capitalist society of which they were a part.

Social Construction of the Rural Neighborhood

Family, Work, and Landownership

While the family was the preeminent social and economic unit, the rural neighborhood ran a close second.[22] Recent studies of midwestern farm women's lives during this period reveal that while the farm household was of prime importance in direct production, the extended family was central in the other social relationships of the rural neighborhood.[23] The rural neighborhood was small both territorially and demographically. It usually consisted of fewer than two dozen households linked through kinship and marriage into a smaller number of extended families occupying a territory of only a few square miles. Since the relationship between the extended family and the neighborhood tended to be a reciprocal one, kin who left the neighborhood were often no longer functioning members of the family. As the frontier had moved westward and as conflicts between disparate groups gave way to the emergence of shared attitudes among persistent families, rural neighborhoods became more rather than less important social institutions.[24] Neighborhoods were the institutional means of organizing communal and individual work exchanges, the sharing of farm and household implements and other economic resources, and the trading and marketing of products produced by women. All of these activities helped farm families overcome inequalities in access to needed labor and capital resources. While rural neighborhoods in the Midwest tended to be homogeneous ethnically, mutual need among those sharing a common territory, not ethnicity, was the principal basis upon which neighborhoods were constructed.

Landownership was critical in the linked processes of family and neighborhood reproduction. In accumulating land, persistent families also accumulated social power and status. This usually received expression in the social landscape by the boundaries of rural neighborhoods conforming to geographical concentrations of these families. Often neighborhoods were named after their dominant families.[25] Given the high levels of fertility, the accumulation of additional land was essential to the reproduction of the lineal family. Only in this way could all or most of the (male) children be assured of a good start in life.[26] As long as the family's economic success remained tied to agricultural production, securing landownership remained far more important than providing one's children with an education above the rudimentary level already provided in the country school. By the beginning of the twentieth century, landownership became harder and harder to achieve. In many neighborhoods, particularly ethnic ones, farms were less and less frequently put on the open market and were instead increasingly exchanged only between family members (typically from father to son or son-in-law). While this helped ensure that particular farms remained in a family line, the rise of these "family land markets" made it more difficult to ensure the reproduction of that family in the home neighborhood. Farm children upon reaching adulthood had little choice but to seek land in other farm neighborhoods if they wished to remain in farming or to seek employment elsewhere.

Family gave social definition to the neighborhood, and the neighborhood became the locus of the family's social activity. Neighborhood building, like estate building, however, was gendered. While persistent families wielded disproportionate social and political power in a neighborhood, male heads of these families were those who exercised it. Men also controlled land and the money income from the sale of a farm's commercial products. It was the women, however, who typically forged the social and economic bonds through which these extended families became neighborhoods. Indeed, the primary means by which women could gain social power was by their influence in organizing neighborhood exchanges and social activities. Farm people, especially farm women, built neighborhoods in four ways: "visiting, exchanging work, exchanging products, and sharing life events." Of these, visiting or neighboring was probably the most important. Visiting provided a key social basis for the sharing of neighborhood resources, especially labor and equipment, that was crucial in the survival strategies of family farms.[27]

Neighborhood work exchanges were particularly important because they permitted the temporary expansion of the local labor force without adding the cost of hired workers. They included such activities as corn gathering, corn husking, wood chopping, hog butchering, threshing, haying, barn raisings, and road work. Men and women appeared to operate in separate economic spheres. Men focused on commodity production for extralocal markets, and women focused on producing goods needed in local markets and for the daily maintenance of the household. The boundaries of these spheres, however, were permeable, with women more likely to engage in boundary crossing than men. Most of a farm woman's work was in "maintaining a household production system that enabled the reproduction of the farm labor force. This work connected her to other women who were doing the same kind of work and with whom she exchanged her goods and services, but these exchanges were coordinated in an informal, decentralized way" in the rural neighborhood.[28]

The point of a woman's production and many of her "social" activities was to meet the needs of her household and those of other people (friends, relatives, and neighbors) with whom she was bound by local ties of reciprocity. Women exchanged labor and their products in neighborhood networks. Included in the former were gardening, caring for children, and sewing, while the latter included local trading in eggs, butter, sausage, sauerkraut, and so on. Although these exchanges sometimes involved cash payments, they were not market exchanges governed by the impersonal law of supply and demand. When the farms of a rural neighborhood had unequal resources, these exchanges and those organized by men could help offset inequalities rather than compound them. The opportunity to repay obligations over an indefinite time horizon and in many different forms "made it possible for neighbors to feel an equality in exchanges and to feel that exchanges were freely made between neighbors, not in an economic trade relation."[29]

Another key element of neighborhood "exchange" was the sharing of farm and household equipment that was too expensive for all farms in a neighborhood to procure for themselves. In well-integrated neighborhoods, this sometimes involved the creation of an intricate system for informally coordinating the buying and borrowing of major pieces of equipment by the various households in a neighborhood. While such borrowing did not require exchange per se, it did require mutual trust and reciprocity between neighbors. Both men and women built neighborhoods through these forms of social cooperation, but women "organized the symbolic social rituals" that helped institutionalize the mutual trust and reciprocity necessary for making them work over the longer run. The social relations characterizing neighborhoods were not limited to close kin. Through the locally structured relationships of neighboring, farm people could build ties that transcended their differences, or they could create an intimate core of families that exacerbated them. "Neighbors pooled local resources, and neighboring helped people preserve their family farms." But it "often made it difficult to organize broad coalitions, and excluded more marginal farm people. Those who were not part of neighborhood networks and those whose networks had few resources had more difficulty remaining on the land."[30]

Church and School

In areas settled by families of differing ethnicity, ethnic groups identified themselves according to their country of origin and religion as well as by neighborhood. Ethnic groups, as well as the native born, typically had their own rural churches. Within a set of contiguous rural neighborhoods any two adults of the same ethnic or cultural background were almost invariably linked to each other through multiple ties of kinship. These larger, extended-family groupings typically came together through their membership in a common rural church.[31] Church membership was by family. Men, as heads of families, controlled the formal organization. The activities of women, however, kept the church a vital part of rural communities and their constitutive neighborhoods. The rural church was not only a key institution linking many nonmarket, local social relations with those of the outside world, it also helped define and divide rural communities and neighborhoods territorially. Throughout the nineteenth century the relationship between the various Protestant denominations was primarily one of rivalry, which frequently led to a large number of rural churches serving smaller and smaller parishes. By the turn of the century, inter-Protestant rivalry and debate had subsided considerably. It had nonetheless left a legacy in the social landscape — a large number of rural churches, many with parishes that were no longer congruent with the rural neighborhoods in which they were located. While inter-Protestant rivalry had subsided, Protestant-Catholic conflict had, if anything, intensified and was soon to spill over into debates over the public schools.[32]

Just as important as the rural church, if not more so, in both defining rural neighborhoods and in linking them to the larger society was the rural school. The social relations characterizing the operation of the rural school were remarkably similar to those characterizing the rural church.

Run by a board of (male) directors, a country school brought together people of all ages. In the absence of paid assistants for the teachers, directors' wives cleaned the schoolhouses each fall and tended to the non-routine housekeeping matters. Students, parents and family members packed the schoolhouses for the parties, programs, and benefits, which were held at least monthly. The directors' wives and pupils' mothers worked together to provide for these gatherings and to assist with the arrangements. The collective work and leisure put neighborhood women in contact with each other and provided a sense of common purpose. . . . [C]ountry schoolteachers, nearly always unmarried women, lived in farm homes, where they became friends with the farm women, as well as models for young girls.[33]

Almost invariably operating on a territorial scale smaller than the rural church, the country school typically was the key institution in bonding rural people together in the common pursuit of goals and in fostering common values in rural neighborhoods.[34] Although appearing to be controlled by the heads of dominant landowning families in a rural neighborhood, the social cooperation required for this institution to function effectively demanded that it facilitate the reproduction of the neighborhood system of social cooperation and local structures of identity. Conflicts deriving from religious differences, particularly anti-Catholicism, were not uncommon in rural areas settled by persons of different ethnicities and national origins. However, they tended not to interfere with the operation of the country school as a neighborhood institution. Rural school districts were so small territorially that when ethnic and religious differences threatened neighborhood harmony, conflict could often be contained by redrawing school attendance area boundaries and/or moving the school building. This also had the effect, however, of changing neighborhood boundaries.

The country school was also a place — the place where formal education occurred, as well the central site at which all members of the rural neighborhood came together to decide important neighborhood matters. The schoolhouse was almost invariably the only genuinely communal property a rural neighborhood possessed and served as an important reminder of the social cooperation necessary for family farming to remain viable socially and economically. The boundaries of the country school district not only determined which school a child attended, they also tended to delimit the boundaries of rural neighborhoods, if only by default. The exception was when almost all families in a locality attended the same rural church. Country school districts (and subdistricts) invariably became etched in the collective and individual identities of rural people.

In both its educational and communitarian roles, the country school was more a social extension of the family than a fundamental building block of democratic self-government. Although women overwhelmingly composed the bulwark of the teaching force for the country schools of the Midwest, women seldom ran for election to the boards of directors in the country school districts, even in states, like Iowa, that permitted it. The wielding of overt power in rural neighborhoods was patriarchal and no more or less democratic than it was anywhere else in American society.

Recently, educational historian Paul Theobald has suggested that local school board men wielded their authority over the country schools in ways that were fundamentally exclusionary and antithetical to the democratic ideal of educational equality.

The school board men of the rural Midwest served as community guardians in their local neighborhoods. Together with other taxable residents, they had the power to make sure that the school promoted intergenerational stability. The various forms of intolerance that were manifested in decisions about where to locate the school, who would be allowed to vote in a school meeting, who could use the schoolhouse during non-school hours, who was eligible for instruction in the school, and what language this instruction would be in were not based on arbitrary likes and dislikes. These decisions hinged on traditions that evolved according to what certain farmers supposed would be the best set of neighborhood circumstances. Institutional manipulation at the local level was a small part of the process whereby a minority population came to own land and possess the ability to pass it on to their descendants.[35]

Specifically, Theobald suggests that persistent landowners used their social power to manipulate local school policy to keep women and tenants from competing with them for the control of local land markets. While correctly identifying the school as a key neighborhood institution, he overstates the extent to which control over it could be used to pursue the parochial material interests of dominant families in rural neighborhoods. As will be seen in later chapters, the rural church was a much more effective institution of exclusion, particularly if it could wield its influence over a local public school system. There is no doubt that male heads of persistent families were attentive to questions of neighborhood maintenance and intergenerational reproduction and often sought to perpetuate locally dominant ethnic and religious values as well. However, they certainly did not have an economic incentive to make their neighborhoods unattractive to tenants, as Theobald suggests, but quite the opposite. Family farmers, concerned as they were with intergenerational persistence, almost invariably owned or attempted to own more land than the conjugal family unit alone could work. They did so for the simple reason that they had to buy land that their children would eventually farm when it came on the market, not when their children needed it. For the intergenerational objectives of the traditional family farmer to be realized in an increasing capitalist land market, landowners needed tenants just as much as tenants needed economically rational landlords. Furthermore, for farmers subscribing to the logic of capitalist accu-

mulation rather than to preindustrial traditions (like intergenerational persistence in a locality), choosing tenancy over landownership was often the
economically more rational choice (see chapter 6).

In short, Theobald is probably right about school board men resisting
educational reform because they perceived it as reducing their ability to preserve their rural neighborhoods. However, he is probably wrong about the
specifics of what they were trying to preserve and why.[36] If neighborhood
patriarchs wanted to manipulate school policy to exclude potential com-
petitors entering a local land market, then control of an open-country consolidated school district was a better means of achieving that than control
of the traditional country school. The reason for this was simple: the consolidated district had the potential for controlling a larger land market.
Could it not be that, in fighting rural school consolidation, farmers were
trying to preserve a broader set of values and that among these was an
authentic desire to preserve their rural neighborhoods for reasons of economic survival, personal worth, and identity?

*Progress: Progress is electricity, school consolidation, church remodeling,
second farm tractors, second farm cars, hay bailers, cornpickers, grain
combines, field choppers, and indoor plumbing.*
— Ollie in the motion picture Hoosiers

3

THE COUNTRY LIFE
MOVEMENT AND MORAL
LANDSCAPES OF MODERNITY

The "Agrarian Myth" into the New Century

One of the taproots of American culture has long involved
an idealization of rural life and living and a sentimental attachment to the
rural as somehow more "natural" and moral. Richard Hofstadter refers to
the complex of notions upon which this attachment and idealization were
based as the "agrarian myth." Essentially the myth contended that agriculture was the nation's basic industry — the one upon which all others depended — and that farming was a morally and spiritually superior way of
life. Farmers, it was maintained, were more independent, self-sufficient,
honest, dependable, free, and devoted to high moral principles, including
those of democracy. Ironically, as the myth became increasingly fictional as
the nineteenth century wore on, people clung to it even more widely and
tenaciously.[1]

In the last decades of the nineteenth century, as agricultural production
lurched through cycles of boom and bust of ever-increasing amplitude,
midwestern cities experienced an industrial and business boom of unprece-
dented proportions. During the 1880s alone, the populations of Chicago
and Omaha more than doubled, while that of Kansas City more than quadrupled.[2] While larger places such as these became the nation's archetypal

industrial centers, small- and medium-sized cities — Cedar Rapids, Water-loo, Davenport, Rockford, Peoria — were growing equally, if not more, vigorously.[3] A greatly accelerated process of rural-to-urban migration and a vast influx of non-English-speaking immigrants from southern and eastern Europe fueled urban growth. Rural-to-urban migration provided a labor force acculturated to accept the commercial and acquisitive value system that undergirded both commercial agriculture and industrial capitalism. Indeed, industrial capitalism in the cities of the Midwest developed concomitantly with the growth of petty agricultural commodity production on its family farms, at least partially justifying the contention that the American road to capitalism passed directly through the gate of the family farm.[4]

Millions, however, were leaving the farms, including those in the supposedly prosperous Midwest where even some of the richest farming regions registered rural population losses for the first time in the period 1900–1910.[5] Rural migrants flocked to the larger towns and cities in search of jobs, even though these were the places that according to the agrarian myth were filled with temptation, vice, and corruption. Materially, the reality of the situation seemed to be that "agriculture could not compete with industry and urban life."[6]

Those leaving the farms did not necessarily abandon their agrarian values. Many took them to the city and sought to render urban spaces more like the rural, providing political support for the City Beautiful movement and the beginnings of city planning. At century's turn, when the United States was poised to assume a position of industrial leadership in the world economy, the agrarian myth still dominated most middle-class Americans' view of themselves and their society. The situation in midwestern rural neighborhoods, however, was different. Here the myth appeared to be losing ground quite rapidly, a trend that began with the defeat of agrarian populism in the 1890s. The prominent Henry A. Wallace of *Wallace's Farmer* noted that the midwestern farmer increasingly appeared to be living in two quite different worlds.

One is the world of the handicraft period, of the American frontier. In this world, he objects to limiting production because he does not like to see his neighbor hunger. He looks on the farm as a home, rather than as a business. He hopes for a good living, but does not look for any great amount of wealth. But he lives also in another, the world of modern business. There he learns that adjusted production is only sound business; the capitalization of earning power in the form of land or stock values is the conventional thing with all great industries; that shrewd dealing on the market will make up for lack of skill in production.

Wallace maintained that the "standards of the handicraft age" had the greater social value, but worried about whether, in the "clash between the two," the older standards could hope to survive? "Perhaps they might," he opined "but certainly not until the farmer learns to see far more clearly than now the difference between the two worlds of economic thought to each of which he now pledges an impossible allegiance."[7] Only in some ethnic communities did the older standards appear deeply enough ingrained and reinforced by the social relationships of neighborhood to withstand the allure of a more urban modernity.[8]

While the period 1900–1914 is usually referred to as the golden age of U.S. agriculture, the term could just as appropriately be applied to the entire period 1900–1920. Although there was a mild downturn in agricultural prices in 1913–14, the big discontinuities in price levels occurred at the very beginning and end of this two-decade period.[9] This longer period was "golden" not just because of the high and stable farm prices throughout its duration, but because they were high and increasing. Although the Midwest remained the nation's leader in agricultural production, the golden age wrought a number of significant economic changes in the countryside and in the relations between town and countryside.[10] The market value of farmland was increasing rapidly, as was the incidence and extent of mortgage indebtedness. As family farms became more commercial and devoted less effort to satisfying household and neighborhood consumption needs, they became more dependent upon external distribution agencies. The processing of agricultural products that had earlier passed from rural neighborhood and village to the town became concentrated in a small number of large cities. Although the prices of farm products rose dramatically in the pre–World War I period and outstripped the rate of increase in nonfarm commodities, the per capita incomes of farm people continued to run below those of the rest of the population. Most farm families remained reliant on the social and economic security net provided by the rural neighborhood. Agricultural prosperity, however, led to growing income disparities and an increasing fragmentation of family farmers along new lines of class division. What had previously been a relatively cohesive class of family farmers began to divide into subclasses based on crosscutting dimensions of tenure status, economic status, and their receptivity to the individuating ideology of "progressive" agriculture. Although it took the onset of agricultural depression in the early 1920s to render them transparent, these new class divisions emerged in the spatially uneven manner characteristic of capitalist development. The terms applied to class divisions varied from one locality to another, but such terms as traditional family farmer, progressive farmer, hired men, and absentee landlords were common.

Tenant farmers had been a significant and slowly increasing minority of the total population of family farmers in the Midwest ever since the region was first opened for settlement and agricultural development. In 1880, almost 24 percent of all farm operators in Iowa were renters; a figure that increased each decade until the 1930s. In 1920, tenants made up approximately 42 percent of all farm operations in the state.[11] Tenancy, however, had never been a very good indicator of either the income or class status of a farm family in the Midwest. Tenant status also had little impact on the operation of the neighborhood system of family farming.[12] Tenant farmers were as likely to have relatives in a neighborhood as were landowners. There were few barriers to their participation in neighborhood exchanges; indeed, their neighbors expected them to participate. The neighborhood system required economic and social reciprocity among those sharing geographical proximity. As long as incoming renters were also dependent on this system to help ensure their survival and showed a willingness to participate in their new neighborhoods, they were seldom excluded from its activities. More important to the continued significance of the neighborhood in family farming was its stability in terms of the in- and out-migration of families and the economic status of those who persisted. Neither of these varied very directly with tenure status.

Farm families whose economic needs were greatest were those most likely to participate in exchange and neighboring practices.[13] Therefore it was the newfound rural prosperity characterizing the golden age, not increasing levels of tenancy per se, that posed a threat to the neighborhood system of family farming. With increased money incomes, more farmers sought economic security by capitalist means through increases in acreage and investments in equipment rather than through social investments in the neighborhood-based system of exchange and support. This trend was more pronounced among the native born and nonethnic. As the market value of prime agricultural land increased, choosing to rent rather than own became an attractive "capitalist" means of achieving economic security. The result in many localities, particularly in richer agricultural states like Illinois and Iowa, was that tenants increasingly worked the best land and occupied the largest farms. Farmers in such areas, both landowners and tenants, were those who were less likely to be reliant on neighborhood exchanges. They were also more likely to subscribe to the tenets of progressive farming, including evincing a preference for owning (or renting) a neighbor's farm rather than having that person as a neighbor.[14]

Other changes in the geography of rural social and economic life during this period also deserve emphasis. Before the turn of the century, small villages and country towns had been sites for a considerable amount of artisanal manufacturing activity, most of which catered to local markets. As such, they were more than the mere service centers many of them would later become. Millers, coopers, harnessmakers, shopkeepers, and bankers provided local employment for those farm children who either could not or chose not to take up farming. This enabled the extended family to remain more cohesive geographically than it otherwise would have.[15] However, improved transportation, RFD, mail-order shopping, and the concentration of manufacturing in the cities from the 1880s onward, resulted in the loss of population and nonfarm jobs in most villages and small towns. Furthermore, the nature of nonfarm jobs in the towns changed from preindustrial artisanal/apprentice systems of employment to those more dependent on skills taught in the high school. Increasingly, the better jobs were available only in the larger towns and cities of the region.

Under these changed social and economic conditions, the alternatives for the intergenerational reproduction of the farm family and neighborhood were limited. A farmer and his wife could help their children secure their own farms as close to the home farm as possible. Alternatively, they could help them buy farm machinery and livestock so as to obtain favorable share agreements as renters. There was another possibility, one favored by middle-class reformers: investing in additional education for one's children to give them a different economic basis upon which to form and launch their own households elsewhere. Here the investment of the farm family was not in land, not in capital goods, but in "human capital." Investment in it became the analogue of the more traditional investment in the accumulation of land to eventually transfer to one's children. The problem with this alternative was that it did not ensure the extended reproduction of family farming and contradicted a corollary of the agrarian myth — that opportunity lay in the land and not in education.

Rise of the Country Life Movement

While many midwesterners welcomed the material advantages wrought by rapid industrialization and urbanization, others worried about whether industrial growth was sustainable both socially and economically or whether it would lead to new and sharper class divisions and class conflict. The hegemony of the agrarian myth in the American consciousness had been an effective antidote to these fears throughout the nineteenth century, but it was not clear that that hegemony would carry into the twentieth. To help ensure that it would, a small but influential cadre of urban elites from agrarian backgrounds coalesced into what became known as the Country Life movement. It became one of the more important rural reform movements and ideological forces gripping intellectual circles during the Progressive Era. In the Midwest, Country Lifers concentrated their intellectual efforts on finding some means of preserving the great farming class on the region's rich prairies. If such a means could not be identified and implemented, they feared that the core values of agrarianism might be lost forever.[16]

The Country Life movement also attracted considerable support from three other groups driven by related, but different, considerations. First was a large group of leading businessmen who realized that the competitive position of U.S. firms in the world economy would be endangered without the continued availability of cheap foodstuffs.[17] Second was a rising cadre of social scientists enamored with conceptions of efficiency and with the possibility of applying social engineering to problems of agricultural production.[18] Third were the leaders of several of the mainline Protestant denominations. They saw the demise of agrarianism as a portent of crisis for the country church and of rural social decay more generally.[19]

Despite their apparent heterogeneity, these groups agreed that American agricultural production and the nature of rural life that sustained it were antiquated and in need of modernization. Otherwise, farming would not remain competitive with other occupations and ways of living. Even the social composition of the farming class seemed to be undergoing a significant transformation. The region's most productive farmers, it was claimed, were deserting agriculture for urban occupations, while their places were being taken by those lacking in entrepreneurial spirit or by those otherwise unsuited for any other occupation. According to this view, "progressive" farmers were being pushed out of the countryside by its economic backwardness and social stagnation with greater force than they were being pulled out by the social and economic attractions of the city. The latter was one of the main conclusions of the 1909 report of the Country Life Commission appointed by President Roosevelt.[20] Those who remained were thought to be inattentive to the means for increasing yields being pioneered in the new agricultural sciences and ill-equipped educationally to take advantage either of them or of the improved business and marketing practices that could make family farming more efficient. This seemed to account for why increases in agricultural productivity in the early years of the twentieth century were meager compared to those of the late nineteenth century or to agricultural productivity in the United Kingdom and Germany — the United States's major economic rivals in the world economy. "In the decade from 1900 to 1910, the United States produced an average of 14.1 bushels of wheat per acre, on land that had been farmed less than a century, while Germany produced 28.9 bushels and the United Kingdom 33.1 bushels per acre, on land that had been cultivated for a thousand years or more."[21] The concerns of Country Life leaders, however, ran deeper than this. They felt that the American farm family had not participated in the social and economic progress of the urban-industrial age as fully as had urban residents. Instead, farm families bore the costs of urban progress. Rural social structures, institutions, and values disintegrated through rural depopulation and the in-migration of European immigrants subscribing to values alien to those previously dominant. The cities attracted public investment in their social and physical infrastructures, while rural areas languished from neglect. To make matters worse, the shortage of farm workers seemed to be compelling farm people to work harder and for longer hours simply to remain in farming. Insofar as Country Lifers recognized the existence of the neighborhood system of family farming at all, they argued that it had been thoroughly undermined by the changed circumstances of country life. Even if it could be resuscitated, it was thought to be an aberrant system belonging to an earlier era of agricultural development, one antithetical to any modern concept of progress. Country Life leaders, however, could agree that unless trends were reversed, social and economic life in the country's great agricultural regions would disintegrate even further.

If the social and economic disadvantages of country life seemed clear enough, ways of overcoming them without also destroying the supposed advantages were not. The Country Life Commission recommended a few specific reforms such as federal road building, parcel post, and federal public health initiatives, but more fundamental changes seemed necessary. In particular, new rural institutions needed to be created to stem the flow of persons, especially of farm youth, to the cities and to retain the "better class" of farmers in the countryside.[22] Many of those affiliated with the movement feared that, without the creation of new institutions, class conflict might spread from the cities to the countryside and undermine American economic progress as a whole. That a class alliance might be forged between farmers and the urban working class, along the lines envisioned by some

Populists only a few years earlier, was viewed with particular dread. Leaders of the movement sought new institutions that would modernize rural life, yet preserve what they saw as the more physically beneficent and aesthetic aspects of country life. The new institutions would be engineered by those in positions of power, not by farmers themselves.[23] While the movement reached no consensus about what specific forms these new institutions should take, its impact in setting limits for the subsequent discourses of rural reform were enormous.

Preserving the Agrarian Myth

Almost from its beginnings the Country Life movement split into two groups advocating mutually antagonistic objectives. One group stressed "making farmers into businessmen," and the other was nostalgic for those "days when farmers enjoyed a higher, more secure status" and a distinctive "way of life."[24] Those in the first group did not mourn the increasing gap between the agrarian myth and the realities of turn-of-the-century commercial agriculture. Wilbert Anderson, for example, writing in 1906 greeted what he called the "new industrial order" in American agriculture with considerable enthusiasm, even celebration:

> It is often forgotten that the materialism of the present day is most wonderfully allied to ethics. What we see is not so much a new material development as a new embodiment of the moral life. Never has the world seen such an environment for the production of the noblest character as that which now presses upon men in every part of the great workshop in the midst of whose din they live. In the case of the country people the struggle for adaptation means the remaking of character. The indolent, passive, meditative, vegetative man must give place to the alert, virile, strenuous man.
>
> Economic adjustment may be won in either of two ways. On the one hand a man may lower the price of his product by lessening the expenditure upon himself. This low-cost laborer is everywhere; he appears in every vacant place, abhorring a vacuum like the air. He is in the country as well as the city. One great movement in the country is the effort to meet the demands of the situation by cheapening men. This is the significance of the displacement of the old stock by the immigrant. . . . But there is another and a better way to meet the exactions of the market by new thrift, by better management, and by higher intelligence. The farmer

must do the one thing or the other; he must be a better farmer or an inferior man. The downward tendency will have a limited field; in the main the new adaptation will be won by a higher intelligence. This means an uplifting of great masses of the country people, and for this process the instrumentalities are at hand.[25]

New Instrumentalities: School Consolidation and the Country Town

According to Anderson, the "instrumentalities" available for hastening the arrival of a new industrial order in agriculture were four. They included the introduction of the "new agricultural education" in rural schools, political action to regulate monopolies, the widespread investment by farmers in joint-stock corporations and the subsequent expenditure of their new-found wealth locally, and rural school consolidation.[26] The transformation of farmers into modern capitalist actors practicing scientific agriculture would help the country town recover its lost prosperity and place the regional economy as a whole on a sound footing. Rural school consolidation centered on a town or village in each township would bring "dignity and importance" to the township as a new and needed political institution in the territorial articulation of a more interventionist state. Unlike some Country Lifers, Anderson thought that rural-to-urban migration was draining the countryside of both its best and worst farmers. He thought that the loss of the better farmers could be reversed if a new rural consciousness could be created among farm people. Consolidating rural schools in small towns, each dominating township-sized territories, appeared to him to be the ideal first step in instilling such a consciousness. In his words, "The consolidated school has powerful influence for good: the children from different sections are educated together; their acquaintance is wide as the town; life for them is in a larger world; they escape the provincialism of the remote school district. Children growing up with the town consciousness promise much for the uplift and enrichment of the community."[27]

Like Anderson, most Country Lifers agreed that a significant restructuring of country life was necessary for the survival of agriculture. Few, however, were willing to abandon the agrarian myth altogether. The movement's more influential leaders in the Midwest clung to their belief in the moral superiority of family farming as a means of organizing agricultural production. They could agree with Anderson, however, that rural social and economic relationships needed to be reorganized spatially. Farmers needed to better recognize their interdependencies with others involved in the increasingly attenuated chains of economic transactions entailed in getting farm products to market. The first step was to bring farmers and the people from the lowest level of urban places — those serving as the primary markets and retail centers for farm families — together in new, more spatially extensive, yet still "local" communities or jurisdictions. This accomplished, both farmers and townspeople would recognize their common social and economic problems and seek appropriate solutions to them. These small urban places were economically dependent on agricultural production in their tributary areas. They served as "central places" in the collection, preliminary processing, and transshipment of farm commodities. They served as retail centers supplying farmers with those goods necessary for the extended reproduction of family farming that farmers did not produce themselves. They served as the places of residence for the increasing numbers of retired farmers. Country Lifers also claimed that these places were "rural-minded" in the sense that all or most of their residents had an objective economic interest in local agriculture and its continued vitality. Finally, Country Lifers claimed that these places were the most appropriate sites for consolidating the social, religious, and educational activities of rural communities.

The crossroads rural church and rural school had served their rural neighborhoods well in earlier times, when the poor conditions of transport and the heavy labor inputs of the farm often limited the spatial extent of the rural community to the rural neighborhood. The space-time convergence brought on by recent revolutions in transport and communications technology required a recentering of rural economic and social life. Country Life reformers saw the neighborhood system of family farming as aberrant and premodern, necessarily giving way to progressive farming freed from the strictures of locality and embracing the social relations of urban middle-class modernity reconstituted in a rural context. Country Lifers, however, confronted a practical problem. Subjectively, farmers and townspeople often failed to recognize their interdependencies or, when they did, they resented them rather than using them as a springboard for effective collective action. Practical problems, however, could be overcome. In principle, midwestern Country Lifers had found what they thought was the key element of an institutional solution to the central problem of country life. What was needed was a new kind of place, the "country town," a rural community combining the advantages of both city and country. Powerful social and economic forces were already transforming rural life and articulating it more closely with a regional hierarchy of urban places. Leaders of the Country Life movement believed that the problems of country life could be solved through appropriate spatial and economic planning and public investment.

They saw the reform of two rural institutions — the rural church and the rural school — as central to that process.

Church, School, and State

Two years after the national Country Life Commission offered its report, a rural sociologist at Iowa State College, John Lewis Gillin, informed readers of the *American Journal of Sociology* that the key rural institution holding farm people on the land, the country church, was in trouble and that its demise spelled the end of community life in the open country. The causes of this state of affairs were the reduction in interdenominational rivalry and rural population loss. No longer were new Protestant denominations blanketing the midwestern countryside with churches as they competed with one another for relatively fewer and fewer parishioners. As even more rural areas registered rural population losses in the first decade of the twentieth century, "overchurching" of the countryside became even more apparent. It also became increasingly difficult for rural churches to pay the salaries necessary to attract resident pastors. In Gillin's words,

> Together with this softening of the ecclesiastical attitude toward other religious bodies there went the great social changes which the attractions of the towns were making in the country congregation. Here one and there another family moved to town. They came back to the country to visit their neighbors oftener on Sunday than any other day because they could best get away that day. Perhaps they went to church at first, but after a time they got out too late to get to the service, and the family stayed at home to have the dinner ready for them when they came. Thus began a tendency to find one's social interests satisfied outside the church. Then some of the young people began to drift off to the town. When they came back their stories made restless the other young people. Soon the drift to the town was on. That broke the social solidarity of the young people of the community and put the church down from its predominating social leadership in the community. The church had ceased to be the only social center of the community. Communication between town and country was increased when some of the older people retired from the farm and moved to the neighboring town. In all these ways the church ceased to be the social center it had once been. It lost its hold upon the people.[28]

Gillin was not alone in this view. Indeed by 1911, it had become the dominant one in the new field of rural sociology — whose philosophical roots can be traced to the rural branch of the social gospel movement of mainline Protestantism in the 1890s, but whose academic legitimacy stemmed directly from the work of Liberty Hyde Bailey and Kenyon Butterfield, the co-founders of the Country Life movement.[29] Rural sociologists argued that rural neighborhoods had broken down and the rural church was rapidly losing its importance as the chief spiritual and social meeting place for farm families. According to this view, the newfound agricultural prosperity, which had put discretionary income in the pockets of operating farmers, had hastened the process. The town was the place where social relations were increasingly becoming commodified, where the additional income was usually spent, and where more and more farmers relocated upon their retirement. Compared to town churches and town schools, country churches and country schools were less edifying and more old-fashioned. It appeared that "new interests had taken the place of the old. New ideals had come to dominate in everything else but the country church and the country school."[30]

According to this characterization of the changing nature of rural life, the drift to the cities and larger towns could be arrested only by making the church and rural school the centers of a thoroughly modern rural community life. In 1912, Warren H. Wilson, Superintendent of Church and Country Life for the Presbyterian Church, himself trained in both sociology and theology, maintained that rural churches held the "key to the problem of country life. If they oppose modern socialized ideals in the country, these ideals cannot penetrate the country." If, however, they "undertake constructive social service in the country, the task will be done."[31] Following a variant of social Darwinism, he argued that that there had been four "economic types" of farmers in midwestern agriculture, each the result of successive evolutionary transformations of the rural economy: the *pioneer*, the *land farmer*, the *exploiter*, and the just emerging *husbandman*. Each of these types, he argued, was characterized by a particular way of earning a living and by its own kind of community and church, but that all four types could coexist contemporaneously. The then dominant type, the exploiter, he argued, was simply a transitional phase in the development of midwestern agriculture, "created in the period of re-distribution of land. The characteristic of the exploiter is his commercial valuation of all things. He is the man who sees only the value of money. . . . The commercial exploitation of land dissolves every permanent factor in the farm economy. The country community of the land-farmer type is being undermined and is crumbling away under the influence of exploitation." Wilson suggested that the exploitation of land was a process with which the church in the country could deal by persuasion. "It is an economic condition," he argued, that needed to be understood and reacted to by rural teachers and preachers alike as a transition through which country people had to go before they would recognize the necessity of "an organized and scientific agriculture."

> Gradually the influence of science and the leadership of the departments and colleges of agriculture are being extended in the country. Little by little, whether through landlord or tenant, farming is becoming a profession requiring brains, science and trained intelligence. The country church should promote this process because only through its maturity can the country church in the average community find its own establishment. The reconstruction of the churches now going on corresponds to the exploitation of the land. The duty of the church in the process of exploitation is to build the community and to make itself the center of the growing scientific industry on which the country community in the future will be founded.[32]

The rural church, however, could not accomplish this social transformation on its own. Also required was the implementation of a new type of rural education and perhaps even a new kind of rural public school. On this, Country Lifers, professional educators, and national leaders of the mainline Protestant churches could all agree. The secular nature of the public school made it the only institution capable of producing the desired results. Rural churches, however, could and should take the lead in mobilizing support for scientific agriculture and for a transformation of the rural school curriculum. The following excerpt from Herbert Quick's unabashedly reformist novel, *The Fairview Idea*, published in 1919 illustrates these sentiments well. Quick was an Iowan who wrote a series of quite popular novels championing the social programs advocated by the leaders of the Country Life movement. The dialogue is between a farmer, Uncle Abner, and a rural minister imbued with the social gospel preached by the leaders of the Country Life movement.

> "Aren't you afraid," I asked, "that a big consolidated school, with an auditorium and all that will do a lot of the work we are doing through the Meeting House Association [of our interdenominational country church] — and sort of weaken us?"
>
> "Uncle Abner," he said, "if that turns out to be the case, it will prove that we are doing what the community ought to do for itself through taxation. Our church may live forever, or it may die with us who have established it; but the school, based on government and supported by taxation lasts as long as the government lasts. And I can see things enough to do to keep the congregation busy when the school takes off

our hands some of the work we have done because there was no other agency to do it. If I have children to bring up in Fairview, I shall want a good school. And I'm for it now."[33]

In the early years of the movement, not all Country Lifers and their allies had given up on the educational possibilities of the small, one-teacher school. In many instances the same farm people who controlled the rural church also controlled the rural school. Since he was often the only agent of modernity in a rural community, the charismatic preacher trained in the methods of rural sociology could be a powerful instrument of rural social change, including school reform. By 1919, however, almost everyone affiliated with the Country Life movement had agreed on the necessity of rural school consolidation and on also finding a comparable way of reducing the number of rural churches. Unlike other regions of the country, the Midwest possessed a large number of local trade and service centers. This ensured that few families lived farther than a few miles from a village or town of some description. This helped ensure that "country towns" and not the countryside became the favored sites for consolidated schools among Country Life advocates in the Midwest.[34] This view is apparent in the pioneering religious-sociological work of Benson Landis in two counties in the Midwest — one in Iowa and the other in Indiana. Landis concluded that the effort to consolidate rural churches had much to learn from the study of rural school consolidation.

The rural school and its leaders are far ahead of the country church and its administrators. The school leaders are endeavoring to build up few and strong institutions at the trade centers that will employ fewer teachers and yet have an abler staff. The consolidated school gives greater opportunity to the rural child. The trained superintendent can get closer to the pupils. Instead of having a large number of small ungraded schools scattered over the trade area, one efficient school center is rapidly taking their places. The lessons of efficiency are being learned in the schools. How long before the rural church will begin to move in this direction? The movement for consolidation in the schools will, however, serve as an object lesson to young and old in the churches in the Middle West. They should now plan to eliminate the large number of extra churches which are not worth what they cost. This weeding-out process cannot begin too soon. Many churches deserve extinction. They are sectarian in spirit, lack community vision and exist for the worship of a mere handful of individuals. In getting rid of the extra churches local desires should be consulted. If the community wants a federated church, then let it have all assistance possible from the respective denominations. If an undenominational community church is desired, then let it be tried, at least. If all but one denominational church should withdraw, and this one be made responsible for a certain program in the field, then all the forces which have to do with rural church administration should help in such a readjustment. Usually trading of local churches can be accomplished with benefit to the communities and the denominations concerned.[35]

The Country Town as a Protestant Place

The concept of the "country town" was probably the principal ideological legacy of the Country Life movement's efforts to recreate the social geography of the midwestern landscape.[36] If the traditional agrarian myth could not be preserved in the countryside, then it should be recreated in a more modern form by creating a new kind of place, country towns, possessing the properties of both the rural and the urban and defined physically by the trade areas of the small village or town. To do so required an institutional means; both the mainline Protestant churches and the consolidated school located in the country town filled the bill almost perfectly. Rural school consolidation, however, also seemed to possess some added advantages over the rural or small-town church. It could improve the educational level of farm children, better preparing them to assume the urban-industrial jobs that many of them would have to fill as the number of farmers dwindled. It could introduce the methods of scientific agriculture, modern business practices, and home economics to the next generation of farmers, thereby not only enhancing agricultural productivity but also improving the quality of farm life. It could help revitalize other rural institutions, especially the rural church, now also suitably relocated in or consolidated with those of the country towns. It might even be instrumental in convincing the next generation of farmers of the need for cooperative organizations to lower the costs of capital inputs and to increase the farmers' share of profits from the sale of agricultural products.[37] In short, it seemed to be a key institution in the reengineering of country life — not in preserving the traditional agrarian myth, but recreating it in a more modern form.

Although the Catholic church in the United States would eventually develop its version of the Country Life movement, the preoccupation with the consolidation of rural life in the country town had its origins in American Protestantism. The country town was to be a nonethnic, Protestant place. This ideology and the close relationships between the home missions work of the mainline Protestant churches, rural sociologists, and the emergence of rural school consolidation as the preferred solution to the problems of country life were not lost on most Catholics and many Lutherans in the Midwest. Each of these churches had well-established traditions of maintaining parochial schools whenever concentrations of adherents made that possible. Not surprisingly, the efforts of the mainline Protestant denominations (especially Baptists, Methodists, and Congregationalists) to push for rural school consolidation engendered considerable skepticism and conflict in areas in which Catholics or Lutherans were numerous. Catholics and Lutherans in the Midwest were well aware that anti-Catholicism and nativism ran deep among many Protestants in the Midwest. They remembered their struggles in the early 1890s to repeal antiparochial school legislation in Wisconsin and Illinois — the Bennett and Edwards laws, respectively — that had been pushed through the Wisconsin and Illinois General Assemblies by nativist Protestants in 1889.[38] To most Catholics and many Lutherans, rural school consolidation appeared to be an alternative means of coercing rural German-American and Catholic schoolchildren into attending public schools, especially the public high school, rather than attending parochial school, thereby destroying the viability of parochial education and undermining ethnic communities. Although this may not have been one of the intended consequences of rural school consolidation, it was one of its effects. As such it was to become a significant, but underplayed, dimension in the political economy of public schooling in the Midwest and in the attempts to reform rural education.

Whenever we differentiate greatly between the education of boys and girls in the country and those in the city, we are in danger of engendering class distinctions, castes, and social strata that work dissension and strife. Rural life and rural education are at present suffering from lack of real leadership, and the country boys and girls of America are not getting a square deal. . . . The system is at fault and must be reorganized until every rural school . . . shall become part of a larger school system having a graded school of more than one teacher — in brief, a centralized or consolidated school.

— Julius Bernhard Arp, Rural Education and the Consolidated School

4

THE POLITICAL ECONOMY OF
PUBLIC SCHOOLS IN THE MIDWEST
DURING THE GOLDEN AGE

In the early nineteenth-century Midwest, the school was a place not much different from other local institutions composing civil society. In any locality the boundaries between institutions were highly permeable and educational tasks were quite casually shifted from one setting for social interaction to another according to local needs and availability.[1] Collectively, the various institutional settings — the household, church, school, shops, and so on — operated in parallel, giving social meaning and definition to neighborhood and community. By the middle of the nineteenth century, however, the urban middle-class family was much more sharply differentiated from other social institutions, and a more sophisticated system for socializing succeeding generations appeared desirable, if not necessary. "The capacity of the family to socialize the child may not have changed, but the society the children would be entering had." It had become bifurcated into the familial world of gemeinschaft and the impersonal, more commodified world of gesellschaft. The large graded school, drawing its pupils from territories much larger than the neighborhood, served as a bridge between the worlds. In urban areas, the role of the school was not "to take over the family's educational functions, but rather to perform new ones that the family could not accomplish."[2] The family taught children about "community," while the school introduced them to the larger, increasingly urban, class-divided society and their likely roles in it. In rural areas, this bifurcation was far less apparent in people's everyday lives. There was no rush among people living and working in the countryside to transform the rural school to resemble its urban counterpart more closely.

The first two decades of the twentieth century witnessed the emergence of a new, more clearly national conception of public schooling in the United States. Forged as it was primarily to meet the needs of a rapidly industrializing, class-divided, increasingly urban society, this national conception had to be modified and adapted to meet the rural social conditions of the Midwest. Even though rural social relations were changing rapidly during this period, agricultural production remained a vibrant and central element in the region's economy and the basis for much of its continuing urban growth. The ascendant, national conception of education that had emerged in the late nineteenth century dominated educational reform in the towns and cities of the Midwest and gained popular support there as well. However, it failed to make much headway in the rural neighborhoods of the countryside. There the traditional country school and the neighborhood system of family farming of which it was a part persisted. In relative numbers, the rural population of the Midwest lost ground to the urban during this period, but as a group farmers remained a political force that reformers could not ignore. At the beginning of the twentieth century the Midwest had more one-room country schools than any other region of the country. For more than a generation these numbers had been the source of great pride in the dispersed rural communities that blanketed the region.

The Rise of a New Philosophy for the Public Schools

Dating roughly from the depression of 1893, a new educational philosophy began to transform the nature of public schooling in the cities and larger towns of the United States.[3] It had been forged by a relatively small number of national leaders — prominent educators, and not a few industrialists and businessmen. They pointed to Germany and its system of technical and industrial schools as a model worthy of at least partial emulation in the United States. Leading educators from John Dewey down to the most humble of urban district superintendents flocked to the "continent" to witness the miracle of German education.[4] The new German schools with their direct curricular linkages to the needs of industrial firms, in particular, were singled out as the reason for that country's avoidance of overproduction and depression in 1893 and for its rapid rise to prominence in the world economy.[5] Most American educators, however, were not interested in forming direct links between the public schools and American industry. Instead, they sought changes in the organization of public school systems that emulated those that had recently occurred in the scale and organization of industrial production in both Germany and the United States. Educational reformers were quick to adopt the ideas and rhetoric of industrial efficiency experts to articulate what they saw as needed reforms in public school systems.[6] They were quick to suggest that a key failing of the common schools was that ordinary people without training in educational administration controlled them. The way to achieve organizational "efficiency," they argued, was to shift the direct control and organization of teaching to those expert in such matters.[7]

According to this view, just as the new, large-scale "consolidated" industrial firms needed to retain experts to manage them, so too did the public schools. The "high" school, with a nested system of graded elementary schools (as opposed to common schools) feeding it, was the analogue of the new type of industrial firm. As Robert Wiebe has argued, in the new system of education, schools became surrogate communities. Reformers maintained that industrialization and urbanization had resulted in the breakdown of nineteenth-century society. Training provided in a fully modern public school system was necessary to prepare the youth for entry into twentieth-century society on competitive terms. In this new system, common schooling was demoted to "elementary" status, serving as an "appendage that prepared pupils and fed them into the high schools" — the real core of the new system. That this system became a popular one is undeniable. From 1890 onward, attendance in high schools mounted. Between then and the mid-1920s, high school enrollments increased fifteenfold, and "it seemed that overnight much of the nation had gone to school and the rest was talking about it."[8]

The premises of the common school movement of the nineteenth century held that equality of opportunity would be the joint result of common schooling and the smooth operation of competitive labor markets. The common school was "common" in a dual sense. First, the children of all social classes attended it. Second, the quality of the curriculum offered did not vary much from one school to another. According to the new philosophy, schools in the twentieth century should remain equally available to all, but no special effort should be made to ensure that the quality of education they provided would be approximately equal. To do so would have violated the central, arguably mythic, tenet of local democracy in America — the local control of public schooling. Competition was still to be important in the educational process, but its locus would shift from the labor market to the schools themselves.[9] As Wisconsin sociologist Edward A. Ross put it, "The chief aim of the 'free-high-school' movement has been not so much national efficiency as social democracy. Thoughtful Americans realize that, so far as possible, all should have an equal chance to show what they can do in the race of life. Hence, society should adopt the policy of equalizing opportunities. We do not yet see just how to correct the inequalities arising from the inheritance of property, business, or family influence. At any rate, however, a system of public education which is free clear to the top will do much to open doors to the poor man's children."[10]

Leaders of urban educational reform appeared willing to abandon the ideals of democratic equality and the creation of a classless society that had underlain the earlier common school movement and adapt public schooling to the decidedly urban and industrial social structure that had emerged in the last decades of the nineteenth century. "The high school was to become the place where each student would have an equal opportunity to assume his 'proper' position in society. That proper position was to be determined not by class or ethnic background but by the natural, yet nurtured, abilities of students and the needs of the larger economy and society."[11] Professional educators were to play central roles in the requisite nurturing and in the supervision necessary for meeting the labor and ideological needs of society. It was in this sense that educational reformers of the period were advocates of social "efficiency." However, professional educators were not to have the determining role in deciding what these needs were. Local control of public schooling ensured that professional educators had to defer to local elites on this matter. Herein lay both the professional educators' power and their weakness. Their power was mystified. Schools appeared to be locally controlled and hence democratic. The reality of the situation, however, was that in the new larger — often citywide — school districts, middle-class elites who formally controlled power subscribed to the same middle-class values as the professional educators themselves. Hence, they willingly ceded most authority over the means and content of public education to the professionals. Because of the appearance of local democracy, working-class parents acceded to this transfer of class power. The professional educators' weakness derived from the impossibility of the educational system to live up to its billing as the key institution ensuring the equality of opportunity in the larger, class-structured society.[12]

Rural areas, especially those of the Midwest, presented reformers with a quite different set of circumstances and challenges. It was clear that rural school consolidation would be a hard sell in the rural neighborhoods of the Midwest. The class structure of rural areas bore only a faint resemblance to that found in the larger urban areas, and the dominance of middle-class values in school decision making could not be taken for granted. Also, most midwestern farmers viewed the consolidation of economic power in the large corporations with skepticism, if not alarm. Hence, even the term "consolidation," or its synonym "centralization," lacked the discursive power it held for many city residents.

The Country Life Movement and Rural Education in the Midwest

Those in the Country Life movement came to champion rural school consolidation principally as a sociospatial means of engineering new forms of rural community.[13] They were, however, also attracted to the idea that the consolidated school would be a new kind of rural school — one offering the type of rural education needed if agriculture was to hold its own in an increasingly commercial, industrialized society.[14] While Germany did not provide a possible model easily adapted to the needs of the great agricultural heartland of the United States, Denmark's rural schools did. In the last half of the nineteenth century, the Danish state, with the support of its churches and rural communities, had established an elaborate system of rural elementary, local agricultural, and folk high schools. This school system, with its emphasis on Danish folk culture, agricultural science, and cooperative agricultural enterprises, had been successful in stemming the flow of Danish youth from the farms to the cities and in transforming Denmark into western Europe's leading agricultural producer. While the Danish educational system arose out of a quite different set of cultural, economic, and environmental circumstances, the Danish experience nonetheless seemed to demonstrate that it was possible to modernize agriculture and preserve the beneficent aspects of rural culture at the same time. A new kind of rural public school and the rural church were the key institutions in the transformation. Perhaps they could be in the Midwest as well.[15]

Country Life reformers argued that the midwestern farmer, like the Danish farmer, needed to become more "confident of his mastery over the forces of nature" without losing belief in the moral superiority of rural over urban life. They thought that this confidence could be nurtured through agricultural extension services for adults and by making the study of scientific agriculture and modern agricultural life the centerpiece of the rural school curriculum. The apparent vocationalism of their agenda did not mean that these reformers had completely severed their ties to the older agrarian ideology. Instead, they articulated a more modern, more fully commodified version of it. Their faith in the inherent advantages of country life and in farmers (now transformed into petty capitalist entrepreneurs) as the economic foundation of the nation remained intact. However, the economic health of that foundation and the continued superiority of rural over urban life could no longer be taken for granted.[16] Rural school consolidation was attractive for several reasons. First, it would make revenue available for the expansion of the public school curriculum to include instruction in agriculture and domestic science. Second, it would force cooperation between rural neighborhoods and reduce the apparent isolation and parochialism of rural life. Third, it would provide a forum for those expert in solving the problems of rural life to assume leadership in the rural communities. The automobile, in particular, made rural school consolidation a practical possibility in those areas with improved roads.

Rural school consolidation appealed to educational leaders for different reasons. They saw it as a necessary step in achieving the efficient supervision of teaching in the rural schools and a way of achieving equality of educational opportunity for rural and urban children alike. In consolidation lay a convergence of interests between these two sets of reformers and potentially a basis for effective political collaboration. In 1912, Mabel Carney, then director of the Country School Department of the Illinois Normal University, asserted that "the fundamental problem of country life is the problem of keeping a standard people upon our farms" and that the solution required that country life be made "adequately and permanently satisfying." "Country life," she continued, could "be made adequately satisfying only through the rebuilding of the country community. . . . The chief agencies for community are the home, the state, the church, the farm organization, and the school. Of these, the school, because it is the agency of education, and because the whole farm problem is largely a matter of education, is best suited for immediate institutional leadership, and most capable of initiating rural social progress. The school, in other words, makes the best and most generally available center for the rebuilding of the country community." Other prominent educators of the period echoed similar, if less tautological, sentiments. There was very broad agreement among them about the nature of the problem and that rural school consolidation was the most effective way to solve it. In this, educators subscribed to the discourse of rural community reform being articulated by those in the Country Life movement.[17]

The "rural school problem," as it was called, entailed a veritable litany of educational sins of omission and commission. Teachers were inexperienced, poorly trained and underpaid, unsupervised, their tenure too short, and their teaching methods dated. Singled out for special ridicule was what most of the new educational experts thought to be an overreliance of teachers on the recitation method and the use of older pupils to help instruct younger ones. The school year was too short and regular attendance levels too low and irregular. There were too few students to permit the grading necessary for converting education from a cooperative to a competitive endeavor. School facilities were too small, unkempt, unsanitary, outdated, and ill-equipped.[18] Most of all, the rural school was criticized for having remained essentially unaltered for more than a generation, standing still, paralyzed and incapable of fulfilling the new mission that had been set for public education.[19]

The properly graded rural school, reformers maintained, would help foster the competitiveness needed for success in an increasingly capitalist, achievement-oriented society, as well as better prepare rural students for success in high school. The modern high school was where students would have equal opportunities to develop the skills necessary to achieve success in society. Only their native intelligence and abilities limited the opportunities available to students. Experts skilled in pedagogy and knowledgeable of the needs of the larger society should be responsible for organizing and administering systems of rural education.

If the rural school had any advantages over other types of schools, they went unmentioned.[20] The leaders of educational reform at the state and national levels thought any more thorough investigation of the country school quite unnecessary.[21] To those leaders setting the parameters of the problem, rural neighborhoods, their people, and their schools symbolized the traditional and parochial and a host of other negative stereotypes. Elwood P. Cubberley, probably the most prominent rural education reformer on the national scene during this period, implied that the nature of rural life had been so transformed in the preceding several decades that farmers would embrace rural school reform, if they could be persuaded or made to try it. Cubberley noted,

> With the urbanization of rural life, . . . there has been a marked breaking-up of . . . close social relationship[s] in the rural communities. . . . The urbanization process has also greatly changed the farmer himself. He is no longer so peculiar in his dress, his manners, or his speech. . . . The farmer comes to feel himself a part of a larger society, — a county, a state, or the nation, rather than of a district or a township, — and he takes an interest in the affairs of the larger unit. Farm specialization, scientific management, and improved machinery have given him more time to read and think, and more time for personal enjoyment, and he travels

farther and more. The result has been a great weakening of the old personal ties.[22]

Cubberley was more explicit than most reformers in enunciating a theory of social change, but he felt there was a gap between the reality of the changes he described and the farmer's consciousness of them. He held out little hope that rural educational reform would occur very quickly, arguing instead that progress would be slow because the rural school was "controlled largely by rural people, who too often do not realize either their own needs or the possibilities of rural education." Progress and improvement in rural education could not occur, he cautioned, "until the district system, with its local taxation and control and its multitude of little schools, is subordinated by general law to a better system of organization and management."[23]

Although a midwesterner by birth, Cubberley was writing for a national audience of aspiring professional educators. Safely ensconced in his position as head of the education department at Stanford University, he did not need to convince recalcitrant midwestern farmers of the educational errors of their ways.[24] If anything, the story of the farmer he told seemed like a page from a description of the urban school-reform movement — expressing concerns that the "intelligent, thrifty, and law-abiding" American farmer of northern European stock was in danger of being replaced by the "ignorant and usually wretchedly poor" from southern and eastern (and obviously Catholic) Europe.[25]

The rising cadre of experts in the new field of educational administration was ready to use its newfound expertise to help transform the rural school into a model for achieving rural social efficiency. Just as the national leaders in urban education had met with success in making the public school a principal site for mediating conflict between the two great urban classes — capital and labor — it fell to rural education reformers to seek a harmonization of relationships between the farmers and urban capital. In so doing, they hoped to mute and/or redirect agrarian variants of class struggle.[26] By the end of the first decade of the new century, they had articulated the broad outlines of a new philosophy for rural education. The "new" system of public schooling introduced in the nation's cities had as its implicit objective the intergenerational reproduction of the class structure of industrial capitalism through the school rather than through the family and urban neighborhood. The new rural education would prepare farm children to reproduce the family farm as a social and economic form in an increasingly commercial, industrialized society. Such a philosophy was consistent with the objectives of both professional educators and Country Life leaders.

Urban school reformers had succeeded by convincing the urban middle class of the need for changes both in the nature of public education and in the class composition of those who would control and administer it. Urban neighborhoods were important institutions of socialization. They were among the chief places where people learned who they were in terms of class, race, ethnicity, and gender. Those advocating a redirected rural education tended to see rural neighborhoods differently, as aberrant institutions and places, comprising primarily persons aspiring to middle-class values. These places were too small to provide the educational facilities necessary to convert aspiration into realization. While recognizing rural neighborhoods as a means to an end in a reconstituted rural life, rural education reformers failed to view rural neighborhoods themselves as significant social entities in that rural life. The reformers were, however, also consummate pragmatists and realized that as a group, farmers still wielded considerable power politically. Not all farmers were ready to abandon the rural neighborhood; most would need more than a little convincing.

In struggles over the control of urban schools, educational leaders had learned that as long as the public schools remained firmly under the control of local communities, education as a profession would not achieve the status and social power it deserved. Without that power, there could be little educational progress.[27] Reformers had succeeded in convincing school boards in most of the nation's larger cities to cede them supervisory authority in the running of schools. They had, however, made little progress along these lines in rural schools, except in the South. For the most part, rural schools remained tightly under the control of farm families in their rural neighborhoods.[28] To succeed, reformers somehow had to break this vicious circle and, as they saw it, save farmers and their neighborhoods from themselves.

The first national study of rural schools in the United States was undertaken in 1896–97 by a committee appointed by the Educational Council of the National Education Association. It included leading educators as well as those others who would soon become identified with the Country Life movement. Henry Sabin, Iowa's superintendent of public instruction, chaired the committee. Judged by late twentieth-century standards of rigor, the committee's investigation appears to have been primarily an effort to legitimate rural reform efforts within the fledgling educational profession and within state legislatures. Prior to this report, few professional educators openly questioned the quality of education provided in the rural schools.[29] To most educational leaders, however, the committee's report contained few surprises. Indeed, it seemed to confirm what they had known all along: "compared with the apparent efficiency and standardization of the urban schools, the rural schools at the turn of the century were as individualistic, inefficient, and chaotic as ever." The report harshly criticized the rural school, noting that "on the whole it may well be doubted whether any money that is expended in the people's interest is expended more wastefully than what goes to the country schools."[30]

The report argued that only a new, redirected, and more competitive system of public education in rural areas could persuade the farm boy to stay on the farm. Needed curriculum changes, however, could not be made without first putting in place a better system of rural school supervision. The prevailing custom of an elected superintendent overseeing the country schools of a county was seen as little better than no supervision at all. As the necessary first step in reform, the report urged that one-room schools be closed and that pupils be transported at local public expense to larger, centrally located, graded schools. While the commission maintained that population decline required rural school consolidation in some areas, it argued for consolidation principally because it would improve the quality of rural education. This was the first salvo in the efforts of leading educators to implement what Tyack has aptly called the "one best system" for organizing public schools in the United States.[31] These new schools, while adopting the appearance, form, and organization of urban schools, were to build upon the distinctively rural and agrarian interests of their students. Manifesting the social Darwinist view that society was an organic whole, the committee's report stated that "the schools must not confuse or destroy . . . by trying to 'citify' the country or by seeking to 'countrify' the town. The city and the country express the equation of life; a weakness in one member means the ruin of both."[32] In this sense the report clearly rejected one of the central tenets of the Populists: that the city was dependent on the country. Like other Progressives, members of the committee sought to restore a semblance of social and economic stability in a society that had seen very little for more than a generation. While raising an important issue, the committee's report begged far more questions about what these new rural schools and the education provided within them might (or should) be like than it provided answers.

Even the concept of a central school was ambiguous. Only spatially extensive entities with clearly defined boundaries have centers. What were "central" schools to be central to? To the dispersed rural population served by the country schools that were to be closed? To some territorial conception of "community"? Or what? Additionally, what form would the improved supervision in the central school take? How would the distribution of discretion between parents, teachers, school administrators, and school boards change, if at all? On all of these issues the debates were just beginning at the turn of the century. Most of these issues would be resolved to the satisfaction of the Midwest's educational leaders before World War I. Convincing farmers of the merits of the resolution turned out to be quite a different matter.[33]

Consolidation may have been an effective administrative means of achieving "social efficiency," but the problem of convincing farmers that they should cede some of their autonomy in school matters to the state remained. The federal government did its part by passing the Smith-Lever Act in 1914, authorizing the establishment of a system of county farm and home demonstration agents in the counties of states agreeing to provide the requisite matching moneys. The U.S. Office of Education continued to act as a clearinghouse, providing state and local leaders with information about educational and administrative innovations that were being tried in the various states. The rest was left up to national nongovernmental organizations and movements within the individual states.

School Consolidation:
A Threat to the Persistence of Family Farming?

There is no disagreement that the country school was an integral part of neighborhood life in the rural areas of the Midwest at the turn of the century. Not all families and neighborhoods, however, placed a very high priority on the form of education provided within them. The importance accorded "schooling" varied significantly across ethnic groups, with, for example, Germans tending to place a lower value on it than the Irish.[34] Nevertheless, irrespective of the ethnicity of a rural neighborhood,

> rural people knew, however instinctively, that to lose their school meant to lose the focus of their community. Boards and trustees of one-room schools went to great lengths to try to keep their schools open; they specifically hired teachers with children of their own who would attend the school and augment the declining enrollment. The loss of a one-room school symbolized an abrupt entry into the 20th century and a shattering of the community spirit of the original settlers. Parents feared that if their children left the community to attend school elsewhere, they might one day leave permanently. And as country schools consolidated, the exodus from the farms increased.[35]

For rural people subscribing to the neighborhood system of family farming, the loss of a school entailed more than simply shattering some nostalgic sense of neighborhood or place. For them, removing the country school from the rural neighborhood also meant that the education of rural children became entrusted to an arbitrary unit of civil society under the aegis of the state and severed the direct tie between the school, the family, and the rural neighborhood. Controlled as it usually was by the prominent families in a rural neighborhood, the country school could be depended upon to reproduce the social relations necessary for the perpetuation of a rural ideology and class structure in which the family farm and the rural neighborhood were the preeminent social units. There was no assurance that this would also be the case in the consolidated school, where children from the farms would mingle and compete with children of town merchants, clerks, and workers and where farm parents had to share power with those who subscribed to different values. It also tended to be true that rural students experiencing the shift from the one-room country school to the consolidated school at least initially often experienced disorientation and a profound unhappiness.[36]

Reformers correctly claimed that the schools in the larger, consolidated districts would be community controlled. However, it was also clear that the relevant community doing the controlling would no longer necessarily be a constellation of rural neighborhoods. Adult males would retain the right to vote for school directors and all the other prerogatives they had enjoyed under the "district system" of one-room schools.[37] This much was true, but what was not emphasized was that the new "community" would no longer be that of the extended family and necessarily dominated by family farmers. Instead, the community would in most cases be village- or small-town-centered and authority would have to be shared among farmers of the different rural neighborhoods, town elites, and professional educators. This attenuation and partial severing of the ties to the family and rural neighborhood also meant that more control over this key aspect of the social reproduction of family farmers as a class would shift from farm women to male educational professionals and administrators. The shift involved changing the territorial locus of the production of education from the family-dominated, rural neighborhood to a secular place more dominated by middle-class educational experts. Viewed from this perspective, struggles over educational reforms, including school consolidation, take on a deeper, more vibrant meaning.

Most rural people did not expect that the educational opportunities they provided for their children would be the same as those provided in cities and towns. Hence, the argument that increasing the territorial size of rural school districts would result in the costs and benefits of public schooling being shared more equitably between rural and urban people often carried little weight. Instead, they preferred to entrust decisions regarding the education of their children to their friends and neighbors rather than to professional people they either did not know or did not know well. They preferred their patriarchal variant of local democracy, however imperfect, to a more bureaucratic electoral democracy.

Given the political strength of traditional farmers at the turn of the century, legislation imposing rural school consolidation on rural neighborhoods that objected to it could not be enacted anywhere in the Midwest. However, as farm incomes increased and as more farmers subscribed to the tenets of the new, more business-oriented system of farming advocated by the Progressives, such legislation gradually gained support. It was only when members of this new farming class had risen to prominence in a locality that consolidation had much chance of local success. These were the farmers more likely to view their future success and that of their children as tied to enhanced educational facilities. Doubtless this was one of the principal reasons why resistance often became quite virulent and why rural school consolidation for a time became one of the rural Midwest's most divisive social issues.[38] While opponents of rural school consolidation could articulate their resistance in terms of class, they could just as easily frame it in terms of place. This raises the possibility that some farmers may well have viewed rural school consolidation as a threat to the continued sociocultural importance of the rural neighborhood as much as a class threat. Addressing this question requires more detailed analysis of rural school consolidation at the state and local levels — at the geographical scales in which battles over consolidation in the Midwest were actually fought. For the reasons discussed earlier, Iowa is a particularly interesting state in which to situate such an analysis.

The best schools in this state are found in Davenport, Des Moines, and Mason City, that is, the buildings cost two or three hundred thousand dollars. We have some nice buildings costing from forty to one hundred thousand dollars.

— *A. M. Deyoe, superintendent of public instruction, to C. S. Risdon, superintendent, Independence, Kansas, 20 November 1916*

5

EDUCATIONAL REFORM IN EARLY TWENTIETH-CENTURY IOWA

Iowa's Educational Apparatus Before 1913

At the turn of the century, a formal, state-level educational apparatus with significant juridical clout simply did not exist in Iowa. There was a state superintendent of public instruction and a state board of educational examiners. Neither possessed much real authority. The state superintendent was an elected state official, serving two-year terms of office. He was charged with the "general supervision of all the county superintendents and the common schools of the state," but had no specific authority to supervise either.[1] With only one deputy and a stenographer to assist him, the general supervision exercised could not involve the actual inspection of schools; for this he was entirely dependent upon the various county superintendents.[2] In practice he acted as a conduit for the flow of information on educational matters between the county superintendents and the state legislature. Candidates seldom actively campaigned for the position in either primary or general elections. Typically, each of the two major parties selected as its candidate the most highly regarded educational figure in the state it could persuade to run; whichever party won the governorship (usually the Republicans) "won" the state superintendency as well. The winner then spent much of the next two years helping county superintendents organize annual county teachers institutes and in attending as many of these as possible. He also prepared an annual report advising the General Assembly on educational matters, particularly regarding "needed" legislation.

The Board of Educational Examiners was charged with holding at least two state teachers examinations annually and with passing upon the qualifications of those applying for state teaching certificates. Since only a few of the larger urban districts in the state required teachers to hold state certificates in order to teach, the board did not have much to do. Members of the board consisted of the state superintendent, the president of the State University of Iowa (now the University of Iowa), the president of the state teachers college (now the University of Northern Iowa), and two other persons, one of whom was required to be a woman, appointed by the governor to serve four-year terms.

County superintendents wielded more power. They were elected in partisan elections to serve two-year terms; most served three or more consecutive terms. Their principal responsibility was to examine applicants who did not possess a state certificate for teaching positions within their respective counties and to issue certificates of various "grades," the lowest of which was the one-year "provisional" certificate. Although county superintendents possessed the authority to visit all the schools in their counties, in practice they restricted their supervision to the many ungraded, country schools.[3] For this reason, the county superintendent tended to function as the superintendent of the rural schools in the county. Town and city school districts had their own superintendents who enjoyed considerably greater prestige in educational circles, commanded higher salaries, and had little reason to interact with county superintendents.[4]

Real authority in school matters rested with the myriad local school districts. Prior to 1913, three general types of districts were recognized: (1) *independent districts*, consisting of any territory containing a village, town, or city, incorporated or unincorporated, with 100 or more inhabitants; (2) *school townships*, consisting of all the rural territory of a civil township (thirty-six government sections) not otherwise organized into independent (i.e., "urban") or rural independent districts, which in turn were further subdivided into an average of nine subdistricts, each with its own school and the prerogative of electing a school director to the township's school board; and (3) *rural independent districts*, consisting of any territory formerly composing a subdistrict in a school township that had in effect legally seceded from the township by majority vote of its electors. In 1900, there were 461 independent districts, 1,187 school townships (with 9,423 subdistricts), and 3,225 rural independent districts. According to the reports of the county superintendents, in these 13,109 units there were a total of 12,615 ungraded and 5,766 graded schools.[5] Although a few of the independent districts undoubtedly maintained ungraded schools, overwhelmingly the ungraded schools were one-room country schools. At the time, Iowa had more of these than had any other state in the nation.

State law granted sweeping powers both to the voters of these districts and to their elected representatives. Male voters, assembled at the annual meeting of a school district, had the power to select textbooks; to direct the sale or disposition of any property belonging to the district; to determine what subjects would be taught; to determine what other uses could be made of schoolhouses; to transfer surpluses from the capital expenditures fund to the general operating fund; to authorize the board of directors to expend funds for building and maintaining roads to ensure access to schoolhouses; and to authorize a schoolhouse tax for the purchase of grounds, construction of schoolhouses, and payment of debt for same. School directors, on the other hand, were delegated such responsibilities as fixing the length of the school term, determining school sites, retaining and discharging teachers, maintaining the condition of schoolhouses, managing the district's fiscal affairs, deciding whether the district would maintain a kindergarten or one or more schools of higher order (e.g., high schools), and adjusting boundaries with adjacent school districts. Women could not vote in school elections, including school board elections, or in elections proposing the formation of new districts. They could, however, vote in school bond issue elections (or any other election on increasing or decreasing tax levies) and could serve as school board directors and vote on matters coming before the board once elected.[6] In practice, few women served on the boards of directors in either rural or urban school districts. The General Assembly constrained the levels of expenditure and debt that a district could incur and required that instruction be in English; but otherwise, the state was anything but intrusive in educational matters. Public schooling was decidedly a local affair, particularly in the rural districts. The rural school district or subdistrict was typically the key neighborhood institution binding neighbors and linking them to the larger social and cultural world around them. If ever there were neighborhood schools, these one-room country schools were they. Chauncey Colgrove, Head of the Education Department at the Iowa State Teachers College, summarized the situation well when he commented that "it cannot be said that the state really creates a complete school system for any community. Each community makes its own school."[7]

For more than a generation the large number of country schools had been the source of great pride in the rural neighborhoods that blanketed the state — too much pride from the perspective of some of the state's educational leaders. Amos Currier, a professor of education at the State University in Iowa City, in his 1898 presidential address before the Iowa State Teachers

Association, opined that he believed there was "a real peril for Iowa education in the general pride in the schools of the state and the consequent satisfaction with things as they are." His concern was that "the opposers of reforms in educational methods and the objectors to larger provision for schools, public and private" almost invariably pointed to Iowa's large number of country schools as the reason why Iowa had the highest literacy rate in the nation.[8]

Iowa's Version of the Rural School Problem

Currier and other educational leaders in the state evaluated the situation quite differently. Like regional and national leaders, they viewed the country school as a carryover from Iowa's pioneer days, ill-suited to meet the demands of twentieth-century farm practice and rural life. While they felt that the educational opportunities afforded children in the rural school districts had fallen further and further behind those of the cities and towns, most educators felt powerless to do much about it. For example, Homer H. Seerley, then president of the Iowa State Teachers College, proclaimed

> a self-satisfied hopeless condition exists among the patrons and the directors of most rural school districts. This situation has developed from social, economic and industrial causes in general and from local, legal and governmental causes in particular, and they do not see any way of relief thru [sic] official action. The authority of the local units is absolutely effective and the interest in the possible education obtainable in the schools is confused with many modern ideals and theories that are now emphasized by a multitude of writers, speakers and promoters, most of whom are not under any central supervision or control. . . .
>
> Efficient standards of school management would require a school district to pay for actual results. This is quite generally impossible because the rural schools boards are inclined to assume that they are not elected to office in order to enlarge the public investment by adopting standards for efficiency as such a policy would increase the expenditures . . . [and instead] . . . insist that taxation be kept at a minimum. The few who have different ideals and who would prefer a more satisfactory condition yield to the majority as they recognize the weakness of the rural school to consist chiefly of the incompetency of the teachers who are obtainable.[9]

Although there was no formal state educational apparatus at the turn of the century, a de facto one had existed since the late 1870s. At that time, the Iowa State Teachers Association (ISTA) stepped into the void and appointed a six-person council to serve as an advisory council to the state superintendent. In many respects, it seems to have been an attempt by the emergent educational "establishment" to use the platform provided by the state superintendency to embark on what they saw as a program of educational modernization for the state. The relationship between the office of state superintendent and ISTA grew even closer in 1894 when then state superintendent Henry Sabin persuaded the governor and the General Assembly to underwrite the publication of the annual proceedings of the association and distribute it to the governor, to all members of the General Assembly, and to ISTA members.[10]

The Iowa State Teachers Association was a misnomer. The ISTA was controlled by school administrators, principally the "college men" in the state's colleges and universities and the superintendents of schools in the state's cities and larger towns. Within the ISTA, rural school teachers were not considered part of the education profession. Country school teachers tended to be treated with disdain. Even though they composed the largest group of teachers in the state, country school teachers were neither recognized nor represented in the ISTA's organizational structure or on the programs of its annual meetings. Country school teachers were even denied participation in selecting members to serve on the all-important Education Council.[11] Part of the reason for this was that teaching in the country schools did not require any formal training. Other than the annual county teachers institutes, the state had no formal system for training country school teachers at all until 1911, when a program providing state aid to public high schools offering a state-approved program of normal training was initiated. Henceforth, whatever special training country school teachers obtained was in these normal training courses provided in the state's larger city high schools. Indeed, the state's teacher certification laws provided no incentive for prospective rural school teachers to participate even in these normal training high school courses. By passing an examination in elementary school studies, anyone of the required age could receive a license to teach. After completing five years of satisfactory service a teacher was eligible to receive a "life certificate."[12] The state's only public normal school, the Iowa State Teachers College at Cedar Falls, offered no program, or even a course, specifically designed to help prepare teachers for their work in the one-room country schools.[13] Instead, the teachers college trained teachers for the graded, urban schools. Not surprisingly, few country school teachers joined the ISTA, and hence few had any voice in its operations.

In 1900, the office of superintendent of public instruction was little more than an extension of the collective interests of the ISTA's leadership. From the time the office first became firmly established as a part of state government in 1864, six of the nine superintendents had been past presidents of the ISTA. The ISTA's leadership effectively shaped the state's lean education apparatus to its wishes and through its legislative committee actually constituted part of that apparatus. Seldom did a state superintendent urge a change in the school laws, however small, without first obtaining the support of this powerful committee. Almost invariably, the recommendations of the ISTA's legislative committee became the ones the state superintendent urged the General Assembly and governor to adopt in his biennial report.[14]

By 1900, reformers within the ISTA had been instrumental in modernizing the public schools of the state's larger towns and cities — a task made relatively easy because it required enacting new laws that affected only the larger urban school districts. Local businessmen had been influential in expediting this process. The high school movement, for example, swept the state like a firestorm from the late 1870s onward. Small-town boosters lobbied the General Assembly successfully to permit progressively smaller and smaller urban places to be organized as independent districts. In 1858, an urban place required 1,000 inhabitants before it could organize as an independent district; by 1894 this figure had been reduced to only 100.[15] Gaining the status of an independent district gave towns access to the more liberal taxation and bonding limits accorded such districts, thereby enabling them to build their own high schools. At the turn of the century, the reality of the situation was that Iowa possessed two school systems — a modern one for its almost 800 cities, towns, and villages and a traditional one for rural children.

The period 1895–1911 was one of considerable ferment — politically, economically, and educationally. In trying to chart a course for the future of rural education in the state, Iowa's education leaders started out from widely disparate positions. Some argued that the rural school should remain essentially a rural institution; others maintained that it should mimic the urban school; and still others that it should become a new hybrid institution. They could agree, however, that a new kind of rural education was necessary and that the old country school had to go. During the first decade of the new century, state education leaders made little effort to convince farm families of the advantages of a "new" rural education. Instead, they chose to follow the model of educational reformers elsewhere by mounting a full-scale attack on the country school as an aberrant, premodern, even antimodern institution. The first line of attack was to argue that country schools were inefficient in multiple ways. Reformers had criticized the quality of teaching in the country schools for more than a decade. The new claim was that the problem of the country school was a structural one, deriving directly from the highly decentralized nature of the district school system itself. In this regard, educational reformers in Iowa conformed to the views of their counterparts elsewhere in the Midwest and nationally. They argued that the state had a rural school problem as severe as that found anywhere; the major difference was that in Iowa there was no excuse for it.[16] Iowa was the richest agricultural state in the nation; it could and should do better by its rural children. The rural school, so characteristic of the Iowa countryside, seemed to be standing still, paralyzed and incapable of fulfilling the new mission that educators everywhere had set for the public school, while farmers were steadily accumulating wealth — wealth sufficient to have rendered them members of the middle class had they lived in the city. This stereotype was so firmly entrenched in the ideology of reform that few of Iowa's educational leaders found it necessary to conduct elaborate investigations to convince anybody otherwise.

More than anything else, Iowa's educational leaders argued that rural schools lacked appropriate supervision. This too was not a new criticism, having been voiced in one form or another by all of the state superintendents and many of the county superintendents since the turn of the century. In 1901, for example, T. M. Clevenger, the Iowa County superintendent, opined that,"One of the greatest needs of the rural schools is supervision. Nothing can contribute more to the successful operation of the public schools than wise supervision. . . . The only way rural schools can feel the benefits of intelligent inspection and direction is by consolidation."[17] What most education leaders meant was that the wrong people controlled the education that farm children received. As one prominent Iowa educator put it, "a stream cannot rise higher than its source."[18] Some educators were also surprisingly candid about what they thought to be the appropriate class composition of school boards and the proper delegation of authority between the local elites in a school district and school professionals. State Superintendent John F. Riggs, for example, in his annual address to the ISTA, maintained that [school] "boards should be composed of men or women of high character; earnest, progressive, duty-loving citizens; clean, successful, competent business or professional men. . . . The proper course for a board of education is to entrust large powers in professional matters to superintendents and other general officers. . . . In business matters boards should retain a much larger share of authority. They are composed of business men vitally interested in the welfare of the community and presumably as well posted on material matters as the average official they might select, hence delegation of authority is here unnecessary."[19]

While Iowa's education leaders may have disagreed on the specific directions a new rural education should take, they all agreed on the evils of continuing to leave the control of education to the rural neighborhood. During this period, they focused most of their overt political activity on changing the school laws that permitted the small rural neighborhood to have its own independent school district. In its place they advocated a return to the township-unit plan, wherein all rural independent districts would be abolished and their former territories aggregated into new school townships governed by boards of directors elected at-large. The new township districts were to possess all of the powers granted urban school districts in the state. Although this plan seemed simple enough, it was so fraught with geopolitical difficulties as to be unimplementable.

In having earlier pushed successfully for educational reform in the cities and towns of the state, reformers had foreclosed on any possibility of simply returning to the township-unit plan. Most towns and all of Iowa's cities already had their own independent school districts and were providing graded elementary and high school privileges to their patrons. Indeed, many had formed their own independent districts so that they could provide graded elementary and high school instruction without having to secure the approval of farmers in the surrounding countryside. Similarly, farm families in the various rural neighborhoods valued the control they exercised over their schools. It should have been apparent to everyone that any attempt to extend the types of educational reforms that had been implemented in the towns and cities of the state to entire townships would be opposed vigorously by residents in both town and country alike. The practical politics of the situation required that any preexisting urban districts would remain independent and exist as territorial enclaves in the new school townships. The state's educational leaders, however, were slow to recognize this. When they finally did, they tried to persuade the state's political leaders that the school laws needed to be rewritten from top to bottom.

In 1908 they were successful in getting Governor Albert Cummins to appoint a special commission to devise a complete recodification of the Iowa school laws to be acted upon in the 1909 General Assembly. The bill recommended by the commission proposed doing away with all preexisting school districts and reconstituting school governance and administration at the county level. It was subject to essentially the same criticisms as was the township-unit plan and attracted the wrath of almost every political organization in the state. More petitions were filed against this bill than against any other piece of legislation related to the public schools introduced in the period 1895–1925. The chair of the Senate's education committee, himself a strong supporter of the bill initially, put it succinctly and bluntly when he declared: "Unanimous opposition to the commission's bill from rural districts will make its passage absolutely impossible. The people are up in arms against the bill and an attempt to pass it out would result in defeat for the entire measure because of this crystallized sentiment against the bill as a whole."[20]

After this failure, it was obvious to reformers that they would have to proceed under existing laws or attempt to change them while working within the constraints of local democracy. Any changes in the organization of rural school districts would need to be initiated in localities and subjected to local voter approval. In retrospect, it was clear that any semblance of spatial rationality in the design of school governance had been sacrificed the moment reformers took the politically expedient path and acceded to the popular view that the urban and the rural were separate social spheres warranting different political and economic treatment. What had been put asunder could not be easily joined together.

The Geography of Social and Economic Change and the Need for Reform

Iowa's rural population had peaked in 1880 and remained relatively constant until the end of the century.[21] In the first decade of the new century, however, the rural population declined by 114,750, or 6.9 percent.[22] Population changes in rural areas, however, were highly uneven geographically (see figure 1). Despite this, in 1910 almost 70 percent of the population was rural (and small town) and overwhelmingly accounted for by farm families. The populations of all cities in the state increased over the decade, but not as rapidly as in other midwestern states.[23] Although Iowa remained "rural," it was losing rural population more rapidly than the industrial bases of its cities were expanding to absorb the rural surplus.[24]

Concomitant with these demographic changes was a 5.1 percent reduction in the number of farms and a 9.9 percent increase in average farm size (from 151 acres in 1900 to 164 in 1910).[25] The distribution of farm sizes was very strongly regionalized by 1910 (figure 2), and by the mid-1920s the state could be divided into five distinct regions of agricultural production (figure 3). In each of them corn and hogs were the principal products. They differed, however, in cropping systems, the proportions of grain produced for feed and sale, the importance of cattle versus hogs, the importance of

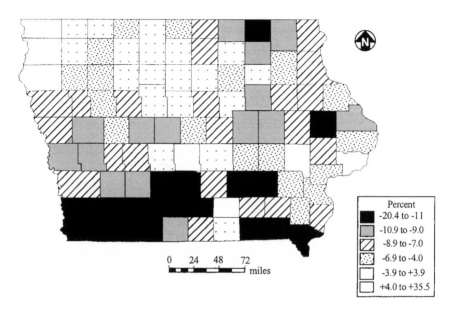

FIGURE 1. *Percent change in rural population in Iowa counties, 1900–1910. Map by Peter Li.*

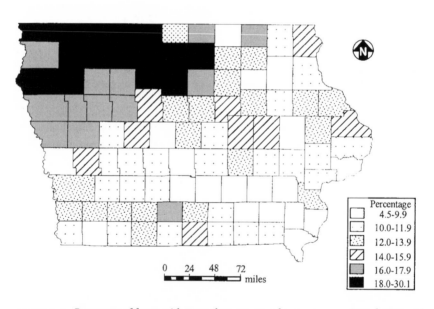

FIGURE 2. *Percentage of farms with more than 260 acres by county, 1910. Map by Peter Li.*

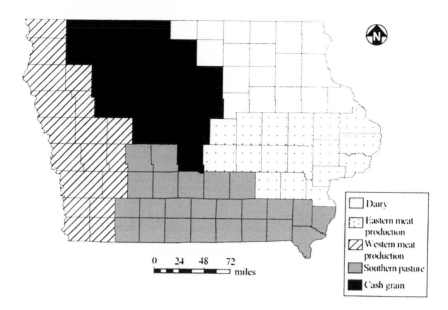

FIGURE 3. *Agricultural production regions of Iowa, 1920. Map by Peter Li. Adapted from C. L. Holmes, "Types of Farming in Iowa," Iowa Agricultural Experiment Station Bulletin no. 256 (1929): 152–206.*

dairying, the extent and use of pasture land, and systems of land tenure. These changes were accompanied by even more dramatic decreases in the number of school-aged children in various parts of the state.[26]

As the rural population decreased and agricultural prices increased, agricultural land values rose sharply. They increased by 123 percent between 1900 and 1910 and continued to soar for another decade.[27] The value of real property subject to taxation for the support of the rural schools increased much more rapidly than the number of pupils decreased. Therefore, rural population loss was not accompanied by any fiscal incentive for farmers to abandon their one-room schools in favor of some alternative means of providing public schooling.

While state educational leaders pondered the future of rural education and the role of rural school consolidation in it, rural sociologists at Iowa State College in Ames or affiliated with the Agricultural Extension Service there began a series of rural community studies designed to chart what seemed to be the major social and economic changes occurring in the Iowa countryside.[28] In particular, these studies chronicled the impact of the automobile on the economic and social organization of the countryside. The negative impacts included the gradual disappearance of the crossroads general store; decreased rural church attendance; decreased supply of farmworkers; and the increased pace and burdensome nature of farmwork. Even the traditional practice of neighboring seemed to be decreasing as farm families eschewed visiting in favor of joyriding in their automobiles. Most rural sociologists of the period seemed to subscribe to the view that fundamental changes were occurring in the countryside and that the general drift of this change was in the direction of farm families becoming increasingly materialistic, middle class, and urban. Influenced by the arguments of the Country Life movement, they pointed to the need for developing a reconstituted conception of rural community — one based on the small market town, not the rural neighborhood. Such places were where farm families sold their agricultural products, bought an increasingly broad array of consumer goods, and attended church, if they attended at all.

Some even described these changes in apocalyptic terms as constituting a breakdown of rural life. Iowan Horace Boies Hawthorn, a rural sociologist at Iowa State College was one of these.[29] Hawthorn argued that these changes were alarming principally because they had not been accompanied by the development of new institutions capable of instilling a modern, expanded conception of community based on a more intensive set of social and economic transactions between the family farm and the small market town. He maintained that an objective transformation of rural life was occurring without a transformation in the consciousness of rural people to sustain it. Farmers were retaining their old values and forms of consciousness while adopting many of the material trappings of modernity. Furthermore, these changes were not producing new forms of community life that were sustainable over the longer run. Like other country life experts of the period, Hawthorn was also distrustful of the rural neighborhood as an appropriate unit for social action. Because rural neighborhoods, in Iowa, as elsewhere, were often homogeneous ethnically, he assumed that any collective action undertaken at this scale would perpetuate ethnic distinctiveness and slow the transition from neighborhood loyalty to a more modern national loyalty — one based on a nation knit together primarily through capitalist exchange. To him the neighborhood was not a "natural" community, whereas those based more exclusively on market transactions were. To hasten the development of modern rural communities, he called for the new "school men" to take charge of a new type of rural school — the rural consolidated school — and assume the role of "social engineers." In his words, "The teaching of community sociology in the consolidated school should be a powerful factor in building community patriotism among the new generation of farmers. . . . One of the weaknesses of rural organization work is neighborhood rivalry which often wrecks community spirit. In addition there is anti-town spirit to contend with. Our future contests will use rivalry between communities, rather than rivalries within communities, while inter-community competition will tend to supplant intra-community competition."[30]

Hawthorn had no illusions, however, that the task of overcoming neighborhood rivalry and establishing the new schools would be riven with conflicts. He situated the principal difficulty not just in rural culture but in one of the core values of the Republic:

> At the very heart of the trouble is our small, inadequate unit of administration and taxation. Because of the American's personal liberty and self-determination complex, he fails to see education as the task of society, and thereupon assumes that every locality, rich or poor, must educate its children. It never occurs to him that children do not "stay put," but migrate to cities and other states to invest their educated lives. He does not realize that, like the army or navy, the school is the first line of national defense not defense against dreadnaughts [sic] or gas bombs, but certainly against the more insidious invasion of destructive, social philosophies that undermine democracy.[31]

Hawthorn did not elaborate on how territorially larger school district units, congruent with "natural" communities and focused on small market centers, would redress inequalities in access to taxable property. The reason he did not was simple. Forming consolidated districts centered only around small market centers — the country towns — would not redress these inequalities: the tax-base advantages of the bigger towns and cities would remain. His notion of consolidated districts forming a bulwark of defense against the "insidious invasion of destructive social philosophies" is more difficult to fathom. It appears that he had two things in mind. First, he subscribed to essentially the same perspective as the state's education leaders — that territorially larger districts would more likely be controlled by middle-class, urban-minded people with backgrounds that prepared them better than farmers for making informed decisions on educational and budgetary matters. Second, he sought to put an end to the well-known tendency for country schools to mimic the moral and religious leanings of their rural neighborhoods. He thought that institutionalizing proper moral and "nondenominational" religious training could best be accomplished in the consolidated school. The anti-Catholicism and antinonconformism implicit in this perspective surely did not go unnoticed. Nevertheless, he contended that both of these effects — one linked to class and the other to ethnicity and/or religion — would help buttress a form of American nationalism based on the expansion of capitalist social relations and the demise of more traditional forms of ethnic or community identity.

School Consolidation in Iowa:
A Response to Population Decline?

In 1906, with little fanfare and no apparent urging from the state's education leaders, the General Assembly passed a bill permitting the formation of new, territorially larger school districts without the explicit approval of the boards of directors of the preexisting districts affected. Such "consolidated" districts could be proposed by a petition signed by as few as one-third of the voters in the proposed district and voted into existence by the dual majority vote of those in the urban and rural portions of it. The intent of the law was to provide a simple, less politically cumbersome means for the school district of a town or city to expand into an urbanizing countryside.

Having failed at persuading the General Assembly to consolidate rural school districts by legislative edict in the 1900s, the state's educational leaders, under the leadership of a new state superintendent, Albert M. Deyoe, devoted much of their attention in 1911 and 1912 to devising a new strategy. Their objectives were to expand the size and authority of the state superintendent and to secure a change in the 1906 consolidation law so that it would not only permit consolidation but actively encourage it. In 1911, they took the first major step along these lines. They introduced and helped secure passage of a change in that law, requiring that whenever an urban place with a school population of twenty-five or more was included within a consolidated district, the school had to be located in that place. This appeared to remove the location of the school from "politics." By ensuring that consolidated districts would include at most only one "urban" place, it also guaranteed the almost unanimous support of the residents of small towns for any and all consolidation proposals that included them. The implicit assumption was that these were the "natural" centers around which local consolidation movements could be organized. The desired effect was not long in coming. Almost overnight, school consolidation became a central element in the growth strategy of most small-town boosters. Consolidation was especially popular in the smallest of the small towns, and it was here rather than in the larger places or in the open country that they were usually located (see figure 4).

In 1911, the so-called free-tuition law also secured passage in the General

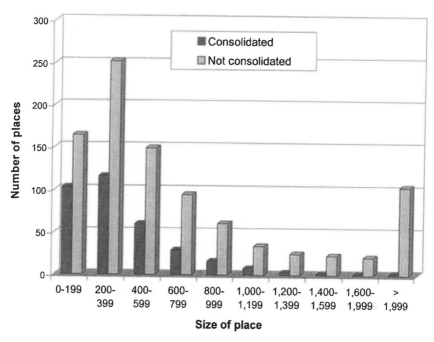

FIGURE 4. *Number of consolidated schools by size of place, 1925. Figure by Peter Li.*

Assembly. It required every school district not having its own high school to pay the tuition for its students to attend any public high school in the state, provided that the tuition paid did not exceed that charged at the nearest high school. Deyoe and other educational leaders actively lobbied for the bill. They expected that it would provide the additional stimulus necessary for rural people finally to see the advantages of rural school district consolidation, while at the same time it would create a justification for state regulation of the high schools.[32] History was to prove otherwise. While the free-tuition law did encourage more students from country districts to attend high school in one of the larger towns in their vicinity, it did not result in any immediate upsurge of interest in rural school consolidation.

Creating a Dominant Alliance and Rendering Its Discourse Hegemonic

By mid-1912, there was widespread agreement among the state's education leaders that the improvement of rural education would require something more than simply closing the country schools with low enrollments and reallocating the students to a smaller number of one- or two-teacher schools. Inserting nature study or other studies related to life and work on the farm into the rural school curriculum, although necessary, was also insufficient. Reform needed to be far more fundamental than this. Leaders finally agreed that a new type of rural school, qualitatively different from the traditional country school, was necessary and that it should be linked to the creation of a new kind of rural-minded urban place — what the Country Life reformers had been referring to as the "country town."[33]

It had finally dawned on the leaders of reform that they ought to take a page from the opposition's songbook and argue that farmers should create their own new communities with their own high schools. Farmers should no longer be required to send their children "away from the farm home," even if the student's home district did pay the tuition.[34] The new farm communities should not only have their own high schools, they should also have schools providing the proper preparation for high school. As leading educators had been arguing for more than a generation, only the graded elementary school was up to the task. The most efficient solution was not simply to build new farmers' high schools but to build somewhat larger facilities and house the elementary grades there as well. If farmers lost their old neighborhood schools — the country schools — they gained a rural "community" high school as well as a new elementary school. The consolidated school would contain both schools and would be controlled by an elected board of directors, most of whom would presumably be farmers. The logic was simple and designed to appeal to the farmers' sense of cultural distinctiveness, pride, and, most of all, to the newfound wealth and middle-class aspirations of some of them.

In 1912 the consummate political maneuverings of Deyoe succeeded in building a powerful alliance between the state's education reformers and economic and political elites. They were united in the belief that a redirected rural education, supervised by professional educators, was necessary for social and economic progress. Organizationally the alliance took the form of a nonpartisan commission appointed by the ISTA — the Better Iowa Schools Commission.[35] All but one of the major reform bills proposed by this group were passed and signed into law in 1913. Of these, by far the more significant were (1) a bill granting state aid to consolidated school districts, if they included courses on agriculture, domestic science, and other vocational subjects taught by state-approved teachers, and (2) a bill granting the state superintendent's office full departmental status in state government. Collectively, these new laws signaled a clear break from the tradition of direct popular control of the public schools. The amount of state aid a consolidated district received was based on the number of classrooms contained in its school building. The maximum amount of aid provided was just sufficient to offset the anticipated cost of adding the teaching of these subjects to a school district's curriculum. To receive any state aid, however, the district had to provide transportation for rural students, and all twelve grades had to be housed in a single facility. Small-town newspaper editors across the state now found it easier to argue that the demise of their country schools was inevitable. As the editor of the *Pocahontas County Sun* opined: "It is evident to all that consolidation is sure to come. The legislature is holding out inducements now for the schools to consolidate in the way of bonuses, but in the near future it is evident that the matter will be dealt with in a different manner. The laws will compel consolidation and the people will have nothing to say."[36]

Implementation and the Containment of Resistance

From mid-1913 to U.S. entry into World War I, the locus of struggle over educational reform shifted from the legislature to the small towns and rural areas across the state. The state's newly created Department of Public Instruction (DPI) under the indefatigable leadership of Deyoe now possessed a corps of school inspectors, as well as the full support of experts from the state's educational establishment. The DPI worked closely with leading businessmen, bankers, small-town boosters, and a few large-scale farmers in a massive effort to persuade family farmers across the state to abandon their country schools in favor of the state-aided consolidated school. The focus of these efforts initially was in the rich, cash grain area in the north-central and northwest parts of the state. It was here that conditions seemed most favorable for consolidation. The farms were larger; there were fewer people and fewer towns. In delimiting consolidated districts, Deyoe and his assistants urged local boosters to include enough taxable property to build and operate a school of a size qualifying for the maximum amount of state aid, while gerrymandering to ensure that the district did not include too many opponents. In 1912, there were but 12 consolidated school districts in the state. This number grew to 80 by the end of 1914, 187 by 1916, and 235 by 1917 (see figure 5).[37]

Almost from the outset, the campaign borrowed some of the rhetoric of the Country Life movement to build local support for "modernizing" rural life. It was argued that open-country communities based on reciprocity and neighboring were either already defunct or fast disappearing and that a resuscitated rural community life was urgently needed. Improvements in transportation and agricultural technology and increases in farm prices suggested that rural social relations were becoming more town-centered, commodified, and modern anyway; rural society was inexorably being incorporated into mass society.[38] With fully up-to-date schools, it was claimed, small towns and villages would become the "community centers" of coun-

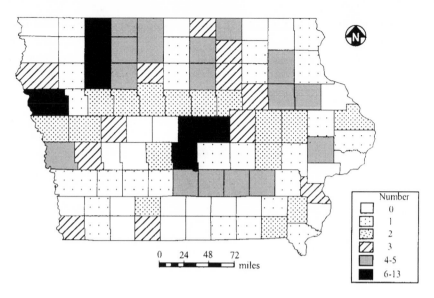

FIGURE 5. *Number of consolidated schools by county, 1917. Map by Peter Li.*

try life — the new "country towns." [39] The consolidated school could temper excessive materialism and play a pivotal role in retaining key features of traditional rural life without impeding social and material progress. In the campaign, the central tenets of both the Country Life reformers and more urban-oriented leaders in the field of educational administration were conjoined in a single discourse of rural reform. Beginning in 1913, Iowa became the center of national attention by providing what reformers hoped would become the new model of rural education to be emulated throughout the rest of the northern agricultural states.

More than 1,000 villages with populations below 800 were identified as the "natural centers" for consolidated schools — as the new country towns that Country Life reformers hoped could be engineered through consolidation. [40] Unlike larger towns, which served more as major marketing centers, villages were more closely linked in their social relations with surrounding rural areas because they were the principal places of retirement for farmers. Towns above this size, it was argued, were not "rural-minded" and were the very places to which rural teenagers migrated prematurely in search of jobs.

Silencing Dissent

From the outset the rhetoric of consolidation found a receptive audience primarily in villages and small towns that either did not have a four-year high school, yet wanted one, or that already had one but could not afford to bring it up to the new state standards. It was in such places that the reformers targeted their efforts. This strategy was contradictory both educationally and territorially. It meant that those country school districts nearer to larger urban places would retain their country schools while paying the tuitions to send their students to high schools in the very towns that reformers argued would undermine important rural values. Apparently, those living in wealthier farm areas where the farms were larger, the population less dense, and the towns more widely dispersed were to be the primary beneficiaries of school consolidation.

The new political geography of school districts was fraught with spatial and economic inequalities and was politically contentious locally. Most regions of the state had far too many villages for all of them to be viable sites for consolidated schools. Elsewhere, so few existed that consolidated districts needed to be exceedingly large territorially. The school consolidation movement produced sharply different controversies from one part of the state to another. In communities with strong ethnic identities or where farm sizes were smaller and incomes low, consolidation was a political dead letter right from the start.[41] The hegemony of the consolidation discourse in reform circles, if not in the countryside, limited the organizational capacity of rural people to respond except in a fragmented, place-based manner.

Reformers realized that as long as the consolidation laws remained general laws focused exclusively on the procedures through which persons in a locality might initiate proceedings to form a consolidated district, persistence by local proponents would win the day politically. Through trial and error, local proponents would eventually hit upon a set of boundaries that could gain majority support in the rural portions of a proposed district. With at least 1,000 locations from which to launch consolidation efforts, far more potential consolidated districts existed than were required or desirable. This created a powerful incentive for various forms of "defensive consolidation." The residents of many neighborhoods felt compelled to seek inclusion in a consolidated district focused on a village of their choosing before they were forced into that of another. There were, however, other alternatives. If the residents of a neighborhood wanted to unite with other rural neighborhoods without locating the school in a town or village, they could try to form an open-country consolidated district. Rural places that did not consolidate retained the traditional country school. Ironically, in some parts of the state, the only sure way for rural districts to avoid losing territory to a consolidated district was for them to join forces, forming a consolidated district of their own for the expressed purpose of not establishing a consolidated school.[42] Importantly, local debates over consolidation were almost invariably presented in local newspapers as if they were solely concerned with the location of district boundaries rather than with community, class, or educational issues. Given the nature of the legislation governing the formation of the consolidated districts, it could not have been otherwise.

Despite billing to the contrary by the educational reformers, school consolidation was never an "experiment." Once a consolidated district had voted the bonds to build a new school, consolidation was essentially irreversible. By the end of World War I, reformers billed consolidation as inevitable — the next step in social progress. School consolidation had been set within a discourse in which experts, townspeople, and some farmers could see no other solution to the "rural school problem" — the consolidation discourse was hegemonic. Was rural school consolidation in Iowa simply a rational response to enrollment decline in rural areas? In a word, no.

The Discourse of Consolidation:
Assumptions, Misunderstandings, Effects

In many respects, Country Life and educational reformers alike misinterpreted the nature of the changes that were occurring in the Iowa countryside. Probably most serious was their failure to understand that rural-to-urban migration in Iowa during this period was not a simple case of rural depopulation in which farmers and their children left the farm in search of a better life in the city. Instead, migration flows generally conformed to one of three patterns: the movement of retired farmers to nearby villages and small towns; the migration of young and middle-aged men, who either had not obtained or did not expect to obtain their own farms, to low-status occupations in nearby cities and towns; and the temporary movement of young people to the city for higher education and then into high-status occupations in urban places near home.[43] Contrary to what was occurring in the East and South, the rural people who migrated to the larger towns and cities of the region moved into occupations vital to the integration of a vibrant regional economy, benefiting both rural and urban people alike. Family farmers in Iowa usually had better relations with merchants and townspeople in the larger towns than they did with those of the villages and small towns that reformers spied as the appropriate sites for consolidated schools. If anything, class-based antagonisms between farmers and the residents of small towns were the more severe. Farm people did not want to be forced into new communities dominated by those who had abandoned residence in the country — typically wealthy "retired" farmers who retained ownership of farms in the surrounding neighborhoods — and engaged in other business and banking ventures that often exploited those who remained family farmers in the locality.[44] An example drawn from a rural school consolidation controversy in Pocahontas County in northwest Iowa illustrates that strained class relations between farm families and the small towns, typically hidden from view and unacknowledged by those in power, could occasionally flare up in school consolidation conflicts of the period.

What Kind of Place for What Kind of School? The Plover Controversy

Late in the summer of 1914, the school board in the small town of Plover began to agitate for consolidating Plover's school district with much of the territory of the surrounding school township. By mid-November, the requisite number of signatures had been obtained, the boundaries of the proposed districts delimited, and the county superintendent's approval obtained. James Woodruff, the Department of Public Instruction's new inspector of consolidated schools, had met with local leaders and had provided them with materials about the advantages of consolidation for distribution and publication in the local newspaper. He had assured them that the district would receive the maximum amount of state aid if the effort was successful and had promised that State Superintendent Deyoe himself would appear at a public meeting in Plover to boost the issue shortly before the consolidation election. Deyoe appeared before the gathering on December 8.[45] Deyoe appears to have mishandled some rather pointed criticisms of the plan made by farmers in the area. The *Rolfe Arrow* published a letter to the editor from Andrew Simonson, a local farmer who opposed consolidation and the new kind of community he thought consolidation would foster. In an apparent attempt to convince other farmers to oppose consolidation, Simonson contended that consolidated schools,

> if they are to benefit the people in the country, must be located in the country. By voting to consolidate our school into a town we are helping to build up the town schools at the expense of the country schools. . . . We don't need consolidation. . . . The rural schools are just what we make them and if they are not what they should be someone is to blame. . . . The reason that some one-room country schools are "going to the dogs" is because they are not receiving the support that belongs to them. . . . Don't let them convince you that consolidation is a good thing simply because there are more of them now than there were a few years ago. . . .

Don't vote for consolidation because someone tells you to. In nine cases out of ten there is some selfish motive back of the proposition, and you don't have to look very far to find it. . . . They say that the school should be the social center of the community — even Mr. Deyoe says that. Where would our social center be if the schools were all located in towns? At Pikertown [Plover]? . . . Why is it that the country school can and does furnish the town school with nearly all their best scholars? . . . The one-room country school explains it. Do you want your boy or girl to associate with a street loafer or a street walker? They have just as many or more of them [proportionately] in the small town as they have in the city. . . . It beats all how much interest some town people seem to take in how our country children should be educated. Are the town people very much interested in establishing consolidated schools out in the country? . . . [A] vote for consolidation is a vote against the country schools.[46]

Another farmer, Charles Stroufe, also entered the debate, arguing that if the 1913 legislation granting state aid to consolidated school districts applied only to those with schools built in towns, it was "class legislation" and should be repealed. If all rural schools in the state were closed and replaced by consolidated schools, he went on, the job opportunities for the daughters of farm families would be greatly reduced. He asked farmers what chance they thought their daughters would have of getting jobs in consolidated schools. Town and city girls, he suggested, would end up teaching in them and farm girls would end up in their kitchens.[47] The issue had been politicized in both class- and place-based terms. In the election to consolidate the country school districts with that of Plover, held on January 30, 1915, the proposal was defeated.[48]

Iowans valued their rural neighborhoods, even when they were no longer their permanent places of residence. Reformers either ignored or seriously underestimated how important the rural school was in institutionalizing the sense of collective identity rural people had with their local communities. When a school is institutionalized in this way, "its perpetuation is seen as an end in itself. . . . [P]arents do not regard the school merely as a place to send their children to learn how to read, but as 'our' school."[49] Resistance to rural school consolidation was usually not perceived of by reformers in communitarian terms, and when it was, it was deemed illegitimate or otherwise unworthy of serious consideration. Instead they viewed resistance either as stemming from an unthinking, shortsighted clinging of farmers to an aberrant educational philosophy or as a form of social degeneration engendered by social and cultural isolation. These misunderstandings and misinterpretations were to have unfortunate consequences for both the rhetoric of rural school consolidation and the way in which its implementation was attempted. Conflict over rural school consolidation would largely determine the nature of the state's educational apparatus in Iowa for the rest of the century.

II

RESISTANCE AND PLACE

[I]n this day of modern inventive genius, with our eighteen hour trains, our wireless telegraphy, the automobile and the flying machines, we are inclined to boast of having annihilated space, but there is space that has quite successfully withstood all attempts at annihilation — the broad expanse of space that many fancy to exist between them and the schoolhouse of a consolidated district.

— Fred Mahannah, *"Factors in Rural School Improvement"*

6

RURAL RESISTANCE TO CONSOLIDATION: WHO? WHY? WHERE?

Opposition to Consolidation and Its Interpretations

Rural school consolidation produced more conflict than any other educational issue placed before Iowa voters in the twentieth century. No issue dealing with public schooling before or since has produced as much litigation as school consolidation did when it was being contested in the hustings from 1906 to 1925. During these years, seventy such cases were appealed to and heard by the Iowa Supreme Court. Countless others went unappealed. Even in the relative "hotbeds" of support, like Buena Vista, Clay, Story, and Marshall Counties, it usually took several elections before a consolidation would pass. When a proposal failed, proponents would simply note where the opposition was concentrated and redraw the boundaries to exclude enough opponents for it to pass at the next election, which until 1917 could be held as little as two weeks later. In the early years of the movement, the state superintendent encouraged local boosters to propose districts territorially much larger than necessary or even desirable simply "to gauge the opposition." [1] Battles over school consolidation could be long and bitter, but, unless proponents were easily tagged as representing "town interests," or the spatial distribution of opponents led to an exceptionally impractical gerrymander, the law favored the eventual formation of a consolidated district. All proponents needed to do was be persistent.

To gauge the prospects for consolidation in various parts of the state, state superintendents of public instruction began surveying county superintendents as early as 1901 about local objections to, and support for, various consolidation schemes. Such surveys were conducted on a regular basis from then until the General Assembly passed major new legislation on consolidation in 1913. Farmers also were not hesitant to write to one of the farm journals (e.g., *Wallace's Farmer* or *The Iowa Homestead*), or to the state superintendent himself, to make their concerns known. Their list of objections to consolidation was a long and varied one. Underlying these were at least six major issues. Although not mutually exclusive, they do represent the chief grounds upon which opposition was politicized once the consolidation movement was fully underway.

First and most basic was the issue of "forced consolidation" — that school consolidation was being thrust upon rural neighborhoods that neither needed it nor wanted it. Voters of rural districts who were satisfied with their existing country schools expressed incredulity when they discovered that their neighborhoods could be forced into a consolidated district even if all voters in the neighborhood opposed consolidation. The law simply required the support of a majority of voters in both the urban and rural portions for a consolidation proposal to pass. It was common for petitions objecting to consolidation proposals to be signed by every eligible voter in a rural neighborhood. Frequently a proposed consolidated district took in only portions of those districts or subdistricts on its boundary, leaving these districts or subdistricts with too little territory and taxable property to function as viable school districts. This led to the charge that consolidation, billed as a means of improving rural education by reformers, frequently "killed" the best country schools. Even the more vociferous advocates of consolidation admitted that the county school could perform credibly, if it was conducted by a good teacher. While it was often possible for local boosters of consolidation to identify contiguous areas of sixteen square miles in which a majority of the voters would support consolidation, it was usually quite difficult to find enough support in territories much larger than this. There were too many highly regarded country schools in most areas of the state for reformers to risk proposing that the General Assembly increase the minimum size of a consolidated district above sixteen sections — the minimum size of a consolidated district, first set in 1906. To do so would have rendered rural school consolidation a dead letter politically in almost all localities. In many instances, gerrymandering was necessary for a district to reach even the sixteen-section minimum.[2]

Second, residents of rural neighborhoods realized that the selection of a teacher was the key decision they made regarding the quality of education their children received in the one-room country school. They were loath to surrender or share this authority with people they did not know well or otherwise had grounds to mistrust. The little country schools were very important to rural families, and most were unwilling to relinquish their control of them without strong justification.[3] Reformers argued that the nature of education provided in the consolidated school would be quite different from what they were familiar with and valued. If the rhetoric was to be believed, this new education would train farm boys to become modern, scientific farmers and farm girls to become the domestic scientists. The latter in particular represented a geographical narrowing of a farm women's "sphere." From being the central figure in building and maintaining rural neighborhoods, the farm women became spouses, responsible primarily for modernizing their husbands' homes. Traditional family farmers tended to be skeptical of the need for these kinds of training and often resented any attempt of the public school to meddle in what they saw as a family responsibility. Some even argued that the "book farming" and "domestic science" taught in the consolidated school would "educate the farm child away from the farm," or at least transmit aspirations to children that would damage their conception of farming as a way of life.[4] A related concern was the fear that if consolidated schools were located in towns, town children and adults would discriminate against farm children even more than they already did. Educational leaders themselves advocated that consolidated schools be located in the small "country town" or village. They almost invariably recommended that consolidated school districts not include towns with more than 2,000 inhabitants. While this assuaged the fears of some farmers that their interests would be dominated by those middle-class townspeople, it also tended to confirm suspicions that consolidation necessarily involved a shift in the control of education away from farm families and their neighborhoods.

Third was the issue of increased taxes. Although early boosters maintained that consolidation would lower the costs of rural public schooling, this claim could not withstand scrutiny. By the time consolidation began to gather momentum in 1913, the issue was not over whether consolidated schools cost more than one-room schools, but whether the benefits of the consolidated school were worth the additional cost. The best estimates available indicated that the shift from the rural-independent to consolidated form of school district organization entailed a threefold increase in school tax levies per acre of farmland in 1915 and a fourfold increase by 1921.[5] The actual determinants of tax levy increases were the size of the district, the numbers of teachers and supervisory personnel, the costs of school equipment, and the geography of assessed valuations. In the best agricultural areas, farmland values were higher, making it easier to raise a given amount of revenue for school purposes with a smaller district. Here also was where residents were more likely to subscribe to middle-class values and judge the additional costs of a consolidated school worthwhile. Instead of reducing variation in per pupil expenditures in rural areas across the state, rural school consolidation actually increased them. Consolidation efforts tended to succeed in richer farm areas and to fail in poorer areas, shattering the approximate equality of country schools, which previously had so clearly distinguished rural education from urban education.

Fourth, the exclusive reliance upon property taxation, coupled with the rapidly escalating farmland values of the period, meant that the tax burdens for building and operating consolidated schools fell disproportionately on farm owners rather than on the owners of urban property.[6] Many farmers were already skeptical about the value of education beyond that provided in the country school. Inequities like these tended to stiffen their resolve, leading some to argue that rural school consolidation was a scheme to coerce farmers into paying for the construction and operation of "town" schools.

Fifth, rural parents were particularly skeptical about the advisability of transporting small children by wagon or bus over the generally miserable back roads in the Iowa countryside. Even reformers conceded that the poor condition of roads placed limits on the feasible size of a district. However, they viewed this as only a temporary impediment, soon to be swept away by the merging of two great Progressive movements — the rural school consolidation movement and the "good roads" movement. Rather then sending their young children to distant consolidated schools, most rural parents preferred sending them to country schools (albeit perhaps ones with better teachers and more modern facilities). The country schools were highly accessible geographically and socially; many feared that consolidated schools would be neither. They had fewer objections to the transportation of older children. Even here, however, the preferred option for most was to send teenage children to a nearby or otherwise accessible city high school with their tuitions paid by the rural school district.

Last, farm families often opposed consolidation because they were unconvinced that the country school was beyond redemption. Many wondered why no effort was made to upgrade the country school through higher minimum wages for teachers or through state aid earmarked for improving their physical plants and educational apparatus. If the primary objective of consolidation was to improve the accessibility of rural students to "rural-minded" high schools, others wondered why no effort was made to encourage the formation of rural high schools.[7] Evidence dating from the 1890s onward was available suggesting that this alternative to consolidation was both successful and popular in many localities in the Midwest, even in Iowa.[8]

In the early years of the movement, reformers conceded the legitimacy of the transportation issue alone. They alleged that the consolidated school was more efficient than the country school in every conceivable way. "It produced the better product — better health, better social life, better living conditions, better roads, and opportunity for a practical high school education for every boy and girl." It was only a matter of time, they argued, before farmers realized that the consolidated school was the better value. The consolidated school was "in line with American progress." It was "coming to bless the rural community" as had the "telephone, the rural mail carrier, the automobile, the electric motor and the gas plant." Indeed, the "hope of perpetuating the small town," it was claimed, lies "in the establishment of better schools and better churches in these communities." The consolidated school in conjunction with the consolidated church would "complete the transformation of rural life conditions."[9] Farmers who argued otherwise were either irremediably ignorant or incredibly short-sighted, bent on selfish accumulation with little regard for the future welfare of their children.[10]

Educational reformers tended to view most farmers as rich and getting richer. Those who were not had only themselves and their lack of appropriate education to blame. Reformers billed the consolidation movement as a means of ensuring that the reproduction of aberrant rural values and agricultural practices would not be continued into the next generation. The country school, unimproved roads, unimproved livestock, unkempt farmsteads, poor business practices, and a host of other rural ills had to give way to social progress.[11]

The Missing Rhetoric

Buried in the hoopla promoting consolidation, and unpublicized by the reformers, was the success of the free-tuition law the General Assembly had enacted in 1911. It required that every school district without a high school pay the tuition of its students to attend any high school in the state. The only limitation was that the amount of tuition paid could not exceed that levied by the nearest high school. For many farmers, the free-tuition law seemed a better way of increasing the accessibility of the modern high school to rural children than rural school consolidation. It enabled farm children to attend one of the better city high schools rather than be limited to a local high school. Furthermore, sending a child to the high school department of a consolidated school often conflicted with farmers' conceptions of what an appropriate high school education entailed. Only in those rural neighborhoods in which many children of high school age had already exercised the option of attending the high school of a nearby town was consolidation with that town usually feasible politically. Even then the attraction of consolidation was that it gave farm parents a means of retaining some control over the education process. In 1919–20, "tuition" students made up 26.7 percent of the state's total public high school enrollment of 63,217 — a figure considerably higher than the estimated number of rural high school students attending consolidated schools in 1927–28.[12] There were a large number of nonconsolidated high schools in the state; these were attended by a relatively high proportion of graduates of the one-room country schools.

Consolidation and Tax Increases: How Burdensome Were They?

Educational reformers were undoubtedly correct about the potential educational value of the consolidated school. Where they were wrong was in assuming that most Iowa farm owner-operators were rich and getting richer. Given the hyperinflated land values of the period, many farmers appeared rich. In terms of money incomes and the rates at which they were accumulating capital, however, average farm owner-operators were "rich" only in comparison to their economic standing in earlier decades. During the period 1913–20, the average farm owner-operator in Iowa could have accumulated capital at a faster rate in almost any other line of business, or by stepping down a rung on the agricultural ladder and opting for tenancy.

A conservative estimate of the average additional tax levy in a consolidated school district in 1921 compared to that in a country school district was $.84 per acre. For an average-size farm, this represented a tax increase of $140 per year, shrinking average profits of its owner-operator to only $105 per year.[13] Henry A. Wallace estimated the additional tax cost for one of the better consolidated schools to be $3.50 per acre. The average owner-operator in such a district would have paid an additional tax of $585 and incurred a significant yearly loss from farm operations.[14] Whatever the estimate, clearly the shift from the traditional one-room school to the consolidated school entailed a significant increase in school taxes for the average farm family. Given the growing number of additional demands on their net yearly income, it was an increase many farm families felt they could not afford.

The Geography of Support for and Resistance to Consolidation

One of the significant changes occurring in the transformation of family farming in Iowa during this period was the emergence of a new subclass of tenant farmers (see chapter 3). Tenant farmers became much more numerous in many localities as the farmland market boomed, fueling further land speculation and squeezing many would-be farmers out of the market. The relative scarcity of land and high commodity prices made renting prime farmland an attractive accumulation strategy for both landlord and tenant alike during this period.[15] This helped produce some localities in almost all parts of the state where accumulation-oriented tenant farmers, adopting modern production techniques, operated the biggest farms on the best land available. Tenant farm families were usually younger than traditional family farmers and more receptive to rural school reforms, including rural school consolidation. They, more than other farmers, tended to be less parochial in their economic and social outlooks, embracing more of the tenets of progress and modernity, including the expectation that as farms became larger, fewer farm children could expect to become farmers themselves. They were also less tied to traditional power structures based on kinship and neighborhood and were more enthusiastic supporters of a redistribution of that power to new state-level bureaucracies.

Increasing tenancy and the more widespread acceptance of this new logic of accumulation in a locality did not necessarily predispose a locality to favor consolidation. Usually, however, it was a good indication that the new agrarian ideology had already undermined the traditional neighborhood-reliant system of family farming there. As social relations in a locality became increasingly commodified, nearby towns necessarily became more important in the daily lives of farm families. Thus, the territory over which new rural communities might operate expanded. Following this logic, one is led to hypothesize that these "progressive" localities should have been the ones more easily mobilized in support of rural school consolidation.

The relative numbers of tenant farmers and owner-operators in a locality should have been largely irrelevant in producing local discourses favorable to school consolidation. What was important was whether the farmers owning and operating their own farms subscribed to a logic of accumulation similar to that of the tenants. Rural neighborhood socialization processes should have helped ensure that such was the case when the owner-operators in neighborhoods were also relatively young.

While the transformation of local social relations created the necessary conditions for predisposing a locality toward consolidation, local contingencies were also important. The relative wealth and its distribution, the magnitude of additional taxation associated with consolidated schools, and the perceived quality and social importance of the existing country schools were also critical factors in some locales, tipping farmers to either support or oppose consolidation. Other conditions also had to be right for even the new type of tenant to become mobilized behind a local consolidation effort. It was usually important for there to be a small town nearby and that it not already possess a high school or that its existing one be perceived as inadequate. If a larger town was more accessible than a small town and thereby the more reasonable location for the consolidated school, it was essential that it not have a history of exploitative relations with the farmers in the surrounding area.[16]

If contemporary historians and anthropologists are correct about German ethnicity inducing a cultural bias favoring the accumulation of capital in the form of land rather than in other forms, then German localities could be expected to have resisted the introduction of tenancy in the more purely capitalist form described above and to have opposed school consolidation on the grounds that additional investment in education was a poor substitute for investment in land.[17] In localities otherwise characterized by high land values and progressive farming practices, particular mixes of ethnicity, religious affiliations, and historical patterns of group conflict could often thwart the collective action necessary for the formation of a consolidated school district. Local traditions of support for parochial schools could also be important in producing active struggles against local consolidation movements.

If tenancy was indeed the leading edge of a more capital intensive system of production based on the family farm, and a new class of tenants was influential in creating localities characterized by modern, more impersonal, and more fully commodified social relations, then consolidation should have developed earlier and had its greatest support in the northwestern and north-central part of the state where cash grain farming was dominant. This was the most recently settled part of the state, having been taken up by farmers with enough capital to incur the costs of draining the area's rich prairie soils. U. S. Vance, the county superintendent of Pocahontas County, noted in his report to the state superintendent in 1901 a relationship between the generally high economic status of farmers in his county and a concern with "progressive" education:

> The schools in this county have been made and systematized in the last ten or twelve years. During this period, the county has made great material ad-

TABLE 1. *Number of Consolidated School Districts by Agricultural Region and Date Formed*

	Region				
Date Formed	Cash Grain	Dairy	Western Meat	Eastern Meat	Southern Pasture
1913 or earlier	20	4	5	5	3
1914–17	62	33	31	25	27
1918–19	23	5	17	17	12
1920–23	28	10	15	23	20
Totals	133	52	68	70	62

Source: Calculated by author.

vancement and the schools have kept up with the progress in other things. . . . People from the older counties of the state, from Wisconsin, Illinois and Indiana began to flock to this county in 1893 and 1894 and land advanced by bounds from ten dollars per acre to seventy dollars and more. The constant addition of vigorous, enterprising blood to the community has had a corresponding influence upon the schools. There has been what may seem an abnormal growth in school sentiment, school interest and in the schools themselves. To-day there is a greater interest in the school affairs of this county than is found in many of the older communities. There is a popular demand for better school officers, better school buildings, better schools, and better teachers and the demand is being filled.[18]

Table 1 provides further evidence in support of this. From 1911 to 1922, almost twice as many consolidations occurred in the cash grain region as in any other region. In the early years of the movement, consolidated districts here formed four times faster than in any other region in the state. While this is consistent with the foregoing interpretation, it is far from conclusive empirical evidence. It is possible to subject this interpretation of the linkage between increasing tenancy, the creation of distinctively "progressive" locales, and local support for or resistance to consolidation to much more rigorous analysis. The next two sections summarize two such analyses, one conducted at the county level and the other at the school district or township level. The nonstatistically inclined reader may wish to skip ahead to the last section of the chapter.

Correlates of the Geography of Success or Failure: County-Level Analysis

Did the geography of social and economic change in the countryside, including development of this new form of tenancy, account for the geography of rural school district consolidation? To answer this question in a statistical sense, a series of multiple regression models were specified and calibrated. Unfortunately, these models had to be calibrated at the county level with variables unlikely to be very sensitive to small-scale social differences within counties — differences likely to be important. It should also be recalled that school district consolidation as it was implemented was a profoundly geopolitical process. School district boundaries were seldom drawn so as to include only localities desirous of inclusion. Instead, they were drawn to include as much valuable agricultural land as possible and without engendering defeat at the polls. Also, there is no reason to believe that people in localities not included in a consolidated district were necessarily opposed to consolidation. Surely some areas were excluded from consolidated districts for other reasons — the poor quality of roads, ethnic conflicts, or low assessed valuations. As a result, it was inevitable that each of the models calibrated would contain very large "error terms" and that all would be characterized by relatively low levels of statistical "explanation."

Dependent Variables. To measure the geographical incidence of the consolidation movement's success from the perspectives of the reformers, four indicators were developed, each capturing a dimension of the success of the consolidation movement at the county level. These are defined in table 2 and are mapped in figures 6–10. Each of these measures was utilized sequentially as a dependent variable in a series of multiple regression analyses.

Theoretically Relevant Independent Variables. The selection of independent variables to include in the regression models was dictated by theoretical relevance and data availability. The indicators developed follow reasonably straightforwardly from the theorization of agricultural change and its relation to support for or opposition to rural school consolidation presented earlier. They are listed and defined in table 2.[19]

Control Variables. Four additional independent variables were included in the models, either because they were thought to be reasonable surrogates for important contingencies affecting local consolidation efforts or because they represented the types of evidence that leaders of consolidation pointed to in justifying consolidation. These too are defined in table 2.

Results. Altogether a total of fifteen regression models were calibrated, three for each of five indicators of consolidation success. The results are presented in table 3. While the levels of statistical explanation are modest, these analyses clearly demonstrate that three of the five indicators of greatest

TABLE 2. *Definitions of Variables Included in Regression Models*

Dependent Variables

NUMDIST: Number of consolidated schools in 1927–28 (compiled from *Iowa Educational Directory*, 1927–28, and from Stone 1928).

RURSTUD: Percentage of the total students residing in the open countryside attending a consolidated school in 1927–28 (estimated from 1927–28 enrollments from *Iowa Educational Directory* based on data from Kaldenberg 1922).

OCCONS: Percentage of the total students residing in the open country attending an **open-country** consolidated school in 1927–28 (calculated as in RURSTUD above).

PCTAR17:   Percentage of the total county area included in consolidated school districts in 1917 (calculated from Stone 1928).

PCTAREA: Percentage of the total county area included in consolidated school districts in 1927–28 (calculated from Stone 1928).

Independent Variables

Theoretically Relevant Variables

FARMTRAC: Percentage of farm operators with tractors in 1925 (calculated from 1925 Census of Iowa).

TENANT20:   Percentage of farms operated by renters in 1920 (calculated from 1920 U.S. Census of Agriculture).

SURROAD: Percentage of all roads in 1925 hard surfaced (with bituminous, gravel, or shale and sand clay) (from Shupe 1947, table 17).

BIGFARMB: Percentage of farms with more than 260 acres in 1920 (calculated from 1920 U.S. Census of Agriculture).

SHFARM20:   Percentage of farms operated by cash-share renters in 1920 (calculated from 1920 U.S. Census of Agriculture).

Control Variables

PCTRUR: Percentage of the total student enrollment in the one-room country schools in 1911–12 (calculated from *Biennial Report of the Supt. of Public Instruction*, 1912).

SMTOWNS: Number of towns and villages with fewer than 500 inhabitants in 1910 (calculated from *Biennial Report of the Supt. of Public Instruction*, 1912).

RPOPCHNG: Percent change in the rural population (not living in places with 2,500 inhabitants or more) from 1900 to 1910 (calculated from the U.S. Census of Population, 1910).

GERMBORN: Percentage of the total population in 1900 born in Germany (from U.S. Census of Population, 1910).

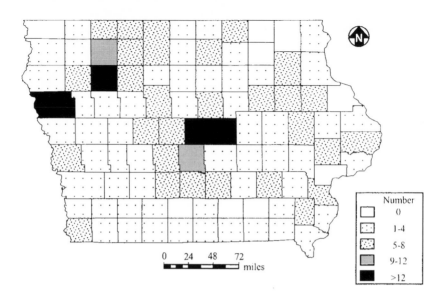

FIGURE 6. *Number of consolidated schools, 1927–28. Map by Peter Li.*

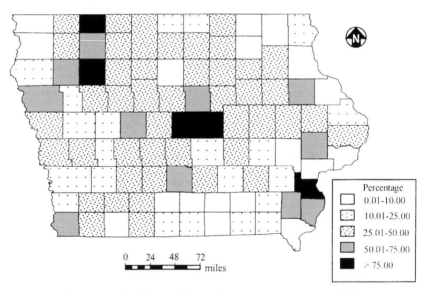

FIGURE 7. *Percentage of students residing in the open country attending a consolidated school, 1927–28. Map by Peter Li.*

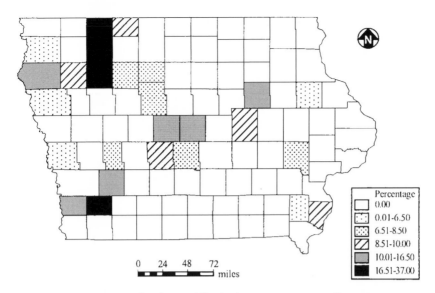

	Percentage
☐	0.00
⋮	0.01-6.50
▓	6.51-8.50
▨	8.51-10.00
▒	10.01-16.50
■	16.51-37.00

FIGURE 8. *Percentage of students residing in the open country attending an open-country consolidated school, 1927–28. Map by Peter Li.*

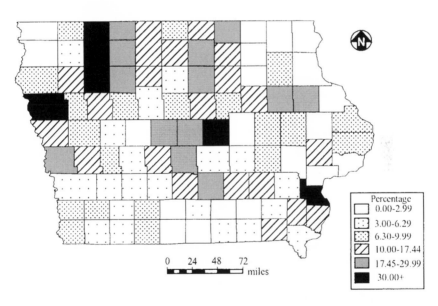

	Percentage
☐	0.00-2.99
⋮	3.00-6.29
▓	6.30-9.99
▨	10.00-17.44
▒	17.45-29.99
■	30.00+

FIGURE 9. *Percentage of county area included in a consolidated district, 1917. Map by Peter Li.*

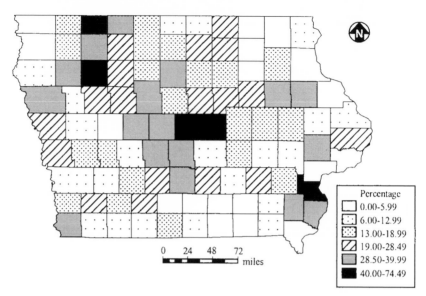

FIGURE 10. *Percentage of county area included in a consolidated district, 1927–28. Map by Peter Li.*

theoretical interest are consistently significant and independently correlated with the geographical incidence of rural school consolidation. The regression coefficients for all but one independent variable have the expected signs (and even those for this indicator have the expected negative value in ten of the fifteen models). Overall, the results suggest that support for consolidation was directly linked to the rise of a new form of tenancy in Iowa and to the uneven penetration of modern, more clearly capitalist, social relations in the Iowa countryside. They also suggest that rural school district consolidation consolidated social changes in the countryside that had already occurred through other means. Thus, there is some indication that school consolidation may have been embraced primarily where even its most vociferous champions claimed it was least needed.

The coefficients for the remaining independent variables are also revealing. First, there is clear evidence that the reformers were correct in anticipating more support for consolidation in the rural portions of counties that were relatively more urban. The message that consolidation would help keep the child on the farm did appear to play better in urbanizing counties. The existence of greater numbers of small towns in a county appears important only in accounting for the number of consolidated school districts and not for the percentage of rural students affected by consolidation. The exceptions are in those analyses attempting to account for the number of students

TABLE 3. *Coefficients of Regression Models*

Variable	NUMDIST 1	NUMDIST 2	NUMDIST 3	RURSTUD 1	RURSTUD 2	RURSTUD 3	OCCONS 1	OCCONS 2	OCCONS 3	PCTAR17 1	PCTAR17 2	PCTAR17 3	PCTAREA 1	PCTAREA 2	PCTAREA 3
FARMTRAC	.243* (.00)			1.393* (.00)			.464* (.00)			.726* (.00)			1.184* (.00)		
TENANT20		.150* (.00)			.835* (.00)			.205* (.02)			.392* (.00)			.712* (.00)	
SURROAD			.205* (.00)			1.014* (.00)			.437* (.00)			.761* (.00)			.929* (.00)
BIGFARMB			.077 (.34)			.530 (.55)			.298 (.12)			.529* (.08)			.524 (.19)
SHFARM20	-.022 (.39)	-.003 (.91)	-.032 (.23)	-.085 (.57)	-.038 (.78)	-.090 (.57)	-.038 (.55)	.028 (.64)	-.088 (.16)	.041 (.69)	.120 (.21)	-.070 (.48)	-.069 (.59)	.035 (.77)	-.104 (.43)
PCTRUR	-.058* (.02)	-.079* (.00)	-.059* (.03)	-.254* (.07)	-.373* (.01)	-.287* (.06)	-.027* (.64)	-.064* (.29)	-.041* (.50)	-.099* (.29)	-.159* (.10)	-.121* (.22)	-.209* (.08)	-.309* (.01)	-.238* (.07)
SMTOWNS	.200 (.15)	.273* (.05)	.216 (.11)	-.391 (.62)	.034 (.96)	-.246 (.76)	-.645* (.05)	-.494 (.15)	-.639* (.05)	-.147 (.78)	.079 (.88)	-.169 (.74)	-.244 (.72)	.116 (.86)	-.149 (.82)
RPOPCHNG	-.046 (.23)	-.051 (.18)	-.063* (.10)	-.366* (.09)	-.391* (.08)	-.433* (.05)	-.004 (.97)	-.014 (.88)	-.047 (.60)	-.096 (.51)	-.098 (.52)	-.195 (.17)	-.233 (.21)	-.254 (.17)	-.308* (.10)
GERMBORN	-.261* (.00)	-.213* (.00)	-.195* (.01)	-1.178* (.01)	-.882* (.01)	-.739* (.08)	-.353* (.06)	-.200 (.28)	-.262 (.12)	-.520* (.09)	-.334 (.26)	-.417 (.12)	-1.118* (.00)	-.868* (.02)	-.781* (.03)
R^2	.322	.316	.350	.275	.210	.259	.186	.126	.255	.204	.176	.307	.277	.261	.287

* Significant at .10 level; significance levels are in parentheses.

attending open-country consolidated schools. It would appear that the presence of larger numbers of small towns simply contributed to the spatial fragmentation of consolidation efforts in a county, probably resulting in more districts than there would otherwise have been. Overall, this is quite consistent with the apparent logic of using consolidation to build and maintain better high schools in small towns — the potential country towns favored by Country Lifers — and to refocus the social relations of rural areas on these places.

As expected, the greater the population loss of a county between 1900 and 1910, the greater the support for consolidation. Again the exception was for open-country consolidations. Somewhat surprisingly, rural population loss was significant in only a third of the models. These results strongly imply that rural population decline was not the principal factor in the success or failure of rural school consolidation in a county.

Finally, the results clearly point to German ethnicity as a negative correlate of school consolidation success. Given other evidence, it is certainly safe to conclude that localities characterized by German ethnicity were not bastions of support for consolidation. Whether this was because of the anti-German sentiment characterizing the period, because of the different accumulation strategies followed by German farmers, or perhaps because many Germans preferred to send their children to parochial high schools (either Catholic or Lutheran) cannot be determined. These alternative explanations are all plausible. German opposition, however, cannot be explained by German farmers having settled in areas with less productive land, or by some other indicator of their lower economic status. Neither was a general characteristic of farming areas in Iowa where Germans were predominant.

The Geography of Resistance: Township and District-Level Analysis

Are there persistent differences in farm size by tenure class and in levels of tenancy between those townships and school districts whose residents voted for consolidation and those whose residents actively opposed it? If the theoretical speculations presented above are well founded, then consolidation should have taken place primarily in those areas where the new form of capital-intensive tenant farming had become most firmly established. Such areas should have possessed three primary characteristics during this era: (1) an increasing number of renters; (2) renters working land that was at least as good in quality as that of owner-operators; and (3) renters operating farms larger than those of owner-operators. In other areas, owner-operators should still have predominated, occupying the best land, while subscribing to more traditional farming practices and ideology, including the more traditional form of tenancy whereby in ascending the agricultural ladder the farmer started small as a tenant. In these areas, the farms of renters should not be larger than those of owner-operators.

Although historical data do not permit a direct comparison of consolidated and nonconsolidated districts in all of these regards, it is possible to do so regarding farm sizes and tenure relations.[20] Unlike in the county-level regression analyses, it is possible here to focus specifically on localities for which it could be documented that rural school consolidation had been either generally supported or actively resisted. Since a consolidated district seldom included an entire township, it was often possible to partition data for a single township into two localities, one in which consolidation was accepted and the other in which it was rejected. In total, the juxtaposition of this information provided thirty-nine localities that had voted to consolidate their rural school districts and thirty-eight in which consolidation was attempted but rejected. Comparable information was obtained for five other townships from several rural social surveys of the period, bringing the total number of "consolidated" and "nonconsolidated" localities to forty-three and thirty-nine, respectively.

The following statistics were calculated for both types of localities: the *average size of farm holdings* for *owner-operators*, for *related renters* (defined as persons renting from an owner with the same surname as the renter), and for *unrelated renters* (defined as persons renting from an owner with a different surname); and the *percentage of the total number of farmers in each of these tenure classes*. Unfortunately, reliable information on land values at the township level does not exist for this period. Therefore, it was not possible to construct a rigorous test of whether renters were occupying land of as high a quality as that of owner-operators. Instead, 1:100,000 USGS topographic maps of Iowa counties and relevant county histories were consulted to make qualitative assessments. Based on these sources, it appears that only a few of the localities supporting consolidation showed any evidence of significant variation in the quality of farmland. In these, there was little doubt that the rented farms were concentrated on higher quality prairie land rather than in the previously timbered or more heavily dissected areas. In localities rejecting consolidation, land was generally of lower quality and the terrain more rugged. Here there appeared to be no tendency for renters to be concentrated on either the better or worse farmland.

Examination of farm sizes by tenure class permits a direct test of the hypothesis that renters in districts supporting consolidation, particularly those who were "unrelated" to their landlords, had larger farms on average than owner-operators; while in areas rejecting consolidation there was either no difference between the average farm sizes of owner-operators and unrelated renters, or the farm sizes of the owner-operators were larger. Attention was focused on the farm sizes of renters unrelated to their landlords, rather than those of renters related to their landlords, because it was expected that this group would be more likely to confront market-based rental payments or share agreements and hence have the financial incentive to farm as much land as possible as part of their accumulation strategies. For the purpose of framing a test of this hypothesis, the average size of the unrelated renters' farms was considered to be significantly greater than that of owner-operators only if the difference was 5 percent or more. Any other difference in these two average farm sizes was considered indicative that there was no significant difference between the farm size values for these two tenure classes or that the farm sizes of owner-operators were greater in these localities.[21]

The numbers of localities, both those approving and opposing consolidation, that met these conditions are summarized by agricultural region in table 4 (the averages upon which this table is based are included in the appendix). Except for the western meat production area, the results lend remarkably strong support for the hypothesis. In the cash grain area (twenty-seven cases) there are only four exceptions, in the eastern meat production area (eighteen cases) two, and in the dairy area (seven cases) one. In the southern pasture area, three of the four cases conformed to the hypothesis. The pervasiveness of the relationship is evident in all regions except the western meat production area, where only twelve of twenty-six cases conform to it. All but one of the localities from this region included in the analysis are in Woodbury, Cherokee, and Monona Counties. At the time, this was the most highly commercialized area of livestock production in the state, with most of its production shipped to the burgeoning stockyards in nearby Sioux City (see appendix). The nature of agriculture in this region, with its emphasis on cattle production and relatively large stock farms requiring greater inputs of both capital and labor than any of the other regions of agricultural production, may account for this apparent anomaly. An established tradition of cash renting in this region, where, relative to other regions in the state, there was much less opportunity for the renter to buy a tractor and the other farm machinery necessary to become a cash grain farmer also contributed. Here, a cash grain farming tenant could compete less favorably with the equally capitalistic production process already dominating the region.

TABLE 4. *Number of Localities Meeting Specified Tenant and Owner Average Farm Size Conditions and Average Percent of Farms Owner-Operated by Agricultural Region and Consolidation Status*

Agricultural Region and Type of Locality	Number of Localities Meeting Conditions		Average Percentage of Farms Owner-Occupied
	I	II	
Cash Grain Area			
Proconsolidation	12	2	46.6
Anticonsolidation	2	11	52.8
Eastern Meat Production Area			
Proconsolidation	8	1	53.1
Anticonsolidation	1	8	55.1
Western Meat Production Area			
Proconsolidation	6	7	50.4
Anticonsolidation	7	6	47.2
Southern Pasture Area			
Proconsolidation	2	0	54.7
Anticonsolidation	1	1	57.3
Dairy Area			
Proconsolidation	5	0	55.9
Anticonsolidation	1	1	57.9

Condition I: Average size of farms operated by renters who were unrelated to their landlords exceeded that of owner-operators by at least 5 percent.

Condition II: Average size of farms operated by owners was either equal to or greater than that of renters unrelated to their landlords.

Source: Calculated by author.

Of what relevance, if any, was the relative proportion of tenant farmers to landowning farmers in localities in the various regions? Was it an irrelevant contingency in local consolidation movements as hypothesized? As indicated in table 4, on average there is a slightly higher proportion of renters in districts supporting consolidation than in nonconsolidated districts, but the differences are not great. Furthermore, those for the southern pasture area and the nonconsolidated localities in the dairy area are based on only two cases each. Again, the exception is the western meat production area, where the average proportion of owner-operators in districts supporting consolidation slightly exceeds the same proportion in the nonconsolidated districts. This is further evidence of the quite different nature of agricultural production in this area during this period. Overall, renters were more numerous than owners in twenty-two of the forty-three localities supporting consolidation and in twenty-three of the thirty-nine localities rejecting consolidation (see appendix). Coupled with the regional averages, it is clear that there was no pervasive relationship between the relative numbers of owner-operators and renters in a locality and the support for or resistance to rural school district consolidation. The key variable was not the relative number of renters in a locality, but whether renters were the more likely to consider farming a business venture. That renters operated bigger farms is certainly consistent with this.

A Tentative Conclusion

Rural school consolidation in Iowa proceeded very unevenly geographically. The leaders of the movement lacked any strong state educational apparatus and were constrained to implement rural school consolidation in a manner roughly congruent with tenets of local democracy. They could not force consolidation on any locality except through the ballot box. Convinced of the necessity of removing the rural neighborhood as the principal site for the determination of rural school policy and of reconstituting rural social relations to focus on the country town, reformers developed an informally constituted, statewide organization, and coordinated it through the office of the state superintendent of public instruction. They pushed for consolidation wherever local conditions seemed favorable. Reformers seem to have badly misdiagnosed the reasons for farm community support for, or opposition to, consolidation. The peculiar nature of economic conditions in Iowa during the period, however, helped forge a new system of production in most areas of the state, in which a new class of tenant farmer was the principal agent of change, providing the new system with its dynamism. The ideology of the consolidation movement held that the consolidated school would play a key role in helping to reconstitute a new, yet vibrant, rural community life. The evidence presented here strongly suggests that this ideology gave way to practical politics and that local consolidation movements followed rather than led social change. School consolidation in Iowa took place primarily where capitalist social relations had already advanced furthest and where, from the perspective of social efficiency then dominating the reform ideology, it was least needed. Although this reform movement may have begun as an attempt to counteract some of the effects of the pervasive spatial unevenness of a more modern capital-intensive agriculture, in its implementation it served primarily to legitimize that unevenness. The evidence is overwhelming that rural school consolidation in Iowa during this period was a place-based class movement.

"Country" and "city" are very powerful words, and this is not surprising when we remember how much they seem to stand for in the experience of human communities.

— *Raymond Williams,* The Country and the City

7

RURAL SCHOOL CONSOLIDATION
AND THE SOCIAL CONSTRUCTION
OF PLACE: A CASE STUDY OF
DELAWARE COUNTY

How did local school consolidation movements actually unfold in the rural neighborhoods and small towns of Iowa during the period under study? How did the dominant proconsolidation discourse of educational reformers play in the hustings? Did it adapt to the politics of local movements? If so, how were these adaptations contested and with what effects? How can such movements best be interpreted? How were they related to one another? This chapter and the next two seek to answer these questions and address related issues by analyzing the interrelated set of local efforts to consolidate rural schools in Delaware County in the period 1915–1922.

Delaware County was not an early leader in the consolidation movement in Iowa. That distinction fell to several counties in the cash grain region of the state. What makes Delaware County important is that it is one of the few counties in eastern Iowa where more than half of the students living in the countryside were attending a consolidated school by the end of the consolidation movement. Located in the dairy region of northeast Iowa, it was the only county to achieve this distinction. If the consolidation movement had a success story in eastern Iowa, it was a Delaware County story. While consolidation was welcomed as an important educational innovation and as a sign of economic progress in some neighborhoods, it was met with vehement resistance in others. By the early 1920s, conflict between contending parties over consolidation throughout much of the county had escalated into open strife with significant class and sectarian dimensions. In Delaware County as a whole, the local press tended to politicize rural school consolidation primarily as a taxation issue, but in the rural neighborhoods and small towns of the county, local battles over rural school consolidation entailed more than this. Here such struggles were over the social and territorial construction of place and social identity.

As we have seen, efforts to consolidate rural schools almost invariably became linked to efforts to create more modern rural places — country towns — without destroying the supposed virtues of rural life with its complicated admixture of communitarianism and self-reliance. Delaware County was no exception. However, efforts at school consolidation here also became linked to attempts at resuscitating and modernizing the dominant church in most of the county's rural localities — the Methodist Episcopal. In localities with sizable concentrations of Catholics, these social reconstructions of place heightened and indeed exploited conflict between Catholic and Protestant, helping to usher in forms of social identity antithetical to communitarian and agrarian class objectives alike. This led some to question whether school consolidation, whatever its educational merits might be, was worth the social cost.

Running diagonally from the northwest to southeast corners of the county, the Maquoketa River approximately bisects the county. To the east lie the earlier settled townships, each with one or more towns or villages of commercial significance, while to the west only two could make such a claim. The quality of its agricultural land was (and is) generally high but subject to considerable local variation. The typical soil, covering two-thirds of the land area, consists of deep black loam derived from Iowan glacial till, and is rich in organic matter and soluble mineral nutrients. The depth and continuity of these soils are greater west of the Maquoketa River, but all townships, except for Colony in the northeast corner of the county, have some areas covered by them. The soils in areas not covered by Iowan drift derive either from loess clays or sands. While some of these soils rival the Iowan drift in quality and fertility, they tend to occur in areas where the topography is more rugged and dissected and hence are less easily worked and more erodible.[1]

Settlement began in 1836 but did not gain much momentum until the opening of the U.S. Land Office at Dubuque, twenty-five miles east, in 1838. Thenceforth, the more easily worked land east of the Maquoketa River was rapidly converted into farms. For rural settlement, the 1850s was the boom

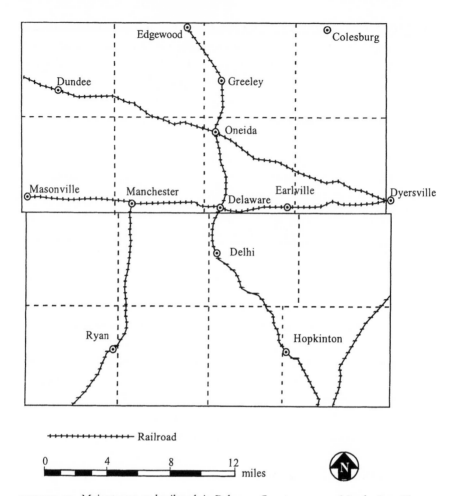

FIGURE 11. *Major towns and railroads in Delaware County, ca. 1920. Map by Peter Li.*

decade. Twelve of the county's sixteen townships had reached their maximum rural populations by 1870, and all had done so by 1880 (figure 11). From 1870 onward, the growth of towns largely accounted for the population increase. Settlement of the countryside and the growth of towns was intimately linked to the development of railroads and the speculative activities of land companies, which often were land-development subsidiaries of the railroad companies themselves. Towns and the boosters of "would be" towns actively courted the railroads, with the larger places typically floating local bond issues to underwrite significant portions of the costs of constructing the railbeds and associated infrastructure. Location on a rail line, particularly a major line, often meant the difference between economic success and economic failure. The Dubuque and Pacific Railroad (later Illinois

Central) reached Dyersville on the county's eastern boundary in 1856 and was extended seven miles west to Earlville (then called Nottingham) late in 1857. Earlville had been laid out and platted by the Iowa Land Company, a subsidiary of the railroad, a few months earlier.[2] Two years later the line was completed westward through the middle of the county with stations at towns platted by the Iowa Land Company at Manchester and Masonville.[3] A second major rail line traversing the county, the Davenport and St. Paul Railroad (later the Chicago, Milwaukee and St. Paul Railroad), a north-south line on the east side of the Maquoketa River, was completed in 1872. It connected the preexisting towns of Hopkinton, Delhi, Delaware, Greeley, and Edgewood. Each of these towns had voted a tax to raise revenues for the construction of the line. Finally, in 1887 the Chicago Great Western Railroad was completed through the northern half of the county, from Dyersville in the east to Lamont near the northwestern corner of the county. It was completed too late to contribute much to town development along its extent. Its location was instrumental in the founding of several small villages. One of these, Oneida, would later play a key role in the consolidation of rural schools in the county.

After the county seat had been moved from Delhi to Manchester in 1880, the Illinois Central developed a branch line connecting Manchester with Cedar Rapids, some forty miles to the south. Ryan, one of the towns along this route, grew rapidly to become the principal market center in the southwestern corner of the county. The new railroad towns and most of the older towns now served by rail lines boomed as they took advantage of the county's agricultural resource base. Manchester grew to be the largest town in the county and its commercial center. The county reached its maximum population in 1900.

In the boom years of the 1850s and 1860s, settlers were overwhelmingly native born, principally from upstate New York but also with sizable numbers from New England, Ohio, and Pennsylvania. A lesser but still significant number came from intervening states. There were, however, sizable concentrations of foreign-born settlers in several localities throughout the county: English in the major towns in the northern half of the county; Germans in several localities in the northeast quarter; Irish in the southwest; Canadians in the northwest; and Scots in the southeast. Of these, Germans and Irish were the most numerous and spatially extensive. The U.S. Census of Religious Bodies of 1906 revealed that 58 percent of the county's church members or communicants were Protestant and 42 percent Catholic. By way of comparison, the ratios of Protestants to Catholics in the neighboring counties immediately east, south, west and north of Delaware County, respectively, were Dubuque — 19: 81; Jones — 73: 27; Buchanan — 61: 39; and Clayton — 66: 34. Consistent with the preponderantly rural, nonethnic heritage of the majority of its inhabitants, Methodists outnumbered the combined membership of the three other principal Protestant denominations represented in the county — Lutherans, Congregationalists, and Presbyterians. The dominance of Methodists, however, slipped somewhat between 1906 and 1915 as the more urban-oriented Presbyterian and Lutheran churches gained in membership. The 1915 Census of Iowa revealed that the ratio of Protestants to Catholics was 61 to 39, little changed from the 1906 figure. Manchester was the county's leading commercial, cultural, and political center and was the only place in the county that approached being "urban" in a cultural sense. By the turn of the century, Manchester had earned a reputation as a producer of high-quality butter for eastern markets.

The first quarter of the twentieth century was to usher in significant economic, demographic, and social changes in Delaware County and northeast Iowa. The agricultural depression of the late 1880s and early 1890s had had a less severe impact on dairying than it had on grain or livestock farming. It had not resulted in the massive abandonment of small-scale family farming as it had elsewhere in Iowa and the Midwest. The rural population of the county began to decline after 1890 and continued to decline quite steadily, averaging about 7.5 percent per decade throughout the period (table 5).[4] While it is less easy to characterize the changes in the populations of urban places during this period, the growth of population in the towns of the county was not sufficient to offset the loss of rural population. The county as a whole lost 6.6 percent of its population between 1900 and 1925.

Manchester's growth occurred in fits and starts throughout the period (see table 6). Dyersville, in Dubuque County but only a stone's throw from the Delaware County line, presented a different growth dynamic, growing at an increasingly rapid rate. Smaller urban places presented a still different picture. Some, like Hopkinton and Ryan, grew modestly early in the period and then began to decline. Others like Colesburg and Edgewood grew more rapidly later in the period. Still others followed a growth path more like Manchester's, declining early in the period and then recovering to achieve modest growth toward the end of the period. Indeed, among the smaller towns and villages, population growth between 1870 and 1920 appeared quite chaotic and far from uniform spatially. Town and village growth possessed the properties of a zero-sum game: those that grew did so at the expense of nearby places. Even here, however, the gains were short-lived. None of the smaller places were successful in achieving sustained popula-

Population	1890	1900	1905*	1910	1915*	1920	1925*
Total county	17,349	19,185	18,761	17,888	18,564	18,183	17,927
Urban (incorp.)	3,581	5,259	5,973	6,187	6,857	7,071	7,258
Rural (unincorp.)	13,768	13,926	12,788	11,701	11,701	11,112	10,669

Population Changes (%)	1890–1900	1900–1910	1905–1915	1910–1920	1915–1925
Urban	46.9	17.6	14.8	14.3	5.8
Rural	1.1	−16.0	−8.5	−5.0	−8.9

* The population of the Delaware Country portion of the town of Edgewood is estimated based on the proportion of the town's population in 1910 that was in Delaware County.

Source: U.S. Census of Population, Iowa Census of Population.

tion growth. To Protestant church leaders in Delaware County, Earlville, Ryan, and Dyersville were viewed as growth centers from which Catholicism was spreading into formerly staunchly Methodist territory.

In 1911–12, there were 4,147 students enrolled in Delaware County's 146 one-room country schools — an average of 28 per school. On average, 69.7 percent of the students enrolled in the country schools attended regularly. In addition 1,742 students were enrolled in the public schools of the county's nine towns and villages, each with its own independent school district.[5] Attendance in the town schools averaged 80.3 percent of their total enrollment. Delaware County had, with very few exceptions, retained the school township form of rural school organization and governance. This had the effect of fostering a somewhat stronger identification of farm families with their townships than was the case elsewhere in eastern Iowa, where the rural independent form of organization was the norm. Subdistricts of school townships, however, operated very much like rural independent districts and were even referred to as "districts" by county residents. Each township elected a board of directors, one director from each of its several subdistricts. Directors were responsible for the maintenance of the school in their subdistricts, for securing a teacher for each of the three terms in the school year, and for negotiating the teacher's salary. Although there was a common

TABLE 6. *Populations of Towns and Villages within or Easily Accessible to Delaware County, 1900–1925*

Major Towns (pop. average > 1,000)	1890	1900	1905	1910	1915	1920	1925
Manchester	2,344	2,887	2,978	2,758	3,102	3,111	3,455
Monticello	1,938	2,104	2,156	2,043	2,259	2,257	2,215
Dyersville	1,272	1,323	1,446	1,511	1,885	1,933	2,083

Small Towns (pop. average 500–1,000)	1890	1900	1905	1910	1915	1920	1925
Hopkinton	668	767	816	797	863	759	729
Lamont	—	636	580	571	592	495	560
Earlville	569	618	571	552	582	619	613
Edgewood	—	565	538	553	625	617	659
Coggan	—	498	506	471	569	553	516

Villages (pop. average < 500)	1890	1900	1905	1910	1915	1920	1925
Greeley	—	488	416	383	370	410	372
Ryan	—	—	371	511	483	397	326
Delhi	—	—	—	375	438	390	407
Colesburg	—	274	286	271	320	337	331
Masonville	—	—	289	282	268	250	228
Dundee	—	—	—	—	—	195	192
Delaware	—	—	—	—	—	194	191
Oneida	—	—	—	—	145	127	114

Source: U.S. Census of Population, Iowa Census of Population.

TABLE 7. *Number of Grades (Yrs.) Provided in the Public Schools of the Towns and Villages of Delaware County, 1906–7 to 1914–15*

City/Town	1906–7	1907–8	1908–9	1909–10	1910–11	1911–12	1912–13	1913–14	1914–15
Manchester	12	12	12	12	13	13	13	12	12
Edgewood	12	12	12	12	12	12	12	12	12
Dyersville	10	10	9	10	—	9	—	—	11
Earlville	11	11	11	11	12	12	12	12	11
Greeley	10	10	10	10	11	11	11	11	11
Delhi	9	9	9	9	12	9	10	10	10
Colesburg	9	9	9	9	10	10	10	10	10
Hopkinton	11	11	11	11	11	12	11	11	11
Delaware	9	9	9	9	11	9	9	10	10
Ryan	9	10	9	9	10	10	10	12	10

Source: *Biennial Reports*, Department of Public Instruction, State of Iowa, 1906–1916.

tax rate throughout each school township, the locally elected township assessor usually adjusted the assessed values of property in the various subdistricts so that each raised revenue sufficient to cover whatever variations in teacher salaries existed across subdistricts. The school township provided an organizational infrastructure through which a modicum of cooperation in educational affairs between contiguous rural neighborhoods could be achieved. Cooperation extended to such matters as hiring teachers, adjusting subdistrict boundaries to accommodate local demographic changes, and relocating or building new schoolhouses when conditions demanded.

In 1911–12, the only towns having full, four-year high schools were Earlville, Edgewood, and Manchester (tables 7–9). Greeley and Hopkinton provided a three-year high school, Colesburg and Ryan two-year high schools, and Delaware, Dyersville, and Delhi only one year of high school. Less numerous, but nonetheless significant, were the several parochial schools serving the children of Catholic families in the county. Dyersville and Manchester each had full twelve-year parochial schools, while the hamlet of Petersburg in Colony Township had a parochial grade school. In 1911–12, the Catholic parish centered on Ryan was actively involved in a campaign to build a graded elementary and high school to serve the growing number of Catholic families in the southwestern corner of the county. The campaign

TABLE 8. *Enrollments in the Public High Schools of Delaware County, 1904–5 to 1913–14*

City/Town	1904–5	1906–7	1907–8	1908–9	1909–10	1910–11	1911–12	1912–13	1913–14
Manchester	131	143	144	169	177	178	199	212	228
Edgewood	37	41	50	60	60	66	79	81	74
Dyersville	16	24	13	—	21	—	17	—	6
Earlville	40	44	47	47	42	30	25	37	41
Greeley	14	16	26	20	23	12	16	15	18
Delhi	14	54	33	22	35	36	19	27	20
Colesburg	26	31	11	3	12	10	8	10	12
Hopkinton	29	46	36	37	43	55	—	37	41
Delaware	24	18	23	34	13	26	18	32	6
Ryan	6	29	16	21	20	15	26	32	30
Totals	337	446	399	377	446	428	407	483	476

Source: *Biennial Reports*, Department of Public Instruction, State of Iowa, 1904–1914.

TABLE 9. *Total Enrollments in the Public Schools of Delaware County, 1904–5 to 1913–14*

City/Town	1904–5	1906–7	1907–8	1908–9	1909–10	1910–11	1911–12	1912–13	1913–14
Manchester	687	694	735	725	721	686	759	993*	754
Edgewood	127	202	189	222	239	227	230	225	225
Dyersville	83	57	56	56	47	—	40	—	45
Earlville	172	171	153	164	156	137	153	172	162
Greeley	121	110	104	121	116	100	82	114	98
Delhi	128	123	122	158	148	166	107	185	169
Colesburg	63	86	87	95	126	91	82	94	118
Hopkinton	237	218	164	182	189	227	227	221	231
Delaware	96	100	86	131	97	67	70	65	76
Ryan	104	122	90	159	162	137	143	144	153
Totals	1,818	1,883	1,786	2,013	2,001	1,838	1,893	2,213	2,031

*The large increase in Manchester's enrollment in 1912–13 is probably due to the new high school being completed in 1912 and freeing up more space for use in the elementary grades.

Source: *Biennial Reports*, Department of Public Instruction, State of Iowa, 1904–1914.

was successful and a parochial school opened there in 1913. It quickly became the largest parochial school in Delaware County, with an enrollment of 139 in 1914–15. The only other parochial school in the county then was a small Lutheran school in Delaware covering only the elementary grades.[6] By 1914–15 the parochial school systems of both Dyersville and Ryan were considerably larger than their public school counterparts. German and Irish Catholic families, respectively, were predominant in these towns and in their surrounding rural neighborhoods. Dyersville retains a large parochial school system even today. In 1921, both towns seriously explored the possibility of discontinuing their public schools by merging them with their parochial schools under the management of their respective parishes.[7]

Unlike some counties in the cash grain region of the state, where farms were considerably larger, population more sparse, and towns more widely spaced, the residents of Delaware County showed little interest in rural school consolidation until 1914 when the newly created Department of Public Instruction (DPI) first sent representatives to the county to campaign actively on its behalf. Before that time, cultural dominance by the northeast with its emphasis on civic virtue and the importance of common schooling ensured that few, if any, rural schools in the county conformed to the caricature of them often drawn by reformers. In short, most were thought to be of high quality and were well-supported by their patrons.

Farm children wishing to attend high school had several alternatives of high repute available. They could choose between the public high school in Manchester, the parochial high schools in Manchester, Ryan, and Dyersville, and the academy affiliated with Lenox College in Hopkinton. Additionally, the public high schools of Edgewood, Earlville, and Greeley also attracted tuition students from the surrounding rural areas. According to the records of the state superintendent, there were 111 rural students in Delaware County attending a town high school on a tuition basis in 1911–12. The public high schools of choice were those of Manchester and Edgewood. These two schools alone accounted for approximately 70 percent of the county's tuition students.[8] Because of the generally poor conditions of the roads and difficulty of travel, students from outlying districts attending high school in these towns usually arranged to board "in town" throughout the week, returning home for weekends. Manchester, Edgewood, and Hopkinton had several rooming houses to accommodate rural tuition students.[9]

An argument in favor of the consolidated school frequently heard in Delaware County after 1915 was that it enabled farm children to obtain twelve years of schooling without having to leave their rural communities. As the *Monticello Express* put it, "consolidation is a benefit to the village and country equally, since each may thus be able to maintain standard school education without sending them [their children] from the parental roof during the high school period, a very important consideration." [10] Carl Wellemeyer, a highly successful young farmer from the Colesburg area, and member of the county board of education, expressed it even more forcefully: "redblooded American citizens living in small towns and on the farms . . . do not relish the idea of sending their children of tender years out of the home and home community to get a high school education." [11]

A key issue was how such "home communities" were constituted in the consciousness of the citizens, and in particular, whether they included both farm families and the residents of the smaller towns. In the parlance of the rural sociology of the day, what distinguished the country town from the urban town? Rural sociologists and Country Life philosophers had their answers, but they did not necessarily conform very well to those of farm people in Delaware County.

Replanting the Consolidation Idea in Delaware County

Before the DPI was established in 1913, the state superintendent could provide little more than rhetorical support to local efforts to consolidate rural schools with those of neighboring villages and small towns. The DPI had no coercive means at its disposal to mandate consolidation and had no mass support from farmers themselves. Even with its new inspectorships after 1913, it still had to depend on its contacts with local elites and local institutions to initiate action on consolidation in the hustings. The DPI sought and found support for rural school consolidation not only among civic and business leaders of small towns but also among rural church leaders, both ecclesiastical and lay. Just as educational leaders argued that the changing nature of rural social and economic conditions required a new system of rural public schools, leaders of the mainline Protestant denominations argued that these changes also required that the rural church's mission be transformed and modernized. They maintained that the rural church needed to take a more active interest in the social and material well-being of its members and that cooperation between churches of different denominations needed to be encouraged. The particular form of cooperation most often advocated was rural church consolidation, involving the merging of rural and small town parishes of the same denomination and the merging of rural churches of different denominations. Just as the rural school problem was one of too many small, inefficient schools, the rural church problem was one of too many small, inefficient churches — "over-churching" as it was usually called. If overchurching were not eliminated, the rural church would become as much a derelict from a bygone era as the country school was already thought to be (see chapter 3).

These ideas found a particularly receptive audience among Methodist church leaders in northeast Iowa. The Methodist Episcopal Church was the dominant Protestant church in northeast Iowa, as it was throughout most rural areas and small towns in the state. In 1914 it still remained a powerful force in the daily lives of ordinary people. Delaware County was no exception.

In 1913, the deputy superintendent of public instruction was Frank D. Joseph. Joseph, a native of Hopkinton, had achieved notoriety in eastern Iowa as the quarterback of the Lenox College football team that beat the University of Chicago and tied the State University in 1899. After graduating from Lenox in 1899, Joseph became principal of the graded public school at Walker (in nearby Linn County). He went on to become superintendent of schools at Edgewood (in Delaware County) shortly thereafter, before being elected county superintendent in 1904. In 1907 he had been instrumental in getting local civic leaders in Delhi to agitate for the consolidation of Delhi's school district with most of the rural subdistricts in the surrounding school townships. It was the first attempt at rural school consolidation in Delaware County. Had the effort been successful, the new district would have contained the forty sections and become the largest school district in eastern Iowa. In the consolidation election, the proposal passed 47–4 in the village but lost 35–79–1 in rural areas.[12] Business leaders in Manchester viewed the effort as an attempt by Delhi to recapture some of the prominence it lost when the county seat was shifted to Manchester some twenty-seven years earlier. Whatever the case, it earned Joseph a reputation as a strong proponent of rural school consolidation in the state. Joseph had served three terms as county superintendent when Deyoe tapped him to become his deputy superintendent; he was only thirty-eight years old at the time.

When the DPI began its drive to consolidate the rural schools of the state in 1913–14, Joseph was expected to utilize his political and professional contacts in northeast Iowa and his knowledge of local social conditions, especially in his home county, to help initiate and implement consolidation in this part of the state. Indeed, Joseph was to become a key figure in coordinating action between Country Life activists, local civic and business elites, the county superintendent, and the DPI.

The DPI's first attempt to stimulate interest in rural school consolidation in Delaware County came in early January 1914 when James A. Woodruff, assistant state superintendent of public instruction, was a featured speaker in the first Country Life conference held in the county. The conference was organized by Gilbert J. Chalice, the pastor of the Buck Creek Methodist Episcopal Church, a rural church in Union Township in the southern part of the county. It consisted of a series of three two-day seminars held at the Buck Creek Church, at the Methodist Episcopal Church in Delaware, and jointly at the Methodist Episcopal and Congregational churches in Earlville. Woodruff spoke on "The Value of Centralized Schools."[13] Joseph had recommended Woodruff to Chalice as an effective and authoritative speaker on the topic of rural school consolidation and its role in revitalizing country life. As events transpired, Woodruff's performances also served as a warm-up for a rousing address from State Superintendent Albert M. Deyoe before the Delaware County Farmers Institute held two weeks later in Manchester. The *Manchester Press* gave front-page coverage to the addresses of Professor W. J. Kennedy, chief of the Extension Department at the State College at Ames and of Deyoe. Both of them emphasized the advantages of rural school consolidation in their speeches. It was Deyoe, however, who stole the show. As the *Press* put it:

> people will remember the address by State Superintendent A. M. Deyoe . . . as having had the greatest general appeal of the entire program. . . . He hurried through an analysis of the underlying causes in the discontent manifested by the young people of the rural communities, saying that too much hard toil, too little in the way of social advantages, and inadequate schools were important reasons. He observed, however, that he believed in hard work and that he thought many lines of business and many of the professions offered as much toil as the farm, but he wanted the drudgery of the farm done away with. . . . He said that progress was apparent at this time in nearly every other side of the country life question in all communities, except where the schools were concerned. Advancement has lagged there, he said, and the time of the little white schoolhouse on the hill has gone by, though it still offered its inadequate facilities to the country boy and girl.
>
> He contrasted one community in which the small relic of pioneer times stood, with its old time equipment, unattractive yard and necessarily limited educational advantages, with another in which the modern consolidated structure stood, offering its scholars the best teachers, the

best equipment, and courses in agriculture and domestic science. Then, he also held as extremely important the advantages the larger school offered as a possible social center, as well as its far broader possibilities for well balanced education.

Where the small district school may have a good teacher, it is left no advantages over the consolidated institution, in Mr. Deyo's [sic] argument. As a matter of efficiency, the consolidated plan offers every advantage. . . . Twenty districts have been consolidated in this state during the past year. Out of 300 districts consolidated in the entire country, but two districts [have] abandoned the plan. Pretty fair evidence, it appears, that the scheme is all that its supporters have contended. In a nutshell, it means educational facilities for the boys and girls in the farm homes that equal those of the towns, and there is no reason, said Mr. Deyoe, to prevent the establishing of such an equality of opportunity.[14]

Deyoe directed his message not only at farm families but also at the residents of the county's many small towns and villages whose school districts lacked the tax bases necessary to provide high school instruction on a par with that found in the larger towns and cities. In 1914, only Manchester had a four-year high school in the county approved by the DPI. Hence, the Manchester district was the only one eligible to receive tuition from rural districts for their students to attend there for a full four years (table 7).[15] Deyoe's message was that the children of the farms, villages, and small towns were unnecessarily being denied access to the educational advantages of places like Manchester. Fully modern schools could be accessible to all children in the county if the rural districts consolidated with those of the county's small urban places. The burgeoning farm economy freed farm families from any fiscal necessity to cling to their aberrant country schools. The drudgery of the farm and the lack of modern amenities in rural areas could be overcome. This, however, would require that previously isolated rural communities be transformed into fully modern rural ones possessing all the advantages of urban life without also gaining its disadvantages. The first step in this transformation should be rural school consolidation.

As the winter of 1914 gave way to spring, campaigns for the modernization of country life had begun in several localities in Delaware County. While the topic of school consolidation was discussed, ways of strengthening the rural and small-town Protestant church received more attention, perhaps because Delaware County was seen by some church leaders as being invaded from the east and south by Catholic farm families. These efforts took concrete form in a second series of Country Life conferences organized under the general auspices of the district superintendent of the Methodist Episcopal Church. The emphasis of these conferences was on modernizing the rural church, rendering it a more central agency in building new rural communities. Topics discussed included modern business methods, securing adequate support, coordinating religious and social forces, the relationship between the church and rural community, the use of the social surveys, and modern child rearing. Conferences were held in Colesburg, Greeley, Oneida, Earlville, Delhi, and at rural churches as well — Silver Creek Church in Adams Township and the Buck Creek Church in Union Township.[16] The idea of community that was propounded at the conferences was based on an updated variant of Protestant evangelism — one quite hostile to the more ethnically grounded conception of Catholics in the area. On the one hand, the concept of community was an inclusive territorial one; on the other, it excluded those who did not publicly accept a new set of beliefs. While all persons in a locality were potential members of a Protestant community, to actually become members they made a public declaration of faith, thereby setting up a contradiction. How could community be ascribed based on the sharing of a common territory and yet somehow also be voluntary? Clearly it could not. Instead, what seemed to be advocated was for each territorially defined rural community to have but a single religious center, with all adult members subscribing to a common faith. On achieving adulthood, each person had to choose between joining the church (community) or leaving it. For a community and a church parish (the two were synonymous) to thrive, all or most of those in a locality had to become members.

In addition to extending the benefits of a modern high school education to more rural children, the principal attraction of rural school consolidation to people subscribing to these views was that it provided a secular means of ensuring Protestant social control over a larger territory than would have been the case had Protestants had to share power with Catholics in a locality. In Delaware County, Methodists were the dominant religious group in most small towns, including Delhi, Earlville, Greeley, Oneida, and Colesburg, and in a number of rural localities, such as Silver Creek and Buck Creek. Methodist dominance, however, was not as great as it had been in times past. Furthermore, in some parts of the county a number of the better farms had been bought or leased by Catholic families who were moving in from Dubuque and Jones Counties. This was reputed to be a burgeoning phenomenon in almost all of the older settled localities east of the Maquoketa River, including Delhi, North Fork, Oneida, Bremen, and Colony Townships, and in Union Township in the southern part of the county.

Agitation for Rural School Consolidation Begins in Earlville

Elites in most of the smaller towns of Delaware County were predisposed to consider rural school consolidation. Consolidation offered a means of providing a larger, more modern high school without significant tax increases in the independent town districts already in existence. It offered a means of preserving and extending existing patterns of religious dominance. It even had attractions as a viable economic growth strategy for small towns. But some spark was needed to ignite concrete action. That spark occurred in Earlville in June 1914. The occasion was a visit by the DPI's new high school inspector, F. E. McClenahan. McClenahan was there to examine whether Earlville's newly implemented high school facilities and course would be approved to receive tuition students for a full four years. According to the *Manchester Press*, McClenahan appears to have accomplished more than simply scrutinizing the high school course at Earlville during his visit.

> A recent visit of the state school inspector has created an interest toward the movement for a consolidated school at this place. The state gives financial aid to approved consolidated schools and the inspector highly recommended such a change at this place. The large beautiful school grounds and up-to-date building are said to be ideal for a modern consolidated school as approved by the state department. The local board of education and rural school directors in nearly all the outlying districts favor the plan of consolidation. The high school building could be remodeled and equipped with but little expense to be among the best public schools in the state. The plan is for the betterment of all schools and is generally favored by all desirous of more efficient and modern schools.[17]

McClenahan was implementing what had become the explicit policy of the DPI: promoting rural school consolidation wherever it would likely pass, especially if that success was also likely to serve as a model for others in the same general area.

Earlville was a propitious place to initiate a drive to consolidate the country schools of Delaware County. The town had built a modern two-story brick school in 1912 and, through a fortuitous set of circumstances, located it on a large plot at the edge of the town.[18] The total enrollment in Earlville's public school peaked at almost 200 students in 1902–3 and then declined every year save one until 1910–11 when it reached a low of 137. It had recovered to 153 in 1911–12, and, thanks largely to the free-tuition law and a doubling in the number of tuition students from the surrounding rural districts, its total enrollment had reached 162 in 1913–14 and 172 in 1914–15 (see table 9). The prospect for future enrollment increase from within the Earlville district itself, however, was not bright. The Catholic populations of rural districts to the north, south, and especially east of Earlville were growing. Some feared that the Earlville school would increasingly lose students to Xavier High School in nearby Dyersville in the future. Furthermore, the priest from Dyersville who conducted services in Earlville was working tirelessly to establish a parochial school at Earlville.[19] The surrounding rural districts, however, were still predominantly Protestant, with most farm families members of the Methodist Episcopal Church in Earlville or the Congregational churches of Earlville and Almoral Station, a hamlet 2.5 miles north of Earlville.[20] All this lent credence to McClenahan's claim that, with only a modest outlay for remodeling, the Earlville school could be converted for use as a consolidated school and receive state aid for doing so.

McClenahan approved the high school program for only three years, instead of the hoped-for four. He assured the Earlville board that it would receive state approval for a four-year high school course immediately if the surrounding rural districts consolidated with Earlville. This idea received the wholehearted backing of Earlville's leading merchants, especially Samuel Wesley Klaus and William Hunt, both of whom were also active in real estate dealings in Earlville and surrounding areas. Albert Voit, the publisher of the *Earlville Phoenix*, the town's only newspaper, was also enthusiastic about the idea. Klaus and Hunt were also members of the Earlville school board, leading figures in the Methodist Episcopal and Congregational churches, respectively, and in the Republican Party. Klaus was chair of the county's Republican Control Committee. He subsequently launched a successful secondary career as a member of the General Assembly, based to a significant degree on his championing the cause of rural school district consolidation in his home county. The idea was given further impetus in late August 1914 when it was rumored that Delhi was again trying to form a consolidated district, this time to help pay for replacing the Delhi school, which had recently been destroyed by fire. What was lacking was any groundswell of support for the idea in the surrounding rural districts.

Three interrelated factors combined to create a heightened interest in consolidation early in 1915, not only in the Earlville area but in most of the school townships and small towns in Delaware County. The first was that effective on July 1, 1915, all schools in the state were required to teach courses in agriculture, domestic science, and manual training.[21] The second factor was the serious shortage of teachers brought on by the industrial boom in midwestern cities stimulated by the war in Europe. The third factor was the need for local elites to identify a new basis for the sustained growth of towns in the area.

Under intense pressure from rural legislators, who argued that rural schools neither wanted nor needed instruction in agriculture, domestic science, or manual training, the General Assembly backed down and exempted rural schools from the requirement that these subjects be taught.[22] This prompted a flood of letters to the DPI from the directors of small-town districts seeking information about whether they too qualified for the exemption. If the earlier law was to be enforced in the independent school districts of small towns, it was clear that a means of satisfying this requirement without incurring unnecessary expense had to be found. F. P. Walker, the newly elected Delaware County superintendent, was quick to point out that the state would, in effect, pay for introducing these new subjects if an independent district merged with surrounding rural districts and adopted the consolidated form of school district organization. As the DPI had been reminding county superintendents and secretaries of small-town school boards throughout the state, the yearly state aid granted to consolidated districts could be used to cover the additional costs of teaching the new subjects.

The shortage of teachers first became apparent in the 1914–15 school year and worsened as World War I wore on. More and better paying jobs were open to women in the larger towns and cities of eastern Iowa — Cedar Rapids, Clinton, Dubuque, and Waterloo. For a country school district to obtain a teacher with a reputation for producing good results, it had to pay higher salaries. Coupled with this, the rising prices of almost everything made it evident that the increased costs of public schooling in rural areas was unlikely to be a temporary, war-induced phenomenon.

In addition, something else of significance was happening in the regional economy. Smaller towns were losing out to larger places in the competition for significant capital investment. While small towns continued to attract retired farmers from the surrounding countryside, this was hardly a way of ensuring the long-term growth and economic viability of a town. Instead, the future growth of the small town became more dependent on attracting the retail patronage of the dispersed farm population. The result was that the small-town merchant and his employees were at least as interested as the so-called progressive farmer was in putting family farming on a sound business basis and for keeping up with recent advances in the application of science to agricultural production. These changed economic circumstances also helped make the economic elites of small towns more attentive to the commercial opportunities implict in the prospect of hundreds of farm families making more trips to the town in which their children attended a consolidated school.

From Trial Run to Institutionalized Response?

In early 1915, the prospects were generally favorable for rural school consolidation in a number of localities in Delaware County. Earlville, however, took the first concrete action. Albert Voit, the publisher of the *Earlville Phoenix*, came up with what was to prove to be a fail-safe strategy for success. After consulting with Joseph in early March, he proposed that Earlville try consolidation on a two-year trial basis. He argued that if rural patrons were in any way dissatisfied with the system of transporting grade school students to Earlville, the status of the district could be shifted to that of an ordinary independent district covering the same enlarged area, but with the reintroduction of the country schools for the elementary grades. Joseph responded:

> I believe the plan to consolidate your schools is a good one. It, however, is of more benefit to the people outside of Earlville than it is to the people residing within the town. It may be difficult to make the surrounding communities see the force of this statement as yet. I have every reason to believe that after two years of trial they would not think of going back to the old plan.
>
> I am by separate mail sending you such material as we have in favor of the consolidated school. We think those who are opposed to the plan will think up enough arguments against it without this department furnishing any. We believe it would be unwise too for us to offer any reasons why a consolidated school should not be established, particularly since we are urging the people to establish this class of schools. You know the Bible says: "A house divided against itself shall fall." In our judgment, the arguments for a consolidated school outweigh those against. In the final analysis there are two things that will be most strongly urged against the consolidation: one is expense and the other is transportation.
>
> The matter of taxation is a local issue entirely. If the people want to pay more and get better results, they will probably vote for the consolidation. It is just the difference of opinion as to whether you want a woolen coat or one made of cotton.
>
> The matter of transportation is very largely a bugaboo. Thousands of children are transported every day in the United States, and it is being

done successfully. In fact, there is not a consolidated district in the state of Iowa where transportation is a failure and we believe it would prove successful at Earlville.[23]

Joseph's response provides key insights into the DPI's policy for encouraging local consolidation efforts. While admitting that rural school consolidation was usually a contentious issue locally, the DPI refused to grant the legitimacy of any arguments against consolidation for fear that it would ipso facto weaken the case for consolidation. Of the two most frequently raised arguments against consolidation, the "matter of taxation" was billed by the DPI as an individually subjective matter. Some people, presumably the enlightened ones, would be willing to pay more for a better quality education and some not. The second argument — that rural students would be subjected to hardships associated with travel in public conveyances over unimproved roads under widely varying weather conditions — was an objective matter, but one easily refuted by empirical evidence. The transportation of students, the DPI maintained, was a success wherever it had been tried. It would be a success in the Earlville area as well.

Just what constituted success or failure was left unspecified. Apparently, it involved local judgments about any inconveniences associated with transporting students being more than offset by the receipt of the superior education provided in the consolidated school. That the DPI's reasoning on this matter was potentially contradictory was largely irrelevant because Voit's trial-run strategy appeared to remove both matters from the local political equation altogether. Although the influx of new students from the surrounding countryside and the teaching of agriculture, domestic science, and manual training would necessitate a larger capital outlay than McClenahan had implied nine months earlier and might even require a new high school building, Voit and the Earlville board still maintained that the additional costs would be modest. If the school board of the new consolidated district proposed a capital outlay that voters thought extravagant, they could simply reject it in a state-mandated school bond election. In the event that farm families found teaching in the elementary grades of the consolidated school less satisfactory than in the old country schools, or if the transportation of young children proved burdensome, then the school board could put the country schools back into service and provide transportation only for rural high school students. It appeared to be a win-win proposition.

Within the month, proponents had decided upon the territorial configuration of the proposed district — 23.5 sections, consisting of the Earlville district and the five rural subdistricts contiguous to it. County Superintendent

Walker approved the petition before it had even been circulated. The *Manchester Press* reported that the directors of the subdistricts involved would use their influence on their respective school township boards to have their "districts" annexed by Earlville if the consolidation effort failed.[24] The result was anticlimactic. It passed 75–7 in the Earlville district and 44–16 in the area outside the Earlville independent district. The *Dyersville Commercial* heralded the event as evidence of the "progressive spirit of the voters of this community . . . and sets the pace for other towns to follow."[25]

When the board of directors of Earlville's new consolidated district began planning for the 1915–16 school year, it soon was apparent that the existing school building was not large enough to accommodate existing students and still allow for any future growth in enrollment in the district. This created a dilemma. How could consolidation be treated as an experiment or trial run, as voters had been led to believe, if the new district had to incur significant indebtedness before the trial was even begun? The board finally decided to submit two bond issues to the voters for their approval or rejection: $1,000 for an addition to the old building and $24,000 for constructing a new building.[26]

Other villages near Earlville had begun giving serious thought to undertaking consolidation drives of their own as soon as agitation for consolidation began in earnest in Earlville. The first to fall in line was Delhi. Having carefully monitored events in the Earlville area, and seeking to avoid losing territory to either Earlville or Hopkinton, boosters of consolidation in Delhi began work on forming their own consolidated district. On June 24, 1915, voters approved it. It was contiguous to the new Earlville district.[27] Shortly thereafter, voters of the Earlville Consolidated School District voted overwhelmingly in favor of both of their bond proposals.[28] Any thought of treating rural school consolidation in the Earlville area as a two-year experiment became a distant memory.

Consolidation proponents in Delhi had also severely underestimated student enrollments in their new consolidated district. The district had been in operation for little more than a year when its board, taking a page from the Earlville script, decided to call for an election on a $20,000 bond issue to construct an addition to the school that had been built less than two years earlier.[29] Unlike in Earlville, voters in the new Delhi district were far less enthusiastic about shouldering the added tax burden required to build the addition to the new school. It would be several years before Delhi area voters finally approved a bond issue to build the addition. In the meantime, the consolidated district continued to operate several of the one-room country schools in outlying portions of the district. None of these difficulties, however, were apparent in the summer of 1915.

Consolidation Movements in the Remaining Small Towns of Eastern Delaware County

The electoral success of the Earlville and Delhi consolidations and the favorable publicity they received in local newspapers prompted interest in consolidation in several other localities in eastern Delaware County. Within a short time, County Superintendent Walker received requests for information about consolidation from school boards and civic leaders throughout the county. Sensing that Delaware County could become the model for other counties in northeast Iowa, Deyoe sent Deputy Superintendent Joseph home for a five-day visit. His mission was to help get underway other initiatives to consolidate rural schools in other localities, particularly in the Hopkinton and Edgewood areas where his social and professional contacts were extensive.[30] Joseph quickly learned, however, that the prospects for consolidation were brighter in the vicinity of Greeley and Oneida, roughly halfway between Edgewood and Earlville. In both places, local notables, A. B. Holbert in Greeley and Sam Knox and John Rector in Oneida, were keenly interested in building modern high schools in their respective communities, even though these two villages were a mere three miles apart.[31]

Neither the DPI nor the county superintendent made any effort to urge leaders in Greeley and Oneida to cooperate with one another in establishing a single consolidated district. Instead, they encouraged the formation of two separate districts. This denied the village of Delaware the possibility of uniting with any of its surrounding country school districts and hence precluded it from becoming the center for a larger rural community. Joseph knew that forming two somewhat smaller consolidated districts focused on the villages of Greeley and Oneida would have a better chance of electoral success than forming one larger one containing both. State Superintendent Deyoe even stepped in to offer Holbert advice on how to organize a successful consolidation drive.[32]

The consolidation law that Deyoe had urged on the General Assembly in 1911 specifically required that if a consolidated district included an urban place containing a school population of twenty-five or more, then the consolidated school had to be located in that place. Had Oneida and Greeley both been included in a single consolidated district, that district would have been required to have two schools. Deyoe had become the prisoner of his own spatial logic. Opposition among area farmers came primarily from those who thought they had least to gain — those who were farther away from either village, who were Catholics, or who operated small farms. Earlville's success created the interest in consolidation, but Earlville's formula for success could not be replicated in either Greeley or Oneida. In both Greeley and Oneida, the organizational infrastructures for the consolidation movements consisted of the men's clubs (or "brotherhoods") of their respective Methodist Episcopal churches.

When the elections to form the Greeley and Oneida districts were held in late July 1915, both propositions passed.[33] Soon after the elections, it came to light that the territory in Oneida and Bremen Townships which had been left out of both of the new Earlville and Oneida consolidated districts, was in limbo with regard to who was responsible for providing school facilities for children residing there. Formerly, these areas had been parts of school townships; now their legal status was unclear. The problem was not unique to these particular consolidations but became a problem wherever consolidated districts formed in the state. This prompted Deyoe to seek a ruling from the attorney general on what should be done concerning the provision of educational privileges in interstitial territories excluded from consolidated districts. The matter was not resolved until mid-autumn 1915. Even then, problems continued for the residents of property-poor rural neighborhoods who wished to retain their country schools in school townships losing territory to a consolidated district.

Despite the efforts of Joseph, Deyoe, and Walker to get consolidation movements underway in Edgewood and Hopkinton, attempts to form consolidated districts in these localities faltered. Edgewood already had the second largest high school in the county, and a four-year one at that. It certainly did not need to consider consolidation as the means of ensuring enrollments sufficient to justify a full-fledged, modern high school. Hopkinton had Lenox Academy and, at least for the time being, seemed content to send its high school students there under a contractual arrangement with Lenox College.

The final effort to consolidate rural and village schools in Delaware County in 1915 focused on the village of Colesburg in the northeast corner of the county. Most of Colesburg's residents were born in England, New England, or New York and had lived for several years in one of the older midwestern states before moving to Colesburg. Overwhelmingly these persons were members of one of Colesburg's two Protestant churches, the Methodist Episcopal or Congregational, with the former being the larger. There was also a small Catholic church in the village attended to by a missionary priest from Elkport, some ten miles north in Clayton County.

The northern half of Colony Township dominated by Colesburg was still largely English, Yankee, and Methodist, but the southern half of the township was overwhelmingly German and Catholic. The Methodist church in Colesburg was active in the Country Life activities of the Methodist Episcopal Church in northeast Iowa and, although not openly anti-Catholic, had been working diligently since early 1914 to help ensure that the Colesburg area remained Protestant. A few people in Colesburg had agitated for school consolidation for several years. It was not until late October 1915, however, that its civic and Protestant church leaders had drawn up the requisite petitions and made plans to push support for consolidation over the top by scheduling a conference on the issue to be held just two days before the election.[34]

The issue carried handily in the village, but by a margin of only sixteen votes in the countryside. Questions about the legality of the new district forced the district to hold another consolidation election in 1916, before it could dispose of the bonds needed to finance the construction of an addition to the Colesburg school, but that too passed.[35] That the new Colesburg district was not contiguous to the other consolidated districts being formed during the period made consolidation a more difficult sell than it had been in Delhi, Greeley, or Oneida. Opposition was particularly virulent in the rural districts between Colesburg and the village of Petersburg, which contained significant numbers of German Catholic families.[36]

With the formation of the Colesburg district, the consolidation movement in Delaware County came to an abrupt halt. The Colesburg elections also raised the specter that for many Protestants, especially Methodists, more was involved in the formation of consolidated districts than simply providing better schooling for their children. School consolidation was viewed by some, perhaps many, Methodist parishioners as a means of ensuring Protestant control of public schooling in the area; the time to consolidate was before, not after, more Catholics moved into Delaware County from heavily Catholic Dubuque County immediately to the east.

Of those towns on the town-rich east side of the Maquoketa River, only Dyersville and Delaware had evinced no interest in exploring the idea of consolidation very fully in 1915. In Catholic Dyersville, consolidation was a political dead letter right from the outset. Delaware, although divided denominationally, was the center of a small but cohesive German Lutheran community whose continuing attempts to maintain its parochial school ensured its hostility to any effort to consolidate Delaware's small public school with those of the surrounding rural districts.[37] On the west side of the river, the towns of Ryan and Masonville, like Dyersville, possessed significant numbers of Catholic families, for whom a proper education, particularly for schooling beyond the eighth grade, was that organized and run by the church. Masonville was the first stop west of Manchester on the Illinois Central line — less than seven miles from Manchester. Catholic children in Masonville could (and did) attend the parochial high school in Manchester.[38]

By the end of 1915, the consolidation issue had lost its political momentum. Delaware County had run out of potential country towns whose social relations with the residents of surrounding rural districts were sufficiently harmonious, especially over matters of religion, for support for consolidation to be mobilized and sustained. The school consolidation movement in 1915 resulted in a dramatic increase in the number of four-year public high schools in Delaware County. From only two in 1914–15, the number rose to seven by the time the new consolidated schools were ready for occupancy in 1916–17. With this increased emphasis on the high school in the small towns, the number of tuition students from the country school districts attending high school in Manchester plummeted from ninety-two in 1913–14 to only six in 1915–16. From then on, more rural high school students attended a high school closer to home. They no longer had to board in Manchester. Whether the quality of the high school programs in the new consolidated schools was really on a par with that formerly available to these students in Manchester or even Edgewood remained an open, even unasked, question. It also remained to be seen whether attending the new consolidated schools would help keep farm boys and girls on the farm over the longer run and contribute significantly to the formation of the new type of rural community hoped for by reformers.

RURAL SCHOOL CONSOLIDATION

AND THE MAKING OF BUCK CREEK

Buck Creek? Where is Buck Creek? It does not appear on any of the official state highway maps published in the last quarter century. According to current United States Geological Survey (USGS) topographic maps, Buck Creek is the name of a small stream originating about 1.5 miles northwest of the town of Ryan. It flows generally eastward for 13 miles until it empties into the Maquoketa River about a mile northwest of the town of Hopkinton in Section 11 of Union Township in Delaware County. It is joined along the way by Golden Branch in Section 11 of Hazel Green Township and by Lime Creek in Section 17 of Union Township. If Buck Creek is a place, someone failed to bring this to the attention of the USGS's cartographers. Likewise, Buck Creek fails to appear on any of the current maps produced for or by Delaware County indicating property ownership, governmental subdivisions, school districts, and recreation opportunities. Nevertheless, as Bernard Thompson's obituary makes clear, Buck Creek is, or was, a rural community of some sort, sharing its name with, or perhaps taking its name from, a Methodist church located in Union Township. Most residents of southern Delaware County know Lime Creek as "Buck Creek" and Buck Creek west of its confluence with Lime Creek as "Upper Buck Creek." From this perspective, it is Upper Buck Creek that originates near Ryan, while Buck Creek has its source in Section 33 of Hazel Green Township. Although this might seem a trivial matter, to those residents, like the Thompsons, whose families have lived and worked in the area for several generations, it

FIGURE 12. *Approach to Buck Creek. 1994 photograph by the author.*

is not. If what the USGS refers to as Lime Creek really is Lime Creek and not Buck Creek, then the personal biographies of many current residents and much of the historical geography of the area need rewriting from beginning to end.

Traveling along County Road D-47 from Hopkinton to Ryan today, the careful observer will notice a small sign by the side of the road announcing the approach of "BUCK CREEK Community POP. 32" (figure 12). The person or group placing the sign there was apparently conforming to the way in which the U.S. Bureau of the Census has helped train us to think about places in the late twentieth century. There probably are thirty-two people who live in the less than half dozen houses huddled around the small Methodist church near where Lime Creek — or "Buck Creek" — crosses the road. Nonetheless, Buck Creek formerly was a much larger place, both in terms of population and territory.[1] About 150 yards west of the church stands a large dilapidated brick building, a former school with gymnasium attached, presently used to store the farm equipment and grain of one of the bigger farm operations in the area. "BUCK CREEK CONSOLIDATED SCHOOL" is emblazoned on a large cement tablet prominently displayed on the front of the building above its main entrance (figure 13). From a census-derived conception of place, this building seems strangely out of place. It is much too large for there not to be some visible evidence of Buck Creek having consisted of many more than the half dozen or so buildings there now. This must be the school referred to with apparent pride in Bernard Thompson's obituary.

This chapter seeks to explain how and why a different place called Buck Creek was created out of portions of Union and Hazel Green Townships beginning almost a century ago. The Buck Creek Methodist Church and the Buck Creek Consolidated School were once imbued with far more significance of place, of community, and even of personal identity for people in southern Delaware County than they are now. The Buck Creek Church and school were once significant social actors in themselves, giving definition and meaning to a larger and, in a sense, far more cosmopolitan place called Buck Creek. In the Buck Creek referred to here, there was no need for a road sign announcing either its approach or its population size. That Buck Creek was visible in the landscape, but one had to know what to look for and realize that place was not a thing but a process.

Before 1912, the predominant social relationships in Union Township revolved around farm work and the various rural neighborhoods composing the area. Being a good neighbor entailed conforming to expected ways of

FIGURE 13. *Former Buck Creek consolidated school. Now used for grain and farm implement storage. 1998 photograph by the author.*

acting toward other people with whom one came into regular contact while working and living in the same small area. These expectations extended to the sharing of capital goods and labor in matters incidental to production, to participation in group-based recreational activities, to cooperation in the structuring of childhood socialization experiences, and in the conduct of leisure time activities of adults or whole families. Good working relationships with one's neighbors were necessary adjuncts to the family- and neighborhood-based system of commercial agriculture then practiced. As a person who grew up in the Buck Creek area during this period put it, "you can't get along without your neighbor no matter what he is, black or white, red or green. You can't get along no matter where you are without your friends."[2]

Although who one's neighbors were was based on spatial proximity and colocation in a bounded territory, the neighborhood itself was socially defined by the juxtaposition of the biographies of individual residents. It was here that country school districts assumed considerable importance, for they provided a dominant context in the spatial structuring of the daily lives of most farm family members. They provided the primary place where neighboring and many other activities occurred. During the two decades bracketing the beginning of the twentieth century, Buck Creek was one such rural neighborhood in Union Township. Its boundaries were coincident with what was then officially subdistrict No. 3 of the School Township of Union, but what locally was referred to as the Buck Creek district — one of the eight subdistricts composing the School Township of Union (figure 14). Until 1912, most of the sixty-seven members of the Buck Creek Methodist Episcopal Church were residents of this neighborhood. There were, however, a few members scattered throughout other neighborhoods in Union Township and a few in the Harrington neighborhood (the No. 6 subdistrict) in Hazel Green Township. While the Buck Creek Church was the only church located in Union Township, it was not the only religious body with a significant number of members there or in the somewhat larger area that would soon become identified as Buck Creek. Others included the Presbyterian church in Hopkinton 5.5 miles east of the Buck Creek Church, the Lutheran and Catholic churches in Ryan eight miles west, the Immaculate Conception Catholic Church in Castle Grove Township in Jones County about four miles southeast, and the new Catholic church in Delhi 6.5 miles north.

Like many rural neighborhoods in Iowa, those in Union, Hazel Green, and Castle Grove Townships experienced significant population declines in

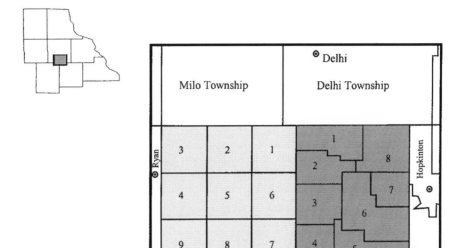

FIGURE 14. *Union and Hazel Green School Townships, 1900–1915. Map by Peter Li.*

the decade from 1900 to 1910. Population decline, however, was not a new phenomenon in the area (see tables 10 and 11). The three townships had all experienced population losses during the depression years of the 1880s and early 1890s and then enjoyed modest increases in the latter part of the decade. In Castle Grove, the population decline of the 1880s was particularly pronounced. During this decade many of the forty- and eighty-acre farms were bought up and consolidated into larger holdings. The only thing unusual about the population decline experienced in the area during the first decade of the new century was that it occurred during a period of generally increasing prosperity for farmers. The total population loss in the three townships amounted to 11.2 percent for the decade, a figure considerably greater than the state average of 6.9 percent. Assuming that the average rural neighborhood consisted of five sections of territory (five square miles), the population loss during this period amounted to 12.5 persons per neighborhood, or roughly three families per neighborhood. In 1910, the average neighborhood in the area still contained roughly 100 persons, or about 25 households.

These losses tended not to be viewed with alarm among those who remained, perhaps because this was a relatively prosperous time for farmers.

TABLE 10. *Populations of Hazel Green, Union, and Castle Grove Townships, 1870–1930*

Township	1870	1880	1890	1900	1910	1920	1930
Hazel Green	752	807	784	857	768	728	743
Union	689	646	611	648	577	556	548
Castle Grove	839	881	750	784	688	663	650

Source: U.S. Census of Population.

TABLE 11. *Population Change from Preceding Federal Census: Hazel Green, Union, and Castle Grove Townships, 1880–1930*

Township	1880	1890	1900	1910	1920	1930
Hazel Green	55	−23	73	−89	−40	15
Union	−43	−35	−37	−71	−21	−8
Castle Grove	42	−131	34	−96	−25	−13

Source: U.S. Census of Population.

Most seemed to agree with local newspapers and farm journals that attributed these population declines to older farmers retiring and moving to town, which in this area was most frequently Hopkinton for Protestant families and Monticello or Ryan for Catholic families. Lending further support to this view was that the enrollments in the country schools of the area had on average remained constant or increased slightly during this period. Furthermore, twenty-five families in a country school district (or subdistrict of a school township) tended to provide more than enough students to keep a country school teacher busy.

Although the rural neighborhoods had lost some of their economic importance in the mixed farming practiced in the area, they still retained their significance as primary referents in a person's individual and community identity. This was because there were (and are) no small towns or villages in any of the three townships. Four general stores and two small creameries were located near the edges of the area, but even these had not formed the nucleus of anything more than the usual crossroads settlement of three or four farm families.[3] Hopkinton was the primary trade and marketing center for most of Union and Castle Grove Townships, and Ryan for most of Hazel Green Township. The distance between these two towns, almost fourteen miles, was traversed by roads that became impassable by automobile for several days at a time during rainy periods, especially in late winter and spring. This left the two churches in the area as the only other preexisting institutions with any potential to become the organizational bases for the creation of a larger, more spatially extensive community consciousness to challenge and transcend the traditional neighborhood. Indeed, if there was any rural "community" in the area that was spatially more extensive than that of the traditional neighborhood, it was the Immaculate Conception Parish. Dominated by several Irish Catholic families, the parish covered most of the territory of the four country school subdistricts surrounding it — two in Union Township and two in Castle Grove Township.

In the decade of most interest here, 1912–22, the Buck Creek Methodist Episcopal Church, under the leadership of a charismatic minister imbued with an evangelical variant of Country Life ideology, set about doing the Catholic community one better by creating a larger, Protestant counterpart. It did so by articulating its own locally nuanced version of how the rural church could become the key agent in rural social and economic change by implementing a series of measures designed to instill in the residents of the area a new kind of rural community consciousness. The effort largely succeeded, but had some important and unforeseen consequences. Perhaps the most significant element in the process was the almost decade-long struggle of leaders in the Buck Creek Church to close the country schools in the area and transport students to a new, thoroughly modern consolidated school to be located near the church. Most other efforts to revitalize rural churches and communities saw religion and education as complementary, but separate spheres, involving different sets of experts. Typically the experts remained silent on the issue of how these spheres should become articulated in concrete social practice in place (see chapter 3). By following the precepts of the new rural sociology then dominant in religious thinking in most Protestant denominations, the Buck Creek Church became a potent "community" force through its many and variegated social activities in the neighborhoods of the area. Indeed, the success of the Buck Creek Church in this regard attracted regional and eventually national attention among the leaders of Protestant home missions work.[4] For a time, Buck Creek appeared to be an exemplar worthy of emulation by rural churches elsewhere in the nation.

The Buck Creek Parish had much more difficulty, however, in successfully promoting rural school consolidation. School consolidation, as we have seen, was being actively promoted by educational leaders in the state not only as an important educational innovation but as a means of creating new rural communities — communities that could stem the flood of the most intelligent and energetic young people to the cities. Leaders of the Buck Creek Church also subscribed to this view but sought to link school consolidation to its own explicitly Protestant (and Methodist) community-building project. School consolidation could perhaps become a central means of retaining Protestant farm families in the area, but what of Catholic farm families? If the country schools were abandoned and school consolidation entailed Methodist hegemony in the day-to-day activities of Buck Creek, it appeared that Catholic families would lose a large measure of control over their children's education and lose one of the principal ways in which they had interacted effectively with their Protestant neighbors for at least two generations. As a community project, the problem with school consolidation was that Catholic families were excluded from participating in it. As the project proceeded, they increasingly became estranged from their Protestant neighbors. Historically, the social relations of neighborhoods in the area had not produced sectarian conflict and hostility; but those of the new Buck Creek "community," based on church and religious affiliation, did. The problem was that Catholics could not become full members of the Buck Creek community and still remain Catholics.

The "Revitalization" of Rural Community Life in Buck Creek

The Reverend Gilbert J. Chalice was born in Plymouth, England, but his age and other details of his life before he and his wife arrived in Hopkinton in 1912 are lacking. According to church records, Chalice was selected as one of 13 from among 180 candidates to be sent by the Methodist Church of England to Ontario, Canada, for further seminary training and "pioneer service" on the Canadian prairies for the Home Mission Board of Canada.[5] From Ontario he was sent directly to the Wesley Seminary in Winnipeg. After graduating, he spent a few months preaching in rural parishes on a circuit on the Canadian prairies, before switching to "city work."[6] It is not clear when he immigrated to the U.S., but he joined the Iowa Methodist Conference in 1909, where he apparently remained in a city church until he was assigned to the Hopkinton and Buck Creek charges in October 1912. He was about thirty-five years of age at this time.

Upon arriving in Hopkinton, Chalice set out to build up both Methodist parishes in his charge. It was clear almost from the start, however, that he thought his talents and interests could be better deployed in the Buck Creek Church. In Hopkinton, the Presbyterian church was clearly the dominant church, a fact reinforced by the presence and prestige of Lenox College and Academy, both Presbyterian affiliated. Presbyterianism was overwhelmingly the faith subscribed to by the social and economic elite of Hopkinton. The Methodist Episcopal Church in Hopkinton lacked the status enjoyed by the Presbyterians and tended to be more the church of the laborer and farmer in Hopkinton and much of the surrounding rural area.[7]

The Buck Creek Church was five miles west of Hopkinton and vied with the Hopkinton church for parishioners in the area in between. Chalice's first impressions of the Buck Creek Church were decidedly unfavorable. As he put it, the "Buck Creek Church . . . had almost ceased to function. The church was picturesquely situated, nestled among the trees which were gay with autumn foliage. Buck Creek, from which the church was named, fed by many springs flowing from the surrounding hills, gurgled and splashed nearby."[8] To his eyes, however,

> the church was hardly in keeping with its surroundings. There were evidences of neglect on every hand. The old wooden approach was in such a dilapidated condition that one had to take care, on entering, lest the boards give way beneath the feet. In the surrounding yard, which was filled with weeds, the "tie posts" were staggering under the pressure of the years.
>
> The church was a simple structure. Just a typical, old-fashioned, one-room building, with old-time pews and the inevitable stoves. Oil lamps, uncleaned and murky, gave forth a feeble light, when any light was required.[9]

Nevertheless, Chalice claimed that as he faced his congregation that first time he began to see the true potential of the rural church in community rebuilding. "Although the church, feeble in its ministry to the community and decadent in appearance, had fallen down on its job, there still existed a most remarkable community spirit. For in that congregation was a large percentage of young people, bright, keen and intelligent, who were only waiting until they should be assigned some definite task to rebuild the community."[10]

Chalice set to work to gain the attention and attract the interest of as many people as possible in the Buck Creek Church. He did this by conducting a series of Methodist camp meetings during which he preached every night for three weeks (including the three Sundays he had to return to Hopkinton for morning services). Many farm families from the surrounding area pitched their tents on land reserved for that purpose down by the creek.[11] Although billed as "special community meetings" directed at the farm families in the area, they were old-fashioned religious revivals, intentionally evangelistic in tone and content. Many came out of curiosity to see the new preacher and his wife and to see how "old-time" religion sounded when delivered with an English accent.[12]

Having aroused the curiosity of people in the area and having captured their attention, Chalice began preparations to launch a program of church revitalization and rural community building. In this work he drew heavily on the writings of American theologians and rural sociologists linked closely to the Country Life movement. Excerpts from some of Chalice's more memorable sermons saved by parishioners strongly suggest that while he subscribed to most of the tenets of the Country Life movement, his philosophy was a complex mixture of traditional Methodism, progressivism, and agrarian utopianism. In one sermon he declared

> The farmer is a custodian of the nation's morality with rural people more susceptible to religious influence because he works in God's soil therefore a great need lies in the pastor's endeavor to supply spiritual help and assist to the higher life. Every rural community has a social craving and this must be satisfied if boys and girls are to be kept on the land. This also calls for attractive homes. No woman should yearn for the city when we equip the home with convenience and labor-saving devices. . . . [W]ith the aid of horticulture, domestic science, and household economics the farm home can be "Heaven on Earth."[13]

Chalice focused first on rekindling interest in the church among Methodist patriarchs and their wives. He created a men's club — the Buck Creek Brotherhood — and, with the help of Mrs. Chalice, reinvigorated the Ladies Aid Society. He also secured their financial support for establishing a local chapter of the Epworth League, a Methodist organization for teenagers and young adults. Through the Epworth chapter, he hoped to develop the lay leadership necessary for the long-run viability of the church. The chapter was especially active in presenting weekly lectures, often delivered by agricultural experts affiliated with the State Agricultural College on topics thought to be of special interest to farmers. Initially, however, attendance at these and at Sunday services was disappointingly low.

Seeking a reason for the low attendance, Chalice decided to conduct a "community survey," then being widely touted by experts as the first step to be taken in any effort of a rural church to expand its service to the community it hoped to serve and revitalize. Almost all households in Union Township and many in the eastern half of Hazel Green Township — Protestants and Catholics alike — were canvassed. In analyzing the reasons people gave for not attending church regularly, Chalice was surprised to discover that many respondents pointed to inconveniences associated with the inadequacy of the church's facilities and grounds and to the generally poor condition of the road leading to the church. This provided the impetus for the Buck Creek Brotherhood to form a committee and apply to the County Board of Supervisors for a grant to cover the costs of material necessary to improve the road. Men in the church donated the necessary labor and even went so far as to "lay a fine strip of macadam, up to the very church door." [14] At Chalice's behest, the Brotherhood completed a number of other projects to improve the appearance and safety of the church building and grounds, thereby removing the major excuse, if not cause, for poor church attendance.

The church introduced new programs designed to appeal to children. The Sunday school was reorganized into grades and "senior class" divisions comparable to the way in which the public schools of the larger towns were structured. Before the end of Chalice's first year, Sunday school enrollments had increased from 52 to 85 and church membership had risen to 87.[15]

In an effort to reach out to farm families who had never had any connection with the church, Chalice organized a series of traveling, "undenominational" Country Life institutes. They began at the Buck Creek Church on January 4, 1914, and continued, in two-day stints, throughout the week at other churches in the county (see chapter 7). Included on the program at the Buck Creek Church were speakers from nearby Lenox College. Talks included "Corn, Alfalfa and Soil Fertility," "Education for the Farmer," "Beef Cattle, Dairying, and Stock Judging," and "The Making of the Country Home." Also included were lectures by the Reverend Albert M. Billingsley, D.D., the district superintendent of the Methodist Episcopal Church on "The Church and Country Life," and by Chalice on "Financing the Country Church." The keynote speaker, however, was Professor J. A. Woodruff, the assistant state superintendent of schools in charge of inspecting the new consolidated schools that were then being established across the state. Woodruff spoke enthusiastically about the value of the consolidated schools in revitalizing rural communities. He illustrated his talk with stereoptically projected views of several of the newly consolidated schools in the cash grain region of the state, several of which had been located in the open country rather than in a village or small town — a fact not lost on either

Chalice or lay leaders in the Buck Creek Church. Thus began the first step in Chalice's rise to regional prominence for his "rural work" and the first discussion of rural school consolidation in Union Township.

From Rural Neighborhoods to Methodist "Community"

During his first two years in the Hopkinton–Buck Creek area, Chalice's theory and philosophy of rural life became much more fully articulated. His reading in the emergent, but overlapping, fields of rural and religious sociology was important in this regard, but so too were his contrasting experiences in Hopkinton and Buck Creek. The works of John Lewis Gillin, a sociologist at the State University of Iowa, Warren H. Wilson, Superintendent of Church and Country Life for the Presbyterian Church, and Liberty Hyde Bailey, Director of Country Life at Cornell University, were particularly influential in his thinking. Like these writers, he saw that significant changes in the rural social fabric had occurred through the adoption of the telephone, rural mail delivery, the interurban railroads, the automobile, and improved roads. Like them, he felt that the isolation of rural neighborhoods from the towns was a thing of the past. As a consequence, the rural church was rapidly losing its centrality in the lives of farm families, both spiritually and socially. Hastening the process was the newfound agricultural prosperity of the Middle West. It had put discretionary income in the pockets of farmers and made the small town a more attractive place of residence for retired farmers. With these changes, the town church began to compete much more effectively with the country church.[16] According to this characterization of the changing nature of rural life, the drift to the cities and towns could be arrested only by again making the church and rural school central foci in rural life. This is precisely what Chalice attempted to do both in word and deed in his work in the Buck Creek Parish over the next four years. In commenting on Chalice's ministry, the *Hopkinton Leader* opined that the Buck Creek "church is waking up to its new problems, interesting itself in the human welfare, exhibiting a real fellowship, and in so doing will halt the hurrying line by its doors. . . . And so Buck Creek is being watched from many angles. . . . Perhaps unwittingly the Buck Creek community has taken up" one of the major "20th century world problems and will carry it to a successful conclusion."[17]

By early fall 1914, the activities and membership of the Buck Creek Church had so expanded that Chalice thought the time propitious to investigate the possibility of securing a resident pastor. He argued that his duties in the two churches — Hopkinton and Buck Creek — had become very heavy and quite divergent. For progress to continue, he argued, it was necessary for each to have its own pastor. This also was an explicit recognition of what most of his parishioners already knew — that the two churches, despite sharing a single pastor, served two quite different communities. Although it served rural residents along with those from town, the Hopkinton church was still a town church whose community-building efforts would need to be different from those of a church located in the open country. This had the result of pulling the single pastor in two directions. Although Chalice attempted to maintain a facade of neutrality, it was clear to all that his greater sympathies lay in the project he had begun in Buck Creek. The Buck Creek charge, however, contributed only $400 toward Chalice's $1,000 salary for the "circuit." At least an additional $600 would be required to cover his salary alone. Furthermore, the Buck Creek Church did not have a parsonage. Chalice or any other resident pastor would need one. The conservative element in the Buck Creek Church doubted whether they would be able to raise the necessary revenue to go it alone. Nonetheless, Chalice was able to convince church leaders that a complete canvassing of families in the Buck Creek area would provide a relatively quick and effective way of determining the feasibility of the plan. To accomplish this, Chalice organized five teams, made up of ten men each, and carefully trained them in the art of canvassing. Considering the survey conducted earlier, the canvassers already knew that approximately 520 persons composing 130 families lived within the area served by the Buck Creek Church. These figures are roughly consistent with the populations of Union Township reported in the U.S. Censuses of 1910 and 1920. Of these, roughly 160 persons were under and 360 over the age of twenty-one. Four hundred and ten were Protestants of various denominations (including 100 who were already members of the Buck Creek Church), and 110 were Roman Catholics. The 4:1 ratio of Protestant to Catholic appears high, perhaps indicating that the survey excluded the almost completely Catholic southernmost tier of sections in Union Township and included the several sections in Hazel Green Township nearest to the Buck Creek neighborhood. Families were asked how much they were willing to pledge yearly for retaining a resident pastor. Existing church members pledged $1,040 and "outsiders and constituents" pledged $247. A similar canvass was conducted in Hopkinton with less beneficent results, but they were able to obtain pledges sufficient to increase the Hopkinton salary to $1,000.[18]

Provided a way could be found to build a parsonage, the Buck Creek Church would have its own pastor and was prepared to pay a salary of almost $300 more than that offered in Hopkinton. Having accomplished this feat, raising the money to buy the sixteen-acre plot of land adjoining the church from the "old bachelor" who lived there was relatively easy.[19] Chalice had already organized a small group of men into an adult Bible class that met each Sunday and again for a "social time" once each month. The men in this group functioned as deacons in the church. Included were several of the wealthier farmers in the area. They agreed to advance the $5,000 needed to buy the land and to build a new parsonage, with the understanding that the church membership would repay the debt. Within a year the debt had been retired.[20]

From the fall of 1914 through the fall of 1918, 137 new members joined the Buck Creek Church, bringing its total active membership to 176.[21] During this period only 15 members died and 33 moved out of the area (most to retire in Hopkinton or Manchester). By 1918, almost every social gathering of any consequence held in Union Township was in one way or another linked to the activities of the Buck Creek Church. The most noteworthy of these was the annual Buck Creek Fair held each year in late August or early September. Usually lasting three days, this was the big social event of the year, attracting hundreds of people from all over southern Delaware County. Consistent with Chalice's Country Life philosophy, the first day of the fair, usually a Sunday, began with a special religious service featuring a noted evangelist. The afternoon featured religious music, more preaching, and religious "carrying on" in the best tradition of Methodist camp meetings and revivals of that era. The second day, designated "Farmer's Day," was devoted to agricultural exhibits, demonstrations, and contests. These were structured by gender. Those for the men stressed agricultural productivity and special achievements, while those for women stressed painting, needlework, and domestic science. Ribbons and prize money donated by the State Department of Agriculture went to the top entries in production and craft categories. The last day of the fair was given over to social, cultural, and recreational events, complete with a parade, band music, athletic contests, a dinner, and lectures designed to provide both entertainment and instruction. The beer tent, sideshows, and games of chance and dancing typically found at county fairs were strictly excluded.[22]

While the Buck Creek Fair was the big event and the one that put Buck Creek on the map, three elements — evangelism, progressive agricultural practice, and "wholesome" recreational activity — permeated all of the Buck Creek Church's many activities. Chalice was a charismatic evangelist as well as a Country Life reformer and his ministering affected the lives of many people in the Buck Creek area quite profoundly.[23] He was even successful in eliminating that anathema to midwestern Methodism, which had hitherto thrived in the Buck Creek area — Sunday baseball. Instead, the church's Epworth League chapter fielded its own baseball team that played on a well-maintained baseball field behind the church every Saturday. Chalice also helped secure the cooperation of the State Library Commission in creating a traveling library for Union Township based in and run by the Buck Creek Church.

At this time roughly half the farms in Union Township were operated by tenants. As was becoming increasingly common in Iowa at that time, tenants occupied farmland at least as good and probably better than that worked by owners.[24] While some tenants in the area moved frequently, they seldom moved very far; most were the sons, daughters, brothers, or sisters of those already there. Intimate local knowledge was a prerequisite for "getting a good farm."[25] Nevertheless, for any strategy designed to improve the quality of rural community life to have a chance of success, it had to be sensitive to who these tenants were and how they might fit into the local social structure. Chalice and leaders of the Buck Creek Church therefore took a particular interest in each year's "crop" of new tenants. Soon after the March 1 "moving day" each spring, the Ladies' Aid Society and the men's Brotherhood held a banquet to welcome newcomers to the area. Not content simply to wait and see who the new renters in the area were each year, Chalice urged major landowners in the church to be proactive and lease only to tenants who would be "good members of the community." Most parishioners interpreted this to mean that they should give preference to those who would become active in the Buck Creek Church. Catholic families, even if they were related to other Catholic families already living in the area, were obviously disqualified.[26] At least initially, this did not lead to any outward manifestations of anti-Catholic sentiment locally. Indeed in his personal relations with Catholic men in the area, Chalice seems to have gotten along well. For example, he befriended Frank King, a major landowner and head of a prominent Catholic family in the Upper Buck Creek neighborhood.[27]

Sensitive to the strong tradition of neighboring in the area and wishing to make the church a vital part of that tradition, Chalice established a "visiting committee" responsible for notifying him of matters bearing on the welfare of the community. Besides informing him of the arrival of any new residents in the area, they also notified him of shut-ins and of those who were sick or otherwise incapacitated. When a farmer was sick or otherwise fell behind in his farm work due to causes beyond his control, Chalice and the male members of the visiting committee offered their help. C. J. "Cliff" Willard, for example, a farmer living about a mile north of the church who had fallen behind in harvesting his corn because of equipment losses suffered in a barn fire, was surprised when Chalice and a team of men arrived to help him complete the harvest.[28] Gradually the Buck Creek Church usurped the role that the rural neighborhood traditionally had assumed in family farming.

Church, School, and Community

As a Country Life reformer and rural community builder, Chalice missed few opportunities to bring innovations in farm management and rural education to the attention of his congregation. Knowing that "no church could thrive in a nonproductive section or in a community where the labor income was small," he actively sought help from the Extension Division of the State Agricultural College in the form of written materials, public speakers, traveling exhibits, and assistance in setting up demonstration projects on a wide range of topics of interest to farmers and their wives: silo construction, herd improvement, fruit growing, poultry raising, canning, rural health, and sanitation. This was relatively easy to accomplish because the Extension Division at Ames was already providing instruction and extension services under the auspices of nearby Lenox College, in Hopkinton.[29] Chalice's interest in the adoption of more scientific agricultural practices and progressive farming was not so narrowly instrumentalist as to be concerned only with augmenting the incomes of his parishioners. He seems genuinely to have believed that the more widespread adoption of these innovations coupled with a spiritual reawakening in the countryside could combine to create something of a rural utopia in the Corn Belt.

Chalice began pushing his congregation at Buck Creek to modernize rural education even before he became their resident pastor. Hence it is not surprising that it was he who first planted the idea that rural school consolidation could be a powerful adjunct in the building of a "heaven on earth" in Buck Creek. It is in this regard, however, that the historical record of church activities is as obscure as it is incomplete. In chronicling Chalice's achievements in the Buck Creek Church, a booklet published by the Home Missions Board of the Methodist Church in 1919 is noticeably silent about his success in spurring educational innovations and improvement in the Buck Creek area. The reason for the silence is simple. There were none to report, even though a movement within the Buck Creek Church to consolidate the rural schools of the area had been building momentum ever since 1915.

Rural Education in the Buck Creek Area Prior to 1915

The area from which the Buck Creek Church drew its membership in 1914–15 included all or part of ten country school "districts." The parish now included all eight of the subdistricts in Union Township and two of the easternmost subdistricts in Hazel Green Township. The voters in Union School Township elected eight directors, one from each of eight subdistricts. The Hazel Green School Township consisted of nine directors elected from nine subdistricts. Directors were usually the heads of prominent land-owning families in their respective subdistricts (neighborhoods). In Union Township, the eight directors in turn selected one of their number president and elected a secretary and treasurer from outside its membership. Ostensibly, the latter two officers were chosen for their record keeping and public relations skills, respectively, but other factors were also important. From the turn of the century until 1920, the officers of the Union Township board invariably consisted of several of the most highly respected men in the township, one from each of the three religious groups in the area. The president was almost always a Methodist and the secretary and treasurer usually a Catholic and a Lutheran or Presbyterian, respectively. Whether maintaining this religious balance in leadership positions on the board was official policy or not, it was good practical politics.

The officers of the Union Township Board of Directors from 1912 to 1921 were Warren H. Winch, president; James Kehoe, secretary; and James A. Johnson, treasurer. These three men commanded the respect of all neighborhood leaders in the area. Their high social and economic status derived from their ownership of land, their kinship, and their commitment to maintaining the social relations of neighborhood upon which family farming in the area depended. Collectively, they represented traditional bases of rural social and political power. Their presence on the board helped ensure that the power to determine basic educational policy would be shared and not the prerogative of any single group in the township. The responsibility for adapting general school policy to the particularities of individual neighborhoods remained with the directors of each of the eight schools.

Warren Winch was the son of one of the well-respected Protestant pioneer families in the area. Although the senior Winch was a Universalist, not a Methodist, Warren was a prominent member of the Buck Creek Church. He was also very active in township politics. James "Jimmy" Kehoe was the son of Patrick Kehoe, a pioneer and patriarch of the major landowning Catholic family in the township. At one time it was said that Patrick owned farms in every section in the southern tier of Union Township as well as some in the northern tier of Castle Grove Township. Patrick had also been a principal benefactor in building the magnificent Catholic church in Castle Grove. James was highly respected in his own right and for a number of years had been chairman of the Delaware County board of supervisors. Johnson too was the son of one of the more successful pioneer families in the area. His father, Alexander, a Scots-Irish Presbyterian noted for his hard work and frugality, had assembled the largest contiguous tract of land under single ownership in the township. One time when asked why he was determined to accumulate so much land, he was reputed to have responded rather matter of factly, "I just want what joins me." His son, James, a prominent Presbyterian in the Hopkinton church, was viewed as one of the most successful and progressive (these terms were seen as synonymous) farmers in the county. Winch and Kehoe were Democrats; Johnson was a Republican but was known to cast an "independent ballot" in local elections. Winch was in his late thirties in 1915, while the other two officers were in their midforties. All had large families with school-aged children.[30]

For the first fifteen years of the twentieth century, the Union No. 1 subdistrict remained largely under the control of persistent, landowning Protestant families.[31] Unlike most of the other subdistricts of the township, the Union No. 1 subdistrict did not constitute a single rural neighborhood in a sociospatial sense. Most of the families belonged to the Bay Church neighborhood, but some identified with and participated in the Upper Buck Creek neighborhood to its immediate south. Bay Church referred to a defunct Baptist church near the northwest corner of the township. In 1915, more than half of its territory was taken into the Delhi consolidated district. Few if any of the families affected were members of the Buck Creek Church, but it was a major disruption to the territorial structure of neighborhoods in the township. The formation of the Delhi consolidated district forced the reassignment of students and families to schools in all four subdistricts in the northern half of Union Township. Upon consolidation, the No. 1 schoolhouse was closed, even though it was located within the portion of the subdistrict that remained in Union School Township. Through a joint agreement of the Union Township and Delhi boards, the schoolhouse was turned over to the Delhi district and sold.[32] In 1914–15, the year before the formation of the Delhi consolidated district, the No. 1 school had the smallest attendance in Union Township. According to the records of the county superintendent, that part of the old No. 1 subdistrict that remained within the

Union School Township continued to elect directors to the township board, even though it had no school until 1918–19. The decision of the Union Township board to open a school in the No. 1 subdistrict in 1918 must have taken the superintendent by surprise. Prior to this, he seems to have assumed that the territory of the old No. 1 subdistrict not taken into the Delhi district had become part of the No. 2 subdistrict and that the No. 2 subdistrict had simply elected two directors.[33] Whether the Union School Township board informally redrew the boundaries of a new No. 1 subdistrict is not clear, but no record of this was filed in the county auditor's office. Whether the No. 1 subdistrict continued to be a legal entity turned out to be a matter of some importance in the controversy surrounding attempts to form the Buck Creek consolidated district in 1920. It was rumored among Catholic families in the area that the designers of the new Delhi district had deliberately excluded Catholics.[34] Whatever the case, there is no doubt that the residents of this residual area were largely Catholic and Irish. With only one exception, Catholics were elected directors in this subdistrict from 1915 onward. When a new No. 1 school opened in 1918–19, it had a Catholic teacher, a practice that was to be continued for many years.

Until the formation of the Delhi consolidated district, the Union No. 2 subdistrict, usually referred to as the "Upper Buck Creek" district or neighborhood, had been a somewhat elongated subdistrict bisected by Upper Buck Creek. Its eastern half was highly dissected and quite heavily timbered land, used mostly for pasture; the western portions contained the better farmland. In earlier years, this neighborhood consisted almost exclusively of Irish Catholic families, but over the years many had intermarried with Methodists from the nearby Buck Creek neighborhood.[35] After 1912, a territorial redistribution of families occurred in this neighborhood, with Methodists congregating in the southern part of the subdistrict (near the Buck Creek Church) and Catholics in the eastern part. Most of this shifting population — both Catholic and Protestant — consisted of tenant farm families.[36] In 1914–15, Catholic families still predominated, but unlike neighborhoods in the southern half of the township, they had no Catholic church nearby. A new Catholic church was built in Delhi in 1914 and many of these families began to attend mass there. Between 1900 and 1914, a Catholic was elected school director every year but one. Starting in 1914–15, the pattern shifted and a Methodist was elected director each year. Although the precise boundaries of the No. 2 subdistrict after 1914–15 are unknown, most of the students from the area of the old No. 1 subdistrict not included in the new Delhi district were reassigned to the Union No. 2 school, at least until 1918–19. It appears that the Union Township board continued to seat a director from the legally nonexistent No. 1 subdistrict so as to give Catholic families in the Upper Buck Creek neighborhood a voice in the operation of the school their children attended. In 1915–16, Mona Hogan, a young Catholic woman from the Castle Grove neighborhood in northern Jones County, was the teacher in the No. 2 school for the fall and winter terms but was replaced by another teacher for the spring term. For the next four years it appears that only Protestant teachers taught in this school.

The Union No. 3 subdistrict, the Buck Creek neighborhood, was overwhelmingly the traditional neighborhood of families belonging to the Buck Creek Church. Like the two subdistricts already described, it was a rolling area of quite good soils and small farms, with significant numbers of renters mixed in with owners. Between 1900 and 1920, its school director was invariably a Protestant, and usually an active member of the Buck Creek Church. Rather than the same director being returned year after year, as was the norm elsewhere in the township, the directorship here rotated among a small group of prominent men in the Buck Creek Church. Not surprisingly, the teacher employed was usually a Protestant. A shifting of the students from the southern part of the No. 2 subdistrict to the Buck Creek school in 1915–16, ostensibly to relieve crowding in the No. 2 school, was an important event in eroding the old neighborhood loyalties of these families to Upper Buck Creek and realigning them more clearly with Buck Creek.[37]

The Union No. 4 subdistrict, the Rose Hill neighborhood, was one in which Protestant families were predominant until early in the 1900s, when for about a decade the neighborhood became home to approximately equal numbers of Protestant and Catholic families. Most of the area consists of rolling prairie land of very good quality. The farms in this area were somewhat larger than they were in the more broken and dissected northern half of the township. Relations between the two religious groups in educational matters appear to have been quite harmonious. From 1901–2 through 1914–15, the director was usually a prominent Methodist, but about one-third of the time a Catholic was elected to the post. During most of these years when property was put up for sale, it was more likely than not to be purchased by a Catholic family with some connection to one of the prominent Irish-American families already farming in the Castle Grove neighborhood. Nevertheless, a few of the old, landed Protestant families remained. From 1914–15 onward, the director elected was usually a member of the prominent Kehoe family either by birth or by marriage. Two-thirds of the time during this period, a Catholic woman, usually a Kehoe, taught in this subdistrict's school. Teacher turnover was low, with one teacher holding the position for thirteen consecutive terms — an unusual feat in Iowa.

The Union No. 5 subdistrict, the Dufoe neighborhood, was composed largely of Irish Catholic families belonging to the Castle Grove Parish. It did, however, contain a few descendants of those who had formed the Protestant settlement of Grove Creek before 1875. The Winches were among these. Warren Winch, like his father before him, was the school director, having first been elected to the post in 1912–13. He remained its director for the next decade, aided considerably by his local prominence in Democratic politics and by having a wife who made no secret of being of Irish extraction. James Kehoe, the secretary of the township school board, was also a resident of this subdistrict and a neighbor of Winch. It would probably be more accurate to say that Winch and Kehoe together ran this subdistrict or neighborhood, even though it was Winch who repeatedly stood for re-election as director. This subdistrict was known to have the best farmland in the township. From 1901–2 until Winch's election, the directorship was held by a member of one of the prominent Irish Catholic families — Kehoe, Evers, Hogan — seven of eleven years. Catholic teachers were employed as teachers about half the time. More so than any other subdistrict in Union Township, Union No. 5 had a tendency to not retain the same teachers for all three terms of the school year. Families in this subdistrict were less fastidious than those of other subdistricts in the area about sending boys to school when there was work to be done on the farm. The result was that boys attended school here in large numbers only during the winter term. During this term, a teacher with a well-earned reputation for maintaining discipline was retained.

The Union No. 6 subdistrict was probably the most socially complex and functioned less like a neighborhood than any of the other subdistricts in Union Township. Indeed, this subdistrict consisted of parts of several neighborhoods. Residents of the two sections in its southeastern corner identified with the Dufoe or Castle Grove neighborhoods. The 2.5 sections along its western edge increasingly became identified with Buck Creek after Chalice's arrival at the Buck Creek Church. Those in the remaining territory tended to see themselves as part of rural Hopkinton. The subdistrict as a whole had more tenant farm families than the other subdistricts in the area — some on farms with very rough land along Buck Creek, and some on farms with the best prairie soils in Sections 26 and 27 of the township. In 1914–15 it had the second highest enrollment and attendance in Union Township. Roy Dighton, a relative newcomer to the area, was elected director in 1912–13; he remained in that position for the next decade. Dighton, like all but one of the others to serve as director in the first two decades of this century, was an active member of the Buck Creek Church. The teachers Dighton hired were invariably Protestants, mostly from families in the general area but not from the subdistrict itself. Teacher turnover in this subdistrict was lower than in most of the other subdistricts; one teacher was retained for three consecutive years.

The No. 7 subdistrict was territorially the smallest in the township, containing the equivalent of only 2.5 sections. Although its enrollments were typically among the lowest in the township, it maintained very high attendance levels. In the religious affiliations of its residents, it was as Catholic as the Union No. 3 subdistrict was Methodist. Here the topography was broken and rough, the farms smaller, and the soils of somewhat poorer quality than in most of the other subdistricts in the township; but it would be inaccurate to refer to the area as poor. The farmers in the area, however, were traditional family farmers and less acquisitive than the progressive farmers of the area. Since the neighborhood was only a short wagon ride from Hopkinton, a number of men in the neighborhood maintained jobs in Hopkinton as laborers while still operating their farms. Neighborhood residents were overwhelmingly Kelleys by birth or marriage. The Kelley patriarch, John Kelley, was elected and reelected director year after year without interruption from 1902–3 through 1918–19. Appropriately enough, locals referred to this subdistrict as the Kelley neighborhood. The school itself, however, was called the Brush Hill school. Even though the subdistrict was overwhelmingly Catholic, Kelley was as likely to retain a Protestant teacher as he was to retain a Catholic. In 1919–20, apparently fearing that the school might contain too many rowdies, he retained male teachers for the year. If any neighborhood in the area had a reputation for not placing a high value on education, this was it. However, this was not well reflected in data for the school on attendance, teacher salaries, and the county superintendent's evaluations of teachers. If families in this neighborhood placed a lower emphasis on education, it was on high school education, not on the traditional common school education. Here they appeared no different from other families in the area.

The Union No. 8 subdistrict, the River Valley neighborhood, was the one most isolated from other neighborhoods in Union Township. It was an area of rugged topography and steep slopes, but it also contained rolling hills and rich bottomland along the Maquoketa River, hence its name. Ethnically and religiously, the area was split three ways between Irish Catholic, German Lutheran, and other Protestant families. Except for one prominent family that converted to Methodism through the influence of Chalice, the neighborhood contained no Buck Creek Methodists. The social life of the neighborhood focused on Hopkinton, which was much more accessible to its residents than was the Buck Creek Church. Support for rural consolidation among the wealthier farmers surfaced quite early in this subdistrict, but it was for consolidation with Hopkinton, not with Buck Creek.[38] Charles Reggentine, Sr., one of its prominent residents, was a vociferous advocate in this effort. The site of the school atop a bluff (locally referred to as Moss Hill) overlooking the Maquoketa River valley provided as magnificent a view as can be found anywhere in Iowa and gave the school its name — the Moss Hill school. The directorship in the subdistrict seems to have rotated among several of the prominent Lutheran families, with either a Reggentine or a Beitz holding the position about half the time during the first two decades of this century. Lutheran hegemony regarding the directorship, however, was not reflected in the choice of teachers. From 1915–16 through 1920–21, a Catholic teacher was retained about 40 percent of the time.

The director of the No. 6 subdistrict in Hazel Green Township was a Harrington — first Dennis and then John — from 1907–8 until the school was destroyed by fire in 1920. Before that, other long-term residents of Irish descent had taken their turn in the post. The Harringtons were Catholics and active members of the Ryan Parish. Appropriately, the subdistrict was referred to as the Harrington neighborhood. Historically the subdistrict had always contained a mixture of Catholic and Protestant families. In 1915 at least half of the families were still Catholic, with the remainder of families about equally split between Methodists and Congregationalists. The last mentioned attended the Golden Congregational Church located one mile west from the northwest corner of the subdistrict. The subdistrict consisted principally of quite small, owner-operated farms (120 acres or less) on a gently rolling prairie landscape. The school here was consistently viewed by the county superintendent as the best in the area, both in terms of his evaluations of the teachers, the school buildings and grounds, and the salaries paid (they were the highest in the area). Unlike most of the other subdistricts in the area, this subdistrict changed teachers relatively infrequently, almost always retaining a teacher for the entire school year and retaining her (the teacher was always a female during the period in question) for two or more years in succession. The subdistrict appears primarily to have recruited local women from Catholic families to teach in the school.

The No. 7 subdistrict in Hazel Green Township was about evenly split between Catholics and Protestants, but Buck Creek Methodists were in the minority. In 1914–15, Frank Houston (a member of the Golden Congregational Church) was the director, having succeeded Will Wilson, a member of the Catholic branch of the locally prominent Wilson family, the previous year. Wilson had held the position for a number of terms before that. Although the neighborhood continued to be referred to as the Wilson neighborhood, its class and religious composition was changing. In 1911, thirty-year-old Clyde Thompson, a native of the neighborhood, and his wife returned from South Dakota after having accumulated some considerable wealth homesteading and operating a hotel. They bought a 120-acre farm next to that of Clyde's older brother, James, on the Union Township line and took up farming. Within a short time, Thompson achieved notoriety in the neighborhood for his outspoken support for scientific farming (later he was the first farmer in the area to produce seed corn) and for his enthusiastic involvement in the activities of the Buck Creek Church. Although he seems to have made few converts to the "book farming" he advocated, his neighbors did think highly enough of him to elect him school director in 1918. Like the subdistrict immediately to its north, the Hazel Green No. 7 subdistrict consisted largely of small, owner-operated farms on land with good quality prairie soils. The eastern half of the subdistrict next to Union Township was somewhat more dissected and broken than that of its western half. Excluding the old Union No. 1 subdistrict, in 1914–15 this school had the lowest attendance levels in the area, even though the enrollments were about average. As in the Dufoe neighborhood, families in this subdistrict appear to have kept many of the boys out of school during the fall and spring terms. In the period 1915–16 through 1920–21, the teachers appear to have been from Protestant families about 80 percent of the time.

In 1914–15, these ten country schools had an average enrollment of 18.6 students, with an average daily attendance of 15.7. The highest enrollment was 23 in the Union No. 8 subdistrict's school, and the lowest was 14 in the Union No. 1's subdistrict. By the next academic year, the formation of the Delhi consolidated district forced the elimination of the school in the Union No. 1 subdistrict, leaving eight subdistricts but only seven schools in the Union School Township. Average enrollments and average daily attendance in the remaining schools stood at 17.4 and 15.8, respectively. The highest enrollment was 27 in the Union No. 3 subdistrict's school, and tied for lowest at 14 were Union No. 7's school and Hazel Green No. 7's school. The jump in attendance at the Buck Creek school (in the Union No. 3 subdistrict) occurred because students from the southern part of the Upper Buck Creek neighborhood (the Union No. 2 subdistrict) had been reassigned to the Buck Creek school to make room for students from the Union No. 1 subdistrict who had not been incorporated into the new Delhi consolidated district.[39]

Monthly teacher salaries varied widely over the subdistricts, ranging from $34.50 to $55.20 in 1914–15; from $35.00 to $51.00 in 1915–16; and from

$48.40 to $54.60 in 1917–18. The narrowing of the range in 1917–18 was the result of the General Assembly passing a law establishing a minimum salary for teachers. School directors tended to follow the usual pattern of not spending any more than necessary to secure and retain teachers who "provided good service." The lower salaries were usually paid to those teachers with less experience. Most directors would pay considerably higher salaries to retain a particularly good teacher. The directors, of course, all knew one another and word invariably got around as to who was and was not a good teacher. Also, the county superintendent for his part was charged with the responsibility for evaluating the teaching performances of all the teachers in the country schools at least once yearly. Provided he discharged this duty, he shared his evaluations with the school directors in each school township.[40] The general sharing around of the better teachers made it difficult for any one subdistrict to retain the same teacher for very long, no matter her (or, less commonly, his) reputation. Interest in school was almost invariably piqued when a school secured a new teacher, especially one who came highly recommended. Enrollment and attendance levels tended to fluctuate accordingly.

In 1914–15, Guy Ribble, the county superintendent, evaluated nine of the fifteen teachers teaching in the schools of the area as "good" or "excellent." Of the remainder, none received a "poor" evaluation; four were adjudged "fair" and two as "fair-good." The next year only nine teachers taught in the schools of the area. Of these the county superintendent evaluated six as good or excellent and the other three as fair-to-good. It was common practice in some neighborhoods for a director to try a new teacher at a low salary for the fall or spring term and hire a proven teacher at a higher salary for the better-attended winter term. However, there were other neighborhoods in which teachers were usually retained for all three terms.[41] Not surprisingly there was a tendency for directors to hire (usually young) women from farm families in the area as teachers, but seldom was a teacher employed in the subdistrict in which her family lived, except in an emergency. Teachers from outside the immediate area were employed about 40 percent of the time.[42] The arrival of a new teacher in a country school was an important event for most young men of the area. It was an important way of recruiting marriage partners for men who hoped to remain on the family farm.

Despite population decline in the first decade of the new century, none of the schools in the area experienced declining enrollments or attendance levels. If anything, several of them were experiencing overcrowding. As a rule of thumb, school directors in the area viewed an enrollment of twenty students to be about the maximum number that could be accommodated without the quality of teaching suffering. Indeed, most of the schools had desks enough to accommodate only about two dozen pupils anyway. If any more students than this attended on a regular basis, arrangements had to be made to temporarily shift some pupils to another school. Almost invariably this was accompanied by grumbling from the families affected. Anticipated enrollments were usually reflected in the salaries that directors paid teachers, with higher salaries generally going to those teaching in schools with higher enrollments.

The physical condition of school buildings and school grounds varied somewhat across the subdistricts, but in general poor conditions one year were remediated by the next. There is no evidence of abject neglect in the case of either school buildings or grounds for any of the schools during the period in question. Of the eight schoolhouses the county superintendent evaluated in 1914–15, seven were rated as "good" or "excellent" and only one as "poor." In 1915–16, the schoolhouse that had been evaluated as "poor" in 1914–15 earned a "fair-good," but there was some slippage in the superintendent's ratings of the school buildings in three subdistricts (see tables 12 and 13).[43]

In summary, with respect to the quality of teaching, the conditions of their buildings and grounds and teacher salaries, the country schools of the area appear to have been about as good as country schools were anywhere

TABLE 12. *Country Schools in the Buck Creek Area, 1914–15*

Subdistrict	Director	Teacher Salary	Grounds	School Bldgs.	Enroll.	Average Attend.
Union 1	W. B. Willard	38.00	Fair	**Excell.**	14	12.45
Union 2	R. Kragenbrink	46.75	**Excell.**	**Excell.**	18	16.08
Union 3	C. J. Willard	49.80	—	—	19	17.4
Union 4	B. A. Moore	45.00	Good	Good	19	16
Union 5	W. H. Winch	34.50	Fair	Good	18	17+
Union 6	Roy Dighton	44.55	Fair	—	20	14
Union 7	John Kelley	38.50	Good	Poor	18	14+
Union 8	John Beitz	44.55	Good	Good	23	20.08
H.G. 6	Dennis Harrington	55.20	**Excell.**	**Excell.**	20	15.8
H.G. 7	Frank Houston	44.00	Poor	Good	17	13.61

Source: Delaware County superintendent records available at the Delaware County Historical Museum, Hopkinton, Iowa.

TABLE 13. *Country Schools in the Buck Creek Area, 1915–16*

Subdistrict	Director	Teacher Salary	Grounds	School Bldgs.	Enroll.	Average Attend.
Union 1	In Delhi Consolo					
Union 2	R. Kragenbrink	37.00	**Excell.**	**Excell.**	16	14
Union 3	T. I. Wilson	45.10	Good	Fair	**27**	**25**
Union 4	B. A. Moore	37.00	Good	Fair	19	14
Union 5	W. H. Winch	35.00	Good+	F/G	15	13
Union 6	Roy Dighton	49.50	Good+	Good−	21	18
Union 7	John Kelley	44.55	Good	F/G	14	14
Union 8	Chas. Reggentine	38.00	Good	Fair	17	17
H.G. 6	Dennis Harrington	50.60	**Excell.**	**Excell.**	14	—
H.G. 7	Frank Houston	42.90	Poor	Good	14	11

Source: Delaware County superintendent records available at the Delaware County Historical Museum, Hopkinton, Iowa.

in Iowa during this period. Importantly, the records of the county superintendent contain no evidence that these schools were visited at all after 1915–16. The reason should be obvious. He expected them to be closed and their pupils reassigned to a new consolidated school.

The Beginnings of School Consolidation in Buck Creek

Although Chalice advocated rural school consolidation, he realized that most people in the area took considerable pride in their country schools. They certainly did not view their schools as in a state of impending crisis. For those who wished to send their children on to high school, the Hopkinton high school was only a few miles away. Practically everyone had close friends or relatives there with whom their children could board throughout the week. The Hopkinton school district contracted with Lenox College to provide facilities and much of the instruction of its high school students. This added luster to the prospect of attending high school in Hopkinton, at least for Protestant families. Indeed, almost all of the Buck Creek Church members who had attended high school had gone to Lenox Academy (as the Hopkinton high school was called) and many of these had attended Lenox College for several terms as well. For Catholic families, there was the new Catholic high school in Ryan (which many had helped pay for with their contributions), or they could continue the long-standing tradition of sending their children to one of several excellent Catholic "colleges" in Dubuque. For Buck Creek area students, the poor condition of the roads prohibited commuting by automobile to Hopkinton. Since students needed to board wherever they went to high school, most reasoned that they might as well go to one of the best schools available. Rail service between Hopkinton and the larger cities and towns in eastern Iowa was very good. If a son or daughter had to be picked up on Friday afternoon in Hopkinton, it did not much matter whether they were met at the train station or at the door of the high school. If support for rural school consolidation was to be forthcoming, it would have to be nurtured and could not be rushed.

In accepting the call to Buck Creek, Chalice's first goal was to make the activities of the Buck Creek Church a central focus in the everyday lives of as many people in the area as possible. This accomplished, he thought the inevitability of rural school consolidation could be faced and the task completed in a manner that would complement and reinforce the church's activities in building a cohesive and progressive rural community. He wanted the material, social, and cultural advantages of the city to be reconstituted in the countryside and available to farm families rather than for farm families to have to relocate, however temporarily, to the town or city to obtain them. In this he had the full complicity of several of the key patriarchs in the Buck Creek Church. Chalice, however, stopped short of openly agitating for the formation of an open-country consolidated school district. To do otherwise would surely have jeopardized his ministry at Buck Creek. Instead, he worked behind the scenes to encourage leaders in the Buck Creek Church to take up the cause. He believed that once the consolidated school was built near the church, then stores and other economic activities would agglomerate to create a village at the site.

Chalice had been in Buck Creek for only a short time when events in Delhi and Hopkinton made rural school consolidation an issue on which almost everyone in the locality staked out a debating position. By the spring of 1915, enthusiasm for rural school consolidation had reached manic proportions and seemed to be sweeping the county. Earlville appeared ready to form a consolidated district; an effort to form one centered on Delhi was well advanced; and even Hopkinton seemed ready to jump on the bandwagon.

It was not until petitions urging the formation of the Delhi consolidated district were first circulated in the Union No. 1 subdistrict of northern Union Township, in late May 1915, that people in the Buck Creek area began to take seriously the issue of rural school consolidation. Once it became clear that the territorial ambitions of Delhi were quite limited in Union

Township, attention in Union Township shifted to avoiding loss of territory to Hopkinton. The only effective way of ensuring against this was to explore the possibility of Union Township forming its own consolidated district, something that Chalice had been urging upon his parishioners for at least two years.

In mid-April 1915, Frank Joseph, deputy superintendent of public instruction, returned to Delaware County on a combination business and pleasure trip. Some aspects of the business purpose of the trip have already been discussed in the previous chapter. One deserves to be highlighted again here because of its relation to the community-building project of Chalice and others in the Buck Creek Parish. Although Joseph's trip to Hopkinton was billed in the local press as a visit with his mother, that purpose was incidental. He was in Hopkinton to help proponents of consolidation in both Hopkinton and the Buck Creek areas get local consolidation movements under way.[44] One of these local proponents was James Thompson, a former Lenox College classmate and member of the football team quarterbacked by Joseph. Thompson owned and operated a farm about two miles southwest of the Buck Creek Church in the Hazel Green No. 7 subdistrict. By late May 1915, sufficient interest in consolidation existed in Hopkinton for school board member W. R. Reeve and other community leaders to propose that Hopkinton form a consolidated district consisting of an undisclosed amount of territory in South Fork Township and fifteen to sixteen sections of territory in the eastern half of Union Township. The portion of Union Township proposed for inclusion included all of subdistrict Nos. 5, 7, and 8 and most of No. 6.[45] Reeve had written to Joseph earlier, soliciting advice on how to proceed with the proposal. Hopkinton's problem was that "people in Buck Creek" had apparently made it clear that they had designs on much of the same territory. Reeve was concerned that the Hopkinton proposal would be vigorously opposed by the "Buck Creekers" (as the more vociferous members of the Buck Creek Church were somewhat uncharitably called by people in Hopkinton and by some members of the Castle Grove Church), and he wanted to have Joseph and the DPI on Hopkinton's side. Joseph suggested that the Hopkinton proposal took in a little too much territory. He urged the Hopkinton board to make some minor adjustments in the location of the western boundary of the consolidated district it had proposed.

I am not surprised that trouble has come from the source you speak of [the Buck Creekers]; in fact, I had anticipated . . . [that] they would stand in the way of any adjustment of territory. I believe it will be better for you to give them the row of eighties along the west side of sections 34, 27, 22 and possibly 15. . . . [N]either the county superintendent nor the inspector, "not even the deputy" [i.e., Joseph, himself] would have any authority to change the boundary lines. I believe I could convince them [the Buck Creekers] that they would have territory enough if they took a little more than the west half of Union Township and a little of Hazel Green Township.[46]

Through his friend James Thompson, Joseph knew that there was at least some support in the eastern part of Hazel Green Township for forming a consolidated school at Buck Creek. Furthermore, he also knew that support for such a proposal was growing among members of the Buck Creek Church. He expressed frustration and disappointment that the Hopkinton proposal was not ready to be submitted to the voters.

I was in hopes your petitions might be circulated and that you might have determined your boundaries fully and have the date fixed for the election before I should speak to the people for, in my judgment, such a course would be the best plan. If you can get your boundary lines adjusted by compromise without sacrificing the best interests of your schools in the future, you had better do so rather than to stir up animosity. I am writing Walker asking him if he cannot assist you in a compromise and have made the suggestions indicated in this letter.[47]

In his letter to Walker, Joseph urged him to use his influence to effect a compromise between the people in the Buck Creek Church and the Hopkinton board. Joseph also opined that support for consolidation at Buck Creek had not yet reached a consensus. He noted, however, that "without doubt at sometime in the future they will have a consolidated school there or near the church." In Joseph's opinion, Buck Creek should plan on taking the western half of Union Township and as much of Hazel Green Township as necessary "to make a good school." The eastern half of Union Township, however, should be set aside for inclusion in a new Hopkinton district.[48]

Joseph's observation that no consensus had been reached on the issue of rural school consolidation in the Buck Creek area was something of an understatement. Members of the Union School Township board of directors were badly split between those who supported the idea of an open-country consolidated school focused on the Buck Creek neighborhood, those who had no interest in a consolidated district likely to be dominated by Buck Creekers, and those who had no interest in consolidation at all. Board president Warren Winch, Roy Dighton, director of the No. 6 subdistrict, and Rudolph Kragenbrink, the newly elected director of the Union No. 2 subdistrict, all prominent members of the Buck Creek Church, favored forming a consolidated district consisting of all of Union Township and the eastern one-third of Hazel Green Township. Board secretary James Kehoe and John Kelley, both Catholics, and Cliff Willard, director of the Union No. 3 subdistrict and member of the Buck Creek Church, and Charles Reggentine, director of the Union No. 8 subdistrict, were opposed. The director of the Union No. 4 subdistrict, James A. Wilson, an active member of the Buck Creek Church, appears to have been undecided. The Union Township board was not even fully agreed in its opposition to the Hopkinton proposal. Reggentine, for example, wanted the Union No. 8 subdistrict to consolidate with Hopkinton. Cliff Willard from the Union No. 3 subdistrict opposed that idea, while Harry Sill from the Union No. 2 subdistrict supported it.

The proponents of consolidation within the Buck Creek Church were apparently willing to concede 1.5 sections of Union No. 6 and one section of Union No. 5 along the eastern boundary of Union Township and perhaps all of the Union No. 8 and Union No. 7 subdistricts (a total of eight sections) to a consolidated district focused on Hopkinton. This was by no means widely agreed upon by others within the larger Buck Creek area. Whatever negotiations took place between the Buck Creekers and the supporters of consolidation in Hopkinton were held strictly in private. The split on the township board and the lack of any consensus within the Buck Creek Church created a serious dilemma for the faction within the church who wanted to build a consolidated school near the church. They could try to agitate for the formation of their own consolidated district, or they could join with those in the area who were opposed to consolidation altogether to avoid losing territory in Union Township to both Delhi and Hopkinton. On this latter course of action, even the members of Union Township board probably would have agreed had the issue come to a vote, but the dilemma was apparent. The first course of action appeared premature. There simply were not yet enough Buck Creekers covering a large enough territory to form a district that would command a tax base sufficient to build and operate a consolidated school of the size advocated by the educational experts. The second smacked of a Faustian bargain that might make it even more difficult to muster a successful consolidation effort in Buck Creek later. From the tone of Joseph's correspondence, he clearly thought that leaders in the Buck Creek Church were prepared to follow the second course of action: "I hope a compromise may be had in the case of Hopkinton. I feel sure that you can arrange this, for the men of Hopkinton will be fair, I am sure, but they ought not to be asked to mortgage the future success of the consolidated school there simply to appease the fellows at Buck Creek, who have done nothing especially when they can get territory that is nearer and easier for them to handle."[49]

As matters progressed, or rather did not progress, in the case of the Hopkinton consolidation effort, a compromise between the competing factions was not necessary. The movement to consolidate the rural schools surrounding Hopkinton with the Hopkinton Independent School District hit a snag that would subsequently doom the proposition there altogether. The snag was that, just as the Hopkinton consolidation movement was getting underway, a Lenox College official announced that the college was experiencing a fiscal crisis and might be forced to close.

On June 14, 1915, Joseph delivered his address in Hopkinton describing the consolidated school movement in Iowa and explaining how the people of the Hopkinton area should go about forming a consolidated school.[50] It did not have the desired effect. In commenting on it in her weekly Hopkinton column in the *Manchester Press*, Mrs. F. C. Reeve simply noted without further comment that Joseph and Walker had been in town and that Joseph had given "an address upon school matters, consolidation, etc." She devoted far more attention to the economic woes of Lenox College: Would it close or be consolidated with Coe, Dubuque, or Parsons College? Or could some way be found for it to continue on its own in Hopkinton? She reported that the college's local board of trustees was strongly opposed to any such takeover and wanted Lenox and Hopkinton "to continue together as they had done in the past."[51]

Just two years earlier, Lenox College had mounted a major fund-raising campaign, obtaining pledges from Hopkinton residents, college alumni, and former students totaling over $75,000. By 1915, however, many of these pledges had failed to materialize.[52] Earlier in the spring of 1915, the president of Lenox College resigned, announcing that he had accepted a position to head Westminster College in Fulton, Missouri. Faced with the loss of their president and aware of the financial woes of the college, all but two of Lenox's eleven faculty members had resigned by early July to accept positions elsewhere. The local board of trustees had to scramble to hire a new president and faculty and persuade local people who had reneged on their pledges of financial support for the college to renew them.

The time was certainly less than propitious for generating support to build a new school in Hopkinton, even if the Hopkinton district did gain access to a larger tax base through consolidation. To many, the choice seemed to be between keeping Lenox afloat and consolidation. Although there was support for consolidation in the No. 8 subdistrict of Union Township, Buck Creekers had voiced their opposition to including any of the other Union Township subdistricts in a new Hopkinton district. In addition, considerable opposition was anticipated from most of the subdistricts of South Fork Township. Nevertheless, the Hopkinton board thought the issue should be put to a vote. They prepared and circulated the appropriate petitions, secured the approval of the county superintendent, and scheduled the election for August 11. Although the board supported the consolidation effort, its rural support was muted.[53] Some proponents thought that the success of the Delhi proposition on July 24 would add impetus to the Hopkinton effort, but they were wrong. James Woodruff, the DPI's inspector of consolidated schools and leading spokesperson on consolidation, was brought in just two days before the election in a last-minute attempt to salvage the proposition. He gave what Mrs. Reeve referred to as a "very forceful argument in favor of consolidation," but it was a case of too little too late.[54] The proposition lost and lost badly. It even failed to obtain a simple majority of the total vote. The vote tally was 80–69 in the Hopkinton district and 43–76 in the area outside. According to Mrs. Reeve's column the next week, "The consolidated school proposition which has been engrossing the attention of our people for some time, was put to death Wednesday by the voters of the districts involved. Opposition was based mainly upon the basis of taxes."[55] One informant recalled that on election day, a large party of men and boys from a neighborhood east of Hopkinton were threshing and "after dinner the whole thrashing crew got up and went and voted against it, every last one of them." Within days of the consolidation issue failing in Hopkinton, Lenox College agreed to take over responsibility for providing instruction in agriculture and domestic science to high school students in the Hopkinton Independent School District.[56]

The threat of a Hopkinton consolidated district encroaching upon the territory of any prospective Buck Creek district was gone. The strength of opposition in the town of Hopkinton itself assured that Mrs. Reeve was right: school consolidation in Hopkinton was "put to death." The issue of consolidation in the Buck Creek area, however, was not. Woodruff's address enjoyed a much more favorable reception by the significant number of the Buck Creekers in attendance. The idea of consolidation had been firmly planted among them; it simply needed time and some tending to grow.

The Rural Church, the School, and the
Transformation of Rural Life

While voters in the Hopkinton area were rejecting consolidation, Chalice attended a district conference of Methodist ministers in Manchester, where he delivered an address describing his activities at Buck Creek. He outlined his vision for making rural churches the center of community life for farm families. The *Manchester Press* referred to his address approvingly as "especially helpful in its suggestions."[57] Indeed, Chalice devoted much of his spare time from pastoral work in Buck Creek to spreading his version of the Country Life gospel throughout the northern part of the state. Over a two-week period from June 21 to July 2, he gave a series of addresses at rural-life conferences sponsored by the Iowa State College.[58] His activity along these lines appeared to be less a case of self-promotion than an integral part of his mission at Buck Creek. He wanted his parishioners to realize that they were involved in something more significant than simply reinvigorating a small country church. Rural leaders across the state and nation were watching their efforts with interest. While education could not be neglected, in Chalice's vision of a reconstituted rural life, the church, not the school, was the central local institution in the reform process. His experience in the Buck Creek Parish seemed to corroborate this. Once the church built the community, the advantages of consolidating the schools serving that community would be obvious to all of its members, or so he hoped.

Also attracting attention in southern Delaware County during the summer of 1915 was the possibility that Ryan might discontinue its public high school and reduce the number of grade school teachers because of the remarkable growth of the parochial school affiliated with Saint John's Catholic Church. In only its second full year of operation, St. John's had become the largest parochial school in the county in 1914–15, drawing Catholic high students from all over southern Delaware County, especially in the Castle Grove area. Prospective enrollments in Ryan's public school were so uncertain for 1915–16 that the secretary of the Ryan school board wrote to the DPI inquiring whether the closure of the public high school and the other retrenchment measures were within the board's prerogative. The DPI replied that they were.[59] As matters turned out, the enrollments for 1915–16 were not as low as anticipated and Ryan maintained its public school teaching staff at 1914–15 levels. However, proponents of consolidation in the Buck Creek Church realized that if they did not act soon on the consolidation issue, even more Catholic families in the Buck Creek area would send their high school children to St. John's. This would make it even less likely that Catholic families in the area would support closing their country schools and building a consolidated school at Buck Creek. It also served to interject the issue of religion affiliation more prominently into the educational politics of the area.

As long as the operation of rural schools in the Buck Creek area remained the prerogative of the various neighborhoods, the religious affiliation of families in a neighborhood was seldom an issue of contention. On those few occasions when it was, voters in that neighborhood usually chose a different director at the next annual meeting. While directors were always prominent men in their neighborhoods, they still had to behave like neighbors; that did not include favoring one religion or denomination over another in the operation of their school. If a neighborhood was predominantly Catholic, the probability was high that the director would also be a Catholic and vice versa for Protestant neighborhoods. Nevertheless, religious affiliation was seldom the conscious criterion used by neighbors in selecting a director. If there was any self-conscious consideration of religion in school politics at all, it was in the selection of the officers of the board. Maintaining religious balance among the officers helped assure that no group could dominate in setting the townships' general educational policy. This amounted to a politics of accommodation, but it also made any change in policy difficult when the attitudes of Protestants and Catholics toward public schooling diverged. Until rural school consolidation became an issue, however, no significant divergence had occurred.

Religion did, however, make a much more obvious difference in the partisan politics of the area. Catholics voted for Democrats and most Protestants voted for Republicans. Therefore, Catholic suspicions were aroused when George Cossan, a candidate in the 1915 Republican gubernatorial primary, was invited to give an address in the Buck Creek Church. Cossan was an outspoken supporter of Prohibition and an enthusiastic supporter of the state's blue laws.[60] Perhaps for the first time, Catholic families in the area realized that the community-building efforts of the Buck Creek Church were not as inclusive as claimed. When activities of Catholic families in the area were mentioned in the *Hopkinton Leader*, they were almost always identified by neighborhood, for example, Upper Buck Creek, Hazel Green, Castle Grove, River Valley, or as residing "west of Hopkinton." On the other hand, when Buck Creek Methodists were mentioned, they were increasingly identified as Buck Creek residents, even though they may have resided in one of these rural neighborhoods.[61]

From the fall of 1915 through 1916, support for school consolidation grew slowly but steadily among members of the Buck Creek Church. Nonetheless, the impetus provided by the threat of Hopkinton forming its own consolidated district and usurping potential Buck Creek territory was gone. The focus of Chalice's activities lay in expanding the size of the parish by preaching his Country Life variant of the social gospel. During the first week of December 1916, the Buck Creek Church kicked off what Chalice dubbed the "Great Forward Movement." It consisted of a series of special meetings designed to celebrate the church's past accomplishments and to expand the scope of its community-building efforts by reigniting interest in rural school consolidation. Chalice and his parishioners appeared confident that what they had accomplished in the way of rural community building in Buck Creek provided an exemplar for other rural churches.[62] Buck Creekers had solved the rural church problem on their terms and were now ready to use the church as a force for social change in the educational arena as well. They would solve the rural school problem and in essentially the same way as they had the rural church problem. The rural school would be revitalized by forming a consolidated school district coincident with the larger Buck Creek community. All its members, Catholic and Protestant alike, would have the advantages of a town or city school, though the school itself would be located in the country. As 1917 began, the politics of accommodation, which previously characterized the operation of the country schools in the area, gave way to a different kind of politics. Precisely what that politics would be was not yet clear, but, whatever its parameters might eventually become, it would rest on some idea of community constructed around the activities of the Buck Creek Church. From about this time onward, all families in the area, Catholics and Protestants alike, realized that efforts were under way to make Buck Creek a Methodist place, to make Buck Creekers of everyone in the area.

In February 1917, the *Buck Creek Messenger*, the church's monthly newsletter, included an article authored by Chalice on the "rural problem" and how it could be solved through the formation of consolidated schools in the open country.[63] W. S. Beels, the editor of the *Hopkinton Leader*, helped publicize the issue by giving extensive coverage to and commenting favorably on a bill introduced by Representative Lenocker of Madison County to correct flaws in the consolidation law: "Mr. Lenocker contends that the original intent of the law . . . was to encourage and establish community centers in rural communities rather than contribute to improving the town and city schools. He says that of the 209 consolidated districts in the state only 39 of them are strictly rural and he believes that if boys and girls are to be encouraged to remain on the farm the fewer rural communities that are hooked up with the town schools the better. For this reason he urges consolidation in rural communities, separate and distinct from towns and cities."[64]

To follow up on these efforts at rekindling interest in school consolidation in Buck Creek, Chalice arranged for Professor K. W. Buell, superintendent of the rural consolidated school at Randalia in nearby Fayette County, to give a lecture at the Buck Creek Church on the role of school consolidation in rural community revitalization. No doubt Chalice invited Buell because the school at Randalia was the nearest open-country consolidated school in an area quite similar to Buck Creek in a number of important respects. There, as in Buck Creek, dairying was the dominant agricultural activity. It was an area of relatively small farms, and, perhaps most important, it was a Methodist community. The announcement of the event in Chalice's weekly column in the *Leader* read: "Don't forget Friday night. Prof. K. W. Buell, superintendent of the consolidated schools at Randalia will give a lecture in the church next Friday, the 9th, on 'Our Rural Schools.' All school directors, parents, and all others interested in the education of the children are invited to the presentation. You that are satisfied with our present schools come. You that object to consolidated schools, come. Let 'em all come. . . ."[65]

In the same column, Chalice also announced that he would lead off a series of Lenten services with a sermon entitled "The Country Slums," dealing "especially with the conditions of home life in rural communities." This was an unusual topic to begin that most holy of Christian seasons, especially for a self-professed evangelist. Nonetheless, it was an appropriate follow-up to Buell's talk two days earlier on rural community modernization. Regarding his sermon, Chalice opined, "Every parent in the community should hear this."[66]

Thus for the first time, open public discussion of the possibility of rural school consolidation in the Buck Creek area was enjoined. This beginning, however, was something less than auspicious. Buell's address was apparently something less than inspirational and may even have helped stiffen opposition to consolidation. The address received no coverage in the *Leader*, not even in Chalice's own column. Whatever the case, it failed to produce any groundswell of support for consolidation in the Buck Creek area. Doubtless part of the reason a consolidation drive failed to get under way was that Albert M. Deyoe, the state superintendent of public instruction, had recently come under attack in the press. Opponents of rural school consolidation in the General Assembly had charged him with using his control over the disbursement of state moneys to force farmers into paying for consolidated schools they neither needed nor wanted.[67] There were, however, other forces at work in the locality dampening enthusiasm for school consolidation.

The Delhi consolidated district, immediately north of the Buck Creek area, experienced a number of difficulties during its first year of operation. Classrooms were overcrowded. The transportation of rural students to Delhi was poorly organized. The travel times were long; buses were late, imposing hardships on children from the more remote parts of the district. Indeed, overcrowding had compelled the Delhi school board to propose issuing bonds to build an addition to the Delhi school. Transportation problems had also forced the Delhi district to continue using the old county schoolhouses for grades one through eight in several outlying neighborhoods. This had led some disgruntled rural patrons to demand that the size of the district be reduced from twenty-eight to sixteen sections (square miles).[68] Opponents in Union Township could point to the apparent failure of consolidation in Delhi as evidence that consolidation would likely fail in the Buck Creek area as well.

Opponents of consolidation in the Buck Creek area tended to possess one or more of four characteristics. They were either members of the generation who had grown up in the troubled 1880s or 1890s (aged fifty or older), they were Catholic, they operated smaller or poorer quality farms, or they were men. Older heads of households, both landowners and tenants alike, remembered the hard times of the late 1880s and early 1890s. Almost as a knee-jerk response, they were opposed to incurring debt, either public or private, for fear that the return of hard times could force them off the land. Catholics tended to oppose consolidation because they saw it as a thinly disguised move to establish Protestant hegemony over the public schools and/or because they were opposed to the additional taxes they would be required to pay for providing a public high school education for the children of their locality. As one opponent of consolidation wrote to Dubuque's *Catholic Tribune Weekly*, "why should we be burdened with still more taxes? We, as Catholics, know that our children belong in a Catholic school, at least for two years and, in my estimation, it isn't near long enough. Why should we vote for Consolidated Schools when we know it is only more or less for the benefit of others."[69] Owners and tenants operating smaller, poorer quality farms, especially those without relatives in the area, also tended to be opponents. They thought that their children would be less available for work during the key periods of planting and harvesting and for "doing the chores" (milking, feeding, and tending livestock on a regular basis). These farmers generally had less capital and were more dependent on the labor power of all nuclear family members, as well as others in the neighborhood, if they were to be economically successful. Finally, the most vociferous opponents to consolidation were invariably male. Some men even subscribed to the specious argument that unless male opponents mobilized, they would be outvoted by women when it came to voting on the bond issue necessary for actually building the school. They feared that women, with their presumed inexperience in formal politics, might follow their "natural" nurturing proclivities and support any innovation, however costly, reputed to enhance the educational advantages available to their children. Women could not vote in school consolidation elections until the Nineteenth Amendment to the U.S. Constitution was ratified on August 18, 1920, but they could vote in school bond issue elections. In short, opposition had generational, class, religious, and gender dimensions; these often tended to reinforce one another.

Proponents of consolidation were younger. They had access to more capital, usually through family connections in the area. They had a more assured labor supply through their church connections. Most importantly, however, they were likely to be active members of the Buck Creek Church. Not all leaders in the Buck Creek Church, however, were enthusiastic about closing the country schools and incurring the additional debt required to build a consolidated school. Those who were outspoken in their opposition were almost invariably either older or members of predominantly Catholic neighborhoods.

In the spring of 1917, there was still insufficient support for consolidation in the Buck Creek Parish for it to carry in the entire township. The most frequent objection to consolidation voiced was that the increased cost of building and maintaining a consolidated school of the size and with the equipment necessary to receive state aid would be prohibitive. Lacking an urban center and consisting entirely of the territory of country school districts, consolidation would necessitate confiscatory taxes. As many of the older farmers in the area put it, the chances were great that building such a school would "bust 'em."

Buck Creek in the National Spotlight

The lack of progress in getting a local consolidation movement under way in the Buck Creek area was surely a source of disappointment for Chalice and his more ardent followers. Professor Paul L. Vogt, Ph.D., National Superintendent of Rural Work in the Methodist Episcopal Church, had scheduled a visit to Buck Creek on April 15, 1917, as part of his effort to see firsthand "the best results of rural and village church work in all parts of the country." [70] Vogt had been informed of Chalice's work and was collecting information on his church's successful efforts at revitalizing rural churches. A successful rural school consolidation movement lead by the Buck Creek

Church would have been the crowning achievement in Chalice's rural-revitalization project at Buck Creek.

Vogt arrived and spent several days visiting with Chalice, collecting some of the materials he wanted to include in a publication chronicling Chalice's community-building success in Buck Creek. Vogt did not appear disappointed, and when he spoke at the Sunday morning service in the Buck Creek Church, he congratulated the congregation for its outstanding work in solving the rural church problem. He also offered some suggestions for continued success, which given his perspectives on rural sociology published in the same year, surely included rural school consolidation.[71]

Whether Vogt's visit would have been enough to rekindle interest in rural school consolidation among Buck Creek Church members had U.S. entry into World War I not intervened cannot, of course, be determined. The patriotic fervor surrounding U.S. entry into the war swept through midwestern farm communities, and Buck Creek was no exception. One of Chalice's first sermons after the declaration of war was entitled "Was Jesus in Sympathy with War?"[72] He argued that Christ would have been in sympathy with the Allies in the war effort. He also introduced the theme that would remain the dominant one for the remainder of his pastorate at Buck Creek — that it was the duty of American farmers to help win the war by dramatically increasing food production. Barely had Vogt left Buck Creek, when aiding the Allied war effort through increased agricultural production became the principal goal of Buck Creek's community-organizing initiatives. An apparent global geopolitical conflict had displaced local and regional conflict over rural school consolidation as the focus of political discussion and debate in the area.

Like others espousing the Country Life philosophy, Chalice believed that the food shortages induced by the war would finally lead to the realization that continued industrialization and urbanization in the United States could not be sustained if the social conditions of rural life continued to languish compared to those of the cities. The economic benefits of a revitalized rural community life, he thought, would become evident in the higher levels of agricultural output forthcoming from such communities. A rural community could demonstrate its worth by getting behind the war effort in a way that resulted in significantly increased production. American farmers, and particularly those in places like Buck Creek, could not only feed the world, but could improve their own level of material well-being in the process. Rural school consolidation, important though it was in improving the conditions of life in rural areas, would have to be shelved temporarily as farmers contributed to winning the war.

In late April 1917, the U.S. government organized a series of "conservation conferences" throughout the Midwest to identify and coordinate local efforts for achieving vast increases in food production. Probably because of Chalice's rapport with farmers in the area, businessmen in the Hopkinton Commercial Club sent him as their delegate to one of these conferences held in Iowa City. Upon his return, he gave a series of rousing addresses, beginning with one at the Buck Creek Church, followed by repeat performances before the commercial clubs of Manchester and Hopkinton. His theme at each was how to organize farmers and farmworkers throughout the county to support the war effort. He urged the expansion of crop acreage and outlined a plan for organizing a county labor bureau to recruit and allocate farmworkers to farms to minimize crop loss during the fall harvest. As he put it, "America is not fighting for territory or money, but to protect the democracy of the world. Every man, woman and child must do his bit."[73]

At the Manchester meeting, he announced that a labor committee and other committees to plan and implement the project had been appointed for the Hopkinton and Buck Creek areas. He urged other communities in the county to follow the Buck Creek example. Buck Creek was no longer synonymous with the old Buck Creek neighborhood. It now consisted of the entire territory from which the Buck Creek Church drew in membership — almost all of Union Township and the eastern one-third of Hazel Green Township. This effort at mobilizing local agricultural production to "win the war" helped institutionalize a new territorially larger Buck Creek as a place with an ostensibly secular identity. Although its activity was secular, its leadership and style remained firmly identified with the Buck Creek Church. No Catholics from Union Township were appointed to the labor committee. The only Catholic appointed to a committee was Chalice's friend Frank King. He was appointed to the publicity committee, along with five Buck Creekers. At a meeting of delegates from all the Commercial Clubs in Delaware County in May 1917, Chalice was again a featured speaker. At his urging, the Delaware County Food and Industrial War Association was formed to organize the entire county into a series of labor committees to coordinate the allocation of farm labor during the August-October harvest season.[74] Directors in the association were "elected" from each township; directors were prominent businessmen in their respective townships. The only exception was Chalice himself, who was appointed from Union Township.

Next Chalice turned his attention to organizing what turned out to be the first step taken in Delaware County toward obtaining a county agent under the Smith-Lever Act of 1914. At his urging, the Buck Creek Brotherhood scheduled a community meeting on the war emergency for May 15. The new county agent from Jones County was the featured speaker. The meeting was announced in the *Hopkinton Leader* and attracted delegations of interested businessmen and farmers from Earlville, Delhi, Milo Township, and Hazel Green Township. The Jones County agent explained that the idea of a county agricultural expert originated in Denmark and Germany, and that these countries had benefited considerably from the practice. By farming intensively and scientifically, Danish and German farmers were able to feed their own people and much of the rest of Europe. He described the full range of services that a county agent could provide farmers, likening the county agent to a farmer's "consulting physician." At the conclusion of the meeting, several of those in attendance signed a petition asking that a county agent be employed in Delaware County.[75] By early summer, the Buck Creek Brotherhood began touring the county trying to create interest in securing a county agent for Delaware County by giving demonstrations for canning fruit, vegetables, and meat. At these demonstrations they also secured signatures to their petition. By fall 1917, Buck Creek could claim to be the most progressive farm community in the county and get no argument from business leaders anywhere in Delaware County. The U.S. participation in World War I had helped forge a new identity for Buck Creek and helped transform the nature of class consciousness among the farmers of the area as well. Farmers and businessmen had reorganized farm labor in such a way as to "win the war," while also helping farmers enter the ranks of the middle class as global commodity producers.

Rural school consolidation had been dislodged from its position atop the reform agenda of Chalice and his Buck Creek followers by the seductive combination of progress, profits, and patriotism. The issue remained alive but dormant. The annual picnic at the Buck Creek country school in June 1917 brought it back into the consciousness of at least one of its frustrated proponents in the Buck Creek Church. In commenting on the loss of the school's popular teacher who found the "work too heavy," the Buck Creek columnist for the *Hopkinton Leader* (probably Mrs. Chalice) noted:

> How long before the people of this community will wake up. It's hard to tell, but seeing there is no race suicide in this community the time is coming when it will be positively impossible to house and educate the children in a dinky one-room school. We shall waken up some of these days to find that whilst other children are making progress intellectually our children are lagging behind. You may be surprised to hear that teaching a one-room school with eight grades and twenty children is hard

work, but all you have to do is to try it and you will be convinced. Well, if you want cheap and inadequate education hold to your little school.[76]

Chalice's success in building up the membership of his parish through his unusual combination of Country Life progressivism and traditional Methodist revivalism had won national attention for Buck Creek and national visibility for him in the new field of religious sociology. His success in forging a coalition between farmers and businessmen to effect higher agricultural production and the more widespread adoption of food conservation measures also won him regional and statewide attention in rural sociology.[77] He was no longer strutting on a local stage. In commenting on Chalice's participation in a national conference on rural church and community problems in Evanston, Illinois, during the week of July 22, 1917, the *Hopkinton Leader* noted on its front page:

> Reverend Chalice has been solicited to take a field superintendency in the Methodist work in this direction and has the matter under consideration. His work at Buck Creek, and the wonderful success which has been accomplished with the hearty cooperation of the people of that community in rehabilitating the church, has become known over the country as an example which other communities are endeavoring to get the spirit of and do for themselves. It is the example of Buck Creek and here and there other sections that have caught the inspiration that has spurred renewed activity in rural community work, and the country church is coming back [in]to its own. The Leader is firmly of the belief that the rural community problem, which means the centralization of community sentiment about the rural church, is the most commanding of any in the social world today, and Buck Creek is one of the pioneer examples of what endeavor and success in that direction means.[78]

Within the month Chalice announced that he would take the field superintendency. At the same time he also announced that he had accepted the call to a much larger parish in West Branch, just a few miles east of Iowa City, the home of the State University of Iowa. In her weekly column in the *Manchester Press*, Mrs. F. C. Reeve praised his good work in Buck Creek and congratulated him on his "appointment to a better charge."[79] W. S. Beels, the editor of the *Hopkinton Leader*, was more effusive in his praise, suggesting that in his new position Chalice would be in a better position to advance his splendid work on the rural church and rural life with the Home Missions Board of the Methodist Episcopal Church.[80]

What makes you think there was only one cross burning in the Buck Creek area? There were plenty of them.

— Mrs. Myron Zumbach, Coggan, Iowa, telephone interview, 26 September 1994

9

RURAL SCHOOL CONSOLIDATION AND THE REMAKING OF BUCK CREEK

In 1918 and 1919, neither the Buck Creek pastors nor the Buck Creek community captured any headlines in the local press. Chalice's replacement, William Baker, came highly recommended from the Methodist Episcopal church in Mechanicsville (population 812 in 1920), but he was unable to pick up where Chalice had left off in carrying forward with the reform of rural community life. Indeed, it appears that he felt there was little more to be done along these lines. Instead, he launched his pastorate with a five-week series of sermons focusing on family life.[1] Apparently this more traditional emphasis was not received with much enthusiasm because at the end of the five weeks Baker announced a list of prominent speakers on various aspects of rural life who had agreed to give addresses in Buck Creek over the next year. Heading the list was the state superintendent of public instruction, Albert M. Deyoe, a personal friend of Baker.[2] Little seems to have come of these initiatives. Deyoe's lecture at Buck Creek never materialized. Deyoe canceled his visit shortly after Frank Joseph announced his candidacy to run against him for state superintendent on the Republican ticket. By midsummer 1918, the Buck Creek Parish was again searching for a new pastor.

A new pastor, W. A. Odell, arrived in October,[3] but he fared no better than Baker. Odell was unable to spark interest in new community-building activities of the sort that Chalice had been so successful in leading. Even his Irish sounding name aroused some concern within the church. He was not reappointed for a second year. Chalice had left very big shoes to fill. Until the arrival of a Chalice protégé, A. R. Grant, in October 1919, nobody could fill them.

In Grant, the Buck Creek Church's board of trustees spied many of the same qualities Chalice possessed — youth, an old-time evangelistic style, and a commitment to obtaining all the conveniences and advantages of urban life for farm families while avoiding the disadvantages. Furthermore, he came highly recommended by Chalice himself.[4] Chalice maintained close personal ties with many persons in the Buck Creek Church, and he and his family frequently returned to Buck Creek for short visits. No doubt he also maintained a keen interest in the success of the community-building effort he had begun but did not fully complete in the Buck Creek area.[5] Although accepting a call to a town church, the regional superintendency he had accepted entailed heading up rural parish work in the Iowa conference for the Board of Home Missions of the Methodist Episcopal Church under the general directorship of Paul L. Vogt. Buck Creek remained the centerpiece, the exemplar, for this work; hence, his success in this capacity was still linked to Buck Creek.[6]

When Grant arrived, the war had been over for almost a year and yet the farm economy continued to boom as agriculture in Europe struggled to get back on its feet. Because of high levels of production at prices guaranteed by the federal government, most farm families in the Buck Creek Parish continued to earn profits at a rate rivaling those of the war years. The most obvious evidence of this continuing prosperity was found in the prices landowners and speculators received from the sale of farmland. As the *Hopkinton Leader* put it, Delaware County experienced the "greatest turnover of dirt" in its history in the fall of 1919 as 345 farms totaling more than 46,000 acres exchanged hands at the then unheard-of average price of $190 per acre.[7] In commenting on the causes of the boom and on the future of the agricultural land market in Delaware County and the Midwest in general, W. S. Beels, the *Leader* editor, opined:

> The waves of landbuying which sweep like a blizzard over the country are popularly charged up to the activities of the landsharks, but this is far from fact. It is a crop of young folks who must get out of the home nest or shoulder out the old folks who start the booms. The young men must have farms and they are willing to pay the price. The old folks must retire and go to the towns. Of course population increases and there are more ambitious young farmers than there are farms, since the free western ranges have been occupied. These conditions follow in periodical sequence, and the young men of today will live to see another land boom

in the course of twenty years or less, when the new crop of youngsters get ready to strike out. . . . When the next boom comes, because of the lack of free lands the large farms of the present will be reduced in size for the convenience of buyers or tenants. Those who have a facility of looking intelligently into the future will realize that a Delaware County farm is a mighty good and a safe investment right now, for in a few years some one is mighty certain to want it real bad at a long price.[8]

As if to signal their confidence in Beels's prediction, the trustees of the Buck Creek Church agreed to pay their new pastor a salary higher than that of any other Methodist pastor in the county. This did not go unnoticed, drawing the following commentary from the editor of the *Manchester Press*: "Big Salary for Rural Pastor — The Hopkinton Leader says that the official board of the Buck Creek Church has decided to pay the pastor a salary of $2,000 per year and house rent. Ever been to Buck Creek? Well, it is purely a farming community, no town to draw on, yet the farmer church goers of that locality feel able to pay a preacher $200 a year more than is received by the pastor of the Methodist church in Manchester. We say that is going some."[9]

Unlike Odell, Grant lost no time in returning to the issue that had been at the top of the reform agenda for Buck Creekers before U.S. entry in World War I — the consolidation of rural schools in the Buck Creek area. In doing so he received a great deal of help from the DPI and ISTA.

Reemergence of the Rural School Consolidation Issue in Buck Creek

During the previous spring, the DPI and ISTA had been successful in pushing legislation through the General Assembly designed to make consolidation more attractive and easier to accomplish politically. By the time Grant arrived in Buck Creek in fall 1919, the ISTA with political support from the DPI had already begun a massive campaign to complete rural school consolidation in the state (see chapter 5). ISTA was ready to supply written materials on consolidation, stereopticon slides of consolidated schools across the state, speakers, forms to be used in organizing consolidation drives, and free legal advice. The campaign was aided immeasurably by the hyperinflation of land values, by high agricultural commodity prices, and by the lure of middle-class modernity seemingly assured by continuing prosperity. In its pamphleteering and exhortation, the consolidation campaign was rivaled in rural areas only by the efforts of the U.S. Department of Agriculture to sign up farmers as members of the Farm Bureau.[10]

Grant did not have to try very hard to create interest in consolidation. Although Delaware County had already experienced its rash of consolidations in 1915, other counties in eastern Iowa had just begun theirs during the summer and fall of 1919. Residents of rural Fayette County, the county immediately to the northwest of Delaware County, for example, jumped on the consolidation bandwagon in August 1919. The movement spread rapidly to other localities in northeast Iowa throughout the fall. As the *West Union Argo-Gazette* reported,

> A Movement towards consolidation of rural schools is agitating almost every part of Fayette County. No less than six proposed consolidated districts are now under discussion, and within a few weeks, when the present rush of farm work is over, there are likely to be formal and legal steps taken to put some of the projects to the test of sentiment in elections in the respective localities. . . . The sudden movement to pre-empt territory by six different localities at once springs in all probability from the conviction that consolidation is coming inevitably, and that the town or neighborhood that is slow about staking out its district lines will find itself compelled to take what is left. . . . Consolidation is upon us; the community that is not awake to this thing may wake up some day in the not distant future to find its territory in another consolidated district. . . .[11]

Buck Creek Methodists were under no immediate threat of losing "their" territory to neighboring consolidated districts. Nevertheless, they realized that if they laid out a consolidated district carefully they could preempt the territory of those districts not yet "awake" to the inevitability of this educational innovation. What was occurring in nearby Fayette County seemed to provide ample evidence that this would be a prudent strategy. There was no indication that Hopkinton could resuscitate a consolidation movement or that the Delhi district would expand southward.[12] Furthermore, they were confident that the new Delaware County superintendent, W. A. Ottilie, would not permit the Catholic neighborhoods to the south (Castle Grove) or west (Hazel Green) to organize purely defensive consolidations.[13] This gave Buck Creekers the organizational breathing room they needed to convince those Methodists who still slumbered to get on with it, provided they were willing to jeopardize the good working relationships they had had historically with their Catholic neighbors in running the schools of Union and Hazel Green Townships.

The members of the Union Township board of education in 1919–20 consisted of Warren H. Winch (president), James Kehoe (secretary), James Johnson (treasurer), John McGinn (No. 1), Harry B. Sill (No. 2), Thomas Wilson (No. 3), W. J. Kehoe (No. 4), Roy Dighton (No. 6), C. J. Edgar (No. 7), and John Beitz (No. 8). Winch, Sill, Wilson, and Dighton were all leaders in the Buck Creek Brotherhood and enthusiastic supporters of consolidation, while James Kehoe, McGinn, W. J. Kehoe, and Edgar were Catholics and equally vociferous in their defense of the country school. Beitz, a member of the Buck Creek Church, was undecided but leaning in favor of consolidation at Buck Creek, provided his neighborhood, the Union No. 8 subdistrict, was excluded. Johnson, too, supported the idea of consolidation but preferred that the eastern half of the No. 6 subdistrict, including his farm, be excluded from a Buck Creek consolidated district so that it might one day be included in the Hopkinton district. According to Johnson, this area was closer to Hopkinton than it was to the Buck Creek Church and on those grounds should be excluded. Numerically then, the Union Township board was as divided on the consolidation question in the fall of 1919 as it had been in the spring of 1915. Only now, the division was deeper and sharply polarized along mutually reinforcing lines of religion. Except for the No. 5 subdistrict, where Winch and James Kehoe in effect were co-directors, every director favoring consolidation was from a subdistrict in which Buck Creek Methodists were in the majority. Every director opposing it was a Catholic from a subdistrict in which Catholics were in the majority.

Unlike in 1915, by 1919 the formation of a consolidated district roughly coterminous with the territorial extent of the Buck Creek Parish was both a political and a legal possibility. The spatial extent of the Buck Creek Parish had expanded to the point where a consolidated school district consisting of somewhat more than the minimum sixteen sections would have a reasonable chance of success with voters. A new district consisting only of contiguous subdistricts in Union Township, with directors known to be enthusiastic supporters of consolidation, plus the eastern half of subdistrict No. 6 in Hazel Green Township, was one such possibility. A consolidated district this small, however, would not have a property tax base sufficient to support a school of the size recommended by the DPI, without exorbitant tax levies. In 1919–20, the total Union Township school levy stood at 14.6 mills (12.9 for the general fund and 1.7 for the schoolhouse fund), which converted to an average tax of approximately 25 cents per acre.[14] At this tax levy, a consolidated district consisting of only sixteen sections would raise a total of only $2,560. By way of comparison, a 1919–20 tax levy of 59.1 mills in the Greeley consolidated district raised a total of $27,000. The Greeley district, however, contained more than four miles of railway rights-of-way as well as residential and commercial property in the town of Greeley contributing to the tax base.[15] Even with a fourfold increase in the tax rate, a sixteen-section district in Union Township would have raised a total of only $10,240. Approximately $8000 of this would be needed for salaries alone if the district was to qualify for the full amount of state aid.[16]

Clearly, any Buck Creek consolidated district would need to be larger than sixteen sections if it was to build and maintain a school comparable to other consolidated schools in the state. The conclusion was inescapable: neighborhoods in which Catholics predominated would have to be included in any Buck Creek consolidated district. The obvious problem with this was that it would surely result in politicizing the consolidation issue in Methodist versus Catholic terms. It would also risk destroying the long-established neighborhood relationships between the two groups based on spatial proximity. In short, any attempt to make Buck Creek a still larger place territorially through a Methodist-led effort to consolidate the rural schools of the area would entail significant social costs. The key question for members of the Buck Creek Church was whether the community and educational benefits of consolidation outweighed the costs of at least a fourfold increase in school property taxes and the further destruction of neighborhood relations with Catholic families in the area. Indeed, some landowners in the area had to do some careful calculations to be sure that the combination of higher tax rates, rapidly inflating land values, and higher costs of living would not push them into bankruptcy.[17] Owner-operators who had bought land recently and were carrying high debt loads were in an especially precarious position.

For most Catholics, the question of whether the benefits of consolidation outweighed the costs was not worth considering. Catholic parents saw few, if any, benefits of any consolidation proposal that ensured Methodist hegemony over the education of their children. For the previous five years they had witnessed their exclusion from much of the social life of the Buck Creek community and their growing marginalization in its political and economic affairs. In the politics of place practiced in Union Township, and increasingly in the rest of Delaware County as well, differences in religion were already politicized. Efforts to revitalize rural life in the county structured around the rural or village church practically guaranteed this result.

Although Grant was Chalice's protégé, he appears not to have been the spellbinding preacher his mentor was. Aided by a quick wit, a warm, outgoing personality, and relative youth (approximately thirty-five years of age), he was, however, equally effective as a community organizer. He won over the young adults in the church almost immediately and set about organizing them into a large, but still cohesive and informed cadre to convince the more recalcitrant Buck Creekers of the merits of rural school consolidation.[18] It is not known whether this group functioned as a formal committee within the Buck Creek Brotherhood, but, given the church's penchant for formal organizing, it appears likely that it did.

By the beginning of the new year, agitation to form a Buck Creek consolidated district gathered momentum. Although the leaders of the effort contained four present and three past directors of the Union Township school board and the director from the Hazel Green No. 7 subdistrict, the Union Township board took no official position on the issue.[19] Instead, the Brotherhood of the Buck Creek Church organized and led the campaign for the new school. A number of women in the Buck Creek Church were also key supporters of the idea, but none assumed positions of leadership in the campaign. As one informant put it, "the Buck Creek Church people they were the ones that began to push to build the school [and] the ones that was awful willing even though taxes would be higher to build this good school. The ones that were agin the school — agin doing it — nine out of every ten were Catholics." [20]

In early January 1920, a large delegation from the Buck Creek Brotherhood attended Professor Macy Campbell's keynote address on rural school consolidation at the Farmers Institute held in Manchester. Campbell was a professor at the Iowa Teachers College and the state's leading proponent of consolidation not in the employ of the DPI. The Buck Creek delegation was not disappointed by what they heard. As the *Manchester Press* editor put it, "Mr. Macy Campbell . . . gave a rattling good talk on 'The Rural School Problem.' . . . Mr. Campbell believes, and we believe with him, that the country boy or girl ought to have just as excellent educational facilities as the boys and girls of the towns and cities, and Mr. Campbell says that so far as Iowa is concerned there is nothing to prevent it except 'human nature,' for the farmers of the state have twice as much wealth per capita as the town dweller." [21]

Members of the Buck Creek delegation spoke with Campbell after his address and obtained his tentative agreement to give a lecture on consolidation at the Buck Creek Church soon after a date for the consolidation election had been set. From mid-January onward, Buck Creek Church leaders organized an intensive word-of-mouth campaign in the parish designed to solidify support and to determine where they could best place the boundaries of the proposed district. Grant gave regular reports on the progress of the movement at church functions. He also made sure that all his parishioners received pamphlets on consolidation produced by the State Teachers College and the DPI. Indeed, the campaign became a virtual crusade. Slowly, members of the church were swung over to support the issue, at least in principle. However, to have any chance for success, most church members needed assurance that a thoroughly modern consolidated school could be built and operated at Buck Creek at about the same total cost as other consolidated districts in the county. This practically guaranteed that the district would have to be large territorially and take in more Catholic neighborhoods than had been envisaged earlier.

A few elders in the church, however, remained unconvinced of the plan's merits. Some thought that the country school was superior to the consolidated school "in the grades." Others thought that the new contractual arrangement between Lenox College and Hopkinton would result in a better high school program, and one provided at a much lower cost, than any that could be provided in Buck Creek.[22] A few, like their Catholic neighbors, also objected to the formation of a consolidated district at Buck Creek because it would coerce a large number of Catholic families in the area into paying taxes for a Methodist-controlled school that few if any Catholics felt they needed or wanted.

In an apparent effort to gauge public opinion on the issue, the Brotherhood leaked word that they were considering the possibility of consolidating all the Union Township subdistricts plus the three easternmost subdistricts in Hazel Green Township — the equivalent of almost forty sections. The clamor that arose from the residents of Union subdistricts Nos. 1, 4, 5, 7, and 8 and Hazel Green subdistricts Nos. 1, 6, and 7 — few if any of whom had ever considered themselves as members of the Buck Creek neighborhood — so reverberated throughout the area that among older residents it is still a topic of conversation even today, over seventy-five years later. Union No. 8 subdistrict was the first to be removed from the plan. John Beitz protested its inclusion because for at least part of the year the only passable roads for a school wagon (or bus) to use in transporting students from this area to and from the Buck Creek crossroads went through Hopkinton. This simple spatial logic was compelling, and the River Valley neighborhood was removed from the proposed district. Residents and landowners in the Hazel Green No. 1 subdistrict viewed their neighborhood, focused as it was at a crossroads where a general store, a country school, and the small Hazel Green Creamery were located, as *the* Hazel Green neighborhood. They argued that to destroy one neighborhood to build up another contradicted a core rural value that people in the Buck Creek Church claimed they had upheld in retaining their rural church. Once it was realized that none of the

Congregationalist and Catholic families of this neighborhood could be persuaded to join in the campaign for the consolidated school, it was quietly dropped from the plan. It contained no active members of the Buck Creek Church anyway.

Omitting the Union No. 8 and Hazel Green No. 1 subdistricts still left approximately thirty-one sections available for possible inclusion in a Buck Creek consolidated district. This was the territory that would eventually be proposed, but the Buck Creek Brotherhood knew better than to circulate any petitions until after moving day (March 1, 1920). They wanted to be more certain that they had enough votes to carry the proposal. Preferring not to leave the matter to chance, the Brotherhood had worked even harder than usual to be sure that incoming renters were the "right sort of people." Grant and others involved most directly in the campaign urged all landowners in the church to rent only to people who agreed to vote for the school.[23] This became another reason to stop any further Catholic expansion in the area. Most Catholic families in Union and Hazel Green Townships did not become aware that this policy had been implemented in the Buck Creek Church until well after moving day. When they did, feelings ran high. Father Bourke, the parish priest of the Castle Grove Church, reputedly denounced the action and urged his parishioners to vote against the consolidation proposal if an election were ever held.[24] Some Buck Creekers claimed that Catholic families in the area, especially in the Upper Buck Creek neighborhood, had been discriminating in favor of Catholic tenants for years. By discriminating against Catholic renters, Buck Creekers were simply "returning the favor." Still others could point to a pamphlet published by the Iowa Agricultural Experiment Station in Ames describing the formation of the Orange Township consolidated school in Black Hawk County. The pamphlet described approvingly the action of the United Brethren church there prohibiting their members from either renting or selling land to anyone outside the church. This may be where Grant got the idea. Macy Campbell billed the Orange Township consolidation plan as a model to be followed in establishing open-country consolidated districts in eastern Iowa.[25] Incidentally, the Glen and Edna Thompson family was one of the families moving to a different farm on moving day in 1920. Nine days later Edna gave birth to Bernard, the person whose obituary introduces the previous chapter.

Chalice returned to Buck Creek for several days in late March to visit with Grant and lend his support to the consolidation effort. During the visit he delivered "a splendid sermon on service" before "a large crowd gathered at the church to hear their old pastor." That same weekend, the Castle Grove

Council for Irish Independence held a mass meeting in the hall behind the Castle Grove Church launching a drive to raise funds to aid Ireland in its war of independence from Britain.[26] The irony of this conjunction of events seems to have escaped observers at the time. While Buck Creek Methodists were busily attempting to oust Irish Catholic influence from their community, the Catholics in the area were mustering support to oust British Protestant influence from Ireland.

The Second Consolidation "Craze" in Delaware County, the Ku Klux Klan, and the First Battle of Buck Creek

On April 8, 1920, the *Manchester Press* carried a piece quoting county superintendent W. A. Ottilie as saying that Delaware County, "one of the richest and most prosperous sections of the globe," would have faced a critical shortage of teachers in its rural schools in the 1920–21 school year had the directors of the county's rural school subdistricts not increased the minimum salaries paid to teachers. The article went on to explain that Ottilie had called a meeting of the officials of the rural independent districts and the school townships and secured from them a resolution fixing country school teacher salaries at a minimum of $90 per month for holders of first-grade county certificates and $75 for second-grade certificates.[27] In most rural school districts and townships this required a rather substantial increase in the local school tax levy, and hence provided yet another incentive for rural school districts to consider consolidation. In Union Township, the school tax levy for 1920–21 was set at 35.0 mills, a 140 percent increase over the previous year. The 1920–21 tax levies were not announced until early July. Consolidation proponents argued that if taxes had to increase by 140 percent just to maintain "inferior country schools," then farmers might as well pay a little more and secure a better education for their children.

Another event in the spring of 1920 helped create interest in the Buck Creek consolidation proposal among voters in the Hazel Green No. 6 subdistrict. Just before the beginning of the spring term, the school in this subdistrict was destroyed by fire, forcing Hazel Green Township to provide transportation for these students to attend another school two miles farther west. There were some suspicions of arson raised by Catholic families in the area, but these could not be proved.

The campaign for the formation of a consolidated district was the principal community activity in the Buck Creek Church during the spring of 1920. Grant and the younger members of the Brotherhood took every available opportunity to agitate for the proposal. They argued that consolidation was needed to relieve crowding in the Buck Creek school. While some of the other schools in the area were not yet crowded, it was argued that they soon would be. Buck Creekers had come to believe in the inevitability of their own community success story. As part of what Buck Creekers hoped would be the final push in a successful crusade for consolidation, Grant organized a series of "community life institutes" focusing on rural school consolidation to be held at several locations in Delaware County. The newly created Rural Life Department of Upper Iowa University, a Methodist college in Fayette County about fifty miles northwest of Buck Creek, assisted in this venture. The first institute was to be held in the Buck Creek Church on April 30–May 1.[28]

The success of the Buck Creek institute was to be measured by more than just the number of people attending. It was also hoped that the petitions then being readied calling for the establishment of the Consolidated Independent District of Buck Creek would be signed in large numbers by those attending the special services on Sunday, thereby obviating any necessity for door-to-door canvassing at a time when farmers were beginning their spring field work. Therefore, it was a serious setback when the institute had to be canceled at the last minute because inclement weather rendered local roads impassable.[29] This opportunity to bring in the experts to help generate enthusiasm had been lost. It was unlikely that a new one could or should be scheduled until later in the spring when crops were in the ground. Furthermore, the poor road conditions that had forced the cancellation of the institute also made it difficult to implement a door-to-door campaign. When the roads finally did improve, farmers would need to be completing their spring plowing. The campaign to form a consolidated school district had to be delayed again.

Although building support for rural school consolidation occupied the members of Buck Creek Church during the spring of 1920, a related activity began to compete for their attention. Seeking to gain a foothold in Iowa by exploiting the anti-Catholic sentiment that had developed over consolidation, the Knights of the Ku Klux Klan secured a member of a well-known family in the Buck Creek Church to be the local organizer — the "kleagle." A drive to enlist members by staging local rallies was soon under way. The extent of Grant's complicity in Klan activity is not clear, but there is no doubt that he did not discourage it either publicly or privately. Most Catholic families in the area believed the widespread rumor that Grant would "whoop it up for the Ku Klux Klan right from the pulpit."[30] Explicit mention of Klan activities during this period was scrupulously avoided in local newspapers. However, R. E. Goss, a local humorist, self-proclaimed social-ist, and contributor to the *Hopkinton Leader*, in commenting on the re-cent invention of a local entrepreneur noted for his dubious get-rich-quick schemes, included a thinly veiled swipe at the support the Buck Creek Church and its pastor were giving to Klan activities in the area when he wrote, "F.A. Bort is some inventor, and the beauty of it is that his inventions are practical. Take for instance his chick feeder. It is just what every farmer wants and what they can now have. They are something that a salesman can sell faster than a Buck Creek preacher can snare suckers, and according to reports, that is going some." Current residents whose families have lived in the Buck Creek area from the 1920s or earlier readily acknowledge that Buck Creek was a hotbed of Klan activity during the "school controversy" and that its activity continued at least through 1924 and perhaps longer. Anti-Catholic sentiment among some residents of southern Delaware and north-ern Jones Counties was not a new phenomenon. Indeed, it dates back to 1854, when members of the Know Nothing Party took credit for burning the first Castle Grove Church.[31]

Acts of actual physical violence perpetrated on persons by or in the name of the Klan in the area during the period in question were few. These were limited to a few instances in which Klan members picked fights with mem-bers of Irish Catholic families who had kept their sons out of the army dur-ing the First World War. Nevertheless, there was a spate of cross burnings. Although details are lacking, most of the cross burnings appear to have oc-curred in Methodist neighborhoods in Union Township, particularly in the Buck Creek and Upper Buck Creek neighborhoods. While these may have been more a ploy to attract new members than to intimidate Catholic fami-lies into supporting the formation of a consolidated school district, there were some important exceptions.

Most historians have interpreted the rise of the Ku Klux Klan in the Mid-west in the immediate post–World War I period as an antimodernist reac-tion against increasing urbanization and the apparent destruction of rural values. Previous research suggests that the attraction of the Klan to many rural midwesterners was that it offered the promise of preserving rural val-ues. It did so by channeling the patriotism and hatred of an external enemy developed during the war and redirecting them against those who would seemingly deny the preservation of these values.[32] This was precisely what the Country Life gospel as preached by Chalice and Grant also promised. The only difference lay in the more explicitly Janus-faced nature of the community-building project of the Buck Creek Church. That project was backward looking in its exaltation of farm life and traditional rural values but forward looking in its insistence on maintaining traditional values under changed social relations and material conditions of rural life. Rural life was to be *of* the city but *in* the country. Anti-Catholic feelings were triggered by the realization among Methodists that Catholics could frustrate the fulfillment of that project by their rejection of rural school consolidation. However, they were also implicit in it right from the beginning. In the attempt to make Buck Creek a Methodist place, Catholic families were denied a role, as Catholics, in that place's future. Yet, they could lay claim to having shaped its history since the earliest days of European settlement every bit as much as the Methodists.

Once a significant number of Buck Creekers joined the Klan, the nature of the controversy over rural school consolidation changed and changed dramatically. In the late spring and early summer of 1920, however, the Klan was just gaining a foothold in the area. Initially, growth in Klan membership among Buck Creekers was greeted with little apparent alarm by local Catholics. For one thing, the Klan was a new phenomenon in Iowa; indeed, its activity in Buck Creek appears to have been the Klan's first serious effort to recruit members anywhere in the state. Many in the Buck Creek area tried to shrug it off as an unpleasant fad, even a new form of rural social activity designed to help enliven an otherwise dull rural existence. Some saw it as a moneymaking scam, either to help line the pockets of particular individuals or to pad the coffers of the Buck Creek Church. As one Catholic who later became active in fighting the consolidation proposal put it, "A lot of the boys that joined the Klan, they reached in their pocket and paid their dues and that's the last they saw of them. It was a sucker deal." [33]

Since the Klan is a secret organization, membership data are nonexistent. It is not possible to estimate with much precision how many members or what percentage of the Buck Creek Church members joined the Klan. Interviews with long-term residents of the area lead to estimates running from half the male heads of families to all but three family heads. There is agreement, however, that almost all members of the Brotherhood who championed the formation of the Buck Creek consolidated school district joined the Klan, with some becoming very active. From early May 1920 onward, interest in the Klan grew among the Buck Creekers as the conflict over the formation of a consolidated school district intensified and increasingly took on religious overtones. Indeed, some people were unable to distinguish between social activities of the Buck Creek Church supporting the consolidation drive and similar activities by the Klan. Simply put, it appears that the Klan became the clandestine arm of the Buck Creek Brotherhood. Speakers at Klan rallies argued that Catholics in the Buck Creek area were opposed to the fully American, rural-minded, consolidated school for one of two reasons. First, Catholics wanted their own parochial schools; they wanted to retain the country schools to save money for the education of their children in parochial schools. Second, Catholics wanted to retain the country schools so they could convert them into de facto parochial schools run and taught by Catholics. Such rhetoric fueled the false rumor among Buck Creekers that the Castle Grove Parish operated a parochial high school at Castle Grove. The fact was that the old school building there had not been used as a school for more than two decades.[34]

Curtis Griggs, one of the few members of the Buck Creek Church who opposed consolidation, remembered attending a Klan rally in the Buck Creek area with a friend who had already joined. Griggs did not join because "it cost $10.00 and I didn't believe in anything that stirs up trouble. . . . It was a fake. They took $10.00 from everybody that joined it and it was just to scare the Catholics about that trouble over the consolidated school. You see the Catholics was against the school and the Klan came in because of that to stir up trouble."[35] Griggs, however, was the exception.

By mid-June 1920, the roads were mud free. The crops had been planted. All was ready for delegations from the Brotherhood and Ladies Aid Society of the Buck Creek Church to call on as many people as possible to explain the consolidation plan and to solicit their signatures on the petitions calling for its implementation. In order for a special election on consolidation to be held, at least one-third of the voters in the area affected had to sign a petition calling for one. The *Hopkinton Leader* gave the issue front-page coverage and indicated that it was pleased to see the movement under way and hoped that it would succeed.[36]

If organizers thought that it would be an easy matter to obtain the requisite number of signatures, they were in for a surprise. First, the proposed district did not correspond with township boundaries. Hence, it was not clear how many qualified voters were in its thirty-one square miles. Second, some Buck Creekers were startled to learn that among voters in the Kelley neighborhood (Union No. 7) and among those whose children attended the "new" No. 1 school, not a single voter could be induced to sign the petition, not even those few, like Curtis Griggs, who were members of the Buck Creek Church. This was particularly troublesome because the farms in these neighborhoods were smaller on average than others included in the proposal and hence they contained proportionately more voters than did the others. In only three of the nine subdistricts included in the proposed district — Union Nos. 2, 3, and 6, where the Buck Creek Church membership was concentrated — was the task of securing signatures relatively easy. Even here, there were some surprises. For example, Cliff Willard, a landowner, respected member of the Buck Creek Church, and former director of the Buck Creek country school, refused to sign. With the excellent Lenox Academy only a few miles away, he was unconvinced that the Buck Creek Parish needed its own high school. He also thought it unfair to force his many Catholic friends and neighbors in Upper Buck Creek into a consolidated district against their will.[37]

Supporters of consolidation were also scarce in the two subdistricts in Hazel Green Township included in the proposed consolidated district. Here only those who were members of the Buck Creek Church signed the petition. Leaders of the effort had thought that voters in the Hazel Green No. 6 subdistrict would support the Buck Creek proposal rather than vote to build a new country school to replace the one destroyed by fire. They were surprised, then, when these voters, like others in Hazel Green Township, voted overwhelmingly for building a new country school. It is not known precisely how many signatures from qualified voters were actually obtained in the territory of the proposed district. Either there were not enough or leaders feared that the proposed district included too many opponents to have any expectation of success in an election. The petition drive was scrapped; the future of Buck Creek appeared to be at a crossroads.

With a little prompting from Grant, Buck Creek Church leaders remembered what had worked eight years earlier when the issue had been the survival of the Buck Creek Church, itself — an old-fashioned Methodist revival led by Gilbert Chalice. Chalice was now posted at West Union in Fayette County. Grant had joined him there for a series of revival meetings over a two-week period in late March and early April. Chalice's relationship with Grant and his continuing interest in the success of the consolidation project at Buck Creek made it relatively easy for Grant to enlist his help in leading off the equivalent of a camp meeting revival to rekindle and expand enthusiasm for the project. Chalice agreed to "preach" at Buck Creek on Monday evening, June 28, in what was billed as the first in a week-long series of "special meetings" to be held "in the interest of the church and Sunday school."[38] Special meetings, indeed. The topic at each meeting was rural school consolidation, and Grant and laypersons in the church spoke almost nonstop on its behalf every night throughout the week. Rather than follow the usual format of a revival service and ask people to come forward and profess their faith at the end of the service each evening, persons were urged instead to come forward and sign the new petition for the creation of the Buck Creek Consolidated School District. The consolidated district described in the new petition deleted the troublesome Union No. 1 and No. 7

subdistricts, but otherwise was identical to the previous one, and retained the heavily Catholic Union No. 4 and No. 5 and Hazel Green No. 6 and No. 7 subdistricts. It contained twenty-seven sections.

Midway through the next week the *Hopkinton Leader* was able to report, "The petitions for the proposed consolidated district at Buck Creek have been generally signed and some of them have been filed. There is a due process of law to follow before the election can be held. Reports are very favorable for the success of the project"[39] By the end of the week enough signatures had been obtained for the proposal to go forward. On Monday, July 5, the *Leader* reported that a picnic for the entire Buck Creek community had been held at the Buck Creek parsonage the previous evening.

The Buck Creek Church had never before had a Fourth of July celebration. What they were really celebrating was the success of the first phase of their battle to form a consolidated school district. On July 23, M. O. Smith, one of the trustees of the Buck Creek Church and a leader in the Brotherhood, filed the petitions for the formation of a consolidated district with the county superintendent. The petitions were accompanied by an affidavit maintaining that there were 120 (male) voters in the proposed district. The petitions bore the signatures of 62 qualified voters — a bare majority of the total number of voters that proponents claimed resided in the district.[40] The Nineteenth Amendment to the U.S. Constitution would extend to women the right to vote in less than a month. One hundred and twenty would prove not to be a very good estimate of the actual number of eligible voters in the proposed district. Despite their week-long revival on behalf of the consolidated school and years of preparation, Buck Creekers knew that the results of the election would likely be very close. If the Nineteenth Amendment was ratified before the election, as appeared likely, women seemed to hold the balance of power in determining the result.

If leaders of the consolidation campaign were worried about the proposal's prospects at the polls, they were careful not to show it. They pushed ahead and signed an agreement with the Hopkinton light plant to extend a line to the Buck Creek crossroads in order to provide electric lighting to the church and parsonage, thereby making it available for a consolidated school at that site as well. Some opponents of the plan, however, had apparently started the rumor that people in Hopkinton opposed formation of the Buck Creek district. Opposition in Hopkinton supposedly arose because the proposed district took in territory that was nearer to Hopkinton and because it would hurt business activity in Hopkinton. The loss of tuition and room-and-board revenue, in particular, was highlighted. The *Leader*, however, lost no time in dispelling the rumor. On August 5, it published an editorial denying that anybody in Hopkinton was inciting opposition to the Buck Creek consolidation effort. Instead, it wished the people of Buck Creek well in their attempt to get a consolidated school because it would "increase greatly to their benefit in the years to come."[41]

While the supporters of consolidation were well organized, opponents were not. Excluding the heavily Catholic eastern portion of the Upper Buck Creek neighborhood and the Kelley neighborhood from the proposal had the effect of silencing, at least temporarily, some of the proposal's more organized and vociferous opponents. It also forced opponents in Hazel Green Nos. 6 and 7 and Union Nos. 4 and 5 subdistricts to devise new strategies. The success the Upper Buck Creek and the Kelley neighborhoods enjoyed in being deleted from the proposal seems to have encouraged other Catholic neighborhoods to follow their example. Instead of joining in a single opposition movement, they argued only for the exclusion of their particular neighborhoods. That the Buck Creekers had been successful in conjoining religious affiliation and territory to create a new place in the collective consciousness of people in the area made it very difficult for Catholic families, who identified themselves with a multiplicity of territorially discrete neighborhoods, to organize on any other basis. While the residents of Union No. 4 and Hazel Green Nos. 6 and 7 were organizing petition drives opposing the formation of the district, most of the families in Union No. 5 were attending a rousing debate in the Castle Grove No. 6 schoolhouse about two miles southeast of the Castle Grove Church. The topic of the debate was whether the tractor was superior to the horse in the general farming practiced in the area. The horse won!

The Opposition Mobilizes

W. A. Ottilie, the Delaware County superintendent, set August 11, 1920, as the deadline for his receipt of "objections to the boundaries or to the formation of the district." He received four petitions protesting the formation of the district.[42] Two of these were filed by Protestant landowners residing in, but also owning several other farms in, the northern half of subdistrict No. 6 in Hazel Green Township. Their objections centered on the microgeography of the proposed district's boundaries. They were concerned that most of the farmland they owned was included in the district while the farmhouses occupied by their tenants were not. In short they objected to paying taxes, the benefits of which were denied to their tenants. The other two petitions were more substantial. Twenty-four men signed the first one. They constituted a majority of the heads of household in each of three subdistricts — Hazel Green No. 6 and No. 7 and Union No. 4. In addition, five persons signed from the No. 1 subdistrict (even though their farms were no longer in the proposed district), two from No. 2 (Upper Buck Creek), and even two from No. 3 (Buck Creek). The reasons for protesting the formation of the district were:

1. It will do away with our local schools, and force us to join a school system that we do not believe can be a success in a district that is several miles from any town when the tendancy [*sic*] of the country schools and churches are to eventually center in the towns of the neighborhood.
2. In the proposed district there are four miles of road along the Union and Hazel Green Township line that is impassable for several months during the school year, and furthermore our road system is not of a standard that will make it advisable to haul children several miles to school during the winter time.
3. We believe the formation of this proposed Independent School District will cause therein a depreciation of land values for the reason that a heavy tax must necessarily be levied to build, equipp [*sic*] and maintain a consolidated school.
4. That in the public notice a copy of which was published in the Hopkinton Leader, a newspaper published and entered into the mails of Hopkinton, Iowa, no limit is fixed on the amount of money that will be expended nor the exact location of the proposed school fixed. We do not believe it right nor just to subject our lands to a tax without limitations.

Ten residents of Union No. 4, six of whom had not signed the first petition, filed a second petition. They objected to the inclusion of their subdistrict in the proposal, claiming that "the present abnormal prices of material of all kinds, the shortage of labor and many other deterring elements including the present conditions of practically all roads in the proposed consolidated district are sufficient justification for our earnest opposition which we register by our signatures."[43]

All told, forty-one persons officially protested the formation of the district in writing. Twenty-nine of these were Catholics. Of the twelve Protestants signing petitions protesting the formation of the district, nine lived in predominantly Catholic neighborhoods. Catholic parents did voice their skepticism about the success of the community-building program of the Buck Creek Church. Although they probably would have preferred to do so, they could not protest the formation of the district on the three grounds that troubled them most. First, that they would be turning the control of their children's education over to a Methodist community that had shown no sensitivity to the wishes of Catholic families. Two, that the Buck Creekers had failed to repudiate the anti-Catholic activities of the Ku Klux Klan in the area. Three, that the proponents of consolidation had included pre-dominantly Catholic neighborhoods in the proposal solely because they needed the additional tax base to build *their* consolidated school. Instead, they protested the formation of the district on the politically more accept-able grounds of cost, fiscal responsibility, property value depreciation, and the poor condition of the roads over which children would need to be transported.

Although consolidated schools were to become the social centers of new rural communities, those in positions of power at the state level considered the issue of how these communities might actually be constituted geo-graphically as irrelevant in the delimitation of consolidated districts. This permitted the taxing power of the state to be harnessed to the community-building efforts of sectarian groups, even if these efforts had the effect of undermining the viability of other communities, including preexisting ru-ral neighborhoods. The school consolidation laws had been designed to encourage the closing of country schools and to foster the building of a different kind of school for farm children. The law was silent on what kind of community these new schools would serve. They would remain "local" in some sense; apparently not as local as the traditional rural neighbor-hood based on routine, but intensive, face-to-face social interaction. In 1920 not everybody in the Buck Creek area — certainly not Catholics — was ready for the new kind of community being constructed by the Buck Creek Methodists.

Ottilie dutifully heard the objections to the Buck Creek proposal on August 16. After "a careful review and investigation of the merits of all claims and objections," giving "due regard for the welfare of adjoining dis-tricts and being fully advised in the premises," he overruled them. Ottilie was concerned about whether the proposal met the letter of the law. It did, and he approved the boundaries as they had been specified in the petition filed by the Buck Creekers.[44] Apparently the tone and tenor of the hearing gave those filing objections no hope that an appeal to the county board of education could meet with success. Ottilie informed the objectors that they and any others who felt like them could more effectively voice their protest by voting against the proposal at the upcoming election. If as many people in the area were opposed to the plan as was claimed by the objectors, then the issue would be defeated.

After consulting with leaders in the Buck Creek Church, Ottilie set the election for September 13. The Buck Creekers urged him not to schedule the election until after the Buck Creek Fair on September 8–11. They wanted to be sure they had enough time to bring in speakers to boost consolidation and "get out the vote." Having a professional stake in the venture's success, he obliged. On September 2, the *Leader*, along with carrying an announcement of the special election as required by law, carried the following two pieces. The first was an editorial regarding the upcoming election. The second was a retrospective on the purpose of education, written by a resident of the Castle Grove neighborhood in northern Jones County immediately south of the Union Township. Taken together they illustrate two sharply contrasting perspectives on public schooling

BUCK CREEK COMMUNITY TO VOTE ON CONSOLIDATION — Those interested will make note of the authorized public notice on the fifth page, of the special school election, to be held at the Buck Creek schoolhouse on Monday, September 13. . . . The project has been under discussion by the community for a number of years past, but one thing and another seemed to interfere with harmony of action. The ambition of the fathers and mothers of the community to give their children an education demanded by the times was not to be denied, and it is hoped that the election will confirm their belief that the community is of one mind on the subject. A fine school would be a wonderful asset to the community.

CASTLE GROVE — School bells will be ringing . . . all this week, calling the children back to their books and blackboard. Let us pause and wonder why. To get an education, to acquire knowledge. . . . Old John Ruskin once said, "Education doesn't mean teaching a person something he doesn't know, it means teaching him to behave as he does not behave." . . . We heartily endorse a rightly disciplined education (excuse our preaching). Boys and girls, go to school and college. Select a school with a reputation; not one that is filling the air with athletic skyrockets; but one that prudently keeps the education of the mind and character uppermost.

The Election

In the week before the election, most political pundits thought the issue would lose, but by a narrow margin. Buck Creekers pulled out all the stops in an effort to push the issue over the top. Grant, in particular, staked the success of his pastorate on its passage. He called on all members of the parish to vote "Yes" both from the pulpit and in personal visits with those people thought to need a "little nudging." Professor Earl Roadman was rescheduled to give the keynote address on that same topic on the first day of the Buck Creek Fair on September 8. Roadman was the rural leadership expert from Upper Iowa University at Fayette who had been scheduled to speak on rural school consolidation at the community life institute that had been postponed in April. Macy Campbell had agreed to make good on his earlier promise and speak on the community benefits of rural school consolidation on September 12, the eve of the election. The issue of the *Leader* announcing these events also contained an editorial urging voters to support consolidation. "Every voter in the proposed Buck Creek district should ponder deeply his obligation to his own family and to his neighbors before he determines to oppose the proposition next Monday. The moral obligation is a hard one to dodge." [45]

The stage appeared set. In Campbell's address on the evening before the election, opponents were depicted as greedy, myopic, educationally backward, unpatriotic, and even immoral. As persons filed out of the Buck Creek Church after the speech, they were startled to see a large cross set ablaze on the hill next to the cemetery about 150 yards west of the church. A small group of men with white hoods and robes cheered and then piled into an automobile that sped northward on the road toward Delhi. One person in the crowd was heard to exclaim, "The fools. They've gone too far." [46] The results of the election the next day perhaps told another story. The cross burning at Buck Creek may have reminded Buck Creek Methodists who might otherwise not have been convinced of the merits of consolidation that the election was about who was to wield power in the area — Protestants or Catholics.

The editor of the *Leader* apparently saw no purpose in reporting the cross burning in its next issue. Instead, the *Leader* reported, "practically every qualified voter in the proposed territory attended the polls. . . . The issue looked doomed to defeat in the weeks before the election. . . . But as the good points of consolidation were presented, one after another of the objections were battered down and numerous voters changed from a negative to an affirmative position when convincing facts were given them." Two hundred and fifteen persons voted, with the final tally standing at 133 for and 76 against, with 6 spoiled ballots. [47] The *Leader* opined that a new school could be built and opened by the next fall, "should everything work harmoniously." The *Manchester Press* carried a similar piece but also indicated that "the new school will be located near the church. This will mean greatly improved facilities for the children of the neighborhood, and we congratulate the good people of Buck Creek upon the wisdom and enterprise shown by them." [48] Lost in the hoopla was any mention of the apparent shift in the power relations between Methodists and Catholics in the area. Buck Creek was now a formally constituted, legally recognized place — a Methodist place. Or, so it seemed to be.

As required by law, the county superintendent posted notices in the *Leader* calling for the nomination of directors and a treasurer for the Buck Creek Consolidated School District. He set the election for October 5, 1920. A slate of five directors was nominated from the Buck Creek Church members, while James Johnson, the long-term treasurer of the Union Township board, was nominated for treasurer. Only one other nomination was forthcoming — that of W. J. Kehoe, the director of Union No. 4 — for one of the two one-year director positions. Consolidation opponents nominated no candidates for any of the other positions. They refused to concede the legitimacy of the district by putting forth a full slate of candidates; their nomination of Kehoe was merely a protest.

One hundred and ninety voters voted in the special election. For the two one-year director positions, Clyde Thompson and Roy Dighton each received 138 votes, while W. J. Kehoe received 52. For the two two-year positions, M. O. Smith and Warren Winch received 138 and 140 votes, respectively. For the one three-year position, Harry Sill received 145 votes; while for treasurer, James Johnson received 150 votes. These results almost certainly indicate that 45 of the 52 people voting for Kehoe voted only for him and no others in the contests for directors. It appears that Catholic farm families in the area finally had some semblance of unity and organization, albeit too late. Along with its report on the election of the new school board, the *Leader* included the following:

> The newly elected officers will go to Manchester next Saturday and qualify before the county superintendent. Following this the necessary steps will be taken to fix upon a location for the proposed school buildings, select plans for the buildings, and hold an election thereafter for authority to issue bonds for the erection of the schoolhouse and the dormitory for teachers.

> The people of Buck Creek community are going about their enterprise with a determination that forecasts decided success in the undertaking. All those with whom the Leader has talked seem to fully realize that they are entering upon an extensive and an expensive enterprise but they feel that it is justified and that the children of the community are entitled to the very best to be had in schools and culture. Buck Creek is one of the very few rural consolidated districts in the state. Most consolidated enterprises have a town as a nucleus for the district, admittedly an advantage in many ways. But the state reports are evidence that the all-rural

schools are being conducted with great success, and that after the initial expense is passed the cost of the schools is no greater than in districts combined with towns. The commendable thing about this community, is that it has reached a point where the people are determined to work out their own destiny and community problems by their own efforts, and such zeal and community inspiration will win for success.[49]

As its first order of business, the new board decided to visit a number of consolidated schools throughout northeast Iowa in an effort to select an appropriate school building design for Buck Creek.[50] Although the leaders of the movement had never publicized the matter, there was never any doubt about where the school would be located. It would be built on the hill just west of the church on land that had already been purchased for that purpose by the trustees of the Buck Creek Church. Ironically, this was the site of the Ku Klux Klan cross burning on the eve of the election. All but one of the teachers then teaching in the soon-to-be-closed country schools was retained for the winter term. The only exception was Katherine McDonald, the teacher in the Buck Creek country school and a Catholic. The board also arranged for the purchase of coal and other materials needed to operate the country schools until the new school was ready for use in fall 1921. It retained an architect to draw up the blueprints for the consolidated school building, and it entered into a contract with a bond company for the printing and issuing of the school bonds.

The Second Battle of Buck Creek: The Opposition Goes to Court

Board members were well aware that Catholic families in the area were angered by the results of the election and by the tactics employed to intimidate voters into supporting the proposition, especially the Ku Klux Klan cross burning on the eve of the election. They had also heard rumors that neighborhood leaders in the Upper Buck Creek, Dufoe, Rose Hill, Wilson, and Harrington neighborhoods had gotten together and retained a lawyer to explore what legal action they might pursue in the matter.[51] However, by late October, the Buck Creek board had heard nothing further on the matter. Hence, they were caught off guard when on November 13, M. J. Yoran, the Delaware County attorney, filed a writ of quo warranto against the Consolidated Independent School District of Buck Creek and its directors. The writ argued that the district was in fact not a legal corporation and that its directors were acting illegally.[52] The *Hopkinton Leader, Manchester Press,* and *Monticello Express* all covered the case, but without much depth. They tended to trivialize the conflict as one of the losing side not taking defeat gracefully and manipulating the complex school laws to their advantage. None contained even a hint that there might be something much more significant that had led to the suit.[53] The board of directors of the new district knew that the battle was not really over minor "irregularities" or inadvertent errors in following the "letter of the law," even though the result of the court case itself might well hinge on such matters.

In August 1920, the federal government announced that it would no longer support the prices of farm commodities at their wartime levels. The golden age of agriculture in Iowa had come to an abrupt end. The economic bubble burst. Crop prices did not drop immediately, but once the fall harvest entered the market, they plummeted. The all-important price of corn kept falling, finally bottoming out at less than one-fourth of what it had been a year earlier.[54] Even more important, the land boom ended, and fear was that boom might turn to bust. Farmers who had borrowed to buy their farms or to add to their holdings during the boom of the preceding year suddenly found that the market value of their new properties was considerably less than they had paid for it. With plummeting crop prices, many of these farmers worried about how they could pay the interest on their debts. Those who had been speculating in farmland — and in the Buck Creek area there had been a number of these — suddenly found themselves in severe financial difficulty. If an election on consolidation had to be held again, financially stressed farmers who had been persuaded to go along with the consolidation project in early September might well vote the other way.

The economic stakes were now higher and the Catholics in the area were mobilized. Maybe the consolidation proponents donning the white robes of the Klan two months earlier had indeed "gone too far." For the first time, local newspapers started to run articles pointing to the virtues of permitting rural schools to be controlled by the rural neighborhoods they served. None, however, published pieces directly critical of rural school consolidation. The *Monticello Express*, for example, wrote approvingly of a situation in Jones County where a country school district retained a teacher even though she was several months short of achieving the required age for receipt of a teaching certificate. Because they knew her and "could trust her with the instruction of their children," the district elected to pay her with private funds rather than accede to the county superintendent's wishes and select from among a list of certified teachers. The article concluded that there were many such women "whose temperament and personality are such as to make them better teachers at seventeen than some other women can ever become at the age of thirty-five" and that it was fortunate that the district exercised such good judgment.[55]

M. J. Yoran, the county attorney, charged that, contrary to the state law, the boundary of the Buck Creek consolidated district did not conform to the subdistrict boundaries of the Union School Township. Hence, it was illegally formed. Yoran maintained that only the county board of education had the authority to change the boundaries of a proposed district from those conforming to preexisting district and subdistrict lines. The county board could change them, however, only if the decision of the county superintendent had been appealed. Even this authority was limited to those instances "when because of meandering streams, irregular boundaries of existing subdistricts or school corporations or the location of highways, the welfare of the consolidated district and the adjoining districts may be better served." [56] The Buck Creek board, the defendants in the case, contended that the boundaries of the district had been established substantially along the subdistrict lines existing on July 23, 1920, the day when the petition was filed with the county superintendent. The key issue turned out to be whether there were eight subdistricts in existence on that date or only seven.

When the Delhi consolidated district was formed in 1915, it took in portions of three subdistricts in northern Union Township (Nos. 1, 2, and 8) — the equivalent of 2.75 sections of territory (see figure 15). With Union No. 1 subdistrict losing most of its territory to Delhi, the township board closed the school. What happened to that portion of the original Union No. 1 subdistrict that remained in Union Township was the key issue in the trial. Two things were clear. First, the voters of Union Township continued to elect eight directors to the township board of directors, even though there were only seven schools to direct. Second, the county auditor's official plat of the taxing units of the county showed only seven subdistricts in Union Township.[57] In fall 1918, the old No. 1 school was purchased by the Union Township board, moved to a site in the Upper Buck Creek neighborhood, and reopened. It operated continuously until the board of directors of the Buck Creek consolidated district closed it. The Union Township board failed to notify either the county superintendent or the county auditor of any boundary changes in its subdistricts in 1918. Until 1918, children living in the old No. 1 subdistrict attended the Upper Buck Creek school (No. 2 subdistrict). This tended to support the plaintiff's contention that the territory of the No. 1 and No. 2 subdistricts not taken into the Delhi district had then been merged to form a single new subdistrict. When the No. 1 school was reopened at its new location, it was with the apparent understanding that the No. 1 school was principally for Catholic children from the Upper Buck

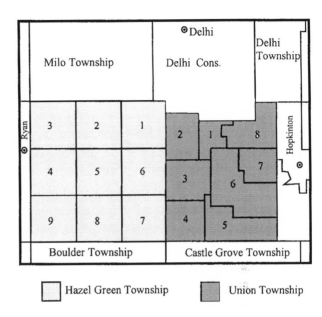

FIGURE 15. *Union and Hazel Green School Townships after the Delhi consolidation in 1915. Map by Peter Li.*

Creek neighborhood and the No. 2 school was for the Methodist children (figure 16).

Yoran argued that the Union No. 1 subdistrict did not exist legally. The election of two board members from the territory of the Union No. 2 subdistrict was within the legal prerogative of the township board, as was the opening of a second school. But, he maintained, neither constituted evidence that a Union No. 1 subdistrict existed legally. Yoran, of course, made no mention of religion in his formal arguments. All participants, however, realized that religion had played a key role in opening the second school in the Union No. 2 subdistrict and that it had also played a role in the formation of the Buck Creek consolidated district itself. He simply maintained that County Superintendent Ottilie, however inadvertently, had acted illegally when he approved the petition asking for the formation of a consolidated district. The boundaries specified in the petition did not conform to those of preexisting subdistricts, and hence the state sought redress by petitioning the legality of that action under quo warranto.

The lawyer representing the Buck Creek board argued that the so-called No. 1 school had been moved to its site to relieve "overcrowded" conditions

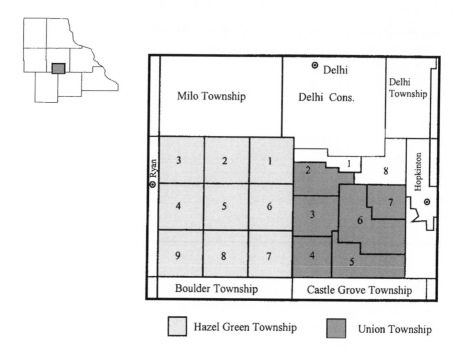

FIGURE 16. *Union and Hazel Green School Townships in 1921. Map by Peter Li.*

in the Upper Buck Creek school and that it was then that the boundaries of the No. 1 subdistrict had been fixed "substantially" as they were indicated in the petition requesting the formation of the Buck Creek consolidated district. Yoran countered with the observation that the minutes of the Union Township board contained no record of this. The Buck Creek board's lawyer pointed out that the plaintiffs had not based their earlier objections to the formation of the district or their appeal of the county superintendent's decision on grounds of the consolidated district's nonconformance with pre-existing subdistrict boundaries. By failing to bring the matter up earlier, he argued, the plaintiff's case lacked substance. Finally, he argued that the court simply lacked the authority to determine the legality or illegality of the Buck Creek consolidated district. The judge disagreed.

On February 21, 1921, Judge E. B. Stiles of the Delaware County District Court ruled against the defendants, holding that the Buck Creek district was illegally constituted and that the board of directors possessed no authority under the law. To make matters worse, the judge ordered the defendants to pay the costs of the court proceedings. The second battle of Buck Creek was over and the opponents of consolidation, comprising mostly Catholics, had won. Another battle was just beginning.

Within a matter of days, Warren H. Winch, the president of the Union School Township board of directors, called a meeting of the board. Winch was the person who only a few days earlier had been the president of the board of directors of the Buck Creek Consolidated School District. By now the board was fully polarized into pro- and antischool consolidation factions. It lost little time in passing a resolution formally delimiting the boundaries of the Union No. 1 subdistrict and directed the president to file a new plat of the Union School Township with the county auditor (figure 16).

The Third Battle of Buck Creek: "If at First You Don't Succeed, Try, Try Again"

The formation of a consolidated school district in the Buck Creek area had been something of a crusade for the Buck Creek Methodists for almost a year. After the cross-burning incident at the Buck Creek Fair, Catholic opposition to consolidation took a similar form. From that time onward, Catholic families, like their Methodist neighbors, increasingly thought of the controversy in Catholic versus Protestant terms. If Catholic families wished to preserve their country schools, they had little choice but to mobilize as Catholics, not simply as members of particular rural neighborhoods. The Buck Creekers were already mobilized as Methodists, but with apparent victory on the consolidation issue seemingly snatched away by the district court, anti-Catholic feelings among them intensified dramatically. Within a matter of a few weeks, the Ku Klux Klan had signed up almost every man in the Buck Creek Church with ten dollars in his pocket. As Buck Creekers flocked to the Klan, cross burnings became more commonplace. Among Catholics, suspicions ran high. Lifetime friendships dissolved as Catholics suspected their Protestant neighbors of belonging to the Klan. Even lifelong friends and neighbors Warren Winch and "Jimmy" Kehoe no longer spoke to each other. The third battle of Buck Creek was on and it was as shrill as it was misguided.

Just as the court case against the Buck Creek consolidated district neared its surprise conclusion, the *Monticello Express* ran a lengthy article describing the success of consolidation across the state. It concluded that "If the progress continues, it may not be long before some of the smaller and even larger cities will have to get a-move-on, if they wish their children to have educational facilities and opportunities at least equal to those of the rural school districts."[58] The article was based either on an interview with Macy Campbell or on one of his many speeches on the subject. Almost surely, it helped steel the resolve of the Buck Creekers to continue in their fight to build a consolidated school. To do otherwise would be to abandon almost a decade of progress in building the Buck Creek community into what was ostensibly one of the most progressive rural communities in the state.

Within a week of the court decision, reports began circulating in Hopkinton that the proponents of consolidation in Buck Creek would begin the consolidation process all over again. This time every step in the procedure would be "scanned carefully to avoid any legal technicalities."[59] The directors of the now defunct Buck Creek consolidated district had initially intended to appeal the decision. However, they abandoned the idea once their lawyer advised them that the errors in the original proceedings were so great as to doom any chance of success. They set to work immediately, first in providing the legal description of the district's boundaries and then with obtaining signatures on the consolidation petition. Despite the dramatic changes for the worse in the farm economy, proponents had surprisingly little difficulty in obtaining the requisite number of signatures. The explanation for this lies in the remarkable growth of the Klan among Protestant, especially Methodist, families in the area. The more spectacular cross burnings occurred in conjunction with the drive to obtain signatures on the petition to form a consolidated district in Buck Creek, but there were others. Several crosses, for example, were set ablaze in or near Catholic neighborhoods, especially in Upper Buck Creek, near the Castle Grove Church, and in the Wilson neighborhood.[60] While the aim of these may have been to intimidate Catholic families in the area, they had quite the opposite effect.

On April 12, 1921, a new petition was filed with the county superintendent. Except for excluding 160 acres that had been ceded to the now formally delimited Union No. 1 subdistrict, the boundaries of the proposed district were identical to those in the original proposal. This small tract of land was highly dissected, of low value, and belonged to Catholic families; hence Buck Creekers were glad to be rid of it. They also argued that it gave Union No. 1 enough territory to continue as a subdistrict in what was left of Union School Township (just over seven sections), if consolidation passed. The petition contained 88 signatures and was accompanied by an affidavit signed by Harry B. Sill maintaining that the proposed district contained 240 qualified voters — twice as many as had been claimed in the first affidavit because women were now counted as "qualified" to vote. Eighty-eight signatures was only ten more than the minimum one-third required by law, indicating that proponents were anxious to get the issue back on the ballot as soon as possible.

A delegation of five or six men from the Buck Creek Church, including

Cliff Willard, Harry Sill, and "Happy" Stead, filed the petition with the county superintendent's office in Manchester. Willard was a new convert to the cause of building a consolidated school in Buck Creek. He swung his support over only after Grant assured him that his Catholic neighbors, the Kings and the Britts, would not be forced into the consolidated district. The Kings and the Britts owned the 160 acres referred to above that had been ceded to the Union No. 1 subdistrict. The delegation must have been confident of success, because on the train trip to Manchester they stopped in Oneida to examine the consolidated school there and to examine the school wagons used to transport students. Of the consolidated districts in Delaware County, Oneida was the only one that transported almost all its pupils to the school — as would also be the case in any Buck Creek district. On the return trip, after having been assured by County Superintendent Ottilie that the petition was in proper order and that he would approve it, the delegation noticed some men from the Dufoe and Rose Hill neighborhoods — Catholics all — at the back of the coach. When the Catholic group noticed the Buck Creek delegation, they began talking loudly about the "damned Klansmen" of the Buck Creek Church who were pushing people around trying to get a consolidated school built. Mike Evers, a fiery Irish American with a reputation as a fighter, was in the Catholic group. As told by Willard's son, "Oh he [Mike Evers] could whip anything he could whip. He was shooting off his mouth about the Klan and the school — that they shouldn't have it and so on. And so my dad got up and walked back there. He says, "Does that include me?" I don't know just what Evers said, but he didn't get up. He knew better. Evers was a fighter, but he wasn't in my dad's class. My dad was a big man and about forty-three at that time."[61] While Evers may well have remained seated because of Willard's size, he was also probably aware that Willard had, at least until recently, been one of the few people in the Buck Creek Church who treated Catholics fairly, even on the consolidated school issue.

Two days later, April 14, the *Hopkinton Leader* carried a notice of the county superintendent's receipt of the petition to form the Buck Creek Consolidated Independent District. The same issue also contained a legal description of the proposed district and a notice that any objections to its boundaries needed to be filed with the county superintendent by April 20. The next day the Hopkinton school board voted to permit all the schoolchildren from the Best district to attend the graded elementary school in Hopkinton. The Best district was a subdistrict of South Fork School Township adjacent to the Hopkinton school district on the latter's east side. The South Fork School Township agreed to pay the Hopkinton district a flat rate of $500 for the next school year, while the Best district provided for the transportation of its students to Hopkinton. Although contractual relationships of this sort had been permitted for more than two decades, this appears to have been the first instance of one being formalized in Delaware County. This served as a reminder that consolidation was not the only alternative available to a rural district or subdistrict interested in having its students attend a modern graded school. In particular, the reminder seemed to be directed at the many families in Union Township to whom Hopkinton was more accessible than the proposed site of the new Buck Creek school. While this helped the anticonsolidation cause, opponents of the Buck Creek proposal had less than a week to organize and file their objections with the county superintendent. To make matters worse, just when opponents began circulating petitions objecting to the formation of the district, a major snowstorm hit the area, making travel difficult and dangerous for several days.[62] Nevertheless, warmed by the thought of those burning crosses, and determined to be heard this time, opponents succeeded in obtaining a remarkably large number of signatures protesting the formation of the district.

All told, 232 persons registered their objections to the formation of the district by signing one of five petitions circulated throughout the area. The first petition, signed by 102 voters and taxpayers from Hazel Green Township, was filed on April 20, 1921. It read quite simply: "We the undersigners, voters and taxpayers of Hazel Green Twp., Delaware Co., Ia. do most emphatically protest against the incorporation of any part of the Hazel Green District into the Buck Creek Consolidation as outlined in your proclamation published in the Hopkinton Leader of April 14, 1921. We also claim that the law does not intend that the interests of one locality should be jeopardized because of the prior action of another."

Most of those signing were Catholics. Some no doubt were loath to lose eight sections of prime farmland to the Buck Creek district because it reduced the tax base available for the provision of schools in Hazel Green Township. Many more, however, mobilized and opposed the formation of the Buck Creek district because of the vehement anti-Catholic sentiment of Buck Creekers. Another petition filed by a second contingent of forty-three opponents from subdistricts No. 6 and No. 7 in Hazel Green Township objected "to being forcibly and against the will of a large majority of the residents and taxpayers included" in the consolidated district. They appealed to the superintendent to "set out and not include" their subdistricts.

Very few men and women in the affected subdistricts in Hazel Green

Township failed to sign one of these two petitions. This served to indicate that if the results of the election hinged on the support it received in the Hazel Green portion of the district, it would be defeated soundly. The only ones who did not sign were a few prominent members of the Buck Creek Church — the Thompsons, the Shovers, and the Houstons. Many people from those portions of Hazel Green not included in the proposed district also signed the first of these petitions. Apparently they were trying to impress upon Ottilie that the formation of the Buck Creek district as proposed would adversely affect the quality of education in the rest of Hazel Green Township.

Two identically worded petitions protesting consolidation were filed by the residents of the Union Township portion of the proposed district. Overwhelmingly the signers were from the Castle Grove neighborhood, but they also included a handful of persons from the Nos. 3 and 6 subdistricts. It stated that the undersigned "emphatically protest against the consolidation of schools . . . for reasons that the taxpayers are hard hit enough at the present time without additional burdens, also the proposed location of the school is inaccessible to a large number of the pupils of said district and for many other valid reasons that should appeal to an unselfish and fair minded adjudication." The first of these was signed by thirty-three people and the second by ten persons, all from the No. 4 subdistrict. Because of the storm, the latter was filed a day late, but was apparently considered nonetheless. At least one adult from every Catholic household in these four subdistricts signed one of the two petitions. Also signing were a number of Protestant tenants not affiliated with the Buck Creek Church and a few Protestants who were either opposed to the township going into debt to build a new school or found the Ku Klux Klan activities on its behalf repugnant.

It is important to note that forty persons, a majority of the voters in the three Union Township subdistricts excluded from the proposed district, also signed petitions objecting to the formation of the district. These were the voters whose silence supposedly had been secured by their exclusion from the proposal the previous year. Now, Klan activities in support of consolidation, coupled with the dramatic change for the worse in the regional economy, forced a reevaluation and political mobilization among the predominantly Catholic families in these subdistricts. Their objections were

1. That it conflicts with the spirit and also the letter of the law as laid down in Acts of the 37th and 38th Gen. Assembly.
2. That because of the outline the Districts in which we live are so iso-

lated that an Independent single school is impossible and that the territory so isolated, being in the form of an ell (L) cannot do justice to the children with less than three schools.

3. That the territory does not comprise but 7 and a fraction sections while the law contemplates 12 sec. for (3) three schools or four for one school.

The "letter of the law" in the first objection referred to the consolidation statute requiring that the boundaries of a consolidated district correspond with district and subdistrict boundaries already established. This provision had been the one upon which the district court's decision had been based. The voters from the now officially delimited Union No. 1 subdistrict maintained that their territory was still simply part of Union No. 2. Its formal delimitation by the reconvened Union Township board the previous month was forced upon them against their will as part of the scheme to create a Buck Creek consolidated district. In short, they maintained that an additional three sections of territory should be excluded from the proposal. This would have brought all of the old Upper Buck Creek neighborhood together again in a single subdistrict. It would also have left the new, but downsized, Union School Township with somewhat more than ten sections of territory. Ten sections was the minimum size territory for a school township to support the three country schools that the protesters felt necessary — a figure still below the twelve sections dictated by tradition. Those signing this last petition included both Catholics and Protestants approximately in proportion to their relative numbers in the three subdistricts. It even included at least two families who were members of the Buck Creek Church. With the downturn in the economy, families in the northern one-third of Union Township genuinely feared that they would be unable to support their country schools with the relatively meager tax base they would have if the Buck Creek consolidated district was formed. The farmland in this area was generally of poorer quality than that found in other neighborhoods in the township. When they claimed that the proposed district violated the "spirit" of the law laid down by the 37th and 38th General Assemblies, they were referring to changes in the consolidation laws intended to ensure that rural school consolidation would not leave adjoining districts or subdistricts with too few resources to provide a good quality education for their children.

The fifth and final petition was filed on behalf of six landowners from Hopkinton who owned land in Union Township along the Maquoketa River south of Hopkinton. Six years earlier, one of the protesters, F. E. Williamson, had been one of the advocates of forming a consolidated district centered on Hopkinton. These protesters did not object to consolidation in principle. They simply opposed having their properties included with the Buck Creek consolidated district. They realized that the children of their tenants could be served by the Hopkinton school district at far less cost on a contractual basis, like that extended to the Best district.

Of the 232 persons protesting the formation of the Buck Creek consolidated district, at least 96 lived within the proposed boundaries of the district. This was 20 more than had voted against the earlier proposal and 8 more than the number signing the petition urging the formation of the district. The sheer number of protesters led the leaders of the opposition to think they might have a good chance of convincing the county superintendent or the county board of education to sustain their objections this time. If all were sustained, there would have been less than sixteen sections of territory remaining for inclusion in the consolidated district, thereby killing the proposal.

At the hearing before the county superintendent on April 25, 1921, ten men representing all of those signing the remonstrances against the formation of the district, except for those signing the fourth petition, testified. Each of these was well respected and came from a family with a long history in the area. These included F. E. Williamson, the president of one of the two banks in Hopkinton and the treasurer of the Hopkinton School District; Reuben Moulton, farmer and former director of the Union No. 3 subdistrict; W. P. Hogan, farmer, major landowner, and former school director from Union No. 5; W. J. Kehoe, farm owner-operator and school director from Union No. 4; Frank G. Kehoe, farm owner-operator and former school director from Union No. 6; W. H. Milroy, farm renter from Union No. 6; Cliff Dighton, farm renter from Union No. 6; John Flanagan, Jr., farm renter from Union No. 6; Thomas Supple, farm owner-operator from Hazel Green No. 7, and J. E. Harrington, farm owner-operator and former director from Hazel Green No. 6. Moulton had been a member of the Buck Creek Church but left it because of his opposition to the Klan. Other Moultons in the Buck Creek neighborhood were staunch supporters of consolidation. Dighton and Milroy were Methodists but attended church in Hopkinton, ostensibly because of Klan involvement in the Buck Creek Church. All the others, except for Williamson, a Presbyterian, were Catholics and members of either the Castle Grove or Ryan Parishes. After listening to their testimony, County Superintendent Ottilie perfunctorily and summarily overruled their objections and informed them that they had ten days to file an appeal of his decision to the county board of education.[63]

Objectors filed their appeal on April 30, well within the ten-day period specified by law. Ottilie set May 10 as the date for the county board to meet. However, in apparent ignorance of the law, he failed to notify each of the objectors of the time and place for the hearing of the appeal by registered letter. Nonetheless, most of the objectors who had testified before the county superintendent on April 25 presented their objections again at the May 10 meeting of the county board called for that purpose.

Overruling both sets of objections, the county board sustained the decision of the county superintendent and approved the boundaries of the district as proposed in the petition of April 12.[64] The objectors from Hazel Green and Union Township who testified were surprised and infuriated when the county board took the time to also hear presentations from the advocates of consolidation from the Buck Creek Church. They maintained correctly that the hearing was supposed to be devoted to hearing and evaluating their objections to the boundaries of the district, not to be a debate on the merits of consolidation. They argued that the hearing was a charade, a "put-up deal."[65] Several of those who had appeared before the county superintendent on April 25 did not attend the appeal. One of these, Reuben Moulton, objected to the fact that the county superintendent had not informed him of the time and place of the appeal. Therefore, he maintained that the hearing had not been a legal hearing. Recognizing that Moulton was correct, Ottilie had no recourse but to go through the whole appeal process again. Therefore, on May 19 a second notice of the petition to form the Buck Creek consolidated district was published in the *Leader*. May 26 was set as the date by which objections to the proposal had to be filed. Except for the Hopkinton businessmen, those who had filed objections to the formation of the Buck Creek district in April refiled the same objections, complete with the same set of petitions they had introduced earlier. On May 31, Ottilie again overruled them and the objectors reappealed the decision to the county board of education. Ottilie set June 14 as the date for the appeal, and this time he notified all of the objectors by registered mail.

Maintaining that the whole process was a sham, none of the objectors attended the appeal. Instead they retained a lawyer, hoping he could identify grounds to contest the legality of the district should it be approved by the voters. The county board minutes indicate simply that "the matter of establishing the boundaries of the Buck Creek Consolidated School District in Delaware Co. was brought up for discussion and the objections read, the appellants not being present nor represented." The county board unanimously overruled the objections; Ottilie set the election on the proposed district for June 23, 1921.

As if to rally the faithful of Buck Creek, on the day of the election the

Hopkinton Leader carried an announcement that Chalice had received an honorary Doctor of Divinity degree from Upper Iowa University at its recent graduation exercises. The announcement appeared as a headline on the first page. The piece noted that the award was made in recognition of Chalice's "conspicuous service in the rural field." It went on to note that "Doctor Chalice" had "won great credit and wide fame for his work and successes in reviving the Buck Creek Church, now known as one of the most outstanding rural churches in Iowa."

The election turned out to be one of the most hotly contested ever held in Delaware County. Practically every eligible voter, and perhaps even a few more, showed up to vote at the old Buck Creek country schoolhouse.[66] Meetings and rallies in support of the consolidation issue were held at the Buck Creek Church every evening during the week before to the election. Grant, "Happy" Stead, Warren Winch, Harry Sill, and others arranged transportation to the polls for every voter known to support, or who could be persuaded to support, the consolidation project. Grant was overheard encouraging the transportation committee to "bring them in from the cemetery by the cart load if necessary." Later, opponents would claim that more than a few ghostly voters did participate in the election.[67] Reverend and Mrs. Grant, living near the school as they did, kept track of who had voted and were on the telephone throughout the day getting out the vote. Although unconfirmed, it was rumored that the "Catholics" were engaging in similar activities to get out the negative vote. Yes, there were also rumors that crosses blazed almost every night of the week leading up to the election. The *Leader* published its story of the election in somewhat heroic terms as follows:

At the special election held at Buck Creek last Thursday, the vote for a second time on the question of consolidation of schools, the proposition won by a vote of 129 affirmative to 103 negative votes. The opposition to the formation of the district was well organized and brought every possible vote to their assistance. Those favoring the project were equally active, and both sides appeared to be confident of winning. The eagerness of those affected by the question was quickly shown as soon as the hour for the opening of the polls came. The larger part of the vote was in very quickly. Very naturally, there is jubilation on the part of the supporters of the consolidated school, who have fought so long and loyally and for a second time win with a handsome majority in its favor. The first election was held a little less than a year ago. The organizers went promptly ahead with the election of a board of directors and were preparing to function when legal proceedings on the part of the minority discovered technical irregularities which nullified all the work. Nothing daunted, the majority again circulated petitions and the election last week, which is believed to have been reached in conformity with every requirement of the law, is confirmation of their contention that the majority of the people of the territory earnestly desire improved school conditions. A special meeting of the district is called for Friday, July 8, as will be noted by the notice elsewhere in the Leader, at which time five directors will be voted for. The next step following will be that of providing for a suitable building for the proposed school.[68]

The special election to select directors for the new district was held in the Buck Creek Church rather than in the Buck Creek country schoolhouse as was customary. The same board that had been elected a year earlier was reelected by acclamation. If any Catholics participated in that election, they went unnoticed. The struggle was finally over. The Buck Creekers had their consolidated district (figure 17); but realists in the congregation knew that additional hurdles probably lay ahead. The Delhi district consolidated in 1915, but voters there still had not approved the issuance of bonds for build-

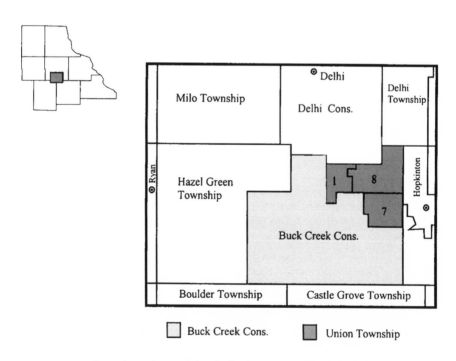

FIGURE 17. *The Buck Creek Consolidated School District, 1921. Map by Peter Li.*

ing an addition to the Delhi school. These faded into the background as the meeting became yet another opportunity for Buck Creekers to celebrate their community accomplishment.

The Aftermath: Paying for the School, Further Legal Complications

The new Buck Creek board was in for a rude awakening. A school building of the proportions they wanted, which in 1915 could have been built for $20,000, was projected to cost approximately $60,000. Furthermore, this figure did not include the dormitory or "teacherage" they had earlier thought would be necessary to attract teachers of a quality comparable to those teaching in the better town schools. Once the Buck Creek school was in operation, eighth-grade graduates would no longer be eligible to attend high school in Hopkinton, Monticello, Delhi, or Ryan at the township's expense. Therefore, to fulfill its promise educationally, the board felt that the high school department of the new consolidated school had to be at least as good as that of these schools. The key question was, however, could they afford it? What level of taxation could be shouldered by taxpayers in the new district, without risking defeat of the bond issue? The election creating the district won by a scant twenty-six votes. Surely those who voted against the district could not easily be won over to support a bond issue for building a school that would, at a minimum, quadruple the taxes of farm families in the area. It was clear that Catholic families opposed building the school. The danger now was that there might be an erosion of support among Buck Creekers themselves, once they realized the actual costs to be incurred. At the very least, the teacherage would have to go. The board felt that they might need to wait to see if the farm commodity prices would rebound later in the summer or fall. The only relatively good news financially, at least for those living in the Union Township portion of the district, was that because of the addition of the high-value prairie farmland in Hazel Green Township to the Buck Creek district, the tax levy in the Union Township portion of the district needed to run country schools until the new school was built could be reduced. The reduction was from 35 mills to 22.1 mills, the levy already in effect in Hazel Green Township.

Ironically, just when the Buck Creekers finally got their consolidated district, local newspapers in the county began for the first time in more than a decade publishing pieces critical of consolidation. On July 28, 1921, the *Manchester Press* reprinted two letters that had appeared earlier in *Capper's Farmer*. The first was written by C. E. Lasley, a farmer from Van Buren County. It suggested that information about the success of consolidation obtained from surveys undertaken by country superintendents was misleading at best and possibly manipulated. Lasley wrote of the tax situation in his district: "We have been consolidated for four years and are sitting on a red hot stove, but we can't rise. We have a big elephant and no feed. Our school levy has increased from 14 mills to 53 mills, and we are going behind every year. My school tax for 1920 on 80 acres of 100-dollar land was $45.52." He also argued that, contrary to the claims of the advocates of consolidation,

> it is harder to sell land in a consolidated district than outside. In 1919 there were about 14 farms changed hands in one of our three consolidated districts in Davis and Van Buren counties and consolidation enthusiasts pointed to this as a great endorsement of consolidation. But while they were singing the praises of the 14 men who bought farms in their district they never mentioned that 14 men who had had the experience had sold out and left the district. Most of us in our district have come to regard our school as a huge and expensive joke.
>
> None of us cares to go back to exactly the old way because we all want good schools for our children, but in my opinion the better way would be to maintain the eighth grade rural schools and have a township high school, centrally located, and when a pupil has passed the eighth grade he is old enough and large enough to transport himself to the center of the township if he wishes to attend high school.

The second letter, written by an unnamed woman, was critical of consolidation and the state's laws dealing with it. First, she pointed to the provision in the consolidation laws requiring that the school be located in a town or village, if one was included in the district. She noted that the flaw in this provision was that it provided no assurance that the school would be centrally located vis-à-vis its rural patrons. Lacking this assurance, excessive travel times had to be borne by some students. Second, she noted that the laws required only that bus routes be laid out such that no student was required to walk more than two miles to get on the bus — a distance that was already the maximum children were required to walk to a country school. Hence, the total travel time could be much greater than it had been under the country school system. Third, if the district included a village of less than 200 inhabitants, then no separate balloting of village and countryside was required. She argued that this gave voters of the village the power to force those in districts and subdistricts outside the village into a consolidated district against their will. She claimed that, on average, farm families were overwhelmingly opposed to consolidation and that they were organizing protests all over the state. Nonetheless, she feared that farmers were fighting "with their backs to the wall." When all was said and done, the "state superintendent has the power to veto an appeal if he sees fit."

On August 11, 1921, the *Manchester Press* reprinted another letter critical of consolidation. This one was from *Wallace's Farmer*. It was written by a farmer living in the New Providence consolidated district in Hardin County who had had children in the consolidated school every year since it opened in 1913. He was very critical of his children having to endure being transported 4.75 miles to school in unheated wagons and sleds, often being gone from home from 6:30 a.m. to 6:00 p.m. He proclaimed that "these conditions are the things that cause farmers to fight consolidation. . . . It is mighty poor business to spend a hundred thousand dollars for a schoolhouse and then thousands more for a faculty; then impose such horrible conditions on the farmers' children that they can not be in condition to receive instruction." He recommended that if consolidation was to be forced on the farmer, then the state should set standards for school buses to assure their safety and comfort. Finally he recommended that the state outlaw large districts. "The state should be redistricted into districts of sixteen sections each, allowing the patrons of each new district to say whether they shall consolidate or continue to use their four small schools." He added:

> This will get us away from one of the evils of the present system. At the present time, some small poverty-stricken town will need a new schoolhouse, and they can't raise sufficient money to build what they want. So they begin to work for consolidation, with a view of forcing the farmers of the community into building the schoolhouse for them, or paying for at least 90 percent of it. Redistrict the state, and the small town folks can have the kind of school they want if they can pay for it, and the farmers can have their own schools and control them. . . . [Farmers] want the system that will give our children the greatest opportunities with as few hardships as possible, and at the least possible cost.

The reprinting of these letters seems to have been sparked by consolidation controversies in the Lamont and Masonville areas west of Manchester. Like the Buck Creek controversy, both of these had become politicized locally as struggles between Catholics and Protestants over who was to control the public schools. What is more important, however, they indicate that the local press was finally willing to give consolidation opponents a forum to voice their concerns. The Buck Creek controversy certainly helped pave the way for this change in policy.

As the summer of 1921 wore on and crop prices dipped still lower, more and more farmers in Delaware County began to wonder if perhaps rural school consolidation was indeed a "huge and expensive joke" on them. In short, rural school consolidation was recognized as having the potential for rending asunder rural neighborhoods and undermining the spirit of neighborhood cooperation upon which family farming had always depended. In early September, the *Manchester Press* also printed a syndicated piece by the *Chicago Tribune* describing the dramatic impact of falling corn prices in the Midwest. It noted that corn in Nebraska was fetching only 28 cents a bushel and was expected to fall to less than 25 cents once the new crop entered the market. Oats were down to 18 cents. With coal prices going up, "farmers will be burning corn to keep warm in the coming winter." [69] The combination of internecine conflict over consolidation and the collapse of the farm economy had finally led the *Manchester Press*, the county's leading newspaper, to question whether rural school consolidation was worth the cost. "In some districts the tax figures are as high as $7 per acre. . . . Are we not in danger of making our rural educational facilities such a burden to the patron as to become insupportable? . . . [I]t is a serious question with us if we are not going to extremes in this consolidated school business," wrote the editor. [70]

The chief selling point of rural school consolidation among Iowa farm families had always been that the consolidated school brought a modern, yet still rural community-controlled high school within easy reach of every farm child, both physically and economically. The disempowering of rural neighborhoods vis-à-vis more expansive communities and conflicts between rival conceptions of community were contentious from the earliest days of the consolidation movement in Iowa. By 1921, however, the economic calculus of rural school consolidation was also centrally on the public agenda. The next week the *Manchester Press* reprinted an editorial from the *Independence Bulletin-Journal*, which argued that the emphasis on the high school was totally misplaced:

> Only a small proportion of our youth go through the high schools and a still smaller proportion of those go to college. And yet our whole system is based upon the latter minor fraction. And the worst of the situation is that the policy is so expensive that the burden of taxation has become crushing. Our schools have not only drilled into the worst possible class methods but their cost increases every year. . . . It is the belief of this paper that the public should look the situation squarely in the face and determine that while every American child should have the opportunity to secure a thorough groundwork in the fundamentals and therefore be-

come fitted for good citizenship, the small minority who aspire to higher education should be allowed to work out their own salvation.[71]

The Buck Creek board found itself in a very difficult position. While the consolidated district had finally obtained voter approval, the issue of consolidation itself appeared to be rapidly losing the support of opinion leaders in the county. On the one hand, the board was tempted to proceed with readying a bond issue proposal to submit to the voters. If they delayed, they risked building costs rising higher, farm prices falling lower, and public opinion switching even more decisively against consolidation. On the other, consolidation opponents and a growing number of Buck Creek Church members themselves argued that the district could not afford to go ahead with the proposal until the economy improved. The board still had not reached resolution on the matter, when, on September 30, Reuben Moulton, acting on behalf of the opponents of consolidation, filed suit against the board in the district court. His petition charged that the district had been illegally formed and that its directors possessed no authority to continue with steps to build the school.[72]

Word of Moulton's case had been leaked the week before. The promise of continued conflict in the Buck Creek area, plus similar controversies at Masonville and Lamont, finally prompted the *Manchester Press* to come out against any further consolidation attempts in Delaware County. It labeled consolidation a "breeder of mischief," contending that Delaware County's experience with consolidation "to date has been a serial story of dissension, bitter controversy and factional hostility. Communities have been rent apart, families divided and resentments aroused which will not [quiet] down in a decade. This paper very seriously questions if it is worth the cost."[73]

This drew a sharp response from a member of the county board of education, who argued that consolidation was a significant step forward. Because of it, there were ten times as many high school graduates in the United States as there had been thirty years earlier. In the same issue the *Press* replied that it remained convinced

that in both High and consolidated schools we are following fads which are not only costly but inefficient. It is the opinion of this paper that instead of giving our children in these schools the solid fundamentals of knowledge, branches of real substance which they will be able to retain and make use of in after life, we are giving them a smattering of this and that, rushing them through to graduation at an early age, cramming them full of hurriedly digested matter which is forgotten as soon as learned, and in effect trying to turn out a university product before the pupil is out of his teens. . . . As to the consolidated school being a provoker of neighborhood contention, that fact is too well established to require elaboration. It is so in all parts of Iowa and in many parts of Delaware County, and we repeat that in its results as a disturber of community harmony and in its effects measured in a practical and lasting education, we could spend our money to much greater advantage.[74]

The *Manchester Press* was correct in its claim that the Moulton case would delay any final resolution of the consolidation controversy. Indeed, it appears that Moulton's purpose in filing suit had been to tie up the matter in the courts long enough for the worsening farm economy to bring enough Buck Creekers "back to their senses." Moulton's case rested on whether the county superintendent's failure to notify those objecting to the consolidation by registered letter in April was corrected by his reinitiating the appeal process or whether that failure resulted in him losing jurisdiction over the matter. The case was heard on November 1, 1921. On November 17, Judge Horrace Boies found that the county superintendent had acted within his authority and that the Buck Creek district had been formed legally. Moulton and his Catholic friends had lost. They needed to regroup and explore their options. After several weeks of meetings held in Catholic homes and in the hall behind the Castle Grove Church had resulted in more than enough pledges to cover the legal fees, they filed an appeal of Boies's decision with the Iowa Supreme Court on December 29, 1921.[75]

At least for the fall 1921 school term, the board of directors of the Buck Creek consolidated district had no choice but to continue operating the existing country schools. They simply took over the operation of these schools from the Union and Hazel Green School Township boards. By the next fall, the supreme court still had not rendered its decision. Apparently confident that the district court's judgment would be upheld, the Buck Creek board went ahead with its preparations for issuing bonds to build the consolidated school. It also had to complete its plans on how to use the existing country schools until the consolidated school was built. Once consolidation opponents, this time lead by "Babe" Kehoe, got wind of this, their counsel requested and received a restraining order from the supreme court on December 14, 1922. The order prohibited the removal of the schoolhouses in Union No. 4 and Hazel Green No. 7 subdistricts and prohibited the Buck Creek board from obligating the district in any way for the construction of a new school building. This buoyed the spirits of opponents, giving them new hope that they might succeed in their appeal after all. It also served to fan the anti-Catholic sentiments of Buck Creekers even further and to stiffen their resolve to see the matter of the consolidated school through to a successful conclusion at almost any cost. The continuing activities of the Ku Klux Klan and its influence in the Buck Creek Church produced a major crisis within the church. The matter came to a head over Grant's retention as pastor and the amount of his (or his replacement's) salary.

Grant had fallen out of favor with the Klan. Klan leaders in the church sought to reduce his salary, claiming that in the depressed agricultural conditions they could no longer afford to pay the highest salary in the county. As Curtis Griggs put it: "The people in the church couldn't pay their minister but they had $10.00 to pay to join the Klan. That made much trouble in the Methodist church."[76] Grant left Buck Creek in October 1922 to assume the pastorate in Geneseo Township in Tama County. Geneseo Township was a Methodist place much like Buck Creek, which had in the previous year completed construction of an open-country consolidated school.[77] His replacement was O. J. Felter, a former pastor of the Colesburg Methodist Church who had been active in the drive to consolidate the schools in that area five years earlier. One widely circulated rumor at the time was that Felter was a member of the Klan.[78]

The case was finally resolved on February 17, 1923, when the supreme court ruled that the Buck Creek Consolidated Independent District had been legally organized.[79] The boundaries of the school districts in Delaware County would remain fixed for the next three decades (figure 18). The board of directors of the Buck Creek consolidated district had already arranged with a contractor to build the school and with a bond company in Davenport to sell bonds in the amount of $60,000 to pay for it, pending the court's decision and voter approval of the bond issue. The bond issue passed handily, apparently with little opposition.[80] By late spring, construction on the new school building had begun and the board was actively seeking a superintendent and a full complement of teachers.[81]

The new school would not be completed until the spring term in 1924. Therefore, for the 1923–24 school year, the Buck Creek board had to hire teachers who were willing and capable of teaching all eight grades in one of the six country schools during the fall and winter terms, before they assumed their more specialized teaching roles in the consolidated school in the spring. Lee H. Campbell was hired as the district's first superintendent at a salary of $255 per month for nine months — approximately three times higher than the salary of any of the country school teachers then employed in the district. Two of the teachers hired were slated to teach in the

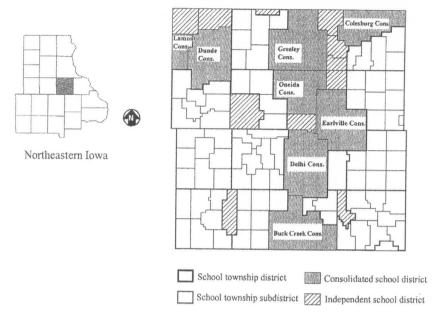

Northeastern Iowa

| | School township district | | Consolidated school district |
| | School township subdistrict | | Independent school district |

FIGURE 18. *School districts of Delaware County, ca. 1925. Map by Peter Li.*

high school department of the consolidated school when it opened. The other four would assume responsibility for two grades each in its grade school department. Only two of these teachers were rehired for the 1924–25 school year.

Beginning in 1924–25, there were two high school teachers. One was a woman who also served as the school's principal. The other was a man, who in addition to his teaching responsibilities in manual training and agriculture, served as director of athletics. The four grade school teachers were all women, each with the responsibility for teaching two grades. This pattern was followed for the remainder of the decade.

All students except those within the immediate vicinity of the school were transported to school in horsedrawn wagons (see figure 19). The wagons were provided by those individuals who won contracts from the school board to provide transportation to students along one or more of the district's eight routes. The lengths of the routes ranged from 2.75 to 7 miles in length. In 1926, the cost of providing transportation in the district was approximately $400.00 per month, with costs of individual routes running from $80.00 per month for the longest route to $29.50 for the shortest.[82] Early each July the board scheduled an afternoon at the school when they would sit and receive bids for the various routes. As was stated in its July 1,

1926, announcement, the board reserved "the right to reject any or all bids."[83] In practice, though, only members of the Buck Creek Church bid successfully.

As had long been the practice in the country schools of the area, a two-week school vacation was scheduled in late October and early November so students could assist in the harvest. Probably the biggest difference between the new Buck Creek school and its predecessors was in the prominence given to organized athletic competition. The Buck Creek school had been open less than a year before it fielded its first basketball teams for both boys and girls. In fall 1926, Buck Creek fielded its first football team.[84]

From 1925, when it graduated its first class, until it was closed in 1959, 345 students graduated from the Buck Creek high school — an average of just under ten per year. The size of the average graduating class was 7.6 in the 1920s, 9.6 in the 1930s, 10.1 for the 1940s, and 10.7 for the 1950s. The largest graduating class was 19 in 1944, and the smallest was 4 in 1931. In 1924, 20 students (9 girls and 11 boys) graduated from the eighth grade of the Buck Creek Consolidated School. Of these, only 7 (4 girls and 3 boys) went on to graduate from the Buck Creek High School. Like many rural Iowans, farm families in the Buck Creek district wanted to have their own high school even though only a minority of their children would ever graduate from it in the years before the end of World War II. Catholic children in the district attended the consolidated school through their grade school years.

FIGURE 19. *Buck Creek school wagon, ca. 1930. Photograph courtesy of Mrs. Gertrude Green, Hopkinton, Iowa.*

They had no choice. Until the 1950s, very few Catholic children, however, attended high school in Buck Creek and fewer still graduated. By early 1926, some members of the Buck Creek congregation appear to have had second thoughts about where the Buck Creek community was heading under the influence of the Ku Klux Klan. They invited Gilbert Chalice, then the pastor of the one of the largest Protestant churches in the state — the Trinity Methodist Church of Cedar Rapids — to speak at the Buck Creek Church's annual father and son banquet on February 20. He also gave the sermon at the regular Sunday service the next day. The title of his sermon was "Who are the leaders of Buck Creek Community and where are they leading Us?"[85]

Between 1925 and 1939, of the 134 students graduating from the Buck Creek High School, only 8 were from Catholic families. Only the King family in Upper Buck Creek seems to have regularly sent its children to high school in Buck Creek. The most prominent Catholic family in the district, the Kehoes, seldom did so. Overwhelmingly, those completing high school in the Buck Creek school were from families in the Buck Creek Methodist Church who had been prominent in the fight to form the consolidated district. Two-thirds of the graduates during this period fell into this category. The board of directors of the district remained tightly under the control of the Buck Creek Church for its almost forty years of existence; throughout the 1920s and 1930s all directors were members of that church. Although it may not have been written into their contracts, all teachers and other employees of the district were either members of the Buck Creek Church or joined soon after securing their positions. The district's first superintendent, Lee Campbell, not only became a member of the church, he also performed as its lay pastor, filling in for the regular minister on numerous occasions.[86]

Catholic families began leaving the district in increasing numbers and as they did their places were taken by Protestants, most of whom became affiliated with the Buck Creek Church. With the onset of the Great Depression, and the decreased ability of farmers to make their mortgage payments, the departure of Catholic families was hastened still further. The residue of bad feelings between Catholics and Protestants caused by the zealotry of the Buck Creekers in their drive to consolidate the rural schools in the area rendered Buck Creek an undesirable place for Catholic farm families. The neighborhood system of family farming was predicated on unequivocal trust and sharing between neighbors. The school controversy had shattered this trust. In so doing it excluded most Catholic families from easy access to the neighborhood-like system of family farming that was still available to most Methodists in the area.

Interest in the Buck Creek school heightened considerably in 1930, when the Buck Creek boys basketball team won the Class B district tournament in Manchester and went on to earn two victories over larger schools in the regional tournament before losing in the championship game. As recorded in the local press, it was "a truly remarkable showing the Buck Creek Team made and one to be proud of. The feat has never been duplicated in the annals of Delaware County basketball, the nearest to accomplish it was the high school team of Hopkinton a few years back who were defeated after playing in the first game at Iowa City. People who had never heard of Buck Creek will remember for a long time to come the fine team put out by the school and the country lads who almost annexed the title. The refereeing was of high class and a large percent of the crowd pulled for Buck Creek to win. Three carloads of fans from the neighborhood made the trip to Waterloo Saturday." [87]

Buck Creek was no longer a place whose identity derived principally from its past successes in creating a vibrant rural Methodist community and the controversy it spawned over the formation of one of the few purely rural consolidated school districts in the state. Buck Creek was now recognized in the record books of the Boys State Athletic Association, and hence, in a larger popular sense, Buck Creek had arrived historically; it had become a real place. Buck Creekers had shown that new purely rural communities could be forged in the countryside and that their farm boys could compete on even terms with those of the towns. No longer did Buck Creekers have to send their children to Hopkinton for high school.

If ever a place was created by following the social policy prescriptions and ideology of the Country Life movement, it was Buck Creek. Indeed, for a time it was held up as an exemplar to be followed by those wishing to conjoin the activities of the local churches and the state in building new rural communities capable of transforming the rural Midwest into a more modern agrarian landscape devoid of class conflict. Much was achieved along these lines in the social construction of Buck Creek, but at what cost? Gone was the rural neighborhood as a place where, irrespective of religion, neighbor was linked to neighbor by bonds of reciprocity, mutuality, and propinquity. A modified neighborhood system of family farming continued to operate for the Methodists in the area, as the Buck Creek Church assumed institutional responsibility for fulfilling needs that had previously rested with the rural neighborhood. Catholics, however, now found the traditional system undermined severely, if not fatally. Many went broke during the depression and left farming altogether. Others moved into Catholic neighborhoods in the Castle Grove area in northern Jones County and closer to Ryan in Delaware County and to Monti in Buchanan County. Of course, the demise of the traditional rural neighborhood in this case cannot simply be attributed to the eventually successful effort of Buck Creekers in linking rural school consolidation with their efforts to build a larger, more Methodist rural community. There were plenty of other forces at work during this period to undermine it as well.

The lesson that Buck Creek teaches is that rural school consolidation was not really about achieving educational equality between town and country or about enhancing the educational opportunities of farm children. It was seen to be an effective means of creating a new kind of place, a place where farmers were better, more modern, richer, even more moral than their town cousins — certainly not merely their equals. Namely, it played to creating social superiority and difference, exploiting whatever implicit differences were already at hand. Perhaps, this was the only way that family farmers would embrace the educational changes that reformers thought necessary for the survival of a family-based system of agricultural production. In Buck Creek, rural school consolidation became a means of creating a Methodist place. Elsewhere in the state, the same laws were coupled with a similar community-building logic to help create Catholic places.[88] The rural school consolidation movement in Iowa was not in principle anti-Catholic. Whatever the case locally, the rural school consolidation movement in Iowa quickly degenerated into a class movement at the state level. The movement attempted to exploit alternative visions of community and place that were as reactionary as they appeared progressive. Unlike in Buck Creek, most farm people in Iowa rejected rural school consolidation, not because they thought it was necessarily poor educational policy but because it was "a provoker of neighborhood contention" and a "disturber of community harmony." They had a point.

If the quality of education in the Buck Creek school was little better than that provided in the country schools it replaced, at least it was offered on the model similar to that recommended by leading educators of the era and hence was modern. It was controlled by a progressive farm community that had been built through the efforts of a rural Methodist church. For most of its patrons, the school itself was the center of community life and community pride, displacing even the Buck Creek Church after World War II, until it was forced to close as a high school in 1959. Ironically, the Buck Creek district was consolidated with those of Earlville, Delhi, Oneida, Delaware, and Hopkinton, and all of the then remaining country school subdistricts in between to form the Maquoketa Valley Community School District. There was also a battle associated with that consolidation, but now the people of Buck Creek fought to retain their "neighborhood" school; this

FIGURE 20. *Buck Creek today. 1998 photograph by the author.*

time they lost. The Buck Creek school was retained as an elementary "atten-dance center" in the Maquoketa Valley district until it was finally closed altogether in 1976. Today the Buck Creek Consolidated School stands aban-doned, a derelict mausoleum providing mute testimony to the struggles over its creation, operation, and demise (figure 20).

Schools are great educational factories set up at public expense. The raw material consists of the children of succeeding generations, helpless and inefficient because of ignorance and immaturity. The school is to turn out as its product men and women ready and able to take up their part in the great world of activities going on about them. It is in this way, in efficient education, that society gets its return for its investment in the schools.
— *George H. Betts*, New Ideals in Rural Schools

EPILOGUE:
RURAL SCHOOL CONSOLIDATION —
MISPLACING EDUCATIONAL REFORM?

Although school administrators have advocated school consolidation for more than a century, it still remains one of the most difficult and contentious social policy issues in rural America. Two of the nation's leading educational researchers, J. B. Banovetz and D. A. Dolan, have recently suggested that consolidation has constituted the "grand debate" in rural education for at least a century.[1] As presently constituted, it pits *what is good for society* — usually defined as the equal availability of educational opportunities — against *what is good for community* — the preservation of distinctive rural community norms and values.[2] While these certainly appear to have been the choices historically, were these real choices or was rural school consolidation a necessary response to the changing nature of rural community wrought by changes in communications technology and by farm consolidation and rural depopulation? Can the analysis of rural school consolidation in Iowa of the preceding chapters provide insights into some of the more fundamental policy issues surrounding rural education today? Might it perhaps also suggest how the grand debate can be transcended? Such are the issues this chapter seeks to illuminate by extending the analysis of earlier chapters into the mid-1960s.

Reconsolidation, Dissolution, and the End of the Consolidation Movement

Before 1921, Iowa school laws permitted the boards of directors of school districts to make territorial adjustments between adjacent districts, including merger, provided the boards of directors of the districts involved concurred. The only means of taking territory from previously existing districts without such approval, however, was through consolidation. This fact tended to produce as many opponents of consolidation as it did proponents. With the deepening economic crisis, local conflicts surrounding consolidation took on new dimensions as more and more districts consolidated multiple times to gain access to additional high-value farmland to augment their tax bases. This reconsolidation phenomenon contradicted many Iowans' sense of fair play. Reformers billed consolidated districts as the rural communities of the future. Yet, the consolidation laws seemed to sanction various forms of predatory and exclusionary behavior that contradicted modern conceptions of social progress.

Perhaps the most perplexing political question involved in the implementation of rural school consolidation was whether rural neighborhoods should have political autonomy in the proceedings and, if so, what form it should take. Should rural neighborhoods be permitted to retain their county schools and opt out of consolidation plans? If so, under what conditions should this be allowed? What if permitting rural neighborhoods to retain their independence would necessarily result in consolidated districts that were either too small to be viable fiscally or too attenuated and/or discontiguous spatially to transport students efficiently? How local could democracy be and still be democratic? These were the specific forms that the grand debate took in Iowa in the years immediately after World War I. The stakes involved rose sharply as the financial costs of building schools and improving the country roads became increasingly difficult for farm families to shoulder as the agricultural depression deepened. Indeed, it was escalating conflict in the hustings over this issue that finally brought the consolidation movement in Iowa to a complete halt in 1921. In that year, the General Assembly changed the consolidation laws to include a proviso prohibiting consolidated districts from expanding their boundaries outward to include additional territory without the approval of the voters in the additional territory.[3] Also deleted was the requirement that school sites be in villages or towns. While the legislative intent of these changes was simply to remove the incentive for defensive consolidation, with its geopolitical incentives to consolidate now removed, consolidation became a dead letter politically.[4]

Consolidation remained on the political agendas in many localities across the state, but by 1922 the principal focus of local school politics shifted from the formation of consolidated districts to their dissolution. New rural school consolidations were no longer viable either politically or economically. In a number of districts that had consolidated after 1919, voters refused to pass the bond issues necessary for building new schools in one bond issue election after another.[5] The bill removing the incentive for defensive consolidations also did away with the disincentive for opponents of consolidation to organize and fight for the dissolution of existing consolidated districts. Gone was the highly unpopular mechanism whereby the county superintendent possessed sole authority to approve or disapprove of a petition requesting that a consolidated district be dissolved. Gone also was the politically fractious stipulation that the dissolution petition contain legal descriptions of the independent districts to be created from the territory of the consolidated district to be dissolved. In their place was substituted what was thought simply to be the mirror image of the procedures to be followed in the creation of consolidated districts. As the language of the bill put it, "A school corporation organized for the purpose of maintaining a central school may be dissolved by following the same procedure as in the organization, in so far as practicable." Perhaps its sponsors thought that this would permit a relatively straightforward return to the structure of districts that had been in place before consolidation. If so, history was to prove them wrong. Legitimizing opposition to consolidation had the effect of changing the parameters of conflict dramatically. Previously, proponents of consolidation had the upper hand in any conflict over the formation of consolidated districts. All they had to do was tinker with the proposed boundaries and keep bringing the issue up for a vote until the opposition was exhausted politically. Now, provided it was sufficiently controversial locally, a battle over consolidation could be extended almost indefinitely. With the severe downturn in the regional economy and this change in the dissolution law, opponents had the upper hand. Now the voice of the traditional family farmer carried greater weight than it had only a short while earlier; family farmers could mobilize a form of class power. The rural neighborhood institutionalized and given social meaning by the country school district (or subdistrict) had for several generations provided family farmers a vital safety net. Controversy over the demise of these districts, coupled with the economic recession, helped family farmers again see the relationship between their power as a class and the control of the spaces and places of that power's reproduction.

In the 1922 general primary election, May E. Francis secured the Republican Party's nomination for the office of superintendent of public instruction over two male candidates, including the incumbent, P. E. McClenahan. The contest was not even close; Miss Francis (as she was called) won over her nearest rival by a ratio of three to one. The *Des Moines Register and Leader* opined somewhat patronizingly that it was largely the women of the state, particularly the women teachers and county superintendents who, having the vote for the first time, had won the position for her.[6] As expected, Francis went on and trounced her Democratic opponent in the general election. The economic crisis had mobilized farmers; more farmers ran for and were elected to both houses in 1922 than in any other election since the depression years of the 1890s.[7] The mobilization of farmers was probably far more important to Francis's success than her sex. Much to the consternation of other educational leaders in the state, upon gaining office she used her position as a platform to speak on behalf of the country school.[8] In doing so, she became the first state superintendent in more than a generation not to tout school district consolidation as the only effective means of improving the quality of rural schools in the state. As she put it during her general election campaign, "[t]he school system is in the hands of the people. If they want consolidated schools they can have them. It is up to the people in the district. I do not expect to use my office to force either the one room rural school type, or the consolidated school on the taxpayers."[9]

Nonetheless, Francis made it clear where she stood on the consolidation issue personally: "I believe in assistance for the 10,000 one room country schools of Iowa."[10] In this sense she was running on her record rather than as populist. She began her career as a teacher in a country school. Later she served as county superintendent in Bremer County, a county in northeast Iowa dominated by small dairy farms and German ethnicity (primarily Lutheran). Bremer County residents had evinced little interest in rural school consolidation; indeed the county was noted for the high quality of its rural schools. In 1919, apparently in recognition of her work in Bremer County, she was appointed as the DPI's first Inspector of Rural Schools. There she was responsible for preparing and administering the regulations for standardizing the rural schools of the state. In the campaign, she was not averse to using populist rhetoric in capitalizing upon the by then widespread popular opposition to any further consolidation. "Due to the financial conditions of this state, I believe that the taxpayers, especially of the rural districts, should not be called upon to expend millions of dollars for palatial school buildings. Rather, should we improve buildings and equipment, and with less of the taxpayers' money, lift the standard rural schools to a place of paramount importance in our educational system." She pledged that if elected "fads and fadism shall not run rampant like a hungry lion, devouring the hard earned dollars of the taxpayers. . . . [M]y motto is, progress and advance for the smallest school unit — the rural school." [11]

With the election of Francis, the educational establishment temporarily lost control of the formal administrative machinery of the state's educational apparatus. The heady days of educational reform in Iowa with rural school consolidation as its centerpiece were over. [12] Educational historians have uncritically accepted the agricultural depression as the cause of the movement's demise. Belying this interpretation is that in other midwestern states, most notably in Indiana, Minnesota, and Kansas, consolidation continued largely unabated throughout the 1920s. [13] In 1928–29, 385 consolidated districts were still operating in Iowa, enrolling approximately 20 percent of the rural students in the state. In its decade-long run from 1913–22, rural school consolidation resulted in the closure of 2,663 country schools. Declining rural school enrollments had not been the driving force or even a significant stimulus in Iowa's consolidation movement. Indeed, consolidation typically resulted in the closure of country schools that had considerably larger enrollments than the ones in districts that resisted consolidation and remained open — an average enrollment of 27.1 versus 16.1. As the number of consolidated school districts decreased, for the first time in over two decades the actual number of rural independent districts increased by 200. [14] Only a handful of consolidations would occur between 1922 and 1945.

Francis remained in office for only one term. An outsider as far as most educational leaders in the state were concerned, she was charged by them as incompetent and unethical in her operation of the DPI. At the urgings of the ISTA in 1924, a special house committee investigated a wide-ranging series of charges leveled at her administration of the DPI. On a narrow vote of the committee, she was exonerated of all charges. She completed the remaining two years of her term, devoting much of her time to campaigning for improving the quality of the country schools and trying to help the large number of small consolidated schools cope with financial crisis. As an economy move, she permitted the latter to combine some subjects and to offer courses in others only every other year. The irony of the situation was inescapable. The state's most outspoken critic of the consolidated school was forced by economic circumstances to work to ensure that school consolidation could be remembered as a success rather than as a failure.

Agricultural depression and the local fiscal crises it produced created the need to rationalize the devaluation of investments in school facilities, particularly the consolidated schools. Many consolidated school districts were forced, sometimes repeatedly, to reissue school bonds at higher rates of interest, to sell them below par, when they could get away with it, or to pay exorbitant issuing fees to bond companies. Some of the districts that had consolidated in the early 1920s were still paying off well into the 1940s the bonded indebtedness they had incurred in building their consolidated schools. A few of the larger consolidated schools fulfilled their promise of providing an education on a par with that of the finest urban schools in the state, but not many. Most struggled through the depression years. In some places, the sheer necessity of struggle help foster a new form of community similar to that hoped for by the Country Lifers a decade earlier. The country schools weathered the depression much better and indeed flourished in most places. Many rural neighborhoods retaining their country schools were glad they had not succumbed to the allure of modernity. After World War II, however, when economic conditions had improved, Iowans were to learn that the 1912–1922 battle over rural school consolidation had not produced clear-cut winners or losers after all. By the standards embraced by a new cadre of educational reformers, all but a handful of the state's consolidated schools were thought too small to be efficient. They were among the first to be recommended for reconsolidation. Most stand abandoned as big buildings in small towns. Others are used to store grain or farm implements (figures 21–28).

FIGURE 21. *Jolley consolidated school (abandoned), Calhoun County. 1990 photograph by the author.*

FIGURE 22. *Beebeetown consolidated school (abandoned), Harrison County. 1998 photograph by the author.*

FIGURE 23. *Bartlett consolidated school (abandoned), Fremont County. 1991 photograph by the author.*

FIGURE 24. *Spring Hill consolidated school (abandoned), Warren County. 1990 photograph by the author.*

FIGURE 25. *Stennett consolidated school (abandoned), Montgomery County. 1998 photograph by the author.*

FIGURE 26. *Thayer consolidated school (abandoned), Union County. 1992 photograph by the author.*

FIGURE 27. *Gardiner consolidated school (abandoned), Dallas County. 1998 photograph by the author.*

Iowa's consolidation movement began in the state superintendent's office in Des Moines in late 1911 and ended on the floor of the General Assembly a decade later. As a progressive movement, ostensibly bringing equal educational opportunities to all, the consolidation movement in Iowa was an abysmal failure. It also created a deep residue of distrust of educational reform and a legacy of mistrust between rural neighborhoods and small towns. Any efforts at reorganizing rural education would have to await a return of economic prosperity after World War II. Iowa may have been a rich agricultural state, but it was not rich enough to become the model for other states to emulate in their efforts to solve the "rural school problem." [15] Iowa began the century leading the nation in its number of one-room country schools; more than sixty years later it still retained that distinction.

The Interwar Years:
What Had the Consolidation Movement Wrought?

The consolidation movement helped create a lively interest in the rural public schools. It resulted in a significant expansion in the number of four-year high schools across the state. It helped improve the access of many rural students to a more "modern" school apparatus. However, it never lived up to its original billing as a means of equalizing the elementary education opportunities of urban and rural children.

What began as an attempt to improve the quality of rural education in all parts of the state quickly and unwittingly was transformed into an effort to improve education in only the most rural of rural areas in the wealthier portions of the state. With the onset of economic depression, the allocation of even fewer resources over more and larger schools ensured on average that the quality of elementary education afforded students was not a great improvement over that provided in the remaining country schools. A study conducted by the Iowa Child Welfare Research Station in the 1920s, for example, showed that country-school students in grades one through three performed better on the Stanford Achievement Test than students in the consolidated schools, while the results were reversed for students in grades four through eight.[16] If the country schools had a weakness, it was in how their students performed in reading and language use. However, the study pointed out that this could have resulted from the generally shorter school terms in the country schools rather than from a poorer quality of instruction. Both types of schools produced students who scored higher than the national norm in arithmetic, spelling, and nature study and lower in history and literature.[17]

Consolidation and the Access of Rural Students to a High School Education

It is also doubtful whether consolidation significantly enhanced the access of rural students to high schools comparable in quality to those of the state's larger towns and cities. In 1912–13, the year before the consolidation movement began and before the state had developed a system for approving high schools, there were 804 public high schools offering one or more years of instruction. Practically every city, town, or village in the state had some form of high school even before the consolidation movement got into full swing. Consolidation was not primarily a means of establishing new high schools in places where none had existed previously. Instead, it was a movement to increase the size and to standardize the curriculum of those already in existence.

Between 1913 and 1930, there was a remarkable increase in the relative and absolute numbers of students attending high school in Iowa.[18] As early as 1920, Iowa was second only to California in the percentage of its school-aged children attending high school.[19] This does not, however, constitute evidence of the consolidation movement's success per se. This was a period in which the popularity of the high school increased everywhere throughout the state, not just in the rural areas.[20] The consolidation movement undoubtedly contributed to this increased interest in the high school. Even more important, however, was the so-called free-tuition law. Far more rural students attended a nonconsolidated high school than a consolidated one.[21]

Beginning in 1911–12, students living in rural districts that did not consolidate could attend any high school in the state at their home district's expense. This was a privilege not granted to other students in the state. In 1912–13, almost 12,000 students took advantage of this law. The number of students availing themselves of this opportunity increased each year until 1930–31 when almost 40,000 exercised the option. As early as 1913–14, tuition students accounted for slightly more than 25 percent of the total high school enrollment in the state. By 1930–31, their numbers accounted for fully one-third of high school enrollment, the vast majority of which comprised graduates of the country schools. Not surprisingly, the residents of rural districts within a reasonable weekend commuting distance from a town or city with a good high school had little interest in consolidation. The financial resources of school districts dwindled as the depression deepened, leading town districts to seek additional numbers of rural tuition students by providing free transportation. This enhanced the attraction of attending a high school under the free-tuition option even further. It quickly became the one preferred over consolidation in most localities. Indeed, this way of providing rural children with a high school education was so popular that as late as 1954 more than 70 percent of the total area of the state was organized into rural school districts that elected to send their students to high school in a nearby town or city of the students' choosing rather than providing high schools themselves.[22]

As demonstrated in the case of Buck Creek, the consolidation movement did help to make *small* high schools more accessible spatially to larger numbers of rural students. Nevertheless, as a state-commissioned study by the Brookings Institution first pointed out in 1933, far too many small high schools existed for them ever to possess local revenues approaching those available to high schools in the larger towns and cities.[23] A movement initiated to equalize the educational opportunities between rural and urban children served primarily to reinstitutionalize urban-rural and class inequalities in a different form. The DPI failed to acknowledge this until late in the 1940s.[24]

Consolidated schools differed from the nonconsolidated schools primarily in that they tended to be smaller and combined the elementary and high school grades in a single facility. More recent studies have shown that most of the long-standing criticisms of the country school applied with equal force to educational conditions in the smaller consolidated and town schools of the state in the 1920s and 1930s.[25]

Rural School Consolidation, Family Farmers, and Class

From its very outset, the rural school consolidation movement was both an educational movement and part of a much broader social movement aimed at transforming the social basis of agricultural production. Convinced of the necessity of removing the rural neighborhood as the principal site for the determination of rural school policy, reformers saw in rural school consolidation a means of expanding modern systems of public schooling into the countryside. As part of the Country Life movement, the consolidated school was to be the key agent for transforming the nature of farm people and the communities in which they lived and worked. Working in tandem with churches and other local institutions, the consolidated school would update and modernize the agrarian myth.

In the new myth, family farms would remain family-owned and family-managed businesses and hence not become faceless capitalist organizations that were insensitive to the needs of those directly involved in production. Some of these family farms would be small businesses; others large. There would still be rich farmers, poor farmers, and many in between. The relative wealth of a farm family would depend primarily on how good its members were as farmers and businesspeople and how hard the family was willing to work, not on the vicissitudes of the market. As in the traditional myth, the attraction of farming lay in its direct contact with nature and the relative simplicity of country life. While farming was a business, it was the most important business of them all; without food, none of the other businesses could exist.

The consolidation movement, reformers hoped, would speed the creation of new kinds of places and communities in which this new agrarian myth could be grounded and sustained materially. The country town was to replace the rural neighborhood as the central institution. The country town would partially insulate the farm family from the harsher realities of the class relations of capitalist society and sustain it during times of economic and natural calamity. As a social movement, rural school consolidation fell short of its objectives. The new type of rural community anchored by the country town envisioned by Country Life reformers turned out to be unachievable. While rural school consolidation was a national movement led by educational and economic elites, the laws guiding and constraining its implementation had to pass muster in the state's General Assembly. The General Assembly, however, was reluctant to impose rural school consolidation and insisted instead that it be left to localities to decide for themselves. Local consolidation movements were usually co-opted by local elites and used to advance some other local initiative. Efforts by church leaders to reinvigorate the rural and small-town church and by businessmen to transform small towns into bigger towns were the principal initiatives. Still, rural school consolidation was rejected in most rural localities in Iowa. It was more readily accepted in the cash grain region where farms were larger and production was more capital intensive. It was also accepted in scattered localities elsewhere in the state where local residents could be convinced that the neighborhood system of family farming had broken down and needed to be replaced by a more modern one. The social safety net previously provided by the rural neighborhood would be found in the institutions of new, more spatially extensive communities focused on the country towns and/or revitalized rural churches.

The rural school consolidation movement may well have helped speed the introduction of scientific agricultural practices and sound business practices into family farming. It did not, however, lead to the creation of country towns, at least not as envisioned by the Country Lifers. Part of the reason was that in most localities in Iowa, class antagonisms between family farmers and townspeople were well entrenched, even when many, if not most, of the townspeople were from farm families themselves. To many family farmers, the act of moving or "retiring" to town was a form of selling out. Rural school consolidation, involving as it did the movement of farm children to towns to receive their education, was seen as class capitulation.

Most rural neighborhoods rejected rural school consolidation. Family farmers, however, failed to exploit their numerical superiority and create an alternative system of rural education — perhaps one based on the rural neighborhood — through which a materially grounded agrarian ideology and politics might have been sustained. They did not get much help from professional educators or social reformers in exploring possible alternatives. The hegemony of the reformist discourse nationally and at the state level contributed to the view, even among family farmers themselves, that the rural neighborhood was an aberrant institution and that in the longer run the system of farming dependent on it was doomed. The wave of patriotic fervor that swept the nation and region during World War I made the survival of rural neighborhoods seem parochial. It also contributed to the view that the social relations of production in agriculture could be reorganized and put on a sufficiently sound economic footing as to make the rural neighborhood expendable.

Economic Hardship and the Rise of a New Sense of Community

The formation of consolidated districts did help contribute to new forms of community, although not quite along the lines that the Country Lifers had envisioned. In many instances, new communities in consolidated districts came into existence in part because of the sheer necessity of rural people having to pull together to make a success of a situation from which there was no turning back. Contrary to the expectations of reformers, the formation of de facto high school districts through the exercise of the free-tuition law had a similar effect. There was, however, another stimulus leading to the creation of a new sense of rural place based on the small town. The gap between the social status and prestige of teachers (and educational administrators) and the longer-term residents of consolidated (and small-town) school districts frequently created a serious cultural tension, which threatened to undermine local support for the public schools. Educators resolved the dilemma by turning the high school into the social and recreational center for the surrounding area, "with basketball teams, marching bands and plenty of hoopla to whip up enthusiasm of residents for a local institution."[26] Grudgingly, educators had come to realize the pivotal role of the school in institutionalizing this form of community identity, thereby engendering broad-based, but not necessarily deep, support for the public schools. Perhaps because they were not permanent members of rural communities (in either their open-country or town-based forms) themselves, professional educators overwhelmingly valued community merely as a means to an end and not as an end in itself. In this way, a new form of community fostering new local identities based on small-town rivalries, institutionalized and legitimated through high school athletic competitions, rose to prominence.[27]

Population and Enrollment Changes: 1930–1950

During the depression and throughout World War II, the consolidation discourse lost none of its hegemony in reform circles either in Iowa or nationally. Reformers assumed that worsening economic conditions had simply forced it off the political agenda. Virtually nothing else, however, stood still. New Deal farm policies and the outbreak of war would eventually bring renewed prosperity to midwestern agriculture. However, it was slow in coming and was accompanied by increasingly rapid changes in the organization of agricultural production. Particularly evident was the decrease in the relative proportion of farmland in the middling family farm sizes (50–179 acres) and an increase in the proportion of large farms (over 259 acres).[28] The population living in rural areas decreased at a rising rate each decade between 1930 and 1970.[29] In 1930, 60.4 percent of Iowa's population lived in rural areas; by 1970 this figure had dropped to 42.8. For the state as a whole, the population aged 5–14 years decreased by 12.9 percent in the 1930s, but increased by 2.2 percent in the 1940s, by 29.3 percent in the 1950s, and by 4.2 percent in the 1960s. By the early 1950s these population changes translated into significant enrollment decreases in both the remaining rural independent school districts and in the consolidated school districts. A few new consolidated districts were formed in the late 1940s, but overwhelmingly the free-tuition option was exercised. In areas where enrollment declines were most severe, two or three country school districts often merged to have enough pupils to justify the continuance of at least one of their country schools. From 1930 to 1950 the number of country schools was reduced almost by half through such voluntary action — most of it coming in the 1940s (table 14). This trend continued into the 1950s.[30] As enrollment in the country schools dwindled, the enrollments in remaining schools were maintained. Although the high school retained its importance in the social life of rural Iowans during the depression, attending high school did not

TABLE 14. *Enrollment in Iowa's Country Schools: 1912–13 to 1959–60*

Year	Number of Country Schools	Enrollment in Country Schools	Average Enrollment
1912–13	12,258	226,880	18.5
1917–18	11,252	204,515	18.2
1921–22	10,828	173,259	16.0
1929–30	9,595	154,594	16.1
1934–35	9,179	135,929	14.8
1939–40	8,533	119,417	14.0
1944–45	7,243	103,673	14.3
1949–50	4,960	86,703	17.5
1954–55	3,232	68,106	21.1
1957–58	2,067	50,942	24.6
1959–60	863	30,861	35.8

Source: Calculated by author from *Biennial Reports*, Department of Public Instruction, State of Iowa, 1913–1960.

lead to appreciably greater success in the job market. Hence, it contributed to a marked decrease in high school enrollments. These losses were even more precipitous than the decline in the number of school-aged children in rural areas. Statewide, while elementary school enrollment decreased by only 5.5 percent between 1930 and 1950, high school enrollment dropped by more than 23 percent (table 15). In districts with their own high schools (the urban independent and the consolidated districts), elementary school enrollments actually increased during this period, at the expense of the country schools. In 1930, country schools accounted for 40 percent of elementary school enrollments in the state; by 1950 this figure was only 23.5 percent (table 14).

Post–World War II Reorganization:
Something Different or More of the Same?

By the 1950s, Iowa had a new rural school problem. Now the small, seemingly inefficient high school replaced the country school of yore as the major focus of concern among the state's education leaders. "Our major concern is not with the rural school. . . . Our most serious problem is in the large number of small, inefficient high schools which we are operating. Three

TABLE 15. *Enrollments in School Districts by Type: 1929–30 to 1959–60*

Year	A	B	C	D	E
1929–30	154,594	231,647	146,629	532,870	40.0
1939–40	119,417	244,654	139,410	503,483	32.8
1946–47	94,894	249,985	114,252	459,113	27.5
1949–50	86,703	278,239	112,778	477,720	23.5
1959–60	30,861	426,125	141,117	598,103	6.8

A: Country school enrollment.

B: Elementary school enrollment in districts with high schools.

C: High school enrollment in districts with high schools.

D: Total enrollment.

E: Percentage of elementary school enrollment in country schools.

Source: Calculated by author from *Biennial Reports*, Department of Public Instruction, State of Iowa, 1930–1960.

years ago we had the dubious distinction of having five per cent of all the high school districts in the entire United States."[31]

The dimensions of the problem were remarkably similar to those first articulated a half century earlier. As happened in the 1910s, following a decade of plummeting enrollments, the 1950s witnessed an economic boom accompanied by an upswing in the number of school-aged children. In both the 1900s and the 1940s, rural children were perceived as not having access to the same quality of education afforded urban children. Quality in both decades was defined by the size of schools and the number of grades and classes into which they were organized. In the earlier decade, rural had been viewed by reformers as the open countryside. By the 1950s, rural had come to conform more closely to the U.S. Census definition of "rural" (i.e., persons not living in urbanized places with populations in excess of 2,500). In the 1910s, reformers were concerned with ensuring greater access to both graded elementary and high schools; in the 1950s access to a quality high school education was the preoccupation. A new generation of educational reformers argued that most of Iowa's high schools were simply too small to offer the breadth and depth of curricula needed to provide rural students with skills that would enable them to compete for the best jobs in the burgeoning postwar economy.

The pursuit of equality of educational opportunity required that schools and school districts be consolidated or consolidated anew, but a new metaphor was needed. The consolidation metaphor was based on the concentration of economic power during monopoly capitalism. What better than "reorganization," a metaphor based on the rise and extension of the welfare state? Labels notwithstanding, residents of those areas that had consolidated their schools at the urging of reformers earlier in the century now made up the bulwark of opposition to it in the 1950s and 1960s. Although a large number of rural independent school districts still remained in 1950, population loss had taken its toll; their residents no longer possessed the political clout enjoyed a generation earlier. The battle over rural school consolidation during the first two decades of the century had not produced community winners or losers after all. Changed economic circumstances in both the state and in American society as a whole combined to produce a state educational apparatus the agenda of which was more transparent than it had been in earlier years.

Local proponents of earlier consolidation efforts now often found themselves prisoners of the old consolidation discourse: if the country school had to give way to educational progress, then so too had the small-town high school. Even these people must have had some regrets. Both the country school and the small high school had been key integrating institutions in their respective place-based communities and had imparted an important sense of collective identity. The community identities fostered by consolidation were based largely on pride of place. They resulted from the simple fact that the high school was the one place where the shared activities of students, parents, and townspeople had been institutionalized. This provided a community identity for almost everyone in the school district, but one based on a social variant of lowest common denominator. That extracurricular activities, particularly athletic events, were a major part of the institutionalization of the school and often engendered intense rivalries between neighboring school districts did not make the community identities any less real.

At long last, the principal issues at stake in the consolidation debate — in both its original form and in its reincarnation — were clear. The choice was between what was good for society — equality of educational opportunity for all individuals in the larger society — and what was good for community — a sense of collective identity and a set of shared values and a means of reproducing them. In the earlier consolidation debate, most reformers had asserted that the goals of equality and community were compatible, provided that new forward-looking communities could be created. Curiously, few if any saw the two goals as mutually essential and none of them articulated a role for the public schools in achieving both simultaneously. Despite the centrality of the school in fostering community identity, educational reformers had left the pursuit of community to the institutions of civil society; school facilities merely provided the infrastructure. They repeatedly stressed that education was a societywide function, and that the pursuit of equality of education, a primary goal of the state, should be achieved through its system of public schools over which it exercised ultimate authority.[32]

The growing materialism of the period, coupled with the widespread belief nationally that educational attainment was the route to material advancement, made it difficult for rural people either to maintain traditional communitarian values or to articulate new ones. The territorially extensive community identities that had been fostered through the extracurricular activities of high schools were easily caricatured and lampooned as distractions from achieving what had become the real mission of public schooling. The choice between society and community had become apparent only when it was clear that community had already lost resoundingly. The consolidation of Iowa's remaining country schools with the newly reorganized community districts was largely complete by the mid-1960s, but the pressure to form still larger districts continued.

Although the discourse of the reorganization movement, like that of its predecessor, remained one of modernity versus tradition, there were some differences in the way in which reorganization was implemented. In the earlier consolidation movement, all the preexisting county schools in a consolidated district were closed. Under reorganization, most of the small-town high schools and the smaller consolidated schools were retained as elementary or junior high attendance centers in newly reorganized districts. Only the remaining one-room country schools were slated for closure altogether. The charade that the new school districts were community institutions was maintained. Under the new school laws mandating reorganization, the districts were specifically referred to as "community" school districts and were required to use this term in their names. New "community high schools," often built in the open country to avoid the appearance of favoring one small town over another, made it clear that whatever concept of community underlay the formation of new districts, it differed significantly from that of most rural residents.

Resistance to school district reorganization was based on community defense sentiments similar to those expressed earlier in the century, but now shorn of any class basis. Previously, the community defended was the open-country rural community typically focused on either or both the country school and church, while later it focused on the small-town high school. Until the mid-1970s, when U.S. education as a whole came under attack for its tenuous connection with parents and the local communities it served, professional educators simply ignored community-based arguments or otherwise denied their legitimacy. From the 1970s onward, an increasing number of studies have documented that the educational advantages of the large over the small high school in Iowa and elsewhere are much less than had been presumed.[33] There is also a growing consensus of what characteristics constitute an effective school educationally. These include relationships between students, teachers, and administrators based on mutual respect; individualized instruction; an emphasis on basic skills; parental and community involvement and support; a tolerance of individual initiative and innovation. There is also a growing realization that none of these have any necessary relationship to school size.[34] If anything, recent work suggests that urban schools have at least as much to learn from rural schools as rural schools have to learn from urban ones.

The Quality of Iowa's Rural Schools in Retrospect

In 1991–92, Iowa students led the nation in average ACT and SAT scores — a position Iowa has held every year save one since these test scores have been published.[35] In an international comparison of high school students' proficiency in mathematics, Iowa students topped those of all other states in 1991–92. In 1992, Iowa eighth graders tied those in North Dakota in having the highest average mathematics proficiency scores in the country.[36] In 1990, Iowa had the highest high school completion rate in the nation (93 percent) and was also closely bunched with four other upper midwestern states in having the lowest high school dropout rates in the nation.[37] In that year, Iowa ranked eleventh in the nation in the percentage of persons twenty-five years old and over with a high school diploma or higher. Additional statistics could be cited, but they would simply confirm what is already clear. In terms of typical measures of the quality of the educational outputs, Iowa schools are at or near the top in the nation. The only standard measure of educational success on which Iowa has never ranked near the top is in the percentage of its population twenty-five years and older with some college education.[38] In 1990, Iowa ranked thirty-seventh among the states on this indicator of quality. Education in Iowa has been high-school focused ever since the early 1920s. In 1990, Iowa was second (to Pennsylvania) in the percentage of its population twenty-five years and older whose highest level of education attained was high school graduation. This is further evidence that both the support for and enrollment in public schools has a pervasive communitarian basis in Iowa.[39] Before World War I, attending the small country schools in high numbers was, to a significant degree, an affirmation of community membership for most rural people in Iowa. After the war, the free-tuition law and the consolidation movement jointly stimulated a greater interest in the high school among rural Iowans. They gradually expanded their community allegiances and identities to include small towns across the state. However, most Iowans still did not accept the reformers' view that the public school was primarily a vehicle for social and economic advancement.[40] Above all, the public school was a community institution and a central element in their personal identities.

High quality is not a recently acquired characteristic of Iowa's public schools. Throughout the twentieth century they have consistently ranked among the best schools in the nation. Iowa has had the lowest percentage of illiteracy in every U.S. census year this century, except for 1960 when it dropped to second. Although many Iowa farm families remained skeptical of the practical value of what they perceived to be higher education, they placed a very high value on their children's acquisition of basic skills. From 1870 through 1950, Iowa invariably was one of the leading states in the percentage of its school-aged population enrolled in school. During those years, Iowa never fell lower than thirteenth and more typically was included among the top five states. Relative to other states, Iowa ranked higher in this percentage before rather than after the consolidation movement began in the 1910s. If only input indicators of educational quality are considered (e.g., per pupil expenditures, state aid per pupil, teacher salaries, teachers' years of experience, and percentage of teachers with advanced degrees), Iowa appears quite average on some indicators, but quite exceptional on others. Iowa has always had low pupil-to-teacher ratios and small class sizes, has invested a relatively high proportion of its average personal income in the public schools, and has a high number of schools per capita. Has the quality of education in Iowa remained high because of, or despite, rural school consolidation? Could both be correct? The foregoing evidence suggests the latter.

Conclusion

While the overall system of public schooling in the United States is now widely perceived to be in crisis, rural education remains preoccupied with consolidation. Most writers on rural education fail to realize that the present discourse of consolidation, like its early twentieth-century progenitor, is only indirectly a debate over the quality of the public schools. Instead, it is the continuation of a much longer hegemonic discourse over consolidation as an end in itself. Failure to recognize this means that we are likely doomed to repeat past mistakes rather than learn from them.

The logic of school consolidation/reorganization has always entailed a simple spatial logic. It assumes that the primary determinants of educational quality are school size, the extent to which the curriculum is determined by professionals, and the amount of revenue available for expenditure. It also assumes that all three of these in turn are directly and positively related to the size and territorial extent of school districts. The issue of quality is otherwise treated as unproblematic. Any linkages between school quality, community vitality, and class are either assumed or ignored, as are any differences between rural and urban communities. The spatial problem is one of assigning and transporting pupils to places where professionals provide education and of assigning taxpayers to those jurisdictions used to generate revenue to pay for that education. Following this logic, if the costs of transportation were to vanish or at least become relatively insensitive to distance, then the logic of consolidation is transformed fundamentally. Historically, the school has been a place where students, teachers, and administrators come into direct physical contact to engage in educational activities. For reasons of spatial efficiency, the numbers of such places have been small relative to the numbers of students involved. If education does not require co-presence of students, teachers, and administrators on the scale required in the past, then the school *as a place* specializing in the provision of education must be reconsidered. What kind of place should it be? If it is a place where lifelong education occurs, how can specialization be justified at all? Also in need of a fundamental rethinking is the traditional concept of school district.

These kinds of questions would be nonsensical were it not for the revolution in telecommunications technology in contemporary society. Advances in such technology have the capability of robbing the grand debate over consolidation of much of its traditional spatial logic. Schools could indeed be almost everywhere there is a port on the fiber-optic "information highway" that can be linked directly to wherever students might need or want to be. Distance learning could become the dominant form of schooling most people receive. Remaining problems — ones that cannot be dispelled by further technological revolutions — include the issues of who will control the system, who will have access to it, how much will it cost, and who will pay for it? These are obviously key sociopolitical issues. How they are resolved will largely determine whether the consolidation debate is transcended or not. It would be a mistake, however, to assume that the advent of distance learning will necessarily obviate any need for further school consolidation in rural areas. If the costs of connecting to a state and/or national telecommunication system are left to already existing school districts, it is likely that the advantages affluent suburban school districts already have over central city and rural districts will be increased still further. This could force rural districts to unite to provide the resources necessary to achieve access to the system — much as small districts are currently urged to merge to meet stricter state standards at a reasonable cost. There is nothing necessarily egalitarian about distance learning. For low-income people, it could well occur only in places strongly resembling traditional schools, while for the more affluent, educational choices could indeed abound.

Essentially, key policy issues in rural education devolve into two general classes: those over the locus of societal/community discretion and those of cost sharing. First and most important is what the relationship should be between local communities and the larger society and how this should find expression in the school. Local communities consist of dense networks of social and economic relations within which people's daily lives unfold. How then can society have meaning if divorced from community? Should the public school seek to instill an appreciation of how local communities are embedded in a class-structured society and give it texture and meaning? Even in the age of telecommunications, the concept of school as an important place where people learn about themselves in relation to their community, to others, and to the structure of society retains its relevance. What, however, are appropriate roles for parents, community members, teachers, and school administrators in maintaining a high-quality school? In rural areas and small towns there is a strong presumption that local communities will be less spatially extensive and that parental and community roles in education can be greater than in urban and suburban areas.

Next is the vexing issue of paying for public education and its infrastructure. Should the state provide all or most of the revenue needed to ensure wide access to communication technology, vitiating the need for large schools? Should the state also pay the salaries of the teachers and administrators still needed, but leave the task of providing support for teachers to parents and community volunteers? Can some more appropriate means of sharing the costs of education between the state and community be found? Answers to these questions may well force a fundamental redefinition of the concept of the school as a place where all or most formal education is obtained. Whether rural and urban communities require different *kinds* (not sizes) of schools to achieve outputs of comparable quality also demands serious reconsideration. The hegemony of the consolidation discourse meant that these questions have been finessed for three-quarters of a century. Only in the 1970s did debate over these matters begin — but all too quickly elided into a contest over the educational advantages of big schools versus small schools.

New technology should not, indeed cannot, determine the answers to these questions, but it has helped reveal what the key policy issues really are. School consolidation has not yet been replaced as a dominant discourse in educational reform, but it has lost its hegemony. Perhaps, more socially constructive reforms in the production and delivery of education can now find a political forum and be taken seriously. The real debates have barely begun. The rural neighborhood is gone but the issue of the relationship between the school, place-based communities, and class is as important as ever.

APPENDIX

AVERAGE FARM SIZES AND PERCENTAGES OF FARMS BY TENURE
CLASS FOR SELECTED LOCALITIES IN CONSOLIDATED AND
NONCONSOLIDATED SCHOOL DISTRICTS: CIRCA 1920

A. AREAS SUPPORTING CONSOLIDATION

Region and Locality (year)	Average Farm Size			Difference (1–3)	Percentage of Farms Operated by Owners
	Related Owners 1	Unrelated Renters 2	Renters 3		
Cash Grain Area					
Boone County (1918)					
Colfax Township	132.2	130.9	155.5	−23.3	47.4
	(55)	(15)	(46)		
Grant Township	138.4	145.1	162.2	−23.8	48.7
	(76)	(35)	(45)		
Jordan Consol.	117.3	138.4	134.3	−17.0	53.0
	(44)	(15)	(24)		
Buena Vista County (1923)					
Barnes Township	162.7	198.7	180.3	−17.6	64.4
	(76)	(11)	(31)		
Brooke Township	211.0	218.7	238.8	−27.8	38.7
	(31)	(25)	(24)		
Hayes Township	173.1	135.7	195.0	−21.9	41.7
	(35)	(7)	(42)		
Maple Valley Township	231.8	140.0	214.4	17.4	27.3
	(6)	(2)	(14)		
Marathon Consol.	148.5	198.3	166.4	−17.9	43.8
	(42)	(15)	(39)		
Varina Consol.	171.3	153.0	190.6	−19.3	48.5
	(16)	(6)	(11)		
Clay County (1919)					
Webb Consol.	145.0	220.0	195.9	−50.9	42.7
	(32)	(4)	(39)		

Region and Locality (year)	Average Farm Size			Difference (1–3)	Percentage of Farms Operated by Owners
	Related Owners 1	Unrelated Renters 2	Renters 3		
Dallas County (1916)					
Adams Township	162.1	133.3	149.1	13.0	60.7
	(17)	(3)	(8)		
Dawson Consol.	191.0	136.4	231.0	−40.0	46.8
	(22)	(8)	(17)		
Gardiner Consol.	115.1	246.0	162.1	−47.0	37.5
	(12)	(6)	(14)		
Washington Township	141.2	146.7	159.3	−18.1	51.4
	(72)	(18)	(50)		
Eastern Meat Production Area					
Marshall County (1924)					
Greencastle Township	132.6	135.1	188.1	−55.5	48.2
	(53)	(28)	(29)		
Jefferson Township	149.8	193.1	162.3	−12.5	54.5
	(60)	(29)	(21)		
Liberty Consol.	191.9	120.0	204.1	−12.2	51.4
	(18)	(1)	(16)		
Tama County (1926)					
Geneseo Township	249.6	220.4	263.5	−13.9	50.6
	(45)	(11)	(33)		
Dinsdale Consol.	233.6	181.2	183.5	50.1	52.4
	(44)	(18)	(22)		
Cedar County (1916)					
Center Township	170.8	210.9	186.4	−15.6	57.4
	(108)	(17)	(63)		
Clinton County (1925)					
Elwood Consol.	158.8	171.3	193.4	−34.6	48.1
	(37)	(14)	(26)		
Center Township	153.5	192.9	184.4	−30.9	61.5
	(59)	(15)	(22)		
Welton Consol.	149.0	177.3	161.4	−12.4	53.6
	(45)	(16)	(23)		

Region and Locality (year)	Average Farm Size			Difference (1–3)	Percentage of Farms Operated by Owners
	Related Owners 1	Unrelated Renters 2	Renters 3		

Western Meat Production Area

Cherokee County (1923)

Afton Consol.	162.1	188.1	177.8	−15.7	41.2
	(35)	(21)	(29)		
Aurelia Consol.	215.8	221.9	216.8	−1.0	31.8
	(35)	(25)	(50)		
Brooke Consol.	193.5	177.2	201.5	−8.0	44.8
	(13)	(8)	(8)		
Grand Meadow Township	148.4	169.6	190.1	−41.7	43.3
	(45)	(15)	(44)		

Harrison County (1922)

Beebeetown Consol.	145.7	144.0	138.0	7.7	64.7
	(33)	(5)	(13)		
Magnolia Consol.	127.9	125.3	107.7	20.2	53.3
	(64)	(16)	(40)		
Mondamin Consol.	184.9	188.3	214.0	−29.1	60.0
	(54)	(15)	(21)		

Monona County (1919)

Castana Consol.	172.1	202.8	160.1	12.0	63.3
	(76)	(15)	(29)		
Maple Township	128.7	280.0	255.7	−127.0	52.9
	(9)	(1)	(7)		
Blencoe Consol.	182.0	163.0	184.8	−2.8	48.9
	(22)	(2)	(21)		

Montgomery County (1920)

Wales-Lincoln Consol.	192.2	192.1	206.2	−14.0	41.7
	(43)	(19)	(41)		

Woodbury County (1917)

Floyd Township	249.2	193.0	203.4	45.8	57.1
	(56)	(14)	(28)		
Willow Township	132.2	204.5	157.0	−24.7	52.0
	(65)	(22)	(38)		

| Region and Locality (year) | Average Farm Size | | | Difference (1–3) | Percentage of Farms Operated by Owners |
	Related Owners 1	Unrelated Renters 2	Renters 3		
Southern Pasture Area					
Taylor County (1923)					
Conway Consol.	140.7	165.0	222.6	−81.9	56.3
	(18)	(4)	(10)		
Warren County (1921)					
Jackson Township	138.9	173.7	157.3	−18.4	53.0
	(71)	(23)	(40)		
Dairy Area					
Allamakee County (1917)					
New Albin Consol.	246.1	343.0	269.0	−22.9	89.3
	(25)	(1)	(2)		
Butler County					
Aplington Consol.	179.3	191.1	205.1	−25.8	41.3
	(26)	(14)	(23)		
Black Hawk County (1921)					
Hudson Township	192.3	243.2		−50.9	43.4
(1921)	(36)	(47)			
Orange Township	139.8	167.7		−27.9	60.6
(1915)	(86)	(56)			
Buchanan County (1921)					
Jesup Consol.	144.6	172.1		−27.5	44.7

Region and Locality (year)	Average Farm Size			Difference (1–3)	Percentage of Farms Operated by Owners
	Related Owners 1	Unrelated Renters 2	Renters 3		
Cash Grain Area					
Boone County (1918)					
Jackson Township	153.3	142.1	146.1	7.2	55.1
	(32)	(10)	(16)		
Peoples Township	154.9	142.7	152.5	2.4	51.8
	(73)	(27)	(41)		
Buena Vista County (1923)					
Coon Township	161.8	170.8	161.9	−0.1	50.5
	(48)	(11)	(36)		
Grant Township	164.8	153.4	161.0	3.8	57.1
	(68)	(17)	(34)		
Maple Valley Township	191.4	154.0	189.0	2.4	44.2
	(34)	(19)	(24)		
Poland Township	141.4	254.0	129.7	11.7	62.9
	(22)	(4)	(9)		
Clay County (1916)					
Freeman Township	205.0	158.4	179.9	25.1	61.6
	(53)	(11)	(22)		
Lone Tree Township	253.7	211.4		42.3	35.3
	(30)	(55)			
Dallas County (1916)					
Adams Township	117.2	124.9	101.8	15.4	64.8
	(81)	(16)	(28)		
Beaver Township	171.8	138.9	150.6	21.2	46.0
	(40)	(13)	(34)		
Colfax Township	139.9	140.2	184.0	−44.1	56.8
	(75)	(23)	(34)		
Dallas Township	174.4	151.1	147.9	26.5	41.3
	(26)	(9)	(28)		
Sugar Grove Township	153.6	146.0	168.7	−15.1	59.6
	(53)	(11)	(25)		

Region and Locality (year)	Average Farm Size			Difference (1–3)	Percentage of Farms Operated by Owners
	Related Owners 1	Unrelated Renters 2	Renters 3		
Eastern Meat Production Area					
Marshall County (1924)					
Bangor Township	160.3	90.0	162.5	−2.2	55.2
	(37)	(9)	(23)		
Greencastle Independ.	149.0	166.5	125.8	23.2	57.1
	(8)	(2)	(4)		
Haverhill District	219.4	195.3	168.2	51.2	57.1
	(24)	(8)	(10)		
Liberty Township	204.8	110.3	165.1	39.7	40.1
	(9)	(4)	(8)		
Marietta Township	175.2	163.6	165.2	10.0	68.2
	(60)	(9)	(19)		
Timber Creek Township	118.0	133.9	128.6	−10.6	51.8
	(59)	(11)	(44)		
Tama County (1926)					
Howard Township	155.6	154.4	145.3	10.3	50.4
	(64)	(22)	(41)		
Lincoln Township	185.4	200.2	191.5	−6.1	37.7
	(40)	(26)	(40)		
Clinton County (1925)					
Waterford Township	188.8	185.4	159.0	29.8	78.5
	(84)	(9)	(14)		
Western Meat Production Area					
Cherokee County (1923)					
Spring Township	233.7	292.9	195.0	−17.8	30.4
	(7)	(7)	(9)		
Wilson Independ.	125.6	232.5	195.0	−69.4	41.7
	(5)	(2)	(5)		
Fremont County (1920)					
Riverside Township	207.4	130.5	164.7	42.7	55.6
	(55)	(14)	(30)		

Region and Locality (year)	Average Farm Size			Difference (1–3)	Percentage of Farms Operated by Owners
	Related Owners 1	Unrelated Renters 2	Renters 3		
Harrison County (1922)					
Washington Township	176.9	160.3	189.7	−12.8	49.5
	(49)	(27)	(23)		
Monona County (1919)					
Center Township	159.0	140.0	208.2	−49.2	44.1
	(15)	(2)	(17)		
Grant Township	145.0	158.3	212.7	−67.7	43.0
	(40)	(9)	(44)		
Kennebec Township	201.0	229.0	203.1	−2.1	49.2
	(29)	(7)	(23)		
Maple Township	144.1	140.0	171.1	−27.0	59.2
	(29)	(6)	(14)		
Sherman Township	172.9	140.0	194.7	−21.8	35.7
	(15)	(2)	(25)		
Montgomery County (1920)					
East Township	122.1	163.0	119.4	2.7	68.6
	(83)	(13)	(25)		
Woodbury County (1917)					
Floyd Independ.	204.2	120.0	173.3	30.9	42.9
	(6)	(2)	(6)		
Morgan Township	241.2	213.3	173.3	69.7	40.7
	(37)	(15)	(39)		
Moville Township	180.6	219.5	178.7	1.9	53.3
	(53)	(10)	(36)		
Southern Pasture Area					
Taylor County (1923)					
Marshall Township	158.6	120.2	166.4	−7.8	63.5
	(40)	(9)	(14)		
Grant Township	152.5	147.4	206.5	−54.0	51.1
	(48)	(14)	(32)		

Region and Locality (year)	Average Farm Size			Difference (1–3)	Percentage of Farms Operated by Owners
	Related Owners 1	Unrelated Renters 2	Renters 3		
Dairy Area					
Allamakee County (1917)					
Jefferson Township	141.7	133.8	155.1	−13.4	82.5
	(113)	(6)	(18)		
Butler County (1917)					
Ripley/Madison	167.7	200.9	173.7	−6.0	33.3
Townships	(33)	(20)	(46)		

Note: The numbers in ( ) are the number of farms in that tenure category.

Sources: Data for Lone Tree Township in Clay County are from Von Tungeln, "A Rural Social Survey of Lone Tree Township, Clay County, Iowa"; those for Jackson Township in Warren County are from Gillespie, "A Social Survey of Jackson Township, Warren County, Iowa"; those for Hudson Township in Black Hawk County and the Jesup consolidated district in Buchanan County are from Von Tungeln and Eells, "Rural Social Survey of Hudson, Orange and Jesup Consolidated School Districts, Black Hawk and Buchanan Counties, Iowa"; and those for Orange Township in Black Hawk County are from Von Tungeln, "A Rural Social Survey of Orange Township, Black Hawk County, Iowa." All other data were calculated by the author directly from farmers' directories published by the Anderson Publishing Company (Mason City and Des Moines) on the dates indicated in the table above.

Preface and Acknowledgments

1. Alexis de Tocqueville, *Democracy in America*, 87.

2. The term "soft fascism" is borrowed from Scott G. McNall, *The Road to Rebellion: Class Formation and Kansas Populism, 1865–1900*, ix.

3. Tocqueville, *Democracy in America*, 514, 511.

4. McNall, *The Road to Rebellion*, x.

5. Ibid., xi.

6. Tocqueville, *Democracy in America*, 506.

7. Lawrence Goodwyn, *The Populist Moment: A Short History of the Agrarian Revolt*.

1. Introduction

1. For a similar perspective, see Lawrence Goodwyn, *Democratic Promise: The Populist Moment in America*, vii–xv.

2. Wayne E. Fuller, *The Old Country School*, 228–239.

3. John Dewey, *Democracy and Education*.

4. Michael B. Katz, quoted in Alan J. DeYoung, "The Status of American Education Research," *Review of Educational Research* 57 (summer 1987): 123–148.

5. Paul Theobald in his *Call School: Rural Education in the Midwest to 1918* provides the most detailed account of these two interpretations in the specific context of midwestern rural resistance to common schools in the nineteenth century and to a lesser extent to township consolidation in the twentieth. See also Paul Theobald, "Democracy and the Origins of Rural Midwest Education: A Retrospective Essay," *Educational Theory* 38 (summer 1988): 363–367. Theobald suggests that Fuller's *The Old Country School* and James H. Madison's paper, "John D. Rockefeller's General Board of Education and the Rural School Problem of the Midwest, 1900–1930," *History of Education Quarterly* 24 (summer 1984): 181–199, are representative of much of the recent work appearing to champion resistance as an expression of local democracy, while he sees educational historians writing earlier in the twentieth century as adhering more closely to the antintellectual-antidemocratic interpretation. Theobald's own perspective falls closer to the latter.

6. Paul Theobald, "Historical Scholarship in Nineteenth Century Rural Education," in Alan J. DeYoung, editor, *Rural Education: Issues and Practice*, 3–25. The quotation is on page 15. Theobald restates this hypothesis in his *Call School*.

7. For a fuller discussion of this issue in the recent geographical literature, see Alan Pred, *Place, Practice and Structure: Social and Spatial Transformation in Southern Sweden 1750–1850*; Edward W. Soja, *Postmodern Geographies: The Reassertion of Space in Critical Social Theory*; Nigel Thrift, "On the Determination of Social Action in Space and Time," *Environment and Planning D: Society and Space* 1:1 (1983): 23–57; Barney Warf, "Regional

Transformation, Everyday Life, and Pacific Northwest Lumber Production," *Annals of the Association of American Geographers* 78:2 (1988): 326–346; and Derek Gregory, *Geographical Imaginations*.

8. Mary Neth in *Preserving the Family Farm: Women, Community, and the Foundation of Agribusiness in the Midwest, 1900–1940*, 290, has recently made a compelling case for the necessity of reconsidering class in the social history of rural America.

9. See McNall, *The Road to Rebellion*, 5.

10. E. P. Thompson, *The Poverty of Theory and Other Essays*, 295 (italics added).

11. James R. Shortridge has identified the depression of the 1890s as the watershed event leading to the social construction of the Midwest as a cultural region distinct from the West. See his *The Middle West, Its Meaning in American Culture*.

12. The existence of large-scale, "progressive" farmers was not a new phenomenon in the Midwest; they had enjoyed prestige in rural communities since the earliest days of settlement. Provided they conformed to community norms in their dealings with other farmers in a locality, they constituted no threat to the stability and reproduction of these norms. As the numbers of such farmers increased in particular localities in the twentieth century, the necessity for conformance to traditional norms was undermined.

13. For a periodization of American history based on long-term demographic characteristics and settlement forms, see Walter Nugent, *Structures of American History*, 111–112. Nugent characterizes the period 1895–1920 in the Midwest as "settled-rural" — a period in which the mortality rate continued to drop significantly, presumably because of improvements in diet, in housing conditions, and in sanitation.

14. Wayne E. Fuller, "Making Better Farmers: The Study of Agriculture in Midwestern Country Schools, 1900–1923," *Agricultural History* 60:2 (1986): 154–168.

2. Family, Neighborhood, Church, and School

1. "If a rural culture means an emotional and craftsmanlike dedication to the soil, a tradition and pre-capitalist outlook, a tradition-directed rather than career-directed type of character, and a village community devoted to ancestral ways and habitually given to communal action, then the prairies and plains never had one." See Richard Hofstadter, *The Age of Reform*, 43, 45–46. Regarding community, Hofstadter notes that the predominance of the "isolated farmstead standing in the midst of great acreage, the frequent movements, the absence of village life . . . deprived the farmer and his family of the advantages of community, lowered his chances of association and co-operation, and encouraged the rampant, suspicious, and almost suicidal individualism for which the American farmer was long noted. . . ."

2. Thomas Bender, *Community and Social Change in America*, 109. Robert Wiebe has described these locality-based communities (gemeinschaft) as "island communities" and has suggested that their disintegration as territorial wholes in the 1880s and 1890s was instrumental in the emergence of the Progressive movement and a new middle class to fill the power voids created by their disintegration. He argues that part of the political success

of the early Progressives derives from their use of the rhetoric of local autonomy and community self-determination at a time when the spatial and social division of labor in the nation ensured that this was not possible without creating and implementing new forms of community and new forms of local control. See Robert H. Wiebe, *The Search for Order, 1877–1920*, 52–58.

3. Bender, *Community and Social Change in America*, 114, 118, 119. Bender also cautions that "To get at the changing meaning of community in the second half of the nineteenth century, historians must focus on tension and interaction rather than collapse. Although the equilibrium between community and society shifted, community never disappeared. It was, however, transformed" (119).

4. See Max J. Pfeffer, "Social Origins of Three Systems of Farm Production in the United States," *Rural Sociology* 48:4 (1983): 540–562. Pfeffer's analysis of the origins of family farming in the Great Plains also applies to farming in the old Northwest and much of the rest of the Midwest.

5. David B. Danbom, *The Resisted Revolution*, 11.

6. The pathbreaking work of John Mack Faragher, *Sugar Creek: Life on the Illinois Prairie*, explodes as myth the view that stable communities failed to develop in the early Midwest. Mary Neth in *Preserving the Family Farm* makes the case that the neighborhood-based social relationships Faragher identified in the nineteenth century in central Illinois remained key attributes of commercial family farming throughout much of the rural Midwest until the beginning of World War II.

7. Neth, *Preserving the Family Farm*, 2.

8. W. J. Cash, *The Mind of the South*, 48 (page citation is to reprint edition).

9. Allan Kulikoff, *The Agrarian Origins of American Capitalism*, 20–21.

10. This is consistent with the argument Max Pfeffer makes regarding the growth of family farming in the Great Plains. See Pfeffer, "Social Origins of Three Systems of Farm Production in the United States."

11. Neth, *Preserving the Family Farm*, 2.

12. There is a very large and contentious literature in rural social history and sociology over the nature of production and the class structure of commercial, family farming as it was (and in some places still is) practiced in North America. Some have argued that family farmers are an intermediate category between capital and labor, possessing qualities of both. See, for example, Patrick H. Mooney, "Toward a Class Analysis of Midwestern Agriculture," *Rural Sociology* 48:4 (1983): 563–584; Susan A. Mann and James M. Dickinson, "Obstacles to the Development of a Capitalist Agriculture," *Journal of Peasant Studies* 5 (1978): 466–481; and Susan A. Mann, *Agrarian Capitalism in Theory and Practice*. Others have argued that it could better be described as a separate mode of production. See, for example, Michael Merrill, "Cash Is Good to Eat: Self-Sufficiency and Exchange in the Rural Economy of the United States," *RHR* no. 4 (winter 1977): 42–47; "So What's So Wrong with the Household Mode of Production?" *RHR* no. 22 (1979–80): 141–146; and Harriet Friedmann, "World Market, State, and Family Farm: Social Bases of Household Production in the Era of Wage Labor," *Comparative Studies in Society and History* 20 (1978): 545–586. Still others have argued that family farm production, although embedded within the ide-

ology of yeomanry was nonetheless petty commodity production. See, for example, Kuli-koff, *The Agrarian Origins of American Capitalism*, chapter 2.

13. Probably the best description of these exchanges is found in Faragher's *Sugar Creek*, chapter 14. Faragher collectively refers to these exchanges as the "borrowing system" and maintains that they operated quite independently of the market in the mid-nineteenth-century community he studied in central Illinois. Mary Neth in her *Preserving the Family Farm* presents evidence that these exchanges remained a central feature of family farming in the Midwest and one of the defining characteristics of rural midwestern culture well into the twentieth century. See especially chapter 2. It should also be pointed out that by the 1910s there was an acute shortage of farm laborers who were willing to work for wages. Wages paid on the farm simply were not competitive with those paid in the cities.

14. Deborah Fink, *Open Country, Iowa: Rural Women, Tradition and Change*, 24.

15. Neth, *Preserving the Family Farm*, chapter 2, uses the phrase "community system of family farming" instead of "neighborhood system of family farming," but in so doing creates some confusion because of the way in which she defines community elsewhere in her book.

16. This work was pioneered by James Henretta, "Families and Farms: *Mentalité* in Pre-Industrial America," *William and Mary Quarterly* 3d ser. 35 (1978): 3–32, and was extended to midwestern contexts by Kathleen Neils Conzen, "Peasant Pioneers: Generational Succession Among German Farmers in Frontier Minnesota," in Steven Hahn and Jonathan Prude, *The Countryside in the Age of Capitalist Transformation*, 259–292, and Faragher, *Sugar Creek*. In the extended lineal family, "each generation lived in a separate household, but the character of production and inheritance linked these conjugal units through a myriad of legal, moral, and customary bonds." Henretta, 25.

17. Sonya Salamon, *Prairie Patrimony: Family, Farming, and Community in the Midwest*, 93. Salamon presents evidence that an obsession with land and family control of it still characterizes rural communities of German ancestry in Illinois.

18. Hal S. Barron, "Staying Down on the Farm: Social Processes of Settled Rural Life in the Nineteenth-Century North," in Hahn and Prude, editors, *The Countryside in the Age of Capitalist Transformation*, 339, 340.

19. See Henretta, "Families and Farms: *Mentalité* in Pre-Industrial America."

20. William L. Bowers, *The Country Life Movement in America, 1900–1920*, 102–127; esp. chapter 1.

21. See, for example, Michel Aglietta, "Phases of U.S. Capitalist Expansion," *New Left Review* 110 (July–August 1978): 17–28; and John Agnew, *The United States in the World-Economy: A Regional Geography*.

22. See, for example, some of the early rural sociology studies, such as J. H. Kolb, "Rural Primary Groups: A Study of Agricultural Neighborhoods," *Wisconsin Agricultural Extension Service Bulletin* no. 51 (1921); D. Sanderson and W. S. Thompson, "The Social Areas of Otsego County," *Cornell University Agricultural Extension Service Bulletin* no. 422 (1923); and E. L. Morgan and O. Howells, "Rural Population Groups," *Missouri Agricultural Extension Service Research Bulletin* no. 74 (1925).

23. Fink, *Open Country, Iowa*; Neth, *Preserving the Family Farm*.

24. See Barron, "Staying Down on the Farm," 334–340; and Nugent, *Structures of American History*.

25. Faragher, *Sugar Creek*; James M. Williams, *The Expansion of Rural Life: The Social Psychology of Rural Development*; Barron, "Staying Down on the Farm"; and Sean Hartnett, "The Land Market on the Wisconsin Frontier: An Examination of Land Ownership Processes in Turtle and LaPrairie Townships, 1839–1890," *Agricultural History* 65:1 (1991): 38–77.

26. Henretta, "Families and Farms: *Mentalite* in Pre-Industrial America."

27. Neth, *Preserving the Family Farm*, 44, 54–55.

28. Fink, *Open Country, Iowa*, 37.

29. Neth, *Preserving the Family Farm*, 62.

30. Neth, *Preserving the Family Farm*, 71–72.

31. Fink, *Open Country, Iowa*, 40.

32. See Theobald, *Call School*, 81–82.

33. Fink, *Open Country, Iowa*, 90.

34. Mabel Carney (*Country Life and the Rural School*, 142) believed that this characterization of the country school was descriptive of an earlier time; but with the arrival of the industrial age and the exodus of the better class of farmers to the city at the turn of the century, she argues, it was no longer an accurate one. "There was a time when the country school was the center of attraction: when spelling-bees, literary societies, singing schools, and debating clubs made it the life of the neighborhood." In addition to Carney's *Country Life and the Rural School*, valuable descriptions of the centrality of the country school in rural neighborhood life can be found in E. R. Eastman, *These Changing Times*; Williams, *The Expansion of Rural Life*; and Faragher, *Sugar Creek*.

35. Theobald, *Call School*, 83.

36. Although Theobald's primary attention is on farmer resistance to the common school movement of the mid–nineteenth century, he also implies that the explanation he offers for the nineteenth century extends to at least 1918.

3. The Country Life Movement and Moral Landscapes of Modernity

1. Hofstadter, *The Age of Reform*, 23–46.

2. Arthur M. Schlesinger, *The Rise of the City, 1878–1898*, 64.

3. Historian William Reese has shown that for the six smaller midwestern cities he investigated, rates of investment in factories more than quadrupled between 1880 and 1900; while geographers Brian Page and Richard Walker indicate that "between 1870 and 1900, ten Iowa cities exhibited percentage increases in manufacturing employment that rivaled or surpassed the regional metropolises of Chicago, Cleveland, St. Louis, and Detroit." See William J. Reese, *Power and Promise of School Reform: Grassroots Movements during the Progressive Era*, 18–22; and Brian Page and Richard Walker, "From Settlement to Fordism: The Agro-Industrial Revolution in the American Midwest," *Economic Geography* 67:4 (1991): 281–315, 302.

4. Page and Walker, "From Settlement to Fordism," 292; C. Post, "The American Road to Capitalism," *New Left Review* 133 (1982): 30–51.

5. See, for example, Nugent, *Structures of American History*, 100–101.

6. Gilbert C. Fite, *American Farmers: The New Minority*, 10.

7. Henry A. Wallace, quoted in Don S. Kirschner, *City and Country: Rural Responses to Urbanization in the 1920s*, 248.

8. See Salamon, *Prairie Patrimony*.

9. M. L. Primack and J. F. Willis, *An Economic History of the United States*, 294–296.

10. For an excellent summary of the major changes, see James H. Shideler, *Farm Crisis, 1919–1923*, esp. 4–19.

11. W. G. Murray, "Struggle for Land Ownership," in *A Century of Farming in Iowa, 1846–1946*, 12.

12. After weighing the available evidence, Neth (*Preserving the Family Farm*, 73) concludes that "Although rural institutions and organizations depended on a stable and prosperous farm population, informal neighboring practices flourished among those who were neither stable nor prosperous. . . . Neither land ownership nor tenancy alone determined whether a farm family would participate in neighborhood exchanges."

13. Ibid., 73.

14. See Hartnett, "The Land Market on the Wisconsin Frontier." The observation about the preference for owning a neighbor's farm rather than for having that person as a neighbor is from Wendell Berry's "A Defense of the Family Farm," in Gary Comstock, editor, *Is There a Moral Obligation to Save the Family Farm?* 356.

15. A number of studies have draw attention to the importance of this phenomenon historically in other parts of the United States. See, for example, Henry J. Fletcher, "The Doom of the Small Town," *The Forum* 19 (1895): 214–223; Williams, *The Expansion of Rural Life*; and Barron, "Staying Down on the Farm." Henretta ("Families and Farms: *Mentalite* in Pre-Industrial America," 11) provides a valuable analysis of how these forms of local production in colonial America should be interpreted as "social necessities" in rural communities, all "intimately connected to agriculture" and "supported by communal action."

16. Bowers, *The Country Life Movement in America, 1900–1920*. Rural historian David Danbom has dubbed those adhering to this perspective as "urban agrarians" and has shown that this description is certainly an apt appellation for Liberty Hyde Bailey, Kenyon L. Butterfield, and Theodore Roosevelt, the movement's principal rhetoricians. See Danbom, *The Resisted Revolution*.

17. Danbom, *The Resisted Revolution*, 36–37. See also David B. Danbom, "Rural Education Reform and the Country Life Movement, 1900–1920," *Agricultural History* 53:2 (1979): 462–474.

18. See Samuel P. Hays, *Conservation and the Gospel of Efficiency: The Progressive Conservation Movement 1890–1920*; Samuel P. Hays, *Businessmen and Reform: A Study of the Progressive Movement*; and Wiebe, *The Search for Order, 1877–1920*.

19. Roger Finke and Rodney Stark, *The Churching of America, 1776–1990: Winners and Losers in Our Religious Economy*, 202–216. See also James H. Madison, "Reformers and the Rural Church, 1900–1950," *Journal of American History* 73 (Dec. 1986): 645–668.

20. U.S. Senate, Special Message from President Roosevelt, *Report of the United States Country Life Commission*. Senate Document 705, 60th Congress, 2d Session, 1909, 21–22, 30–36, 37–51.

21. Eastman, *These Changing Times*, 152; Shideler, *Farm Crisis, 1919–1923*, 4. The quotation is from Julius Bernhard Arp, *Rural Education and the Consolidated School*, 16.

22. Danbom, *The Resisted Revolution*, 44, and *Born in the Country*, 169–175; and D. J. Boorstin, *The Americans: The Democratic Experience*, 134–135.

23. Neth attributes the political conservatism of the Country Life movement to the social agenda of agricultural professionals in the movement who "sought to create a prosperous class of farmers who would practice the tenets of scientific agriculture and modern farm living." They eschewed political movements like those linked to the Populist revolt of the 1890s which tried to ally farmers and laborers because they saw these as undermining the goals of commercial agriculture. They "believed that wealth was available to farmers if they abandoned the old ways and became efficient businessmen." See Neth, *Preserving the Family Farm*, 104.

24. Bowers, *The Country Life Movement in America*, 28, 29. Bowers argues that making farmers into businessmen was "necessarily destructive of the fundamental values of the traditional agrarian way of life. . . . [P]roof of this is the fact that farmers cannot be urged to organize and still maintain their ageold individualism. Furthermore, one could not ask the government to intercede on the farmers' behalf or aid them without the independent and self-help image of agrarians being violated. Nor could one urge farmers to imitate urban business counterparts without doing something drastic to the unique aspects of rural living. Regrettably for those who would have the best of both worlds, the urbanization of farmers destroyed the rural way of life."

25. Wilbert L. Anderson, *The Country Town: A Study of Rural Evolution*, 215–216.

26. Ibid., 217–221, 230–233, 237–238, 253. Anderson saw the class interests of the farmer to be allied with the petty bourgeoisie of the market towns rather than with the working class of the cities.

27. Ibid., 253–254.

28. John Lewis Gillin, "Discussion of the Church and the Rural Community," *The American Journal of Sociology* 16:5 (1911): 697.

29. Lowry Nelson, *Rural Sociology: Its Origin and Growth in the United States*, 3–33. For a good treatment of the social gospel movement among American Protestants, see Winthrop S. Hudson, *Religion in America: An Historical Account of the Development of American Religious Life*, 310–317. For early statements of Country Life ideology, see Liberty Hyde Bailey's *The State and the Farmer* and *The Country Life Movement*.

30. Gillin, "Discussion of the Church and the Rural Community," 699.

31. Warren H. Wilson, *The Evolution of the Country Community*, xvi.

32. Ibid., 32, 34, 44, 46–47.

33. Herbert Quick, *The Fairview Idea*, 52.

34. There were a few advocates of consolidation who remained adamant in their conviction that consolidated schools had to be located in the open country as far removed from any town influence as possible if they were to become the basis for the creation of new

rural life and consciousness. Perhaps the best example of this is Arp, *Rural Education and the Consolidated School*, esp. 91–110.

35. Benson Y. Landis, *Rural Church Life in the Middle West*, 70.

36. Other descriptive terms for essentially the same concept were "rural town" and "rural-minded" town.

37. By no means did all, or even most, advocates of rural school consolidation aligned with the Country Life movement advocate linking rural school consolidation with movements to form agricultural cooperatives of one form or another, but there were several influential educators who did. See, for example, Harold W. Foght, *Rural Denmark and Its Schools*; and Macy Campbell, *Rural Life at the Crossroads*.

38. For an analysis of the conflicts over the Bennett and Edwards laws and their legacies, including a detailed history of nativism and anti-Catholicism in American public education, see Lloyd Jorgenson, *The State and the Non-Public School, 1825–1925*, esp. chapter 9.

4. The Political Economy of Public Schools in the Midwest during the Golden Age

1. Cf. Lawrence A. Cremin, *American Education: The Colonial Experience, 1607–1783*, 237.

2. Bender, *Community and Social Change in America*, 138–139.

3. See, for example, Joel Spring, *Education and the Rise of the Corporate State*; David B. Tyack, *The One Best System*; S. Bowles and H. Gintis, *Schooling in Capitalist America*; and David R. Reynolds and Fred M. Shelley, "Local Control in American Public Education: Myth and Reality," in J. F. Kodras and J. P. Jones, editors, *Geographic Dimensions of United States Social Policy*, 107–133.

4. Reynolds and Shelley, "Local Control in American Public Education: Myth and Reality," 120.

5. David Nasaw, *Schooled to Order: A Social History of Public Schooling in the United States*, 120–123.

6. The point is made most forcefully in Raymond E. Callahan, *Education and the Cult of Efficiency*. More recent scholarship suggests that a concern with "business efficiency" had been an integral part of the common school movement right from the start. In this regard, see Barbara Berman, "Business Efficiency, American Schooling, and the Public School Superintendency: A Reconsideration of the Callahan Thesis," *History of Education Quarterly* 23:3 (1983): 297–321.

7. See, for example, Fuller, *The Old Country School*, esp. chapter 6; and Reese, *Power and Promise of School Reform*.

8. Wiebe, *The Search for Order, 1877–1920*, 158, 155.

9. Reynolds and Shelley, "Local Control in American Public Education: Myth and Reality," 120.

10. Edward A. Ross, *What Is America?* 66.

11. For further discussion of this, see Reynolds and Shelley, "Local Control in American Public Education: Myth and Reality," 121.

12. Wiebe, *The Search for Order, 1877–1920*, 159, 164.

13. There were a few educators of repute in the Midwest who disagreed about the necessity of rural school consolidation. Ernest Burnham, for example, director of the Department of Rural Schools at the Western Michigan Normal School and a research scholar at the Columbia University Teachers College, argued that the district school was better suited to the needs of country children than the consolidated school because of its stronger, holistic ties to the everyday life of the child, his or her family, and to the larger rural community of which it was a part. His argument was based on detailed evidence from a study of consolidated and rural district school systems in Ohio and Michigan. See Ernest Burnham, *Two Types of Rural Schools*, 105–106. Other professional educators of prominence who doubted whether consolidation was a general solution to rural school problems included John T. Prince, "Consolidation of Rural Schools, II," *NEA Proceedings*, 1903, 933–934; Payson Smith, "Dangers of Over-organization of the Rural School," *NEA Proceedings*, 1914, 256–257; and A. E. Winship, "Some Remarkable Achievements in Rural Schools," *NEA Proceedings*, 1918, 792. The last mentioned was the editor of the prestigious *Journal of Education*.

14. See, for example, Anderson, *The Country Town*, 253–254.

15. Foght, *Rural Denmark and Its Schools*.

16. Anna Marie Keppel, "Country Schools for Country Children: Backgrounds of the Reform Movement in Rural Elementary Education, 1890–1914" (Ph.D. diss., University of Wisconsin, 1960), 142.

17. In addition to Carney, *Country Life and the Country School*, also see George H. Betts, *New Ideals in Rural Schools*; George H. Betts and O. E. Hall, *Better Rural Schools*; Elwood P. Cubberley, *The Improvement of Rural Schools*; Elwood P. Cubberley, *Rural Life and Education*; E. Davenport, *Education for Efficiency*; and I. King, *Education for Social Efficiency*. For a more contemporary treatment, the work of Wayne E. Fuller deserves attention. See, for example, his *One-Room Schools of the Middle West*; *The Old Country School*; "Changing Concepts of the Country School as a Community Center in the Midwest," *Agricultural History* 58:3 (1984): 423–441; and "Making Better Farmers: The Study of Agriculture in Midwestern Country Schools, 1900–1923," *Agricultural History* 60:2 (1986): 154–168.

18. For further discussion of the "rural school problem" as articulated by the educational reformers of the period, see Arp, *Rural Education and the Consolidated School*; Betts, *New Ideals in Rural Schools*; Carney, *Country Life and the Country School*; Cubberley, *The Improvement of Rural Schools*; and E. E. Davis, *The Twentieth Century Rural School*.

19. Unemphasized, of course, was that the professional educators themselves had been instrumental in setting this agenda. See Tyack, *The One Best System*; Carl F. Kaestle, *Pillars of the Republic*; Michael B. Katz, *The Irony of Early School Reform: Educational Innovation in Mid-Nineteenth Century Massachusetts*.

20. As David Tyack has put it, "Schoolmen saw clearly the deficiencies but not the virtues of the one-room school. Schooling — which farmers usually associated with book learning — was only a small, and to many, an incidental part of the total education the community provided. The child acquired his values and skills from his family and from neighbors. . . . The major vocational curriculum was work on the farm or in the craftsman's

shop or the corner store; civic and moral instruction came mostly in church or home or around the village where people met to gossip or talk politics." See Tyack, "The Tribe and the Common School: Community Control in Rural Education."

21. Recently historians have undertaken to reconstruct what conditions were actually confronted in the rural schools of this and earlier periods by students, teachers, and patrons alike. The descriptions provided by Tyack, "The Tribe and the Common School: Community Control in Rural Education" and Fuller, *The Old Country School*, are particularly noteworthy.

22. Cubberley, *Rural Life and Education*, rev. ed., 64–65.

23. Ibid., 106, 229.

24. For more biographical information on Cubberley, particularly his power as one of public education's "managers of virtue," see David B. Tyack and Elizabeth Hansot, *Managers of Virtue: Public School Leadership in America, 1820–1980*, 114–128.

25. Cubberley, *Rural Life and Education*, 55.

26. For recent theory on the emergence of the professional middle class in the United States, see David Harvey, *Consciousness and the Urban Experience*.

27. See Tyack, *The One Best System*; and Reynolds and Shelley, "Local Control in American Public Education: Myth and Reality."

28. Typically this control was exercised by the principal landowning families in a locality; and while it was local, it certainly wasn't necessarily democratic. This is a point recently made forcefully by Theobald in his *Call School*.

29. Keppel comments: "One cannot study the reports of the United States Commission of Education between 1885 and 1895 without being overwhelmed by the obvious fact that the rural schools were regarded as no problem." Keppel, "Country Schools for Country Children," 9.

30. National Education Association, *Report of the Committee of Twelve on Rural Schools*, as cited in Fuller, *The Old Country School*, 106.

31. Tyack, *The One Best System*.

32. Committee of Twelve, quoted in Theobald, *Call School*, 162.

33. There were some dissenters who argued that the principal problem of the country school was not poor administration but the lack of good teachers to staff them. Edward A. Ross, for example, worried about the dangers of speeding up the process of education in the public schools and what he referred to as the midwesterners' penchant more "for regimenting more children in the schools" than "for improving teaching." See Edward A. Ross, *Changing America*, 231.

34. See, for example, Merle Curti, *The Making of an American Community*; Conzen, "Peasant Pioneers: Generation Succession Among German Farmers in Frontier Minnesota," 259–292; Sonya Salamon, "Ethnic Communities and the Structure of Agriculture," *Rural Sociology*, 50:3 (1985): 323–340; and Salamon, *Prairie Patrimony*.

35. A. Gulliford, *America's Country Schools*, 44.

36. In retrospect, the cause is not hard to find: "Moving from a school with perhaps twenty students, all of whom knew each other and probably knew each other's families and how they fit into the community, to a school with two hundred or more students, almost

all of them strangers, would be difficult enough. For many rural children the problem was exacerbated by social pressures. Whatever their position had been in the rural school and community, in their new school they usually found themselves at the bottom of the heap. Consolidated schools were frequently located in towns and villages, and town children, in their own cliques and hierarchies, viewed farm kids with scorn. Whatever educational benefits consolidation might have brought to rural school children, few recall the process itself with pleasure." George Peabody, *School Days*, 135. Peabody is describing the experience of rural school consolidation in Prince Edward Island during the 1960s, but it is also an apt description of the rural student's experience of consolidation in the Midwest a half century earlier. The cultural stereotyping of farm and urban people into such categories as "hick" and "hip" is not a new phenomenon and has always been experienced most intensely by children.

37. In general, the rights of women to vote on matters pertaining to education increased from east to west in the Midwest at the beginning of the twentieth century. In Nebraska, women had full voting rights on educational matters; in Iowa they could vote only on matters relating to increases in the tax levy for education (e.g., on bond issues to build a new school); while in Indiana women had no vote at all.

38. One of the few case studies of resistance to rural school consolidation is Madison's "John D. Rockefeller's General Education Board and the Rural School Problem in the Midwest, 1900–1930."

5. Educational Reform in Early Twentieth-Century Iowa

1. *Code of Iowa*, sec. 2622 (1897).

2. John Purcell Street, "Iowa Department of Public Instruction, Its Origin and Development," *Annals of Iowa* 30:6 (1950): 397–452; and Richard N. Smith, "Department of Public Instruction in Iowa," in NEA, *Education in the States: Historical Development and Outlook*, 401–432.

3. According to data presented in the *Biennial Report of the Superintendent of Public Instruction* 30 (1901), on average there were 127 country schools per county in 1900.

4. In 1900, all but a handful of the town and city superintendents were men (no women held such posts in any of the larger towns or cities), while the office of county superintendent was rapidly becoming feminized.

5. *Biennial Report of the Superintendent of Public Instruction* 30 (1901): part I, 486; part II, 27–38.

6. While women could run for school office and vote on all revenue or tax matters coming before a school district, they could not vote in general or school board elections until the Nineteenth Amendment to the U.S. Constitution was ratified in 1920.

7. C. P. Colgrove, *The Teacher and the School*, 84.

8. *Biennial Report of the Superintendent of Public Instruction* 29 (1899): 243–244.

9. "The President's Special Report on the Plans for the Training of Special Teachers for Rural Schools," Homer H. Seerley to State Board of Education, December 26, 1913, Homer

H. Seerley Letters, Special Collections, University Archives, University of Northern Iowa Main Library, Cedar Falls, Iowa.

10. I. H. Hart, *Milestones*; Aurner, *History of Education in Iowa*, vol. II, 53, 82.

11. Smith, "Department of Public Instruction in Iowa," 414; Hart, *Milestones*, 51–58. In 1900, membership in the ISTA was organized into four departments based on the nature of the member's professional work: County Superintendents and Normal, Elementary and Graded, High School, College and University. A fifth, Superintendents and Principals, was added in 1913. A rural school section to the Elementary and Graded Department was not added until the 1930s, by which time it had become clear that the rural schools would not just disappear through the ISTA's neglect. Ibid., 53–57.

12. William C. Lang, *A Century of Leadership and Service, A Centennial History of the University of Northern Iowa*, vol. I, *1876–1928*, 280.

13. After it had come under intense pressure in 1912 from key members of the state legislature and the state's board of education to assume responsibility for training rural school teachers, the State Teachers College finally instituted such a course of study in 1913. Ibid., 323–325.

14. The close relationship between the office of state superintendent and the ISTA is also indicated by the fact that it had been Henry Sabin, the superintendent, who in 1893 urged the General Assembly that the state should recognize the ISTA and publish its proceedings as part of the state superintendent's biennial report. The General Assembly obliged by enacting a law in 1894 authorizing the annual publication by the state of 1,500 copies of the proceedings for free distribution to the governor, members of the General Assembly, and the membership of ISTA. See Smith, "Department of Public Instruction in Iowa," 414. The 1,500 copies were more than enough to go around.

15. Aurner, *History of Education in Iowa*, vol. I, 264–278, vol. III, 210–255.

16. George S. May, "Iowa's Consolidated Schools," *Palimpsest* 37:1 (1956): 1–10.

17. *Biennial Report of the Superintendent of Public Instruction* 30 (1901): 305–306.

18. Betts, *New Ideals in Rural Schools*. See also Macy Campbell, "A Dying School System for Children Who Are Just Beginning to Live," *Midland Schools* 33:10 (1919): 339–342.

19. *Biennial Report of the Superintendent of Public Instruction* 35 (1910): 27–28. "Professional matters" were to apply especially to the hiring and firing of teachers or other employees, the assignment and reappointment of teachers, the selection of textbooks, the selection of courses and programs, school design and construction, and sanitation. These, Riggs proclaimed, were "matters for experts."

20. *Des Moines Register and Leader*, 7 March 1909.

21. John E. Brindley, "A Study of Iowa Population as Related to Industrial Conditions," *Iowa Agricultural Extension Station Bulletin* no. 27 (1912).

22. J. L. Andriot, *Population Abstract of the U.S. 1983*.

23. Bureau of the Census, *Thirteenth Census of the United States, 1909 and 1910*.

24. Brindley, "A Study of Iowa Population as Related to Industrial Conditions."

25. Bureau of the Census, *Fifteenth Census of the United States, 1930*.

26. C. L. Holmes, "Types of Farming in Iowa," *Iowa Agricultural Experiment Station Bulletin* no. 256 (1929): 152–206; Allan G. Bogue, *From Prairie to Corn Belt*; cf., John C.

Hudson, *Making the Corn Belt: A Geographical History of Middle-Western Agriculture*. While the total population of the state decreased by 115,000 between 1890 and 1910, almost 40 percent of this was accounted for by the decrease in the number of persons aged 5–14 alone — the equivalent of the enrollment of approximately 1,800 country schools. In 1903– 4, the average number of persons between the ages of 5 and 21 years residing in a country school district was 30.5 (*Biennial Report of the Superintendent of Public Instruction* 32 (1905): part II, 117). The comparable figure for 1912–13 was 25.4, a loss of 16.7 percent. In 1912–13 the average enrollment in country school districts was 18.5 (*Biennial Report of the Superintendent of Public Instruction* 36 (1913).

27. Bureau of the Census, *Thirteenth Census of the United States, 1909 and 1910*.

28. See, for example, the case studies of rural communities published by the Iowa Agricultural Extension Station affiliated with the Iowa State College, listed in the bibliography.

29. Hawthorn's *The Sociology of Rural Life* was published in 1926, but drew heavily on social surveys and other observations on rural conditions in Iowa during the pre–World War I period.

30. Horace Boies Hawthorn, *The Sociology of Rural Life*, 349, 290.

31. Ibid., 349–350.

32. As Deyoe put it in a letter to the past president of the ISTA, "I believe also, as you do, that when the country districts find they must pay for the high school tuition of pupils residing in such districts, that they will proceed to establish high schools of their own. It will indirectly lead to consolidation of schools." A. M. Deyoe to E. J. H. Beard, Newton, 23 February 1911, Letter Books of the Superintendent of Public Instruction, Archives, State Historical Society of Iowa, Des Moines (henceforth abbreviated LBSPI).

33. In a widely publicized case in Muscatine County, a rural school township had built a two-room central school in 1906 to replace the existing country schools. The majority of parents in the township, however, refused to send their children to the new "central" school, preferring instead to send them to the one-room schools in their respective rural neighborhoods. The Iowa Supreme Court finally ruled in 1908 that the building of the central school had been illegal (*Kirchner v Board of Directors of School Township of Wapsinonic*, 141 Iowa 43 [1908]). This was not only a major embarrassment to educational reformers, it also convinced them that few parents would willingly agree to the closure of their country schools without assurance that the new consolidated schools would be qualitatively different and arguably better than those which they replaced. Additional information regarding this case was derived from A. M. Deyoe to F. E. Stillwell, Glyndon, Minn., 6 September 1912; A. M. Deyoe to John W. Ross, Webber, Kans., 16 August 1913, LBSPI; and Mary and Frederick Maltus, interview by author, Welton, Iowa, 28 May 1991.

34. Whereas the teaching of agriculture remained an important element in some reformers' arguments for the necessity of a qualitative change in the nature of rural education, agricultural education remained a controversial topic in Iowa, producing at least as much opposition to consolidation as it did support for it.

35. Originally billed as a "Country Life Commission," it was quickly renamed The Better Iowa Schools Commission to avoid being too closely aligned with the national movement headed by Liberty Hyde Bailey of Cornell University in New York. Homer H. Seerley

to Prof. A. C. Page, Branford, Conn., 15 November 1911, Homer H. Seerley Letters, Special Collections, University Archives, University of Northern Iowa Main Library, Cedar Falls, Iowa. For its recommendations, see "Report of the Better Iowa Schools Commission," *Proceedings of the Fifty-Eighth Annual Session of the Iowa State Teachers Association* 58 (1912): 55–118.

36. *Pocahontas County Sun*, 10 April 1913.

37. G. A. Brown, *Iowa's Consolidated Schools*, 101; May, "Iowa's Consolidated Schools," 39.

38. For an elaboration of this perspective, see Daryl Hobbs, "Social Organization in the Countryside," in Emery N. Castle, editor, *The Changing American Countryside: Rural People and Places*, 369–396.

39. Albert M. Deyoe, "The School as an Efficient Factor in the Educational, Social, and Recreational Activities of the Community," *Midland Schools* 26:1 (1912): 46–48. Deyoe, "Factors in the Development of a Greater Iowa," *Proceedings of the Fifty-Eighth Annual Session of the Iowa State Teachers Association* 58 (1912): 37–53 (reprinted in *Midland Schools* 27:6 [1913]: 175–184); Deyoe, "Public School Activities in Iowa," *Proceedings of the Sixtieth Annual Session of the Iowa State Teachers Association* 60 (1914): 36–51 (reprinted in *Midland Schools* 29 [1915]: 147–153).

40. F. A. Welch, "Some Problems of the Village School," *Midland Schools* 35:5 (1921): 147–148; Macy Campbell, "A Brief History of Consolidation in Iowa," *Bulletin of the Iowa State Teachers College*, Department of Rural Education 22 (1921): 3–16.

41. Reformers did not push for the consolidation of rural school districts in parts of northeast and much of southern Iowa on the grounds that the uneven topography there made the transportation of pupils at public expense impractical. Not insignificantly, however, uneven topography also went hand in hand with small farms and relatively low farm incomes.

42. At least thirty and perhaps as many as sixty such consolidated districts were formed between 1913 and 1922.

43. Ricard J. Jensen and Mark Friedberger, *Education and Social Structure: An Historical Study of Iowa*, 6.34–6.35.

44. The exploitation derived not from dominance of the wage-labor relation but from the lack of competition from other entrepreneurs typically found in small urban settlements. The lack of competition within small urban places was aided by the spatial competition with other places. The latter, as any introductory text in economic geography shows, produces spatial monopolies. See also Thorstein Veblen, *Absentee Ownership and Business Enterprise in Recent Times*, 147.

45. *Rolfe Arrow*, 3 December 1914; 28 January 1915.

46. *Rolfe Arrow*, 28 January 1915.

47. *Rolfe Arrow*, 18 February 1915.

48. Although the consolidation election in Plover failed, the boundaries of the proposed district were adjusted several times and finally the issue passed in 1916.

49. Robert R. Alford, "School District Reorganization and Community Integration," *Harvard Educational Review* 30:4 (1960): 350–371.

6. Rural Resistance to Consolidation

1. John F. Riggs to F. T. Clampitt, New Providence, Iowa, 23 February 1905, LBSPI.

2. Brookings Institution, *Survey of Administration in Iowa*.

3. Dorothy Schwieder, "Education and Change in the Lives of Iowa Farm Women, 1900–1940," *Agricultural History* 60:2 (1986): 200–215.

4. Jensen and Friedberger, *Education and Social Structure*.

5. D. P. Phillips, "What Does the Farmer Pay for a Consolidated School?" (master's thesis, State University of Iowa, 1923), 38.

6. This contention was disputed by reformers of the period, but it was later confirmed by research conducted at the agricultural experiment station associated with the Iowa State College at Ames. See William H. Lancelot, "Taxable Property Per Child in Farm and Non-Farm Communities of Iowa," *Iowa Agricultural Experiment Station Bulletin* no. P55 (1943); and Lancelot, "Rural School Reorganization in Iowa," *Iowa Agricultural Experiment Station Bulletin* no. P69 (1944).

7. Regarding "rural-mindedness," see Deyoe, "The School as an Efficient Factor in the Educational, Social, and Recreational Activities of the Community."

8. See, for example, *Biennial Report of the Superintendent of Public Instruction* 30 (1901); Clarence R. Aurner, *Leading Events in Johnson County, Iowa History*; and Aurner, *History of Education in Iowa*, vol. 3. Regarding the success of the rural high school in Illinois, see Horace A. Hollister, *The Township and Community High School Movement in Illinois*, Department of Interior, Bureau of Education, bulletin no. 35.

9. So proclaimed Deyoe in his yearly address before the annual meeting of the State Teachers Association in 1915. See Albert M. Deyoe, "Educational Needs and Tendencies in Iowa," *Proceedings of the Sixty-First Session of the Iowa State Teachers Association* 61 (1915): 11–21.

10. Jensen and Friedberger (*Education and Social Structure*, 7.2) expressed the sentiments of many reformers well when they wrote "Farmers who prided themselves on herds of fat cattle and hogs, high grain yields and large bank accounts were easily satisfied with dirty, dark, dank frame buildings for their offspring."

11. Evidence that reformers may have overestimated how wealthy Iowa farmers were is provided in H. Kyrk, "Cost of Living on Iowa Farmers, Part II: Household Expenditures," *Iowa Agricultural Experiment Station Bulletin* no. 237 (1926): 61–79.

12. *Biennial Report of the Superintendent of Public Instruction* 40 (1920).

13. D. P. Phillips, "What Does the Farmer Pay for a Consolidated School?" (masters thesis, State University of Iowa, 1923). The calculations are based on 1918 data from H. B. Munger, "Farm Management Surveys in Black Hawk, Grundy and Tama Counties, Iowa," *Iowa Agricultural Experiment Station Bulletin* no. 198 (1921): 253–276a.

14. Henry A. Wallace, "What Is an Iowa Farm Worth?" *Wallace's Farmer* 49:1 (4 January 1924): 1, 4.

15. See Ross, *What Is America?* 74–80. In a sense, the increasing tenancy of the period can be viewed as a rational economic response to a new set of more clearly capitalist struc-

tural conditions then beginning to characterize agricultural production in Iowa and much of the rest of the Midwest. For a discussion of the forms of tenancy prevailing in Iowa during this period, see O. G. Lloyd, "Farm Leases in Iowa," *Iowa Agricultural Experiment Station* no. 159 (1915): 152–206.

16. Veblen argued that the latter was often a difficult condition to meet throughout the Midwest. Veblen, *Absentee Ownership and Business Enterprise in Recent Times, 142–165.*

17. See, for example, Jensen and Friedberger, *Education and Social Structure;* and Sonya Salamon, "Ethnic Differences in Farm Family Transfers," *Rural Sociology* 45:2 (1980): 290–308; "Ethnic Communities and the Structure of Agriculture"; and *Prairie Patrimony.* There are of course other reasons related to language preservation and the practice of religion that can also help explain the opposition to consolidation in areas of German ethnicity.

18. *Biennial Report of the Superintendent of Public Instruction* 30 (1901): 328.

19. Given the high intercorrelations between most of these indicators, regression analyses were conducted in sets of three, wherein only selected combinations of the indicators (with low intercorrelations) were included in any one model.

20. The Anderson Publishing Company (Mason City, Iowa, and Des Moines, Iowa) compiled and published township "farmers directories" for about half the counties in the state at various times during the period under investigation. These directories are based on cadastral maps and interviews with farmers. For each farmer residing in the township, the directory lists his or her name, the name of his or her spouse, the given names of all their children, the section number and size (in acres) of each land parcel owned or rented, the names of the owner(s) of the parcels rented, and the number of years the farmer had resided in the county. Based on primary source materials available in the archives of the State Historical Society (in both Iowa City and Des Moines) and supplemented by information gleaned from local and county historical societies, area educational agencies, university libraries, local libraries, county courthouses, and the files of particular school districts themselves, it was also possible to construct a quite comprehensive enumeration of all rural school consolidation controversies occurring in each county of the state during the period in question. While the quality and depth of this information varies considerably, it does permit the rather precise identification of those localities where consolidation attempts met with little or much local opposition. Fortunately, it was possible to locate Anderson directories compiled between 1916 and 1925 covering many of the townships for which reliable information on rural school district consolidation had also been assembled. The townships chosen for analysis were those covered in the Anderson directories for which it was also possible to document some effort to consolidate rural schools.

21. The 5 percent figure used to test this hypothesis is arbitrary and is not meant as a measure of statistical significance; nonetheless, it does provide a fairly rigorous criterion.

7. Rural School Consolidation and the Social Construction of Place

1. John F. Merry, editor, *History of Delaware County, Iowa and Its People,* vol. I, 45–46. (Henceforth referred to as *History of Delaware County,* 1914.)

2. Regarding the tie between the railroads and the Iowa Land Company, see *History of Delaware County*, 1878, 468.

3. A station was also located at Delaware to serve the town of Delhi, then the county seat, by ground transport three miles to the south, but the railroad took no direct interest in its development. See *History of Delaware County*, 1878, 525–526.

4. This decline is not revealed as clearly as it might be because of the unavailability of population data for small towns and villages that had not yet incorporated.

5. These data are contained in the *Biennial Report of the Superintendent of Public Instruction* 36 (1912). The nine urban places with their own independent districts were Colesburg, Delaware, Delhi, Earlville, Greeley, Hopkinton, Manchester, Masonville, and Ryan.

6. It is not clear when this school first began operation, but it was operating in 1914. See *History of Delaware County*, 1914.

7. Regarding Dyersville, see P. E. McClenahan to Mrs. Frank J. Williams, Dyersville, Iowa, 21 May 1921, and P. E. McClenahan to Mr. W. A. McCord, Des Moines, 25 June 1921, LBSPI. Regarding Ryan, see F. M. Joseph to Mr. Walter Locke, Ryan, Iowa, 31 August 1915, LBSPI.

8. Whether this figure bears any relationship to the actual number of tuition students is an open question. Even when school districts did comply with the data collection requests of the state and county superintendents, there was no means of verifying their accuracy. Unfortunately, neither the state superintendent's reports nor the records of the Delaware County superintendent provide any information on the numbers of rural students in the county attending town schools between 1911–12 and 1915–16, the first full year in which any consolidated school district in Delaware County was organized. The 1911–12 academic year was the first time that the state required all school districts without their own high schools to pay the tuition of their students to attend high school in a district of their choosing.

9. Mr. and Mrs. Freeman Smith, interview by author, tape recording, Union Township, Delaware County, Iowa, 24 May 1991.

10. *Monticello Express*, 13 January 1920.

11. *Manchester Press*, 20 October 1921.

12. March 1907 minutes of the board of directors of the Consolidated Independent School District of Delhi (available in the superintendent's office of the Maquoketa Valley Community School District in Delhi, Iowa). Subsequently the size of the proposed consolidated district was cut almost in half and the proposition resubmitted to the voters. It passed but only because the Delhi school board had refused to permit separate voting in the village and countryside. Rural opponents threatened legal action and the vote was set aside as illegal (1 June 1907 minutes). This soured relations between civic leaders in Delhi and farmers in the area for almost a decade. Some farmers in Union Township were still muttering about those "smooth talkers" from Delhi when rural school consolidation was being considered in Union Township in 1920–21 (Leslie Tumey, interview by author, tape recording, Hazel Green Township, Delaware County, Iowa, 24 May 1991).

13. See Centennial Committee of Buck Creek United Methodist Church, *Buck Creek United Methodist Church Centennial 1875–1975* (available in the Delaware County Historical Museum, Hopkinton, Iowa); and *Manchester Press*, 8 January 1914.

14. *Manchester Press*, 8 January 1914.

15. Edgewood also had an approved four-year high school in 1914, but it was located just over the county line in Clayton County.

16. Local newspaper coverage of these conferences gives the impression that similar conferences were also held in several other places in Delaware County and perhaps in neighboring counties as well. *Manchester Press*, 14 May 1914.

17. *Manchester Press*, 16 June 1914.

18. Mary Mathey, *Earlville Centennial*, 1952 (locally published pamphlet, available in the Earlville Public Library, Earlville, Iowa).

19. Ibid.

20. There was a history of collegial working relationships between the Methodist and Congregationalist churches in the area dating back to a fire that destroyed much of the town in 1887. At that time the Methodists were given use of the Congregational church in Earlville until they were able to rebuild. See *History of Delaware County*, 1914, 305.

21. This requirement was part of the legislation recommended by the Better Iowa Schools Commission in 1913. The General Assembly passed the bill at that time but gave school districts two years in which to make the necessary preparations for implementing it.

22. *Laws of Iowa*, Senate File 238 (1917), State Historical Society of Iowa, Iowa City, Iowa.

23. Frank D. Joseph to Albert Voit, Earlville, Iowa, 3 March 1915, LBSPI.

24. *Manchester Press*, 1 April 1915.

25. The *Dyersville Commercial*, 22 April 1915. The *Manchester Press* ran a similar piece a week later, but emphasized that this action ensured that Earlville would receive state aid. It too urged other districts to follow Earlville's lead.

26. *Manchester Press*, 8 July 1915.

27. The vote in Delhi had been expected to be close, but a public address by Joseph in Hopkinton a week before the election on how to organize and implement a consolidation campaign lent credence to the rumor that Hopkinton was about to form a consolidated district and helped ensure that the issue passed in the Delhi area. *Manchester Press*, 10 and 17 June 1915.

28. *Manchester Press*, 5 August 1915.

29. Minutes of the board of directors of the Consolidated Independent School District of Delhi, 28 March 1917.

30. *Manchester Press*, 22 April 1915; and Frank D. Joseph to A. B. Holbert, Greeley, Iowa, 29 April 1915, LBSPI.

31. Holbert was a member of the house in the Iowa General Assembly and the owner of one of the largest stables producing draft horses in the United States. Knox was the mayor and school board director in Oneida, while Rector was a major landowner and president of the Oneida bank.

32. A. M. Deyoe to A. B. Holbert, Greeley, Iowa, 27 May 1915, LBSPI.

33. No record of the actual election results could be found. The *Manchester Press*'s coverage of the elections (29 July and 12 August 1915) gives the impression that both passed by comfortable margins.

34. *Manchester Press*, 25 November 1915; *Edgewood Journal*, 25 November 1915.

35. Records pertaining to this matter are on file in the Auditor's Office, Delaware County Courthouse, Manchester, Iowa.

36. As if in retaliation, a Catholic parochial school was established in Petersburg within a year.

37. According to the *History of Delaware County*, 1914, Delaware contained four churches: Baptist, Methodist, Swedish Lutheran, and Evangelical Lutheran.

38. Frank Allyn, interview by author, Masonville, Iowa, 28 May 1991.

8. Rural School Consolidation and the Making of Buck Creek

1. For a short time in the 1850s when Township 87, Range 4, was separated from South Fork Township, it was referred to as Buck Creek, but the name was changed to Union Township during the Civil War. It is not this use of the term Buck Creek that is being referred to here. See *History of Delaware County*, 1914, vol. II.

2. Tumey, interview by author.

3. The area of concern consists of all of Union Township, the eastern one-third of Hazel Green Township, and the northern one-third of Castle Grove Township. Union and Hazel Green Townships are in Delaware County, while Castle Grove is in Jones County.

4. A booklet chronicling the achievements of the Buck Creek Parish was distributed widely to Methodist churches throughout the country for a number of years (*Buck Creek Parish* [Philadelphia: Board of Home Missions and Church Extension, 1919]). It is available in the Delaware County Historical Museum, Hopkinton, Iowa.

5. Centennial Committee of Buck Creek United Methodist Church. *Buck Creek United Methodist Church Centennial 1875–1975*, 6. This booklet is available in the Delaware County Historical Museum, Hopkinton, Iowa.

6. *Buck Creek Parish*, 10.

7. Dr. Paul Gerhart, interview by author, tape recording, Hopkinton, Iowa, 16 June 1994; and anonymous informant (name withheld at his/her request), interview by author, tape recording, 24 August 1994.

8. *Buck Creek Parish*, 1.

9. Ibid., 1–2.

10. Ibid., 2.

11. From the 1989 *Directory of the Buck Creek United Methodist Church*.

12. Roscoe Willard, interview by author, tape recording, Hopkinton, Iowa, 20 June 1994.

13. *Buck Creek United Methodist Church Centennial 1875–1975*, 6.

14. *Buck Creek Parish*, 6.

15. Ibid., 8.

16. John Lewis Gillin, "Discussion of the Church and the Rural Community," 699.

17. *Hopkinton Leader*, 18 March 1915. This is included in a scrapbook donated by the late Dora Winch, a long-time resident of the Buck Creek area, on file at the Delaware County Historical Museum, Hopkinton, Iowa.

18. *Buck Creek Parish*, 10.

19. Smith, interview by author.

20. According to the *Buck Creek Parish* pamphlet distributed by the Board of Home Missions and Church Extension of the Methodist Episcopal Church, the $5,000 was raised in thirty minutes after a sermon dealing with church finances given by Charles W. Flint, the president of Cornell College, Mount Vernon, Iowa. Cornell was one of four colleges in Iowa supported in part through contributions from the Methodist Episcopal Church.

21. Other sources place the Buck Creek church's membership at 250 at this time. See *Delaware County Leader*, 24 April 1975 (a dated clipping in Dora Winch's scrapbook written by Bernice Moulton, a Buck Creek resident), and Centennial Committee of Buck Creek United Methodist Church, *Buck Creek United Methodist Church Centennial 1875–1975*, 6. Both of these are on file at the Delaware County Historical Museum, Hopkinton, Iowa.

22. See *Buck Creek Parish*, 1, and a newspaper clipping in Dora Winch's scrapbook, dated 1955 entitled "Buck Creek Methodist Church will observe the 50th anniversary of an unusual event — a church-sponsored community fair," available at the Delaware County Historical Museum, Hopkinton, Iowa.

23. Dora Winch's scrapbook of newspaper clippings from the early 1920s through the 1970s focus on the activities of Buck Creek residents, and especially on those of the Buck Creek Church. Some of these are in the Hopkinton Public Library and the rest are available at the Delaware County Historical Museum in Hopkinton. In perusing these, one is struck by the frequency with which obituaries of Buck Creek area residents made specific mention of both the Buck Creek Church and Chalice.

24. Indeed, all of the persons interviewed agreed with this generalization. Some also noted that the fact that Catholic families were renting land previously worked by Protestant families was a major source of concern within the Buck Creek Church at the time.

25. Winona and Jay Flannagan, interviews by author, Hopkinton, Iowa, 3 and 4 September 1994.

26. Willard, interview by author, and Flanagans, interviews by author, 4 September 1994.

27. Smith, interview by author.

28. Willard, interview by author.

29. *Buck Creek Parish*, 11; William R. Ferguson, *The Biography of Lenox College*, 25.

30. Much of this biographical information was obtained from *Delaware County History*, 1914, vol. II.

31. Although the term subdistrict is used here, in almost all of Iowa, subdistricts were usually referred to as districts by their residents.

32. The two boards agreed that the blackboard in the Union No. 1 school be turned over to the Delhi district but that Union Township retain its other contents and that one-third of the proceeds from the sale of the school would go to Union Township (minutes of the Delhi board, 20 August 1915, available in the superintendent's office of the Maquoketa Valley School District, Delhi, Iowa). The schoolhouse was apparently sold to the farmer who owned the surrounding land and sat vacant until it was repurchased by Union Township in 1918 and moved to the east-central portion of the No. 2 subdistrict and became the "new" No. 1 school. It was also referred to after 1918 as the Britt school.

33. The official county map of 1918 showing taxing districts (available in the county auditor's office) reflects this.

34. It should also be noted that most of these families were not distressed about not being included in the district and would have voted against the proposal if they had been included (Tumey, interview by author).

35. Anonymous informant, interview by author, tape recording, Hopkinton, Iowa, 26 August 1994.

36. Curtis Griggs, interview by author, tape recording, Manchester, Iowa, 10 September 1991, and Flanagans, interview by author, 4 September 1994.

37. Smith, interview by author.

38. Minutes of the board of directors of the Hopkinton Independent School District, 30 July 1915, superintendent's office, Maquoketa Valley Community School District, Delhi, Iowa.

39. All information on school attendance, teachers, and school conditions were obtained from the records of the Delaware County superintendent, on file in the Delaware Country Historical Museum, Hopkinton, Iowa. Unfortunately, enrollment and attendance data are not available for earlier or later years.

40. Delaware County bucked the state trend and retained male superintendents much longer than did other counties.

41. There was no correlation between the social and economic characteristics of a subdistrict and this pattern of hiring teachers.

42. This is an estimate based on an analysis of the surnames of teachers employed in these nine subdistricts in the period 1914–15 to 1920–21.

43. In 1915–16, F. P. Walker replaced Guy Ribble as county superintendent. This makes comparisons across subjective evaluations of this sort even more difficult. Based on an examination of pictures of each of the schools taken in the period circa 1915, it would appear that the county superintendent's evaluations of the school buildings were not far off the mark.

44. *Manchester Press*, 22 April 1915. There is some evidence to indicate that Chalice and lay leaders in the Buck Creek Church were initially in favor of exploring the possibility of much of Union Township consolidating with the Hopkinton district. James Johnson, the former treasurer of both the Union Township school board and the board of the Buck Creek Consolidated School District told Herbert Gearhart that the Hopkinton board was opposed to the idea because they "did not want all those farm kids in town." Gearhart, interview by author.

45. Frank D. Joseph to Mr. W. R. Reeve, Hopkinton, Iowa, 2 June 1915; and Frank D. Joseph to Superintendent F. P. Walker, Manchester, Iowa, 2 June 1915, LBSPI.

46. Frank D. Joseph to W. R. Reeve, Hopkinton, Iowa, 2 June 1915, LBSPI.

47. Ibid.

48. Frank D. Joseph to Superintendent F. P. Walker, Manchester, Iowa, 2 June 1915, LBSPI.

49. Frank D. Joseph to Superintendent F. P. Walker, Manchester, Iowa, 5 June 1915, LBSPI.

50. Frank D. Joseph to Superintendent F. P. Walker, Manchester, Iowa, 5 June 1915; to W. L. Peterson, Hopkinton, Iowa, 5 June 1915, LBSPI. Details of the proposal to form a consolidated school district in Hopkinton are lacking because of the unavailability of copies of the *Hopkinton Leader* in the archives of the State Historical Society of Iowa or in any other local repository. Unfortunately, a fire destroyed the *Leader*'s own copies for the period in question.

51. *Manchester Press*, 17 June 1915.

52. Ferguson, *The Biography of Lenox College*, 25–26.

53. *Manchester Press*, 22 July 1915. The whole affair seems to have been conducted in great haste and was of questionable legality given that the board did not run a legal description of the proposed district in the *Hopkinton Leader* far enough in advance and for the appropriate number of times. No legal description of the proposed district was included in the minutes of the meeting of the Hopkinton school board. Among farmers, the most outspoken advocate of consolidation was A. D. LeClere who, according to the *History of Delaware County*, 1914, vol. II, was "recognized as one of the most progressive and enterprising agriculturalists of his locality."

54. *Manchester Press*, 12 August 1915.

55. *Manchester Press*, 19 August 1915.

56. Frank D. Joseph to Prof. E. V. Laughlin, Hopkinton, Iowa, 25 August 1915, LBSPI.

57. *Manchester Press*, 12 August 1915.

58. *Manchester Press*, 3 June 1915.

59. Frank D. Joseph to Mr. Walter Locke, Ryan, Iowa, 31 August 1915, LBSPI.

60. The announcement of Cossan's address was carried in the *Manchester Press*, 9 December 1915.

61. Given that local news was usually submitted by local correspondents or directly by subscribers, this suggests that among members of the Buck Creek Church an identity with a larger Buck Creek area had replaced the form of neighborhood identity still characterizing most Catholic families in the area.

62. The *Hopkinton Leader*, 6 December 1916, carried a lengthy article on the Great Forward Movement, apparently written by Chalice.

63. *Hopkinton Leader*, 1 March 1917.

64. *Hopkinton Leader*, 8 March 1917. Although the editorial went out under Beels's name, it is likely that Chalice either wrote the article or provided Beels with the information.

65. *Hopkinton Leader*, 8 March 1917.

66. As matters turned out, Buell's train was delayed and the address had to be postponed until the next week (*Hopkinton Leader*, 15 March 1917).

67. *Hopkinton Leader*, 15 March 1917.

68. *Hopkinton Leader*, 29 March and 5 April 1917.

69. (Dubuque) *Catholic Tribune Weekly*, 18 November 1920, 8.

70. *Hopkinton Leader*, 12 April 1917.

71. Paul L. Vogt, *Introduction to Rural Sociology*; *Hopkinton Leader*, 19 April 1917.

72. *Hopkinton Leader*, 26 April 1917.

73. *Hopkinton Leader*, 10 May 1917.

74. Ibid. Later members of the Castle Grove Parish set up a parallel, but subordinate set of committees to organize and coordinate the allocation of farmworkers to Catholic farms during the 1917 and 1918 harvests.

75. *Hopkinton Leader*, 17 May 1917; *Buck Creek Parish*, 18.

76. *Hopkinton Leader*, 14 June 1917.

77. The *Hopkinton Leader*, 21 June 1917, reported that "The Reverend Gilbert Chalice is at the State College at Ames, where he will give a series of lectures on Rural Sociology. A large number of ministers and leaders in rural life are expected from all over the state."

78. *Hopkinton Leader*, 26 July 1917.

79. *Manchester Press*, 11 October 1917.

80. *Hopkinton Leader*, 4 October 1917.

9. Rural School Consolidation and the Remaking of Buck Creek

1. *Hopkinton Leader*, 11 and 18 October 1917.

2. *Hopkinton Leader*, 22 November 1917.

3. *Manchester Press*, 10 October, 1918.

4. Mrs. Gertrude Green, interview by author, Hopkinton, Iowa, 30 August 1991.

5. For example, the *Manchester Press* in its "Hopkinton" column on 24 October 1918 contained the following: "Rev. and Mrs. G. J. Chalice and two daughters spent part of last week with friends in this section. He has been returned to the charge at West Branch, where he is doing good work. Their many friends here are always glad to see them."

6. The 11 March 1920 issue of the *Hopkinton Leader* indicated that Grant and Chalice were scheduled to hold revival meetings together in West Union in March and April of 1920. Subsequent issues confirmed that these meetings were held.

7. *Hopkinton Leader*, 8 April 1920.

8. Ibid.

9. *Manchester Press*, 25 September 1919.

10. *Manchester Press*, 27 November 1919.

11. *West Union Argo-Gazette*, 20 August 1919, 22 October 1919, 3 December 1919.

12. In the fall of 1919, the Hopkinton school board had proposed constructing a new high school building for the Hopkinton independent district at a cost of $38,000 (board minutes of the Hopkinton Independent School District, 26 September and 22 October 1919, available in the superintendent's office of the Maquoketa Valley Community School District, Delhi, Iowa). In the bond issue election that followed, the proposition was trounced — with only 44 persons voting yes and 193 voting no. The board then began negotiations with Lenox College, and by late winter had entered into a contractual arrangement with Lenox such that Lenox Academy and the Hopkinton school district would merge and be under the control of the district board, but with an advisory board from the college (*Manchester Press*, 4 March 1920; *Hopkinton Leader*, 25 March 1920).

13. Ottilie was elected county superintendent by the presidents of the independent school districts and townships in the county over two other candidates by only a single vote. The presidents of all of the consolidated districts in the county voted for him, while the support for his principal opponent was primarily in the school townships. Warren Winch, president of the Union School Township board, voted for Ottilie (*Manchester Press*, 4 April 1918).

14. Tax levy figures were obtained from the *Manchester Press*, 30 October 1919.

15. *Hopkinton Leader*, 9 September 1920.

16. This figure for salaries was calculated by using 1924 salary figures when the consolidated school was opened and adjusting the payroll downward to the average salaries paid teachers in the area three years earlier.

17. Rapid increases in the cost of living was a much discussed topic in the area in the fall of 1919. Mrs. F. C. Reeve's column in the *Manchester Press* on 11 December 1919, for example, was captioned "High Cost of Living Soars at Hopkinton" and went on to itemize the recent increases in the cost of various goods and services available in Hopkinton, including a 25-cent/month rise in telephone rates and a 10 percent increase in electric rates.

18. Key members of the group included Roy Dighton, Rudolph Kragenbrink, C. R. "Clell" Moulton, Harry B. Sill, Byron "Binney" Smith, Harold "Happy" Stead, Clyde Thompson, Glen Thompson, Thomas Wilson, and Warren Winch; but there were also some strong supporters of consolidation among the older generation, including Cliff Reed, James A. Wilson, and Harold McBride. This information was derived from church records available in the Delaware County Historical Museum in Hopkinton and from interviews.

19. In 1917 when consolidation had last been seriously discussed in the Buck Creek area, state law regarding consolidation required that petitions calling for an election be filed with and acted upon by the school board of the independent district of the village, town, or city included in the district or the board of directors of the most affected school township. In 1919 this was no longer required; the petition calling for an election could bypass any of the existing schools altogether and be forwarded directly to the county superintendent.

20. Smith, interview by author. The informant's parents were active members of the Buck Creek Church in 1919. He was in his late teens at the time.

21. *Manchester Press*, 15 January 1920.

22. Almost all of the people in the Buck Creek area who had graduated from high school had attended Lenox Academy. If Buck Creek formed its own consolidated school, then the option of attending Lenox Academy under the new arrangement between the Hopkinton independent district and Lenox College, whereby the first two years were spent in the Hopkinton high school and the second two years on the Lenox campus would no longer be available except on a private tuition basis.

23. Green, interview by author.

24. Willard, interview by author.

25. George Von Tungeln, "A Rural Social Survey of Orange Township, Blackhawk County, Iowa," *Iowa Agricultural Experiment Station Bulletin* no. 184 (1918); and Campbell, "A Brief History of Consolidation in Iowa." See also Gillin, "Discussion of the Church and the Rural Community"; and Hawthorn, *The Sociology of Rural Life*. Campbell was appar-

ently impressed with the community-building efforts of the Buck Creekers. "The Buck Creek neighborhood in Delaware County is a thriving country community which has developed a remarkable community church in the open country under the leadership of Rev. Grant. They are conducting an energetic and thorough campaign to consolidate their schools which is part of a far reaching plan to develop the community to the point where it will offer life's best opportunity to the most capable young folks who grow up on its farms" (Macy Campbell, "Sidelights on Consolidation," *Midland Schools* 35:3 (1920): 88–89, 91).

26. *Hopkinton Leader*, 1 April 1920 and 18 March 1920.

27. *Manchester Press*, 8 April 1920. Actually these minima were identical to those called for in a bill then under consideration by the General Assembly. Within days the General Assembly passed the bill. It set the minimum monthly salaries based on certificate grade, ranging from $120/month for those with four years of college to $50/month for the holder of a third-grade uniform county certificate (*Des Moines Register and Leader*, 18 April 1919).

28. *Hopkinton Leader*, 29 April 1920.

29. *Hopkinton Leader*, 6 May 1920. The conference appears never to have been rescheduled, although Professor Roadman, who was scheduled to be the principal speaker, did speak on rural life and consolidation at the Buck Creek Fair on 8 September 1920 shortly before the first election on consolidation. However, a similar conference was held in the Methodist church in Delhi a week later, and apparently some people from Buck Creek attended (*Hopkinton Leader*, 13 May 1920).

30. Anonymous, interview by author.

31. *Hopkinton Leader*, 27 May 1920. Goss was the postmaster of Socialville, a rural crossroads post office south of Hopkinton. He was a self-identified socialist, insurance salesman, humorist, and freelance journalist who traveled throughout southern Delaware County trying to interest farmers in cooperative insurance plans. Each week he wrote a very popular weekly column entitled "Socialville" under the byline "Scrap Iron Dick" in the *Hopkinton Leader*. Its popularity derived from its biting humor and Goss's willingness to tackle topics the *Leader* typically ignored. Without exception, the persons interviewed in the Buck Creek area all volunteered that the Ku Klux Klan wielded influence in the Buck Creek Parish during this period and that the school consolidation controversy was the spark the Klan exploited in its anti-Catholic activities in the area. Regarding the earlier Know Nothing Party activity in the area, see Sister Joan Marie Delay, "The History of the Immaculate Conception Parish," 1969 (mimeo); and Dorothy Martin, "Castle Grove Named for Log Castle," *Cedar Rapids Gazette*, 11 November 1962.

32. See J. M. Mecklin, *The Ku Klux Klan: A Study of the American Mind*; C. C. Alexander, *The Ku Klux Klan in the Southwest*.

33. Tumey, interview by author.

34. Two of the people interviewed insisted that the parochial school behind the Castle Grove Church operated until the Buck Creek consolidated school was built in 1924. The fact that there was a country school across the road from the church at this time, and that the old high school building was used for some social activities connected with the country school as well as for religious instruction, did lend plausibility to the contention that there

was a parochial high school there. For information on the old high school and its operation prior to 1900, see a feature article by Dorothy Martin appearing in the *Cedar Rapids Gazette*, 11 November 1962; and Sister Joan Marie Delay, "The History of the Immaculate Conception Parish."

35. Griggs, interview by author. Griggs's grandfather, a Blanchard, was one of the early settlers in the area, having first settled there in 1849. Copies of the *Hopkinton Leader* are unavailable for 1921–1924, so it is not possible to comment on the extent to which the activities of the Klan were reported in the local press. The 9 July 1925 issue of the *Leader* did contain the following editorial: "That was a significant gathering at Delhi Sunday afternoon, called by the promoters to express a public protest of the county as opposed to Sunday celebration and noisy public entertainments on Sunday in this county. There was some speculation at the beginning as to the response to the call, but as a matter of fact there was a large crowd in attendance and every section of the county was represented by leading members of the several communities. The meeting may have been a synchronized arrangement with the Ku Klux Klan organization which held a meeting and had music and an address on the ground the same evening, but the sentiment represented and expressed during the day should have a salutary effect upon all communities of the county for their future guidance." This was followed up two weeks later under the *Leader*'s "Delhi Dept." with "A meeting of the Ku Klux Klan was held in the park Sunday evening, and a second large crowd was in attendance. The meeting was addressed by a state organizer from Dubuque, songs were sung, and apparently the proceedings were of much interest to the members of the order. There were many spectators who watched the proceedings and heard the talk with great interest and curiosity. The flaming cross was not in evidence" (*Hopkinton Leader*, 23 July 1925).

36. *Hopkinton Leader*, 17 June 1920.

37. Willard, interview by author.

38. *Hopkinton Leader*, 1 July 1920.

39. Ibid.

40. Records of the Delaware County superintendent, on file with the county auditor's office, Manchester, Iowa. The official notice of the county superintendent's receipt of the petition and affidavit mentioned only that the latter contained 62 signatures and that that figure represented more than one-third of the voters in the proposed district. While a map of the district was filed with the county superintendent, none was included in the legal notice or in any newspaper article dealing with the subject. This made it difficult for opponents to determine whether the 120 voters claimed in the affidavit was an accurate estimate.

41. The electricity agreement was announced in the *Hopkinton Leader*, 29 July 1920. Information about the rumored Hopkinton opposition was obtained from the interview with Mrs. Gertrude Green. It should be pointed out that at this time the Hopkinton school district was preoccupied with the process of putting together the terms of its high school's merger with Lenox Academy and had abandoned its earlier interest in rural school consolidation

42. *Hopkinton Leader*, 29 July 1920.

43. All of the petitions mentioned in this chapter protesting the formation of the Buck Creek consolidated district are on file in the county auditor's office in the Delaware County Courthouse, Manchester, Iowa.

44. Records of the Delaware County superintendent on file in the Auditor's Office in the Delaware County Courthouse, Manchester, Iowa.

45. *Hopkinton Leader*, 2 and 9 September 1920.

46. Green, interview by author.

47. Prior to the election, a considerable amount of interest had arisen over what the voting split between men and women would be on the issue. The *Monticello Express* carried a piece opining that it was likely that women would be less influenced "by the dollars and cents" than the men would be (23 September 1920). In the final count, however, the difference between men and women was not great. Seventy-three men voted for the proposition and 44 against, with 2 spoiled ballots (61.3 percent in favor), while for the women, 60 voted for and 32 against, with 4 spoiled ballots (62.5 percent in favor) (*Hopkinton Leader*, 16 September 1920). This lends further support to the contention that the issue of cost was not the deciding issue in the contest. By way of comparison, in the 1917 bond issue election to erect a new consolidated school building in Delhi, there had been a pronounced gender split in the vote, with the men voting it down 77–101, while women voted 81–59 in favor (minutes of the Delhi board, 5 May 1917).

48. *Hopkinton Leader*, 16 September 1920; *Manchester Press*, 16 September 1920.

49. *Hopkinton Leader*, 7 October 1920. The dormitory was never built, probably to cut costs.

50. *Hopkinton Leader*, 14 October 1920 and 4 November 1920.

51. Indeed they had banded together. The Catholic churches in Castle Grove, Ryan, and Delhi had all helped by taking up special collections to help pay the legal fees. They continued to help in this manner for the next several years.

52. Case No. 4796, Delaware County District Court, December Term 1920, on file in the Delaware County Courthouse, Manchester, Iowa. The lawyer retained by the opponents of consolidation had approached Yoran with the particulars of the case and persuaded him of its merits.

53. *Hopkinton Leader*, November 25, 1920; *Manchester Press*, 25 November 1920; *Monticello Express*, 25 November 1920.

54. Thomas J. Morain and D. Miles, *Century Farms of Iowa: The History of Farming in Iowa*, 25.

55. *Monticello Express*, 25 November 1920.

56. W. A. Ottilie, the county superintendent, was apparently unaware that the General Assembly had amended the state's consolidation law in 1919 to include this constraint. *School Laws of Iowa* (1919), Des Moines: Department of Public Instruction.

57. The Delaware County auditor's records indicate that the boundaries of the subdistricts in Union Township had last been modified after the Delhi consolidation in 1915, when all of the previously existing Union No. 1 subdistrict not taken into the Delhi Consolidated Independent School District became part of the Union No. 2 subdistrict.

58. *Monticello Express*, 13 January 1921.

59. *Hopkinton Leader*, 3 March 1921.

60. Mrs. Myron Zumbach, interview by author, Coggan, Iowa, 26 September 1994.

61. Roscoe Willard, interview by author, tape recording, Hopkinton, Iowa, 25 August 1994.

62. *Monticello Express*, 21 April 1921.

63. State law did not require county superintendents to hold formal hearings on objections to the formation of a consolidated district, but Ottilie appears to have done so because of the precedent he had set the previous year when, in ignorance of the law, he did schedule a hearing.

64. *Manchester Press*, 12 May 1921.

65. Tumey, interview by author.

66. At the time there was no formal voter registration process. The detection of voting fraud was dependent upon the success of poll watchers in mounting their challenges after an election.

67. Green, interview by author. Opponents of consolidation maintained that the 240 qualified voters claimed in the affidavit accompanying the petition requesting the second consolidation election was an overestimate of the number of eligible voters. They were probably correct. Given that the population of Union Township was 556 in 1920 and that the proposed district contained twenty-seven sections (as opposed to thirty in Union Township), a reasonable estimate of the population in the district at that time would be 500 persons. Assuming that two-fifths of the population (both men and women) was of voting age, this yields an estimate of 200 for the number of eligible voters in the proposed district. What the Buck Creek proponents had done in filing the second petition was simply to double the figure claimed on the first affidavit because of the newly enfranchised women voters.

68. *Hopkinton Leader*, 30 June 1921, as reprinted in the *Monticello Express*, 7 July 1921. Microfilm copies of the *Hopkinton Leader* are unavailable for the period beginning December 2, 1920, through the end of 1924. A few scattered issues during this period are available at the Delaware County Historical Museum, Hopkinton, Iowa. This forced a reliance on other local newspapers in the area, especially those of Manchester and Monticello, for coverage of the events and reactions to the second Buck Creek election.

69. Quoted in *Manchester Press*, 8 September 1921.

70. *Manchester Press*, 8 September 1921.

71. *Independence Bulletin-Journal* as reprinted in the *Manchester Press*, 15 September 1921.

72. *Manchester Press*, 6 October 1921. Two weeks later, W. J. Kehoe, the leader of the Castle Grove opposition, filed a companion case versus the county treasurer and the directors of the Buck Creek Consolidated School District to restrain the county treasurer from paying into the treasury of the district any of the school funds proportioned from tax receipts, pending the court's ruling on *Reuben v Consolidated Independent School District of Buck Creek* (*Manchester Press*, 13 October 1921).

73. *Manchester Press*, 29 September 1921.

74. *Manchester Press*, 20 October 1921.

75. Tumey, interview by author; and district court records available at the Delaware County Courthouse, Manchester, Iowa.

76. Griggs, interview by author.

77. *Geneseo Community History*, 30 and 44. A perusal of this community history makes it clear that the Methodist churches outside of Delaware County were also active in the formation of consolidated school districts during this period.

78. Green, interview by author.

79. *State v Consolidated Independent School District of Buck Creek, Delaware County*, 195 Iowa 637 (1923).

80. No records of the actual vote on the bond issue are available from records in the Delaware County Courthouse or in the *Manchester Press*. Undoubtedly, the results were published in the *Hopkinton Leader*, but microfilm copies of the *Leader* for the period 2 December 1920 through 31 December 1924 are not available, and the *Leader*'s own copies were destroyed in a fire.

81. By early November most of the bricklaying for the school building had been completed and the work on the roof begun (*Hopkinton Leader*, 8 November 1923).

82. *Hopkinton Leader*, 23 September 1926.

83. *Hopkinton Leader*, 1 July 1926.

84. *Hopkinton Leader*, 12 November 1925; 26 November 1925; 26 October 1926.

85. *Hopkinton Leader*, 18 and 25 February 1926. Felter left the Buck Creek congregation at the end of September 1925 and was succeeded by Virgil Welch. However, the congregation remained badly split over the issue of Klan influence in the church at the time of Chalice's return visit. No doubt, Chalice urged his former parishioners to sever their connections with the Ku Klux Klan.

86. See, for example, the *Hopkinton Leader*, 22 October 1925.

87. From a scrapbook of newspaper clippings on Buck Creek from the early 1920s through the 1980s kept by the late Dora Winch, available in the Delaware County Historical Museum, Hopkinton, Iowa. The clipping appears to be from the *Manchester Press*. It is simply dated "1930."

88. For example, at Cosgrove in Johnson County and Parnell in Iowa County, Catholic parishes used the school consolidation laws to strengthen and reinforce Catholic communities.

Epilogue

1. Allan J. DeYoung, *Struggling with Their Histories: Economic Decline and Educational Improvement in Four Rural Southeastern School Districts*, 232; and J. B. Banovetz and D. A. Dolan, "Rural Education," in W. Jones, editor, *Research in Rural Issues: An Annotated Bibliography*, 99.

2. For a discussion of community in American society, see Bender, *Community and Social Change in America*.

3. *Laws of Iowa*, Senate File 464, ch. 75 (1921). The new law deleted that section of the consolidation law (Code of Iowa, sec. 2524.1 [1919]) requiring the county superintendent to follow the boundary lines of "school corporations or subdistricts already established" in exercising her prerogative to modify the boundaries of a proposed consolidated district.

4. The district courts across the state quickly became clogged with cases brought by opponents of consolidation whose country school districts or subdistricts had been taken into a consolidated district against their wishes. By 1924 the state supreme court made it much easier for opponents to stop consolidation by finally granting standing to claims that the formation of a consolidated district could have negative impacts on the contiguous school corporations that had not been included in the consolidation plan (*Consolidated Independent School Corp. of St Anthony, Marshall Co. v Shutt*, 199 Iowa 111 [1924]). Previously, as long as a school corporation losing territory to a consolidated district possessed at least four sections of contiguous territory "suitable" for forming a new district, the courts tended not to give standing to cases against the legality of a consolidated district brought by those residing outside the consolidated district.

5. These included approximately eighty consolidated districts that had been formed defensively to ward off being incorporated into another consolidated district and at least two dozen districts that had consolidated late in 1920 or in 1921.

6. *Des Moines Register and Leader*, 6 June 1922. Also mentioned as contributing to Francis's success was Superintendent McClenahan's run-in with state legislators in 1921 over the legality of his policy of accepting fees for addressing teachers institutes.

7. In 1923, 62 state representatives (67 percent of the House) listed their occupations as farmers; comparable figures for the Senate were 23 and 46, respectively. Farmers held slim majorities in the House in three other General Assemblies in the period covered by this study: 1907, 1917, and 1921. In each of these General Assemblies, rural education reforms fared badly.

8. See, for example, May E. Francis, "Standardization of Rural Schools," *Midland Schools* 34:3 (1919): 77 and May E. Francis, Untitled note, *Midland Schools* 34:4 (1919): 118.

9. *Des Moines Register and Leader*, 16 June 1922, 4.

10. Ibid.

11. May E. Francis, "Iowa's Three Candidates for State Superintendent of Public Instruction, *Midland Schools* 36:8 (1922): 281, 282. Francis's gender and her populist rhetoric probably explain why her contests for the Republican nomination in the primary and in the general election were the only campaigns for the state superintendency to receive any coverage in the *Des Moines Register and Leader* throughout the period covered by this study.

12. Smith, *Development of the Iowa Department of Public Instruction, 1900–1965*.

13. See, for example, data on numbers of consolidated schools by state in the U.S. Bureau of Education Statistics (1930), and Wayne A. White, "Rural School Consolidation: Rationalization and Social Scarcity" (Ph.D. diss., Kansas State University, 1981).

14. *Biennial Report of the Superintendent of Public Instruction* 41 (1922) and 44 (1928), "School Statistics," 122 and 115, respectively. The only thing surprising about this is that as consolidated districts dissolved, they tended to organize as rural independent districts

rather than as school townships. During this same period, the number of school townships decreased by twenty-five. Ibid.

15. As one student of educational administration in Iowa noted, the "economic instability of these rural people, plus a fear of additional tax burden, during the past few years has made it almost impossible to add more territory to these consolidated schools. As far as cost is concerned, the consolidation movement had failed to solve the problem of bringing equal opportunities to all, in fact, it is probably the factor that is hindering any reorganization that might be brought about at the present time." Richard W. Fobes, "The Rural Elementary and Secondary Schools of Calhoun County, Iowa, and Possibilities for their Reorganization" (master's thesis, Iowa State College, 1938), 10.

16. Reported in Jensen and Friedberger, *Education and Social Structure*, 7.5.

17. Similar results were obtained in a massive nineteen-state study examining the achievement scores of 15,000 students in both consolidated and country schools under the auspices of the National Education Association in 1920–22. See Fuller, *The Old Country School*, 241–243.

18. In 1913, total enrollment in the state's high schools was 48,770; by 1930, high school enrollment burgeoned to 120,526. In 1930, seventy-seven state-approved four-year public high schools accounted for 27.5 percent of the state's public school enrollment (Brookings Institution, *Survey of Administration in Iowa*, 142). The first year for which reasonably accurate high school enrollment data is available is 1913–14. Prior to the creation of the DPI in 1913, no means existed for the state to compel districts or county superintendents to supply these.

19. O. L. Troxel, *State Control of Secondary Education*, 191.

20. In the twenty-year period from 1913–14 to 1933–34, the total high school enrollments in Iowa increased from 48,770 to 129,845, an increase of 166 percent. During this same period the number of rural students attending high school under the provisions of the state's free-tuition law increased from 12,587 to 34,720, an increase of 175 percent.

21. In 1919–20, "tuition" students made up 26.7 percent of the state's total public high school enrollment (*Biennial Report of the Superintendent of Public Instruction* 40 [1920]) — a figure considerably higher than the number of rural high school students attending consolidated schools in 1927–28 (the first year in which all of the consolidated schools had finally been built). Most of these tuition students were graduates of the one-room country schools. In 1921–22, when roughly half of the new consolidated schools had been built, the high school departments of consolidated schools accounted for 24.5 percent of the total high school enrollment in the state as opposed to 29.1 percent accounted for by tuition students. In 1927–28, when all of the consolidated schools had been built, the comparable figures were 22.6 and 27.3 percent, respectively (see *Biennial Report of the Superintendent of Public Instruction* 44 [1928]). The number of "tuition" students in these calculations includes only those whose tuitions were paid by a rural independent district or by a rural school township; hence it surely underestimates the actual number of rural students attending a nonconsolidated high school.

22. Smith, *Development of the Iowa Department of Public Instruction, 1900–1965*, 109.

23. Brookings Institution, *Survey of Administration in Iowa*.

24. Smith, *Development of the Iowa Department of Public Instruction, 1900–1965*, 109.

25. Jensen and Friedberger, *Education and Social Structure*, 7.15–7.16.

26. Jensen and Friedberger, *Education and Social Structure*, 7.17.

27. Cf. Callahan, *Education and the Cult of Efficiency*.

28. Hart, John Fraser, "The Middle West," *Annals of the Association of American Geographers* 62:2 (1972): 273–274.

29. The decreases in the percentages of persons not living in places with 2,500 or more residents for the 1930s, 1940s, 1950s, and 1960s were 2.5, 4.3, 5.5, and 6.7, respectively.

30. By 1957–58, of the 2,545 school districts in Iowa with an average daily attendance of less than twenty-five, 1,240 did not operate any school at all (U.S. Office of Education, *Biennial Survey of Education: 1956–58*).

31. Department of Public Instruction, *Reorganization of Iowa School Districts: 1954–1955 to 1959–1960*, 6.

32. See, for example, Alford, "School District Reorganization and Community Integration," 370; and M. Ingle, *Reorganization of Iowa School Districts*.

33. J. F. Baker, "A Study of the Relationships and Educational Effectiveness of the Upper Levels of School Size and Selected Student Characteristics and Behavior" (Ph.D. diss., University of Iowa, 1970); F. Dunne, "Choosing Smallness: An Examination of the Small School Experience in Rural America," in J. P. Sher, editor, *Education in Rural America: A Reassessment of Conventional Wisdom*, 81–124; J. Goodlad, *A Place Called School*; D. Monk and E. Haller, *Organizational Alternatives for Small Rural Schools*; R. Turner, "Dimensions of Quality in School Education," *School and University Review* 15 (1985): 1–5.

34. Paul Nachtigal, "Rural Education in a Period of Transition: Are the Public Schools Up to the Task," National Rural Studies Committee, *A Proceedings* (1990): 97.

35. U.S. Department of Education, *National Center for Educational Statistics, Digest of Education Statistics*.

36. U.S. Department of Education, *National Education Goals Report*, vol. 2, *State Report*.

37. Ibid.

38. R. A. Teixeira, "Rural Education and Training: Myths and Misconceptions Dispelled," in Castle, editor, *The Changing American Countryside: Rural People and Places*, 419–435.

39. In 1976, Iowa led the nation in the percentage of persons eighteen years and older whose highest level of educational attainment was four years of high school (U.S. Office of Education, *National Center for Educational Statistics, Digest of Education Statistics*). Also contributing to this is that the job opportunities for college graduates are not as great as in more urban states; many of those who do obtain college educations must move out of the state.

40. Jensen and Friedberger, *Education and Social Structure*, 8.1–8.7.

BIBLIOGRAPHY

Aglietta, Michel. "Phases of US Capitalist Expansion." *New Left Review* 110 (July–August 1978): 17–28.

Agnew, John. *The United States in the World-Economy: A Regional Geography.* New York: Cambridge University Press, 1987.

Alexander, C. C. *The Ku Klux Klan in the Southwest.* Lexington: University of Kentucky Press, 1965.

Alford, Robert R. "School District Reorganization and Community Integration." *Harvard Educational Review* 30:4 (1960): 350–371.

Anderson, Wilbert L. *The Country Town: A Study of Rural Evolution.* New York: Baker and Taylor Co., 1906.

Andriot, J. L., ed. *Population Abstract of the U.S. 1983.* Vol. 1. McLean, Va.: Androit Associates, 1983.

Arp, Julius Bernhard. *Rural Education and the Consolidated School.* New York: World Book Co., 1919.

Aurner, Clarence R. *Leading Events in Johnson County, Iowa History.* Cedar Rapids, Iowa: Western Historical Press, 1912.

———. *History of Education in Iowa.* Vols. 1–3. Iowa City: State Historical Society of Iowa, 1914–15.

Bailey, Liberty Hyde. *The State and the Farmer.* New York: Macmillan, 1908.

———. *The Country-Life Movement.* New York: Macmillan, 1920.

Baker, J. F. "A Study of the Relationships and Educational Effectiveness of the Upper Levels of School Size and Selected Student Characteristics and Behavior." Ph.D. diss., University of Iowa, 1970.

Banovetz, J. B., and Dolan, D. A. "Rural Education." In W. Jones, editor, *Research in Rural Issues: An Annotated Bibliography*, 99–152. Macomb, Ill.: Western Illinois University, 1990.

Barron, Hal S. "Staying Down on the Farm: Social Processes of Settled Rural Life in the Nineteenth-Century North." In Steven Hahn and Jonathan Prude, editors, *The Countryside in the Age of Capitalist Formation*, 327–343. Chapel Hill: University of North Carolina, 1985.

Bender, Thomas. *Community and Social Change in America.* New Brunswick, N.J.: Rutgers University Press, 1978.

Berman, Barbara. "Business Efficiency, American Schooling, and the Public School Superintendency: A Reconsideration of the Callahan Thesis." *History of Education Quarterly* 23:3 (1983): 297–321.

Berry, Wendell. "A Defense of the Family Farm." In Gary Comstock, editor, *Is There a Moral Obligation to Save the Family Farm?* 347–360. Ames: Iowa State University Press, 1987.

Better Iowa Schools Commission. "Report of the Better Iowa Schools Commission."

Proceedings of the Fifty-Eighth Annual Session of the Iowa State Teachers Association 58 (1912): 55–118.

Betts, George H. *New Ideals in Rural Schools*. Boston: Houghton Mifflin, 1913.

Betts, George H., and Hall, O. E. *Better Rural Schools*. Indianapolis: Bobbs-Merrill, 1914.

Bogue, Allan G. *From Prairie to Corn Belt*. Chicago: University of Chicago Press, 1963.

Boorstin, D. J. *The Americans: The Democratic Experience*. New York: Vintage Books, 1974.

Bowers, William L. *The Country Life Movement in America, 1900–1920*. Port Washington, N.Y.: Kennikat, 1974.

Bowles, S., and Gintis, H. *Schooling in Capitalist America*. New York: Basic Books, 1976.

Brindley, John E. "A Study of Iowa Population as Related to Industrial Conditions." *Iowa Agricultural Extension Station Bulletin* no. 27, 1912.

Brookings Institution. *Survey of Administration in Iowa*. Des Moines: Institute of Government Research, State of Iowa, 1933.

Brown, G. A. *Iowa's Consolidated Schools*. Des Moines: Department of Public Instruction, State of Iowa, 1922.

Buck Creek Parish. Philadelphia: Board of Home Missions and Church Extension, 1919.

Burnham, Ernest. *Two Types of Rural Schools*. New York: Teachers College, Columbia University, 1912.

Callahan, Raymond E. *Education and the Cult of Efficiency*. Chicago: University of Chicago Press, 1962.

Campbell, Macy. "A Dying School System for Children Who Are Just Beginning to Live." *Midland Schools* 33:10 (1919): 339–342.

———. "Sidelights on Consolidation." *Midland Schools* 35:3 (1920): 88–89, 91.

———. "A Brief History of Consolidation in Iowa." *Bulletin of the Iowa State Teachers College*, Department of Rural Education, 22:3 (1921): 3–16.

———. *Rural Life at the Crossroads*. Boston: Ginn and Co., 1927

Carney, Mabel. *Country Life and the Country School*. Chicago: Row, Peterson and Co., 1912.

Cash, W. J. *The Mind of the South*. New York: Knopf, 1941. Reprint, New York: Vintage Books, 1991.

Castle, Emery N., ed. *The Changing American Countryside: Rural People and Places*. Lawrence, Kans.: University Press of Kansas, 1995.

Centennial Committee of Buck Creek United Methodist Church. *Buck Creek United Methodist Church Centennial 1875–1975*. Monticello, Iowa: The Monticello Express, 1975.

Colgrove, C. P. *The Teacher and the School*. New York: Charles Scribner's Sons, 1910.

Comstock, Gary, ed. *Is There a Moral Obligation to Save the Family Farm?* Ames: Iowa State University Press, 1987.

Conzen, Kathleen Neils. "Peasant Pioneers: Generational Succession Among German Farmers in Frontier Minnesota." In Steven Hahn and Jonathan Prude, editors, *The Countryside in the Age of Capitalist Formation*, 259–292. Chapel Hill: University of North Carolina Press, 1985.

Cremin, Lawrence A. *American Education: The Colonial Experience, 1607–1783*. New York: Harper & Row, 1970.

Cubberley, Elwood P. *The Improvement of Rural Schools*. Boston: Houghton Mifflin, 1912.

———. *Rural Life and Education*. Boston: Houghton Mifflin, 1914.

———. *Rural Life and Education*. Rev. ed. Boston: Houghton Mifflin, 1922.

Curti, Merle. *The Making of an American Community*. Stanford, Calif.: Stanford University Press, 1959.

Danbom, David B. *The Resisted Revolution*. Ames: Iowa State University Press, 1979.

———. "Rural Education Reform and the Country Life Movement, 1900–1920." *Agricultural History* 53:2 (1979): 462–474.

———. *Born in the Country: A History of Rural America*. Baltimore: The Johns Hopkins University Press, 1995.

Davenport, E. *Education for Efficiency*. Boston: Heath, 1909.

Davis, E. E. *The Twentieth Century Rural School*. Indianapolis: Bobbs-Merrill, 1920.

Delay, Joan Marie. "The History of the Immaculate Conception Parish." Mimeo, 1969.

Department of Public Instruction. *Biennial Reports of the Superintendent of Public Instruction*. Vols. 24–45. Des Moines: State of Iowa, 1889–1930.

———. *Iowa Educational Directory, 1927–28*. Des Moines: State of Iowa, 1928.

———. *Reorganization of Iowa School Districts: 1954–1955 to 1959–1960*. Des Moines: State of Iowa, 1960.

Dewey, John. *Democracy and Education*. New York: Macmillan, 1916.

Deyoe, Albert M. "The School as an Efficient Factor in the Educational, Social, and Recreational Activities of the Community." *Midland Schools* 26:1 (1912): 46–48.

———. "Factors in the Development of a Greater Iowa." *Proceedings of the Fifty-Eighth Annual Session of the Iowa State Teachers Association* 58 (1912): 37–53. Reprinted in *Midland Schools* 27:6 (1913): 175–184.

———. "Public School Activities in Iowa." *Proceedings of the Sixtieth Annual Session of the Iowa State Teachers Association* 60 (1914): 36–51. Reprinted in *Midland Schools* 29 (1915): 147–153.

———. "Educational Needs and Tendencies in Iowa." *Proceedings of the Sixty-First Session of the Iowa State Teachers Association* 61 (1915): 11–21.

DeYoung, Alan J. "The Status of American Education Research." *Review of Educational Research* 57 (summer 1987): 123–148.

———. *Struggling with Their Histories: Economic Decline and Educational Improvement in Four Rural Southeastern School Districts*. Norwood, N.J.: Ablex, 1992.

———, ed. *Rural Education: Issues and Practice*. New York: Garland, 1991.

Dunne, F. "Choosing Smallness: An Examination of the Small School Experience in Rural America." In J. P. Sher, editor, *Education in Rural America: A Reassessment of Conventional Wisdom*, 81–124. Boulder, Colo.: Westview Press, 1977.

Eastman, E. R. *These Changing Times*. New York: Macmillan, 1927.

Executive Council of the State of Iowa. *Census of Iowa*. Des Moines: State of Iowa, 1905, 1915, and 1925.

Faragher, John Mack. *Sugar Creek: Life on the Illinois Prairie*. New Haven, Conn.: Yale University Press, 1986.

Ferguson, William R. *The Biography of Lenox College*. Hopkinton, Iowa: The Hopkinton Leader, 1949.

Fink, Deborah. *Open Country, Iowa: Rural Women, Tradition and Change*. Albany, N.Y.: SUNY Press, 1986.

Finke, Roger, and Stark, Rodney. *The Churching of America, 1776–1990: Winners and Losers in Our Religious Economy*. New Brunswick, N.J.: Rutgers University Press, 1992.

Fite, Gilbert C. *American Farmers: The New Minority*. Bloomington: Indiana University Press, 1981.

Fletcher, Henry J. "The Doom of the Small Town." *The Forum* 19 (1895): 214–223.

Fobes, Richard W. "The Rural Elementary and Secondary Schools of Calhoun County, Iowa, and Possibilities for their Reorganization." Master's thesis, Iowa State College, 1938.

Foght, Harold W. *Rural Denmark and Its Schools*. New York: Macmillan, 1915.

Francis, May E. "Standardization of Rural Schools." *Midland Schools* 34:3 (1919): 77.

———. Untitled note. *Midland Schools* 34:4 (1919): 118.

———. "Iowa's Three Candidates for State Superintendent of Public Instruction." *Midland Schools* 36:8 (1922): 281–282.

Friedmann, Harriet. "World Market, State, and Family Farm: Social Bases of Household Production in the Era of Wage Labor." *Comparative Studies in Society and History* 20 (1978): 545–586.

Fuller, Wayne E. *The Old Country School*. Chicago: University of Chicago Press, 1982.

———. "Changing Concepts of the Country School as a Community Center in the Midwest." *Agricultural History* 58:3 (1984): 423–441.

———. "Making Better Farmers: The Study of Agriculture in Midwestern Country Schools, 1900–1923." *Agricultural History* 60:2 (1986): 154–168.

———. *One-Room Schools of the Middle West*. Lawrence, Kans.: University Press of Kansas, 1994.

Geneseo Community History. Iowa Falls, Iowa: Hecht Printing, 1967.

Gillespie, G. "A Social Survey of Jackson Township, Warren County, Iowa." Master's thesis, Iowa State College, 1923.

Gillin, John Lewis. "Discussion of the Church and the Rural Community." *The American Journal of Sociology* 16:5 (1911): 697–700.

Goodlad, J. *A Place Called School*. New York: McGraw-Hill, 1984.

Goodwyn, Lawrence. *Democratic Promise: The Populist Moment in America*. New York: Oxford University Press, 1976.

———. *The Populist Moment: A Short History of the Agrarian Revolt*. New York: Oxford University Press, 1978.

Gregory, Derek. *Geographical Imaginations*. Cambridge, Mass., and Oxford, England: Blackwell, 1994.

Gulliford, A. *America's Country Schools*. Washington, D.C.: Preservation Press, 1984.

Hahn, Steven, and Prude, Jonathan, eds. *The Countryside in the Age of Capitalist Transformation*. Chapel Hill: University of North Carolina Press, 1985.

Hart, I. H. *Milestones*. Des Moines: Iowa State Education Association, 1954.

Hart, John Fraser. "The Middle West." *Annals of the Association of American Geographers* 62:2 (1972): 258–282.

Hartnett, Sean. "The Land Market on the Wisconsin Frontier: An Examination of Land Ownership Processes in Turtle and LaPrairie Townships, 1839–1890." *Agricultural History* 65:2 (1991): 38–77.

Harvey, David. *Consciousness and the Urban Experience*. Baltimore: The Johns Hopkins University Press, 1985.

Hawthorn, Horace Boies. *The Sociology of Rural Life*. New York: The Century Co., 1926.

Hays, Samuel P. *Conservation and the Gospel of Efficiency: The Progressive Conservation Movement 1890–1920*. Cambridge, Mass.: Harvard University Press, 1959.

———. *Businessmen and Reform: A Study of the Progressive Movement*. Cambridge, Mass.: Harvard University Press, 1962.

Henretta, James. "Families and Farms: *Mentalite* in Pre-Industrial America." *William and Mary Quarterly* 3d ser. 35 (1978): 3–32.

Hobbs, Daryl. "Social Organization in the Countryside." In Emery N. Castle, editor, *The Changing American Countryside: Rural People and Places*, 369–396. Lawrence: University Press of Kansas, 1995.

Hofstadter, Richard. *The Age of Reform*. New York: Knopf, 1969.

Hollister, Horace A. *The Township and Community High School Movement in Illinois*. Department of Interior, Bureau of Education, Bulletin no. 35. Washington, D.C.: Government Printing Office, 1917.

Holmes, C. L. "Types of Farming in Iowa." *Iowa Agricultural Experiment Station Bulletin* no. 256 (1929): 152–206.

Hudson, John C. *Making the Corn Belt: A Geographical History of Middle-Western Agriculture*. Bloomington: Indiana University Press, 1994.

Hudson, Winthrop S. *Religion in America: An Historical Account of the Development of American Religious Life*. 2d ed. New York: Scribner's, 1973.

Ingle, M. *Reorganization of Iowa School Districts*. Des Moines: Department of Public Instruction, State of Iowa, 1960.

Jensen, Richard J., and Friedberger, Mark. *Education and Social Structure: An Historical Study of Iowa*. Mimeo. Final Report to National Institute of Education, The Newberry Library, Chicago, 1976.

Jones, W., ed. *Research in Rural Issues: An Annotated Bibliography*. Macomb, Ill.: Western Illinois University, 1990.

Jorgenson, Lloyd P. *The State and the Non-Public School, 1825–1925*. Columbia: University of Missouri Press, 1987.

Kaestle, Carl F. *Pillars of the Republic*. New York: Hill & Wang, 1983.

Kaldenberg, G. "The Consolidated School Situation in Iowa." Master's thesis, Iowa State College, 1922.

Katz, Michael B. *The Irony of Early School Reform: Educational Innovation in Mid-Nineteenth Century Massachusetts*. Cambridge, Mass.: Harvard University Press, 1968.

Keppel, Anna Marie. "Country Schools for Country Children: Backgrounds of the Reform Movement in Rural Elementary Education, 1890–1914." Ph.D. diss., University of Wisconsin, 1960.

King, I. *Education for Social Efficiency*. New York: Appleton, 1913.

Kirschner, Don S. *City and Country: Rural Responses to Urbanization in the 1920s*. Westport, Conn.: Greenwood Publishing Corp., 1970.

Kodras, J. F., and Jones, J. P., eds. *Geographic Dimensions of United States Social Policy*. London: Edward Arnold, 1990.

Kolb, J. H. "Rural Primary Groups: A Study of Agricultural Neighborhoods." *Wisconsin Agricultural Extension Service Bulletin* no. 51, 1921.

Kulikoff, Allan. *The Agrarian Origins of American Capitalism*. Charlottesville: University of Virginia Press, 1992.

Kyrk, H. "Cost of Living on Iowa Farms, Part II: Household Expenditures." *Iowa Agricultural Experiment Station Bulletin* no. 237 (1926): 61–79.

Lancelot, William H. "Taxable Property Per Child in Farm and Non-Farm Communities of Iowa." *Iowa Agricultural Experiment Station Bulletin* no. P55, 1943.

———. "Rural School Reorganization in Iowa." *Iowa Agricultural Experiment Station Bulletin* no. P69, 1944.

Landis, Benson Y. *Rural Church Life in the Middle West*. New York: George H. Doran Co., 1922.

Lang, William C. *A Century of Leadership and Service, a Centennial History of the University of Northern Iowa*. Vol. I, *1876–1928*. Cedar Falls: University of Northern Iowa, 1991.

Lloyd, O. G. "Farm Leases in Iowa." *Iowa Agricultural Experiment Station Bulletin* no. 159 (1915): 152–206.

McNall, Scott G. *The Road to Rebellion: Class Formation and Kansas Populism, 1865–1900*. Chicago: University of Chicago Press, 1988.

Madison, James H. "John D. Rockefeller's General Education Board and the Rural School Problem in the Midwest, 1900–1930." *History of Education Quarterly* 24 (summer 1984): 181–199.

———. "Reformers and the Rural Church, 1900–1950." *Journal of American History* 73 (Dec. 1986): 645–668.

Mahannah, Fred. "Factors in Rural School Improvement." *Proceedings of the Fifty-Seventh Annual Session of the Iowa State Teachers Assocation* 57 (1911): 42–48.

Mann, Susan A. *Agrarian Capitalism in Theory and Practice*. Chapel Hill: North Carolina University Press, 1990.

Mann, Susan A., and Dickinson, James M. "Obstacles to the Development of a Capitalist Agriculture." *Journal of Peasant Studies* 5 (1978): 466–481.

Massey, Doreen. *Spatial Divisions of Labor: Social Structures and the Geography of Production*. New York: Routledge, 1995.

Mathey, Mary. *Earlville Centennial*, 1952. Pamphlet, Earlville Public Library, Earlville, Iowa.

May, George S. "Iowa's Consolidated Schools." *Palimpsest* 37:1 (1956): 1–64.

Mecklin, J. M. *The Ku Klux Klan: A Study of the American Mind*. New York: Russell and Russell, 1924.

Merrill, Michael. "Cash Is Good to Eat: Self-Sufficiency and Exchange in the Rural Economy of the United States." *RHR* no. 4 (winter 1977): 42–47.

———. "So What's So Wrong with the Household Mode of Production?" *RHR* no. 22 (1979–80): 141–146.

Merry, John F., ed. *History of Delaware County, Iowa and Its People*. 2 vols. Chicago: S. J. Clarke Publishing Co., 1914.

Methodist Board of Home Missions and Church Extension. *Buck Creek Parish*. Philadelphia: Board of Home Missions and Church Extension, 1919.

Monk, D., and Haller, E. *Organizational Alternatives for Small Rural Schools*. Ithaca, N.Y.: Cornell University Press, 1986.

Mooney, Patrick H. "Toward a Class Analysis of Midwestern Agriculture." *Rural Sociology* 48:4 (1983): 563–584.

Morain, Thomas J., and Miles, D. *Century Farms of Iowa: The History of Farming in Iowa*. Dallas: Taylor Publishing Co., 1986.

Morgan, E. L., and Howells, O. "Rural Population Groups." *Missouri Agricultural Extension Service Research Bulletin* no. 74, 1925.

Munger, H. B. "Farm Management Surveys in Black Hawk, Grundy and Tama Counties, Iowa." *Iowa Agricultural Experiment Station Bulletin* no. 198 (1921): 253–276a.

Murray, W. G. "Struggle for Land Ownership." In *A Century of Farming in Iowa, 1846–1946*, 1–17. Ames: The Iowa State College Press, 1946.

Nachtigal, Paul. "Rural Education in a Period of Transition: Are the Public Schools Up to the Task." *A Proceedings*, National Rural Studies Committee, 1990.

Nasaw, David. *Schooled to Order: A Social History of Public Schooling in the United States*. New York: Oxford University Press, 1979.

National Education Association. *Report of the Committee of Twelve on Rural Schools*. Chicago: University of Chicago Press, 1897.

Nelson, Lowry. *Rural Sociology: Its Origin and Growth in the United States*. Minneapolis: University of Minnesota Press, 1969.

Neth, Mary. *Preserving the Family Farm: Women, Community, and the Foundation of Agribusiness in the Midwest, 1900–1940*. Baltimore: The Johns Hopkins University Press, 1995.

Nugent, Walter. *Structures of American History*. Bloomington: Indiana University Press, 1981.

Nunnery, G. *The Old Pro Turkey Hunter*. Meridian, Miss.: Portals, 1980.

Page, Brian, and Walker, Richard. "From Settlement to Fordism: The Agro-Industrial Revolution in the American Midwest." *Economic Geography* 67:4 (1991): 281–315.

Peabody, George. *School Days*. Fredericton, N.B.: Goose Lane Editions, 1992.

Pfeffer, Max J. "Social Origins of Three Systems of Farm Production in the United States." *Rural Sociology* 48:4 (1983): 540–562.

Phillips, D. P. "What Does the Farmer Pay for a Consolidated School?" Master's thesis, State University of Iowa, 1923.

Post, C. "The American Road to Capitalism." *New Left Review* 133 (1982): 30–51.

Pred, Alan. *Place, Practice and Structure: Social and Spatial Transformation in Southern Sweden 1750–1850*. Cambridge: Cambridge University Press, 1986.

Primack, M. L., and Willis, J. F. *An Economic History of the United States*. Menlo Park, Calif.: Benjamin Cummings, 1980.

Prince, John T. "Consolidation of Rural Schools, II." *NEA Proceedings* (1903): 933–934.

Quick, Herbert. *The Fairview Idea*. Indianapolis: Bobbs-Merrill, 1919.

Reese, William J. *Power and Promise of School Reform: Grassroots Movements during the Progressive Era*. Boston: Routledge & Kegan Paul, 1986.

Reynolds, David R., and Shelley, Fred M. "Local Control in American Public Education: Myth and Reality." In J. F. Kodras and J. P. Jones, editors, *Geographic Dimensions of United States Social Policy*, 107–133. London: Edward Arnold, 1990.

Ross, Edward A. *Changing America*. New York: The Century Co., 1912.

———. *What Is America?* New York: The Century Co., 1919.

Salamon, Sonya. "Ethnic Differences in Farm Family Tranfers." *Rural Sociology* 45:2 (1980): 290–308.

———. "Ethnic Communities and the Structure of Agriculture." *Rural Sociology* 50:3 (1985): 323–340.

———. *Prairie Patrimony: Family, Farming, and Community in the Midwest*. Chapel Hill: University of North Carolina Press, 1992.

Sanderson, D., and Thompson, W. S. "The Social Areas of Otsego County." *Cornell University Agricultural Extension Service Bulletin* no. 422, 1923.

Schlesinger, A. M. *The Rise of the City, 1878–1898*. New York: Macmillan, 1933.

Schwieder, Dorothy. "Education and Change in the Lives of Iowa Farm Women, 1900–1940." *Agricultural History* 60:2 (1986): 200–215.

Seerley, Homer H. *Homer H. Seerley Letters*. Special Collections, University Archives, University of Northern Iowa Main Library, Cedar Falls, Iowa.

Sher, J. P., ed. *Education in Rural America: A Reassessment of Conventional Wisdom*. Boulder, Colo.: Westview Press, 1977.

Shideler, James H. *Farm Crisis, 1919–1923*. Berkeley: University of California, 1957.

Shortridge, James R. *The Middle West, Its Meaning in American Culture*. Lawrence: University Press of Kansas, 1989.

Shupe, L. E. "History of Public School Transportation in Iowa." Master's thesis, Iowa State College, 1947.

Smith, Payson. "Dangers of Over-organization of the Rural School." *NEA Proceedings* (1914): 256–257.

Smith, Richard N. *Development of the Iowa Department of Public Instruction, 1900–1965*. Des Moines: Department of Public Instruction, State of Iowa, 1969.

———. "Department of Public Instruction in Iowa." In *Education in the States: Historical Development and Outlook*, 401–432. Washington, D.C.: NEA, 1969.

Soja, Edward W. *Postmodern Geographies: The Reassertion of Space in Critical Social Theory*. London and New York: Verso, 1989.

Spring, Joel. *Education and the Rise of the Corporate State*. Boston: Beacon Press, 1972.

State Superintendent of Public Instruction. Letter Books of the Superintendent of Public Instruction. Archives, State Historical Society of Iowa, Des Moines.

Stone, H. E. "The Costs of Establishing and Operating Consolidated Schools in Iowa." Master's thesis, Iowa State College, 1928.

Street, John Purcell. "Iowa Department of Public Instruction, Its Origin and Development." *Annals of Iowa* 30:6 (1950): 397–452.

Taylor, F. W. *Principles of Scientific Management*. New York: Harper, 1911.

Teixera, R. A. "Rural Education and Training: Myths and Conceptions Disspelled." In Emery N. Castle, editor, *The Changing American Countryside: Rural People and Places*, 419–435. Lawrence: University Press of Kansas, 1995.

Theobald, Paul. "Democracy and the Origins of Rural Midwest Education: A Retrospective Essay." *Educational Theory* 38:3 (summer 1988): 363–367.

———. "Historical Scholarship in Nineteenth-Century Rural Education." In Alan J. DeYoung, editor, *Rural Education: Issues and Practice*, 3–25. New York: Garland, 1991.

———. *Call School: Rural Education in the Midwest to 1918*. Carbondale: Southern Illinois University Press, 1995.

Thompson, E. P. *The Poverty of Theory and Other Essays*. New York: Monthly Review, 1978.

Thrift, Nigel. "On the Determination of Social Action in Space and Time." *Environment and Planning D: Society and Space* 1:1 (1983): 23–57.

Tocqueville, Alexis de. *Democracy in America*. Translated by George Lawrence. Edited by J.P. Mayer. New York: Harper & Row, 1966.

Troxel, O. L. *State Control of Secondary Education*. Baltimore: Warwick and York, 1928.

Turner, R. "Dimensions of Quality in School Education." *School and University Review* 15 (1985): 1–5.

Tyack, David B. "The Tribe and the Common School: Community Control in Rural Education." *American Quarterly* 24:1 (1972): 1–19.

———. *The One Best System*. Cambridge, Mass.: Harvard University Press, 1974.

Tyack, David B., and Hansot, Elizabeth. *Managers of Virtue: Public School Leadership in America, 1820–1980*. New York: Basic Books, 1982.

U.S. Bureau of Education. *Biennial Surveys of Education, 1918/20–1926/28*. Washington, D.C.: Department of Interior, 1930.

U.S. Bureau of the Census. *Thirteenth Census of the United States, 1910*. Vol. 2, *Population*. Washington, D.C.: Government Printing Office, 1913.

U.S. Bureau of the Census. *Thirteenth Census of the United States, 1909 and 1910*. Vol. 6, *Agriculture*. Washington, D.C.: Government Printing Office, 1913.

U.S. Bureau of the Census. *Fourteenth Census of the United States, 1920*. Vol. 2, *Population*. Washington, D.C.: Government Printing Office, 1922.

U.S. Bureau of the Census. *Fifteenth Census of the United States, 1930*. Vol. 2, Part 1, *Agriculture: The Northern States*. Washington, D.C.: Government Printing Office, 1932.

U.S. Department of Agriculture. *Yearbook*. Washington, D.C.: Government Printing Office, 1910.

U.S. Department of Education. *National Center for Educational Statistics, Digest of Education Statistics*. Washington, D.C.: Government Printing Office, 1933.

U.S. Department of Education. *National Education Goals Report*. Vol. 2, *State Report*. Washington, D.C.: Government Printing Office, 1933.

U.S. Office of Education. *Biennial Survey of Education: 1956–58*. Washington, D.C.: Government Printing Office, 1958.

U.S. Office of Education. *National Center for Educational Statistics, Digest of Education Statistics*. Washington, D.C.: Government Printing Office, 1981.

U.S. Senate. Special Message from President Roosevelt. *Report of the United States Country Life Commission*. Senate Document 705, 60th Congress, 2nd Session, 1909.

Veblen, Thorstein. *Absentee Ownership and Business Enterprise in Recent Times*. New York: B. W. Heubsch, 1923.

Vogt, Paul L. *Introduction to Rural Sociology*. New York: Appleton, 1917.

Von Tungeln, George H. "A Rural Social Survey of Orange Township, Black Hawk County, Iowa." *Iowa Agricultural Experiment Station Bulletin* no. 184, December 1918.

———. "A Rural Social Survey of Lone Tree Township, Clay County, Iowa." *Iowa Agricultural Experiment Station Bulletin* no. 193, March 1920.

Von Tungeln, George H., and Eells, H. L. " Rural Social Survey of Hudson, Orange and Jesup Consolidated School Districts, Black Hawk and Buchanan Counties, Iowa." *Iowa Agricultural Experiment Station Bulletin* no. 224, 1924.

Von Tungeln, George H., Kirkpatrick, E. L., Hoffer, C. R., and Thaden, J. F. "The Social Aspects of Rural Life and Farm Tenantry in Cedar County, Iowa." *Iowa Agricultural Experiment Station Bulletin* no. 217, August 1923.

Von Tungeln, George H., Thaden, J. F., and Kirkpatrick, E. L. "Cost of Living on Iowa Farms." *Iowa Agricultural Experiment Station Bulletin* no. 237, November 1928.

Wallace, Henry A. "What Is an Iowa Farm Worth?" *Wallace's Farmer* 49:1 (4 January 1924): 1, 4.

Warf, Barney. "Regional Transformation, Everyday Life, and Pacific Northwest Lumber Production." *Annals of the Association of American Geographers* 78:2 (1988): 326–346.

Welch, F. A. "Some Problems of the Village School." *Midland Schools* 35:5 (1921): 147–148.

White, Wayne A. "Rural School Consolidation: Rationalization and Social Scarcity." Ph.D. diss., Kansas State University, 1981.

Wiebe, Robert H. *The Search for Order, 1877–1920*. New York: Hill & Wang, 1967.

Williams, James M. *The Expansion of Rural Life: The Social Psychology of Rural Development*. New York: Knopf, 1926.

Williams, Raymond. *The Country and the City*. New York: Oxford University Press, 1973.

Wilson, Warren H. *The Evolution of the Country Community*. Boston: Pilgrim Press, 1912.

Winship, A. E. "Some Remarkable Achievements in Rural Schools." *NEA Proceedings* (1918): 792.

INDEX

Cedar Rapids, 109

Cedar Rapids Gazette, 131

Centralization. *See* Consolidation, industrial

Central schools, 55–56, 227. *See also* Consolidation, rural school

Chalice, Rev. Gilbert J., 118, 138–140, 142–144, 174–175, 183, 188, 189, 209, 220; Country Life philosophy, 140–143, 144–146, 164, 169–173; views on rural school consolidation, 158, 166–167

Chalice, Sada (Mrs. Gilbert), 140

Cherokee County, 102

Chicago Great Western Railroad, 109

Chicago Tribune, 214

City Beautiful movement, 31

Class: conflict and public schools, xi, 10–11, 36–37, 53, 80, 222; consciousness, 8–9, 13, 172, 236–237; and family farmers, 10–13, 20, 22, 32–33, 35–37, 236–237; and place, 8–10, 58

Clay County, 85

Clayton County, 110, 128

Clevenger, T. M., 65

Colesburg, 110, 113, 116, 120, 129; rural school consolidation, 128–129

Colesburg Catholic Church, 128

Colesburg Congregational Church, 128

Colesburg Methodist Episcopal Church, 128, 129, 217

Colgrove, Chauncey, 61

Colony Township, 107, 113, 120, 129

Common school movement, 5, 48–49

Community, 8–9; based on rural neighborhood, 19; effects of modernization on, 17–18; and family farming, 17–18; as gemeinschaft, 17, 22, 46; as gesellschaft, 22, 46; and revitalization of small-town Protestant churches, 120, 192

Consolidated Independent School Corp. of St. Anthony, Marshall Co. v Shutt, 286 n.4

Consolidation, industrial, 50

Consolidation, rural school; appeal of to educational leaders, 51–54, 236–237; and the "country town" (*see* Country towns); defensive, 77, 177, 227; and ethnic identities, 77, 100; and the Great Depression, 239–240; and increased taxation, 90, 125, 126, 168, 169, 178–179, 183, 211, 212, 213–214 (*see also* Consolidation, rural school: opposition to); laws, in Iowa, 66–67, 72, 74–75, 127, 166–167, 192, 198, 206, 226–227; movement in Delaware County, 106–107, 116–130; movement in Iowa, 67–78, 104–105, 176–177, 226–227, 229; opposition to, xii, 5–7, 11, 13, 57–58, 80–89, 94–105, 128, 129–130, 190–192, 196–208, 211–216, 243–244; post World War II, 230, 240–243 (*see also* Reorganization, school district); and quality of rural education, 4, 6, 12–14, 48–49, 55, 241–246; and the rural church (*see* Country church: and rural school consolidation); state aid for, 74, 80, 121, 123, 179; and tenancy (*see* Tenancy: and support for rural school consolidation); as threat to family farming, 56–58, 237–238; transportation issues, 88–89, 125, 168, 181, 191–192, 212, 213, 218–219, 226, 235–236, 246. *See also* Buck Creek, rural school consolidation

Cossan, George, 165

Country church, 35, 40–42; modernization of, 120; and "overchurching," 40, 116–117; and rural school consolidation, 42–44

Country Life Commission, 35–36, 40

Country Life Institutes (Delaware County), 118, 120, 141, 184

Country Life movement, 4–5, 34–45; and rural school consolidation, 4–5, 39–40, 50–51, 54, 221, 236–237. *See also* Country towns

Country towns, 38–39, 43–44, 57, 70–71, 74, 75–76, 107, 116, 130; as Protestant places, 44; and rural school consolidation, 38, 237–238

County superintendents, authority of, 60, 227

Cubberley, Elwood P., 52–53

Cummins, Albert, 66

Currier, Amos, 61–62

Davenport, 217

Davenport and St. Paul Railroad (Chicago, Milwaukee and St. Paul Railroad), 109

Davis County, 212

Delaware (town), 109, 113–114, 127, 129, 222

Delaware County, 106–130, 159, 171–172, 176, 177, 179, 183, 203–204, 213, 215, 216, 217, 221; Auditor's Office, 283 nn.43, 44 n.57; commercial clubs, 171; county agent, 173; Farmers Institute, 118, 180; Food and Industrial War Association, 171; Historical Museum, 276 nn.21, 23, 277 n.39, 280 n.18; parochial schools, 113, 115; rural schools, 111, 113; superintendent's records, 282 n.40. *See also* Consolidation, rural school

Delaware Methodist Episcopal Church, 118

Delay, Sister Joan Marie, 281 n.31, 282 n.34

Delhi, 109, 113, 117, 120, 122, 126, 129, 134, 158, 161, 163, 168, 172, 211, 222; rural school consolidation, 117, 122, 126–127, 158, 168

Delhi Catholic Church, 134, 149

Delhi consolidated school district, 148–149, 154, 168, 198, 210

Delhi Township, 120

Denmark, 172; educational system, 50

Department of Public Instruction (DPI), 15, 75, 79, 164, 176, 228–229, 236; involvement in consolidation in Delaware County, 115–116, 117–119, 121–125, 127–128, 159–160, 161–163

Des Moines Register and Leader, 228, 281 n.27, 286 n.6

Dewey, John, 6, 47

Deyoe, Albert M., 59, 72–73, 75, 79–80, 117–119, 127–128, 167, 174, 269 n.32

Dighton, Cliff, 207

Dighton, Roy, 151, 161, 178, 195

Dissolution of consolidated districts, 227

Distance learning, 246–247

District system, 53, 57

Dolan, D. A., 225

Domestic science, 51, 74, 119, 122, 123, 125

Dubuque, 107, 110, 158

Dubuque and Pacific Railroad (later Illinois Central), 108

Dubuque County, 110, 120, 129

Dyersville, 109, 110, 111, 113, 115, 122, 129

Dyersville Commercial, 126

Earlville, 109, 111, 113, 115, 120, 222; rural school consolidation, 121–122, 124–126

Earlville Congregational Church, 118, 122

Earlville Methodist Episcopal Church, 118, 122

Earlville Phoenix, 122, 124

Edgar, C. J., 178

Edgewood, 109, 110, 113, 115, 117, 127, 128, 130

Epworth League, 140, 145

Ethnicity: and family farming (*see* Family farming: and ethnicity); and rural neighborhoods, 26; and rural school consolidation (*see* Consolidation, rural school: and ethnic identities)

Evers, Mike, 203

Evers family, 151

Extension Division, State Agricultural College, 146

Fairview Idea, 42

Family farming: and the country school, 12; and ethnicity, 21; and midwestern economic development, 11–12; and the neighborhood system, 19–21, 133–134, 214, 220, 221–222, 227; as petty commodity production, 31, 51; and social isolation, 21. *See also* Class: and family farmers